RADICAL REFORM

RADICAL REFORM

Islamic Ethics and Liberation

Tariq Ramadan

UNIVERSITY PRESS

2009

OXFORD
UNIVERSITY PRESS

Oxford University Press, Inc., publishes works that further
Oxford University's objective of excellence
in research, scholarship, and education.

Oxford   New York
Auckland   Cape Town   Dar es Salaam   Hong Kong   Karachi
Kuala Lumpur   Madrid   Melbourne   Mexico City   Nairobi
New Delhi   Shanghai   Taipei   Toronto
With offices in
Argentina   Austria   Brazil   Chile   Czech Republic   France   Greece
Guatemala   Hungary   Italy   Japan   Poland   Portugal   Singapore
South Korea   Switzerland   Thailand   Turkey   Ukraine   Vietnam

Copyright © 2009 by Oxford University Press, Inc.

Published by Oxford University Press, Inc.
198 Madison Avenue, New York, New York 10016

www.oup.com

Oxford is a registered trademark of Oxford University Press

Library of Congress Cataloging-in-Publication Data
Ramadan, Tariq.
Radical reform : Islamic ethics and liberation / Tariq Ramadan.
p. cm.
Includes index.
ISBN 978-0-19-533171-4
1. Islamic law—Interpretation and construction.   2. Law reform.
3. Ijtihad (Islamic law).   4. Islamic ethics.   I. Title.
KBP470.R36 2009
340.5'9—dc22   2008026901

3 5 7 9 8 6 4 2

Printed in the United States of America
on acid-free paper

To you,
Who through your presence of heart and mind
Have enabled me to go forward and to remain standing
And have offered me energy and hope

Contents

RADICAL REFORM

Introduction

The road has not always been smooth and the research and study have been long and sometimes very difficult. The reflections and proposals that readers will find here are the outcome of a long, deep immersion in the Universe of the "Islamic sciences." For more than twenty years (nurtured by traditional teaching, accumulated readings, personal research, and the writing of books) I have repeatedly stated that the awakening of Islamic thought necessarily involves reconciliation with its spiritual dimension on the one hand, and on the other, renewed commitment and rational and critical reading (*ijtihâd*) of the scriptural sources in the fields of law and jurisprudence (*fiqh*). I have not changed my mind at this point: the luminous heart of Islam is indeed spiritual quest and initiation, and its universal dimension necessarily involves a continued process of reading and rereading, of faithful and innovative interpretation, leading to the formulation of adapted legal rulings (*fatâwâ*). Today's Muslims, both in the East and West, urgently need contemporary *fiqh*, distinguishing what in the texts is immutable and what may be changed. I tackled this issue systematically in three books using different approaches: in *To Be a European Muslim*,[1] I presented a new reflection based on the main classical instruments offered by the fundamentals of law and jurisprudence (*usûl al-fiqh*): critical and autonomous interpretative reasoning (*ijtihâd*), the public interest and common good (*maslahah*), and detailed *fatâwâ*. This approach was meant to enable European (and Western) Muslims to respond to the issues and challenges of their presence in secularized societies where religious reference plays a secondary role in public life. *Western Muslims and the Future of Islam*[2] took up this reflection with a more direct approach to the issue of the sciences and methodologies at the source: the second part of the book took the form of practical, concrete proposals in such fields as spirituality, education, social and political commitment, interfaith dialogue, and so on. Those two works popularized a thought and methodology that spread well beyond what I had hoped for. *Islam, the West, and the Challenges of Modernity*[3] approached the issue from the standpoint of Muslim majority societies, asking which project for which modernity? It also studied the social, political, economic, and cultural dimensions of a possible vision for society. The point was, yet again, to strive to achieve faithfulness through movement.

Limits have, however, been reached. The general vision has indeed been renewed; innovative readings have often made it possible to provide original solutions, to overcome withdrawal attitudes, to put an end to victimlike isolation or to sectarian literalism: another relation to oneself and to the West turned out to be possible. Yet drawbacks remained, making it impossible to carry the reflection further and, above all, turning the reform (*islâh*) movement into a process of continuous adaptation to the order of things...however unsatisfactory they might be. It seems obvious that I had to go further and not only, as reformists had done in the past two centuries, question the productions of *fiqh*, but also its fundamentals, its sources, and the mother science (*usûl al-fiqh*). Centuries of referring to *ijtihâd* certainly did make things progress, but this remains highly inadequate because crises are still there and are even getting deeper, and Muslims seem to be at a loss for a vision and projects for the present and future. We seem to have reached the end of a cycle, that which consisted in thinking through revival merely through a renewed reading and interpretation of scriptural sources. Apt distinctions had been made between *sharî'ah* (the Way to faithfulness including the legal order) and *fiqh*, between general principles (*'âm*) and specific principles (*khâs*), between immutable norms (*thawâbit*) and norms subject to

change (*mutaghayyirât*); this had made a renewal movement possible, as Indian-Pakistani thinker Muhammad Iqbâl (died 1938)[4] had
suggested and hoped. However, as I show in the first section of this
book, this is not sufficient when the world's progress is so rapid, when
challenges are so complex and globalization is so unsettling.

Therefore I must go further and raise the issue of the sources of
usûl al-fiqh, of the categories that organize them, of the methodologies that result from them and, finally, of the nature of the authority all those elements impart to text scholars (*'ulamâ'* and especially
fuqahâ'). This is what I propose to undertake in the present work: it
is, clearly, a new step. The objective is to revisit not only the tools and
concrete, historical implementations of *fiqh*, but also their sources,
their categorization, and at the same time their methods, the range
of their authority and the nature of the approaches that have been
put forward throughout the history of this science (*usûl al-fiqh*). This
approach is the fruit of years of reflection and questioning about the
nature of the crises, difficulties, and drawbacks that paralyze contemporary Muslim thought: why does recourse to *ijtihâd*, so long called
for, fail to produce the expected renewal? Why has the innovative,
bold, creative spirit of early times given way to timid approaches that
only consider reform in terms of adapting to the world and no longer
with the will and energy to change it? How can we explain this divide,
this huge gap between the "Islamic sciences" (or "sacred sciences")
and all the "other sciences," defining distinct and well-secured fields
of authority, but making it impossible to respond adequately to the
challenges of our time? Those questions, among many others, challenge us to go back to the roots of problems, circumscribe their scope
and suggest a new approach and a new methodology regarding the
fundamentals and sources of *usûl al-fiqh*.

This book contains three fundamental propositions: the contemporary Muslim world (both East and West) must reconsider the terms
and modalities of the reform process (*islâh, tajdîd*). It is important to
distinguish between "adaptation reform," which requires religious,
philosophical, and legal thought just to adapt to the evolutions of societies, the sciences, and the world, and "transformation reform," which
equips itself with the spiritual, intellectual, and scientific means to
act on the real, to master all fields of knowledge, and to anticipate the
complexity of social, political, philosophical, and ethical challenges.
To this end—and this is the second proposition—the contents and

geography of the sources of *usûl al-fiqh* must certainly be reconsidered. It cannot be enough to rely only on scriptural sources to examine the relationship between human knowledge (religion, philosophy, the experimental and human sciences, etc.) and applied ethics: the Universe, Nature, and the knowledge related to them must assuredly be integrated into the process through which the higher objectives and ethical goals (*al-maqâsid*) of Islam's general message can be established. The consequence of this new geography is important and it leads to our third proposition: the center of gravity of authority in the Islamic Universe of reference must be shifted by ranking more clearly the respective competences and roles of scholars in the different fields. Text scholars (*'ulamâ' an-nusûs*) and context scholars (*'ulamâ' al-wâqi'*) must henceforth work together, on an equal footing, to set off this radical reform that we wish for.

I recognize, when writing these lines, that criticisms will certainly be expressed. Some in recent years have questioned my competence and capacity to tackle certain issues related to the Islamic sciences (*fiqh, usûl al-fiqh*, etc.) and, *a fortiori*, to suggest solutions. It is worth repeating here that what matters is that such criticisms should stop focusing on the person and instead engage with the only worthwhile debate, that is, to examine the propositions and reflections presented and if necessary to produce a serious and well-argued critique. In launching the *Call for a Moratorium on the Death Penalty, Corporal Punishment, and Stoning*,[5] it was expected that reactions (even those of a few *'ulamâ'*) were going to be passionate and emotional but I was disappointed at the dearth of argued critiques produced after thorough study of the text of the *Call*. This lack of calm critical debate is, I think, one of the evils undermining contemporary Islamic thought.

During the academic presentations (lectures, conferences, or symposia) that preceded the writing of this book, some interlocutors objected that, according to them, those reflections were not new and that the integration of scientists (from the experimental or human sciences) was already a reality in some Islamic legal councils. I have reservations about this and question the modalities. There are indeed, and they are mentioned several times, fields (such as medicine) where platforms are provided for text *'ulamâ'* and scientists to consult with one another and combine their skills, but this reality is an exception far more often than the rule. Besides, my argument is much clearer and more radical than simply calling for punctual "consultation" of experts and specialists (*khubarâ'*) in the different fields of knowledge: the issue here is to question the essence of categorization between the sources of *usûl al-fiqh* and, thereby, to state the need to integrate the scientists (*'ulamâ'*) of Nature, of the experimental and human sciences, *permanently and on an equal footing* when higher objectives and ethical goals are to be determined in their respective fields. This approach enables us to suggest a more elaborate set of ethical results (rather than the traditional five or six main objectives[6]) and an original (horizontal and vertical) categorization of higher objectives. Such an approach offers a framework that does not claim to be definitive but that in effect imposes a critical revision of classical methodologies and typologies.

It might also be objected that I do not always put forward concrete solutions to the various issues raised. Domains must be kept separate: the theoretical work undertaken in the first three parts of this book consists in studying the terminology and categorization of the sciences and the history of the different schools of the fundamentals of *usûl al-fiqh*. As part of this fundamental reflection, I suggest a new geography of the sources of *usûl al-fiqh*: this should lead to integrating the Universe and social and human environments (and therefore all related sciences) into the formulation of the ethical finalities of Islam's message, of which a new presentation and categorization are set forth here. On the basis of this theoretical framework, practical cases are examined, and a number of issues and questions are raised: I have chosen a number of key domains (medicine, the arts and cultures, gender relations, ecology and economy, and secularization, politics, philosophy), which are far from being the only ones but where (within the limited scope of this study) this proposed approach can open new areas for investigation and creativity. The objective here is not to provide answers to each of the questions raised, since the fundamental proposition in this book is to state exactly that specialists must examine those issues, become more involved, and give us the benefit of their skills about matters that are often complex and highly specialized. This present contribution is to question methods rigorously while stating fundamental criticisms involving the formalistic or clearly inadequate nature of the answers proposed. After that, it is up to scholars, scientists, and experts in the various branches of knowledge to provide new, efficient solutions.

Another point must be made clear: this is not a blunt, systematic critique of *'ulamâ'* and *fuqahâ'* in which they are seen as responsible for all the evils that affect Muslim-majority societies and the communities living in the West, in Asia, or in Africa. I address the contemporary Muslim conscience at all levels and strive to make the criticisms constructive and multidimensional. So-called ordinary Muslims must take on their share of responsibility in critical work, in the nature of the issues raised, and in starting in-depth reflection from day-to-day realities. The problem of leadership in the Muslim world is also related to the lack of critical contributions within religious communities, to the passivity of the majority and to their following often exclusively, through emotion or admiration, this or that skilled and/or charismatic scholar or leader. The critique must also include those intellectuals, scientists, or scholars who excel in their fields but who do not take part in intellectual and ethical debates within the spiritual community: they are often content with criticizing "the-incompetence-of-scholars-who-know-nothing-about-the-issues-about-which-they-legislate" but they remain passive observers who fail to take on any responsibility for the crisis of the contemporary Muslim conscience. I therefore call for a general awakening and a critical evaluation of all consciences and all skills, those of ordinary Muslims as well as of intellectuals, scientists, and *'ulamâ'*. Even non-Muslim experts should, as we shall see, have a part to play in the process, by questioning the contemporary Muslim conscience about a number of issues or by contributing with their skills to the possible resolution of some scientific and/or ethical issues (in the experimental or human sciences).

This study has four different parts. The first three are theoretical and determine the framework through which practical cases are approached in the fourth part. I first examine terminology and the nature of the reform already mentioned above. Second, I present the three main classical schools that defined the fundamentals of *usûl al-fiqh*: the deductive school, the inductive approach, and the school of higher objectives (*al-maqâsid*). Third, I suggest "a new geography of the fundamentals of law and jurisprudence" and set forth the basic propositions. Fourth, I discuss a few fields (an arbitrary choice, which moreover did not allow for exhaustive study), in some of which the evolution of Islamic thought has been more or less satisfactory (like medicine, although even more specialist involvement is required), while in others real drawbacks can be observed (the arts, cultures, economy, ecology, etc.). The point is to show how, and why, a new methodology is necessary to take up the different challenges of our time. What is required is not, in each scientific field, to try to adapt to social and scientific evolutions, but rather to offer an ethical contribution, more soul, humanity, and positive creativity, to societies, to the sciences, and to human progress.

The reader who wishes to avoid the technical chapters that analyze the Islamic sciences and the fundamentals of *usûl al-fiqh*, as well as the theoretical development presenting the new geography, can focus on studying the practical cases and the five sections established in part IV. Readers may then decide to read the theoretical part at a later stage. Both a linear reading of the book or an initial approach through the practical cases can be logical, or even complementary, if one keeps in mind the imperative relationships that exist among theoretical criticism, the methodology proposed, and the practical and ethical solutions that this approach aims for. I speak from within a universe of reference whose classical categorizations and methodologies I question so as to be able to reconcile the contemporary Muslim understanding with the universality of its message and the complexity of contemporary challenges. In so doing, the limits and the ambitions of the task at hand must not be forgotten.

I

❧

About Reform

The debate over the question of the renewal, revival, and reform of Islamic sciences, and more specifically of *fiqh*, is a very old one among Muslim scholars. Since the establishment of the first schools of law (*madhâhib*) between the eighth and tenth centuries, intense legal discussions have opposed those who favor strict attachment to the historically constituted schools and those who call for a constant return to the primary scriptural sources: the Quran and the Prophet's tradition (Sunnah). As early as the twelfth century, Abû Hâmid al-Ghazâlî referred to the necessary "revival" (*ihyâ'*) of "religious sciences," in a magisterial seminal work that bears just that title.[1] The deep insight that faithfulness to Islam through history required via a continuous effort of research, renewal, and reform of thought (and of methodologies) has been present in the world of Islamic sciences from their early days to the present, with periods in which it thrived and others when thinkers were hostile to it. Closer to our own times, in the late nineteenth century, with the Nahda and Salâfiyya movements, and the critical output of Jamâl ad-Dîn al-Afghânî and Muhammad 'Abduh,[2] those concepts spread and became ubiquitous in contemporary discourse, of course involving many disputes, from the outright refusal of the idea of reform to the monopolizing of its contents and objectives by some thinkers. For the past twenty years, the parties (whether scholars or thinkers), critics, commentators, and observers of those debates have been expressing different, and sometimes radically opposed, views about the meaning of concepts—that of "reform" in particular—and about whether such or such a scholar or thinker could be labeled a "reformist" or a "reformer."

We are in a sort of terminological haze in which the meaning of words is so variable that one no longer knows exactly what the discourse about "reform" refers to. Therefore, it is necessary to clarify the meaning of the concepts I will use and the aim I have set for myself when using them, to make clear the direction of our reflection.

1

The Concept of "Reform"

Many Muslim scholars (*'ulamâ'*), as well as intellectuals and ordinary Muslims, oppose the use of the word "reform" because they think it represents a threefold danger as far as faithfulness to the Islamic tradition is concerned. For some, "reforming" Islam thus means—or sounds as though it means—changing Islam, perverting it to adapt it to current times, which is not acceptable to a believing conscience. The second criticism comes from those who see in "reform" something foreign, an approach imported from the Christian tradition to cause Islam to undergo the same evolution as Christianity and thereby make it lose its substance and its soul. The third criticism is based on the universal and "timeless" character of Islam's teachings, which, therefore, the argument goes, are in no need of "reform" and can be implemented in all times and in all places.

Those criticisms, which are often set forth in very general terms, raise serious questions and require accurate answers. The laudable and clearly stated intention of protecting Islam from deviation and treachery cannot, however, express nor impose itself through refusing any critical approach as to the nature of the necessary faithfulness to the universal message of Islam. While refusing the alienation caused by thinking about oneself through the categories of the Christian tradition, some people come to express an even deeper alienation, when they identify as "foreign" what in actuality is inherent in the Islamic tradition itself: such self-ignorance, nurtured by fear of change, of losing oneself or more generally "fear of the other," is one of the major dangers that threaten the contemporary Muslim conscience.

Tajdîd *and* Islâh

In addition to the notion of "*ihyâ'*" (revival) I have referred to with al-Ghazâlî's work, the vocabulary of Islamic sciences contains two concepts directly drawn from scriptural sources that directly refer to the ideas of "reform" and "renewal." The term "*tajdîd*" appears frequently in contemporary Islamic literature (and this has been especially true for the past 150 years): it literally means "renewal," or even "rebirth" and "regeneration."[1] The verb root of this noun can be found in a famous *hadîth* of the Prophet: "God will send this [Muslim] community, every hundred years, someone/some people who will renew [*yujaddidu*] its religion."[2]

This Prophetic tradition is highly significant and has given rise, through the ages, to numerous commentaries as to its meaning and impact. What has been unanimously established in the Islamic creed (*al-'aqîdah*) is that the Prophet of Islam is the last of the Messengers and that he represents the final stage in the cycle of Prophethood. What the *hadîth* tells us is that the Muslim community will nevertheless be accompanied and guided through the centuries by scholars and/or thinkers who will help it, every hundred years or so, to "regenerate" or "renew" the religion of Islam. This renewal of religion (*tajdîd ad-dîn*) does not, of course, entail a change in the sources, principles, and fundamentals of Islam, but only in the way the religion is understood, implemented, and lived in different times or places. This is precisely the point: scriptural sources (the Quran and Sunnah) remain the primary references and the fundamentals of faith and practice are left as they are, but our reading and our understanding of the texts will be "renewed" by the contribution of those scholars and thinkers who will point to new perspectives by reviving timeless faith in our hearts while stimulating our minds so as to enable us to face the challenges of our respective times.

"*Tajdîd*," as it was understood by the classical tradition of scholars and schools of law, is thus a renewal of the reading, understanding, and, consequently, implementations of texts in light of the various historicocultural contexts in which Muslim communities or societies exist. Muslims must, at a particular time in history, be able to rediscover the essence, ethical substance, and superior aims of Islam's message to implement them faithfully and adequately in sociocultural contexts that are by essence changing, in constant mutation. It is a matter of recapturing the original essence and "form" of the message, through renewed understanding, to remain faithful to it while lucidly facing the evolution of human beings and societies. The meaning of *tajdîd*, as expressed in this Prophetic tradition, is indeed to "re-form" constantly, to *reform* in the name of faithfulness. In short, no faithfulness to Islamic principles through the ages can exist without evolution, without reform, without a renewal of intelligence and understanding.

This is also the meaning of the concept of "*islâh*" that appears several times in the Quran and in some Prophetic traditions (*ahâdîth*); it conveys the idea of improving, purifying, reconciling, repairing, and reforming. This is the meaning the prophet Shu'ayb conveys to his people when he says in the Quran: "*I do not desire, in opposition to you, to do that which I forbid you to do. I desire nothing but reform [betterment, purification]* (al-islâh) *as far as I am able.*"[3] Thus, divine messages through the centuries came to reform human understanding, and messengers are "*muslihûn*" who bring good, reconcile human beings with the divine, and reform their societies for the better. The notion of *islâh* implies bringing the object (whether a heart, an intellect, or a society) back to its original state, when said object was still considered to be pure and good: it is indeed a matter of improving, of curing, through re-forming, through *reform*.

It can be understood, then, that the two notions of *tajdîd* and *islâh* convey the same idea of reform and are at the same time complementary since the former primarily (but not exclusively) refers to the relationship to texts, while the latter mainly has to do with reforming the human, spiritual, social, or political context. This revival of faith and religion through a constantly reforming approach of the understanding of texts (*tajdidiyyah*) and of the understanding of contexts (*islâhiyyah*) is essential to the Islamic tradition and has been so since its early days. The first scholars who categorized the various spheres and manifold tools of Islamic sciences, particularly in the areas of law and jurisprudence, integrated those dimensions, when, for example, they referred to *ijtihâd* (the critical approach of texts) or to *maslaha* (common good and interest). These latter notions are discussed in more detail later in this book; however, it is important to state at this point that the use of the word "reform" is not at all foreign to the classical Islamic tradition, but that it is essential, from the outset, to define the aim, contents, and limits of the said reform.

The Question of Scriptural Sources

In the contemporary debate over "reform" within Islam's Universe of reference, the law of the Quran is repeatedly stressed. It is as if no reform could actually take place if the law of the Quran itself, as the very word of God revealed to men, was not discussed or questioned. This condition is more or less clearly expressed, and sometimes in radical terms, by some of our Jewish and Christian interlocutors in numerous interreligious circles and by a number of Muslim thinkers. They argue that Islam and Muslims will not "evolve" or be able to "reform" their religion and practices, unless they question the Quran's status as the absolute word of God and undertake a historical-critical reading and exegesis that alone will permit a real *aggiornamento*, or update, of Islam similar to the Protestant Reformation or Vatican II. This argument is highly successful in the West, and the answer one gives about the status of the Quran seems to have become the issue setting "true" reformers apart from "neo-fundamentalist" frauds.

It is indeed important, when starting this general reflection about reform, to clear up some points and to discuss some ideas that are commonly accepted and yet highly disputable. At the heart of the Islamic creed (*al-'aqîdah*), among the six pillars of faith (*arkân al-imân*), lies the recognition of revealed books and the faith and belief that the Quran, the last Revelation, is the word of God (*kalâm Allah*) revealed to mankind as such in clear Arabic language (*"lisânun 'arabiyyun mubîn"*[4]). To the believing conscience, this is one of the pillars of faith and any reform questioning one of the fundamentals of the creed, of the *'aqîdah*, could not be accepted, heard, or promoted by the Muslim faithful. This might be attractive to the restricted circles of rationalists, but it will always be perceived at best as out of place, and at worst as a clear betrayal of Islamic teachings, by the majority of believers, irrespective of their level of practice. Indeed, this "excess of rationalism" on the part of some early or contemporary thinkers has often led to simply disqualifying the notion of "reform" altogether, since it was perceived as dangerous because it undermined the principles of the Muslim faith or was imported from the Christian sphere of reference.

It must be added that the very terms of this debate have generated postulates that need to be questioned. Thus, people tend to believe that dogmatic or literalist approaches are caused by the nature of the Quranic text, and that ascribing a human origin to it[5] would suffice to open the way to a historical and contextualized reading. However, this statement involves two dangerous shortcuts. The first is in assuming that the status of the text alone determines its readers' mode of interpretation, although this is far from obvious or inevitable. The history of religions and ideologies is filled with examples of texts produced by guides or thinkers, texts that have been, and still are, read in a dogmatic way by their adepts or followers. The status of the text can indeed influence the modalities of reading, but in the end, it is the mind and psyche of the reader interpreting it that project its categories and the modalities of its interpretation onto the book. Until very recent times, Marx's works were sometimes read and interpreted in most dogmatic terms by most atheistic Marxists. A text's human source by no means warrants a historicizing reading of its contents, and numerous Christian trends, while recognizing the various historical strata of the Gospels' elaboration, still advocate a literal reading of the New Testament. What must be assessed and questioned is often the outlook, the psychology, and frame of reference of interpreting scholars, and the debate over the status of the text falls far short of resolving the issue of historical and contextualized interpretation.

The other shortcut is methodologically more serious and its consequences are far more harmful. It consists in importing the experience of Catholic theology into the Islamic tradition: because the historicocritical approach was only possible in the Christian tradition, after the human source of the New Testament had been acknowledged, it is assumed to be the same—by natural induction—for the Islamic legal tradition. However, this exogenous imported viewpoint fails to do justice to the great legal tradition of Islam that has never, since the beginning, linked the status of the Quran (as the "eternal word of God") to the impossibility of historical and contextualized interpretation. Indeed, quite the contrary has occurred: from the outset, the Prophet's Companions (*as-sahâba*), the following generation (*at-tâbi'ûn*), then the scholars, the leading figures of the various sciences and schools of law, kept referring to the context, causes (*asbâb*), and chronology of revealed verses. The sciences and commentaries of the Quran (*'ulûm al-Qur'ân* and *at-tafâsîr*), the study of the Prophet's life (*as-sîra*), and the classification of Prophetic traditions (*'ulûm al-hadîth*) are areas of study that were set up while taking into account the historicality of the revealed Word as well as of the Prophet's speech and action. The eternal Word of God was revealed within a specific history, over twenty-three years, and if some texts or injunctions transcend the human History that receives them, some other verses cannot be understood without putting them within a particular time sequence. Human intelligence alone, then, can determine the contents of the timeless principle drawn from the text, while necessarily taking into account its relation to the social and historical context of its enunciation. This critical approach has been known and acknowledged since the beginning by all schools of Islamic law, and what was debated later on was not the legitimacy of the approach itself but the norms and limits of such contextualizing.[6] The debate already involves the elaboration of an applied hermeneutics.

The postulate—increasingly frequent in some academic or interreligious circles in the West that only by questioning the status of the Quran could a far-reaching reform be carried out—thus turns out to be highly disputable both in terms of its theoretical assumptions and of its logic itself; it is unanimously rejected by Muslim masses. The contemporary trend that seeks to disqualify *ahâdîth* (Prophetic traditions) altogether as fundamental scriptural sources (for elaborating Islamic law and ethics) is being similarly rejected by Muslims all over the world, and will most certainly continue to be. The Sunnah is indeed considered as secondary to the Quran, but it nevertheless remains an essential source to determining Islamic norms and practices: for instance, it is impossible to know how ritual prayer—the second pillar of Islam—should be performed unless one refers to the

Islamic traditions (*ahâdîth*) that detail and establish its form and are unanimously acknowledged by scholars and believers alike.

The status of the Quran for Muslims—considering it as God's word—as well as the necessary mediation of the Prophetic tradition (Sunnah), are by no means obstacles to a historical, contextualized, and critical reading. What remains essential in this debate is to determine categories and norms that must make it possible to remain both faithful to the creed as such and coherent as to the questions raised by intelligence when faced with the evolution of sciences and of societies. Only within this frame of reference can the concrete implementation of *tajdîd* and *al-islâh*—as already presented—be efficient and fruitful. That is what I discuss in this book.

The Immutable (Ath-Thâbit) *and the Changing* (al-Mutaghayyir)

Just as the terms of the debate, with certain trends defined as "strictly rationalistic," must be clarified, it is also essential to question the methodological assumptions and some reductions made by contemporary literalist trends that often present themselves as the only true "*salafî*."[7] Those trends, at the other end of the spectrum of interpretations, tend to reduce and level all areas of study and methodological categories established by scholars through the ages. Because the Quran is eternal and revealed, differentiation among the nature of principles, the classification levels of verses or Prophetic traditions, and interpretative methodologies is reduced to a minimum. Literalists do admit that some principles and practices are more essential than others, but historical and contextual data (and, consequently, their influence on the texts' interpretation) are neglected, if not totally absent from the elaboration and fixation of the norms of practice and behavior.

The contemporary literalist approach thus puts into evidence three reductions, or confusions, which restrict interpretation and in effect make it impossible to give adequate answers to contemporary challenges. The first reduction is fundamental and appears, all things considered, as a cause of the other two: it is the failure to distinguish between that which, in the Revelation, is immutable (*thâbit*), absolute, and transhistorical, and that which is subject to change, linked to the temporal evolution and environmental changes (*mutaghayyir*). Several principles or practices remain fundamental and are absolute, true, and/or to be implemented regardless of time or place. Thus the tenets of the *'aqîdah* (the six pillars of faith) and of religious practice (the five pillars of Islam): a practicing Muslim strives to respect those principles and remain faithful to the rules and forms of practice that have never changed since the early days of Islam. Similarly, moral obligations or prohibitions (ethics of behavior, food prohibitions, etc.) are immutable and must be respected whatever the life context. This context must, however, be taken into account to determine the necessarily changing contextual modalities and conditions of application of those transhistorical prescriptions. While this is never necessary for the creed (*al-'aqîdah*) whose principles refer to conscience and faith and rarely pertain to ritual practices—although a number of possible allowances and alleviations (*rukhas*, sing. *rukhas*) exist in various situations and contexts—taking the milieu into account is a constant necessity for implementing moral obligations in the sphere of social affairs and for all that pertains to local cultures and customs.

Injunctions, prohibitions, and recommendations may indeed be absolute and immutable in themselves, but their concrete implementation necessarily takes different and changing forms according to the environment. Scholars who dealt with the fundamentals of Islamic law and jurisprudence (*usûliyyûn*), after Muhammad ibn Idrîs ash-Shâfi'î (ninth century), made this distinction between the immutable and the changing even in the implementation of the "prescriptions defining the duties and obligations of responsible beings" (*al-ahkâm at-taklîfiyyah*):[8] thus, marriage is permitted and recommended (*mubâh* and *mustahab*) in general, but it can become almost an obligation (*wâjib*) according to the person's situation, or, depending on the people involved, it can be considered as a reprehensible action (*makrûh*) or as altogether prohibited (*harâm*). The context can thus make a single action move through the five categories established to define duties and obligations and thereby produce a specific moral judgment. On a less technical level, one can find the same distinction—in social and cultural affairs—between respecting an absolute principle and the form its implementation will take: the principle of modesty and its rules (for both men and women) is established in Islamic ethics, but its implementation in any given society has always had to take into account local cultures and habits (types of clothing, colors, etc.).

By failing to distinguish sufficiently between the immutable and the changing—and never doing so systematically—contemporary literalists bestir a series of other confusions involving especially grave consequences. For on the level of relationships within human societies, distinguishing between the immutable and the mutable makes it possible to draw a fundamental difference between principles and models. Principles can be immutable, absolute, and eternal, but their implementations in time or in history—historical models—are relative, changing, and in constant mutation. Thus, the principles of justice, equality, rights, and human brotherhood that guided the Prophet of Islam indeed remain the references beyond history, but the model of the city of Medina founded by Muhammad in the seventh century is a historical realization linked to the realities and requirements of his time. Muslims must, in the course of history, try to remain faithful to those principles and strive to implement them as best they can according to the requirements of their time, but they cannot merely imitate, reproduce, or duplicate a historical model that was adapted for a particular time but no longer corresponds to the requirements of their own. To confuse eternal principles and historical models is simplistic and, most of all, particularly serious: idealizing something in a moment in history (in this instance, the city of Medina) leads to the thoughtless and guilty denial of that history and reduces the universality of Islam's principles to the dream of an impossible return to the past, to an irresponsible "nostalgia of origins." The same temptation can be found in some contemporary *salafî* trends that advocate an almost exclusively political commitment: they reduce faithfulness to the message of imitating, or returning to, a specific historical political structure, a particular type of "state," or the reference to the "caliphate," which they set against any other possible political organization (dismissively arguing that these alternatives arise from the era of ignorance or opposition to Islam, *al-jâhiliyyah*). Through a binary approach that is both simplistic and, unfortunately, appealing because it is so simple, they set one order against another and find it difficult to look into the nature of the principles on which each order relies.

The greatness and exemplarity of the city of Medina do not lie so much in its form proper as in the adequacy—at that particular moment in history—between the eternal principles stated and the historical implementation elaborated by the Prophet and his community. Thus, the historical model becomes a reference because its authors were able to achieve coherence between ideals and practices. The distinction between principles and models appeals to Muslims' conscience and requires them to display intelligence and creativity to achieve, at each moment in history and whatever their environment, a society model as faithful as possible to the ethical principles they adhere to. Whereas for literalists the act of being faithful to the Prophet, his Companions, and the *salaf* essentially consists in imitating their behavior and simply trying to reproduce their historically dated achievements, it seems to me that essential faithfulness consists in recapturing their spiritual strength and intellectual energy to achieve the most coherent social model for our own time (as they did for theirs). The point is not to imitate the historical result achieved but to reproduce the ethical demand and human efforts through which it was achieved. It is not to repeat its form but to grasp its substance, spirit, and objectives.

The same intellectual stance can be found in the most ordinary everyday realities and produces equally excessive and dangerous legal judgments. A confusion exists between principles and models, between a rule and its form, and this leads to exceedingly rigid and particularly exclusive reductions. Thus, modesty is prescribed to Muslims, but in the eyes of literalists only one way of being modest exists (and thereby also obeying Islamic prescriptions): imitating the Prophet, his Companions, and the *salaf,* and dressing just as they did, with the same clothes—this is the only possible reference. It can be seen here how the principle of modesty is reduced to its actualization within a specific historical context. One could understand and accept such reduction if its advocates only expressed it for themselves. However, they do not, and that exclusive approach has been fitted out with legal constructs to disqualify all other interpretations; thus, dressing in any other way than the *salaf* did is seen as a *bid'a* (plur. *bida'*), one of those guilty innovations the Prophet himself condemned. This is where the third reduction already mentioned occurs: it is the failure to distinguish between, on the one hand, legal methodology linked to the *'aqîdah* (the creed) and the *'ibadât* (worship), and, on the other, that which deals with *mu'âmalât* (social affairs). This distinction, however, is essential, from its very basis. In the two spheres of *'aqîdah* and *'ibadât*, we are confronted with the immutable teachings and practices determined by the Revelation and by Prophetic traditions, and in which human reason can add or delete nothing. We are here on the level of what could, by analogy, be termed "dogmatics": nothing can be said or stipulated in those two fields without relying on a verse, a *hadîth*, or a *dalîl* (evidence). In this area, only what is written is allowed, and any addition or change is considered as a blameworthy, dangerous, or condemnable innovation (*bid'a*).

In the sphere of *mu'âmalât* (social affairs), scholars established from the outset that the rule is exactly the opposite of that concerning *'aqîdah* and *'ibadât*: here, everything is allowed, except that which is explicitly forbidden by scriptural sources or scholarly consensus. The basic principle, in social affairs, is permission (*al-asl fîl-ashyâ' al-ibâha*), thus opening to humankind the fields of rationality, creativity, and research. So long as they remain faithful to principles and respect prohibitions, their intellectual, scientific, artistic and, more generally, social, economic, and political productions are not innovations, but instead welcome achievements for the welfare of humankind. The reduction performed by contemporary literalists consists in failing to distinguish between those spheres (*'aqîdah* and *'ibadât* on the one hand, *mu'âmalât* on the other) and extending the methodology of rule elaboration applicable to the first two ("only what is written can be done") to the totality of human actions. All that does not correspond—in its form—to what the Prophet and his Companions did or produced is thus seen as a *bid'a* that must be denounced. The consequences of such reduction are clear, and even though literalist scholars differ widely from each other in their degree of intellectual and legal sophistication, it remains that the theoretical framework underlying their approach not only opposes reform of models but also adopts legal instruments of judgment that enable it to disqualify Muslim scholars who engage in that endeavor. This is not just a matter of disagreement, but of how one relates to Islamic norms, with the emergence of a scholarly authority that determines what is Islamic and what is not: the outbreak of "innovator" or "*bid'a* promoter" accusations[9] reveals of those tensions that run across the Islamic world about establishment of a framework of Islamic authority. The debate is sharp and the stakes are crucial.

That threefold confusion and reduction (the immutable/the changing; principles/models; and *'aqîdah*, *'ibadât*/*mu'âmalât*) clearly has major consequences on contemporary Islamic thought and in effect tends to disallow any reform of the reading, understanding, and implementation of the texts in a new historical context. It reduces faithfulness to the message to fixed reading, *status quo*, imitation (*at-taqlîd*), and blind reproduction of what had been done previously. Most of all, it results in oversimplifying the message of Islam and implementing its teaching in a way that, although it claims to be faithful to its historical form, sometimes contradicts its eternal objectives.

Ijtihâd

All of the Muslim scholars who have stressed the need for *tajdîd*, for reform, have referred to the central notion of *ijtihâd*. In the field of the classical study of the fundamentals of *usûl al-fiqh*, *ijtihâd* has always consisted in promoting a critical reading of texts when they were open to interpretation (*dhannî*), when the texts were silent about a particular situation, or when the context imperatively needed to be taken into account in the implementation of texts (even when those were explicit, *qat'î*).[10] The debates over the possibility, meaning, and limits of *ijtihâd* have been, and continue to be, numerous and heated, but the legitimacy and necessity of such critical reading are rarely questioned, except by those following the narrowest literalist trends.

As we shall see in the second part of this book, the human, social, political, economic, and cultural environments have always been more or less taken into account by scholars who codified and implemented the principles of the fundamentals of Islamic *usûl al-fiqh* as well as by those who specialized in drawing up practical answers to the new questions of their time (*fuqahâ'* working in the restricted sense of *fiqh*). When the former speak of "consensus" (*ijmâ'*), of "analogical reasoning" (*qiyâs*), of all the secondary sources (*istislâh, istihsân,* etc.), and more generally of common good and interest (*maslaha*),[11] they directly or indirectly refer to the practice of *ijtihâd* that involves reading some texts in the light of the context and requires reforming our understanding of texts as well as of their implementation. This is exactly what jurisprudence scholars (*fuqahâ'*) do when they seek to implement some Islamic rules concretely in a new environment and/or time and sometimes have to draw up specific legal judgments (*fatwâ*). This dialectical relationship between text and context is an appeal to human intelligence to find a way to be faithful through the merging of two levels of knowledge: that of the eternal principles of practice and ethics and that of the ever-changing realities of human societies. Necessary "renewal" and constant "reform" thus lie at the very heart of the requirement of faith and faithfulness that accompanies the believing conscience through life and through history.

It must be added here that from the outset, Muslim scholars set strict, and indeed legitimate, conditions for the practice of *ijtihâd*. Thus, the interpretation of individual texts can only be carried out in the light of knowledge of the general message, of its various levels of enunciation, of the categories of the sciences (*'ulûm*) and methodologies, and of the rules (*qawâ'id*) applied to scriptural texts, grammar (*nahw*), semantics (*ma'nâ*), and morphology (*sarf*). *Ijtihâd* has never been considered a free interpretation of texts, open to the critical elaboration of individuals with no knowledge of Islamic sciences nor of the conventions and norms that text specialists and their procedures are bound to follow. This pertains to the fields of applied science and law that by nature require appropriate training in the knowledge and mastery of the texts and the interpretative rules that apply to them.[12] It must be stressed again that—contrary to the argument one often hears nowadays in some self-termed "progressive" circles, that the "reform of Islam" will only be possible when *every* Muslim (whatever his or her degree of knowledge in the matter) has the right to exercise their own *ijtihâd*—the renewal and reform of contemporary Islamic thought—can by no means imply that one fails to respect the requirements of knowledge and science about our relationship to the Revelation, Prophetic traditions, and productions of scholars in the course of history. The laudable intention to "democratize" Islamic thought here takes on a dangerous aspect of downward leveling that disqualifies the basic conditions associated with the legal understanding of a text and the elaboration of its possible interpretations. In the field of law, such an attitude would amount to hoping that judges and lawyers faithful to the spirit of legal texts could magically emerge without ever having received any training on the subject (or, better still, *because* they never did). It also amounts to stating—most dangerously—that such immediate, free, and nonspecialized access to scriptural texts ensures the emergence of more "open," more "progressive," and necessarily more "modern" readings of the Quran and Sunnah: the violent and extremist actions committed in recent years in the name of Islam, and in general in the name of superficial readings of certain Quranic verses, ought to convince us that this is far from certain.

Ijtihâd must therefore be associated with very precise conditions that scholars have stated many times over. The very story of Mu'âdh ibn Jabal, who was sent as a judge to Yemen by the Prophet Muhammad, is full of such teaching and determines the framework we should adopt when discussing *ijtihâd* and reform. When Mu'âdh was about to set off for his mission, the Prophet asked him: "According to what will you judge?" He answered: "According to the Book of God." "And if you find nothing?" the Prophet asked. "According to the tradition [Sunnah] of God's Prophet." "And if you find nothing?" "Then, I shall exert myself [*ajtahidu*] to my utmost to formulate my own judgment,"[13] Mu'âdh answered. The Prophet then exclaimed: "Praise be to God who guided His Messenger's messenger to what pleases His Messenger."[14] The first two questions and their respective answers directly mention the reference texts and their interpretation: Mu'âdh ibn Jabal, whom the Prophet acknowledged to be one of the most competent in his community in the field of Islamic ethics,[15] states that he will first of all look for solutions in the Quran and in the Prophet's own practice, which he must therefore know perfectly. The third question is of particular interest, because it stipulates that Mu'âdh will necessarily be confronted, in the new environment of Yemen, with situations of which nothing is said in the neither Quran nor the Sunnah. This question itself alone reveals two major teachings: the first is, of course, that not all answers can be found in the Quran and in the Sunnah. The Quran indeed contains verses stating that "*We have sent down to you a Book explaining all things*," and "*We have omitted nothing from the Book*," but that refers to general principles, to essential and immutable rules, the practical implementation of which has to be thought out—through the mediation of the intelligence—according to circumstances and situations.[16] The second teaching is directly linked to these situations: Yemen—although only a few hundred kilometers away and in the Prophet's own time—*already* constitutes a different geographical, cultural, and legal setting, requiring the scholar to produce a reflection, an extrapolation effort, reasoned and reasonable *ijtihâd*, to remain faithful to Islamic prescriptions. Mu'âdh's last answer is no less edifying in this respect, since it directly refers to his own critical intelligence, which will have to face both the texts' potential silence and the new context. In such a situation, merely repeating or blindly imitating the Prophet (*taqlîd*) in the form of his answers or in the practical implementation of rules is impossible: while one must remain faithful to essential and immutable principles (*usûl*), it is no less necessary to take into account the context, culture, and *maslaha* of the society at hand. Mu'âdh, in the seventh century and in the Prophet's presence, thus showed that faithfulness of the heart and mind required lucidity and creativity from a human intelligence nurtured and inspired by the deep meaning of texts, and constantly setting them against the changing complexity of contexts. He was also strongly commended by the Prophet: "Praise be to God who has guided His Messenger's messenger to what pleases His Messenger."

All those reflections about reform lead us to the conclusion that there is indeed, in the classical Islamic tradition, a central reference to the need for a renewal, revival, and consequently, *reform* of our reading and understanding. Debates have often—quite legitimately—concentrated on clearly determining the abilities and limits necessary for the practice of *tajdîd* and *ijtihâd*. When studying the history of Islamic law and ethics, it is clear that the advocates of the different interpretations were sometimes involved in tense, and often highly specialized, contradictory debates. While some scholars called for the practice of *ijtihâd* as a condition to faithfulness, others wanted to forbid it out of fear of excess or because of excessive admiration for the works of the first great scholars who founded the legal schools; others even went so far as to deny its legitimacy in the name of a rigid literalist reading. What nevertheless remains the majority opinion among the critical mass of both Muslim scholars (whether Sunni or Shi'î, and from all legal schools) and Muslim communities, is that the rereading effort (*tajdîd*) and the tool of critical interpretation of texts (*ijtihâd*) are indispensable means to face contemporary challenges. Whether one chooses to be affiliated with a legal school (*madhhab*), and whatever trend of thought one follows, it seems clear that new challenges require new answers. Muslim scholars must assuredly resume possession of the intellectual and legal tools of that renewal, of that necessary reform that stands out as a requirement of faithfulness from the very origin of the message's revelation.

What Reform Do We Mean?

The previous reflections about the legitimacy of using the notion of "reform" from within the Islamic frames of reference themselves—as well as the study of its methodological prerequisites, its conditions, and its possible limits—are important insofar as they compel us to delve into and reconcile ourselves to the Islamic Universe of meaning, and to reach a better understanding of the legal tools it uses to face the evolution of time and the diversity of environments. This is indeed the point: to preserve the meaning offered by the divine, to follow the Way (*ash-sharîah*), through the changing circumstances of time and space in which humankind's destiny is inscribed.

A legal tradition several centuries old is evidence of the tireless efforts put forth by Muslim scholars and thinkers as they strove to reread their sources, to provide suitable, and sometimes bold, answers, to think about the methodological modalities of the required faithfulness, to call for coherence, and to implement *ijtihâd*. *'Ulamâ* endowed with deep spirituality, extraordinary intellectual abilities, rare legal genius, and indomitable courage brought Islam's theological and legal thought to life, then revived and renewed it: we must acknowledge and study their output and take into account, in our contemporary questions, the manifold historical experiences that their works offer us. Neglecting such a fundamental would be not only disrespectful but also, above all, a sort of guilty madness, cutting off Muslims from their heritage under the pretext of having them "move forward" toward the "modern"...in the name of an illusory progress removed from its roots. If modernity, progress in any era, means "breaking away from tradition," then such modernity may very well be the euphemistic expression of a state of being that has no landmarks, no history, no principles, no vision. A modernity that rejoices in its situation without really knowing what it is. That is madness, alienation.

Becoming reconciled to that rich past is the best way of devising new paths toward the future. For years, in the course of my work on law and jurisprudence, I have been reading and analyzing reference works on the fundamentals of Islamic law (*usûl al-fiqh*) and their concrete and practical implementation in different historical periods (*fiqh*), with the aim, of course, of finding new answers to the new challenges faced by contemporary Muslims—and, among them, Western Muslims.[1] Many fields have been investigated by contemporary Muslim scholars, many proposals have been drawn up and the reform of reading and understanding as well as the exercise of *ijtihâd* have been a continuous practice. Today, however, we seem to have reached a limit, so that we shall have to ask ourselves precisely not only what meaning we give to the notion of reform (which was discussed in the previous section) but also what its objectives must be. To put it clearly, what reform do we mean?

Thinking Out Fiqh

The long and rich tradition of the Islamic sciences teaches us that the field of study that has been most open to diverse approaches and to renewal in the understanding and implementation of texts has been the field of law and jurisprudence (*fiqh*). Consequently, that field also gave rise to numerous debates and controversies: it is about *fiqh* that some suggested all the gates of *ijtihâd* should be permanently closed (out of faithfulness to the message and the great *'ulamâ*), and it is with respect to the implementation of law that other scholars answered that the very nature of Islam's teachings forbade such a decision, which, according to them, would mean self-enclosure, regression, or even betrayal. As we have seen, the debate between literalists and traditionalists on the one hand, and reformist traditions on the other, is directly linked to the elaboration of law and norms and dates back to the time of the two Companions of the Prophet 'Abd Allah ibn 'Umar and 'Abd Allah ibn Mas'ûd, who had each opened the way to different approaches of the texts: the *ahl al-hadîth* (the people of tradition and text) followed the former and wanted to keep to the literal meaning of texts, while the *ahl ar-ra'y* (the people of opinion) followed the latter sense and tried to extract the meaning and objective from the terms of a text or saying, beyond literality.

All reformist schools (whether *tajdîdiyyah* or *islâhiyyah*) agreed that Muslim legal scholars (*fuqahâ*) must think through and reconsider *fiqh* in light of the new challenges of their time. There were indeed, as already stated, immutable teachings (essentially in the two fields of *'aqîdah* and *'ibadât*, as well as the explicit injunctions linked to *mu'âmalât*), but it remained imperative to devise a type of law and jurisprudence that would, in social, cultural, economic, and political affairs, take into account the increasing complexity of sciences, techniques, and societies. *Ijtihâd* was considered, as Muhammad Iqbâl[2] put it, as the natural instrument, offered by the Islamic legal tradition, to achieve such renovation and renewal. Centuries of legal elaboration are evidence that many scholars were able to face that challenge of time with exemplary courage and determination, while at times, other scholars preferred protection, self-enclosure, and imitation (*taqlîd*), either because they sincerely feared that Islam's teachings could be corrupted, or because they were unable to provide their contemporaries with both original and faithful answers.

The late nineteenth century, with European colonization and the slow, deep-seated decay of the Ottoman Empire, led some scholars to consider a renaissance (*nahda*) and to try to devise the means for it, particularly in the field of *fiqh*. The two World Wars and their consequences on the world, followed by decolonization and the independence countries were achieving, compelled Muslim scholars and thinkers to carry on their reflections about reform and the need to reread the texts in light of new political as well as scientific challenges. The increasingly important presence of Muslims in the West, gradually becoming Muslim Europeans, Americans or Australians, also raised new questions for present-day scholars of law and juris-prudence scholars. The globalization of the economy and communi-cations, the new relations to world culture and national and regional traditions, have also prompted them to renew their consideration of the stakes and subsequently to produce more appropriate answers. For more than a hundred years, the world of Islamic law and juris-prudence has been in constant turmoil, nurtured by innumerable works and debates, cut across by sharp, ceaselessly renewed ten-sions, and sometimes strife between schools that led to rejection and mutual exclusion. It is no exaggeration to say that the Muslim world—including, of course, all the Western Muslim communities—has been driven by deep-seated questioning that relates both to a real crisis and to the approach of a turning point. That crisis, to which I shall return in the course of this study, is multidimensional and ranges from an authority crisis (who speaks for whom and who is, indeed, a legitimate speaker?) to an adequacy crisis (are the answers of contemporary Islamic law suited to the complex challenges of modern times?). Those tensions are constantly expressed in multiple ways, both in Muslim-majority societies and in the American, European, Australian, Asian, or African communities. Any observer of the Muslim world today cannot help but notice a state of crisis and restlessness accompanied by new, sharp, and most interesting transversal debates. Directly or not, Muslims throughout the world communicate, hear, and answer (or exclude) one another through real, high-stakes reflections and debates—although today these often become chaotic. The questions and answers come from everywhere: Western Muslims no longer merely listen to the "Islamic world," they now interpret, query, sug-gest, and the last—in its turn and in parallel—listens, questions, and accepts, or disagrees. The crisis and questionings are genuine, but at the same time one can feel a change going on, and it is very difficult to foresee how it will develop and what consequences it will have on Islamic law and on the behavior of Muslims in the twenty-first cen-tury. We are at the heart of that transition.

For the past twenty years, my work on contemporary Islam, and on Western Muslims in particular, has led me to delineate the frame-work of the Islamic legal tradition, to define its tools, and to use them to provide specific answers to new questions. That work on *fiqh* and *ijtihâd* was in keeping with the original Islamic reformist tradition: it consisted of rereading the texts in the light of the new context and providing today's Muslims with new and faithful answers. To my mind, that work was and remains essential. However, to me, it has become clear that such work must be associated with basic questions about the modalities of that rereading and of the methodologies brought into play to approach the texts and understand the context. Indeed, the achievements of the renewal of *fiqh* cannot be denied, yet it is compelling to wonder why, after constantly referring to *ijtihâd*, *tajdîd*, and *islâh* for over a century, Muslims—whether in Muslim-majority societies or Western communities—still find it difficult to overcome the successive crises they go through and to provide something more than partial answers, even those answers that remain constantly apologetic or were produced by mostly defensive postures.

It does indeed seem that we have reached limits and that we are now at a loss. The present situation throws light, more vividly than ever, on deep disagreements within the great reformist school itself, which considers *ijtihâd* as the key instrument and reform as its foremost priority.

Adaptation or Transformation

The very old reformist tradition (*tajdîdiyyah*) established a close link, in the field of *fiqh*, between the interpretation of some texts and their implementation in a new or specific context. The context therefore acted as a catalyst and facilitator: it constantly compelled jurists to reconsider their interpretation of texts in the light of the new questions raised by a specific historical situation and to find answers that were both faithful to the texts and suited to the realities of their times.

Taking the context into account has always been essential to the practice of *fiqh* because jurists needed to provide concrete answers when faced with new social or cultural situations or with new scientific and technical challenges. *Fiqh* has always allowed for "adaptation reform," and this is considered as normal by those text specialists who, in the fields of law and jurisprudence, attempt to follow the evolutions of their times. It has been so for centuries, cut across here and there by long periods of imitative timidity, but the principle remained the same: changes and progress were to be taken into account, and legal answers to be reconsidered when the need arose. This was what reformists kept calling for in the late nineteenth century and throughout the twentieth, and rightly so: they had to provide themselves with the means to adapt.

Questioned in the fields of cultural practices, medical science, scientific discoveries, and new technologies, many law scholars and jurists (*fuqahâ*) continuously strove to provide answers, sometimes relying on a more appropriate critical reading of texts (*ijtihâd*), and stating *fatawâ* (legal judgments) accompanied with specific reasoning explaining their choices or decisions. Contemporary *fiqh* literature frequently refers to *maslahah* (common and public interest), *hâjah* (need), or *darûrah* (imperative necessity) to explain how the new challenges of our time should be faced. The point is to adapt to the new realities of the world while taking into account the common interest and the necessities and imperatives of the time: such considerations make it possible to make allowances (*rukhas*); to state context-specific, circumscribed, or marginal legal judgments; or to suggest that the implementation of some particular rules should be temporarily suspended. On the international level, in Muslim-majority countries, the contemporary output of *fuqahâ* in the fields of economics or global communications, for instance, is entirely motivated and nurtured by this adaptive methodology: the worlds of economics and communication have become extremely complex, so that legal judgments are formulated to adapt to the new realities while protecting the fundamentals of Islamic principles. Similarly, the "minority *fiqh*" (*fiqh al-aqalliyât*) that some scholars[3] have been formulating and producing for the past ten years or so to answer the needs of Muslims living in a "minority situation," particularly in the West, is based on the same approach, since it consists in drawing up legal judgments based on the specific situation of Muslims in Western contexts and taking into account the Muslim community's *maslahah* and *hâjât* as well as the *darûrât* to which the faithful are subject (laws, taxes, insurance, banks, marriage, armies, food, etc.).

That effort today enables millions of Muslims throughout the world, including in those societies where they are a religious minority, to remain as faithful as possible to their religion. Yet, it is also highly necessary to look into the consequences and limits of that methodology today.[4] For many centuries, that method was and remained the best means to advance Islamic legal thought. However, the fields of the human, experimental, and exact sciences have now become so complex, and the acquisition of knowledge has developed to such an extraordinary extent over the past century, that it has become urgent to reconsider the nature of the relationship established by scholars between scriptural sources on the one hand and social and scientific contexts on the other.

Because of globalization and rapidly changing fields of knowledge, *fuqahâ'* are now beset with questions linked to the viability of Islam's prescriptions in this new age. The world is moving on and legal scholars are forever lagging behind that constantly accelerating progress that seems to escape them: the legal reforms they advocate are therefore, necessarily, reforms of adaptation to the new order of the world and of knowledge. They try their best not to lose touch, and to keep abreast of new realities. Twentieth-century Muslim reformism was naturally driven by that requirement and that dynamic of renewal and adaptation.

There would be nothing to say against such a healthy approach if one did not realize today what explicit limits that approach and its methodological assumptions have reached. The need to reread the texts when faced with transformed human realities is essential and remains the only way of producing a religious ethics that meets the challenges of human history. Nevertheless, "adaptation reform" constitutes a crucial problem for the contemporary believing conscience, for "adapting" to the order of the world and of the sciences does implicitly express a twofold attitude to reality. Indeed, on the one hand, one admits that the world is changing and one agrees to change with it, but what is primarily expressed on the other hand is that one "adapts" to what the world is becoming as if that were fated. What matters would then be to protect one's ethics in the face of an evolution one acknowledges without going so far as to dispute the very nature of that evolution. The initial attitude—acknowledging the evolution—which is positive but can remain very passive, is associated with a "protective" posture: one adapts to the global system by creating sheltered areas in which Islamic ethics will be somewhat protected. The example of the Muslim intellectual output in economics is most telling in this respect: one takes stock of the nature of the capitalistic order, then one adapts to it by creating banking or financial techniques that protect Muslim firms or individuals and by making some transactions more "Islamic." In the meantime, one does not seem to realize that such reforms, which adapt to the present system, fail to question the system in its essence, in its objectives, and most of all in its consequences. The reverse is true because adapting to such a system amounts to endorsing its reality, or its domination, or both. In other words, the "sheltered areas" of Islamic transactions at the heart of the capitalistic system confirm the domination of that system at the very moment when, inside it, one finds derived means of protecting the Islamic ethics. Adapting does not—or does not necessarily—mean questioning, criticizing, or challenging. Such are the limits and contradictions inherent in the adaptation reform that has nurtured contemporary Islamic reformist thought for the past decades, and it is the rapidly increasing complexity of knowledge that has naturally exposed this dilemma to the believing conscience. Should we refer to an ethics only to *adapt* to the requirements of a changing world, or should we, more deeply, refer to an ethics with the requirement of *changing* the world... because that ethics precisely questions its justice?

If one answers the second part of the question in the affirmative, then the very nature of the reform changes completely. "Adaptation reform" is indeed imperative, but its scope is limited: it means observing the world, noting its changes then coming back to the texts to suggest new readings, alleviations, or exemptions in their implementation. "Transformation reform" is more exacting, in that it adds a further step, and condition, to the whole process. It aims to change the order of things in the very name of the ethics it attempts to be faithful to, in other words, to add a further step going from the texts to the context to act on the context and improve it, without ever accepting its shortcomings and injustices as matters of fate (to which one would simply have to adapt). That further step requires that a fundamental condition be fulfilled: acquiring deep knowledge of the context, fully mastering all areas of knowledge including the human and exact sciences, which alone can make it possible to act adequately on the world and its order. The further step, down the line in the process, thus reveals an axial condition up the line: a reform aiming to change the world—as well as providing a new reading of the texts—cannot rely only on text expertise, but requires a full and equal integration of all available human knowledge.

It is no longer a matter of being subjected to the world's complexity and stopping to produce an ethics for the occasion, with the hope of protecting believers as best as we can from the immoral realities of the present world order: what we must do now is attain better knowledge of the world, its history and its sciences to provide ourselves with the means to act on it. This, as we shall see, requires restoring knowledge about the Universe and societies to its proper place in relation to mere knowledge about the texts, as a reference for ethics and its implementation. Transformation reform thus involves questioning not only the practice of *fiqh* but also, more essentially, the sources and fundamentals of that *fiqh* (*usûl al-fiqh*). After more than a century of calling for *ijtihâd, tajdîd,* and reform, we seem to have reached the limits of such demands: the renewed reading of scriptural sources has brought about a revival of Islamic thought, it has opened up new horizons enabling Muslims to keep more abreast of their time, but Muslims today clearly appear to lack the means to formulate new prospects for the future and to become a proposing force to reform the world we live in. Contemporary *tajdîd* looks for solutions to the problems raised, it follows, answers, and adapts, but it fails to anticipate and project into the future and it thus has neither the purpose nor the means of transforming reality.

Radical Reform?

I am not, therefore, speaking about the same reform. Contemporary reformist trends use the same concepts (*ijtihâd, tajdîd, islâh,* etc.) but with very different objectives and their disagreements are sometimes important in terms of at least three issues, and on three different levels.

What is at stake, before beginning this, is first of all to determine the status of ethics in the lives of societies and individuals. That question indeed applies to all religions, to all ideologies, and to every individual, whether a believer, an agnostic, or an atheist: are our respective ethics no more than a body of principles that we protect away from the world (in the very intimate, if not marginal, sphere of our existence), or are they references through which we try to live coherently in our private and public lives? In this respect, it must be stressed that secularization has never meant removing the moral reference from the public sphere, but instead distinguishing between different spheres of authority. It means opposing the dogmatic imposition, from above and for everyone, of moral and behavioral (and, more broadly, religious) norms, but it does not imply the disappearance of the collective ethics elaborated and negotiated by society's members. Removing ethics from the public space would amount to upholding the darkest Machiavellian political theory, postulating that some areas of political and public practice can remain outside the scope of ethics. For Muslim reformists, as well as for any agent in modern societies, the question is raised with all the power of its simplicity: what is ethics for? In what ways and in what fields should it be referred to?

Even though Muslim scholars do, theoretically, speak of the universal and global character of Islam's moral commands, the thought that "adaptation reform" scholars have produced and that thought's implementation have in fact been "defensive," striving for self-protection, creating "*halâl*" (licit action) areas within a global system that falls short of being moral, and resorting to alleviation and exception to justify their viability in modern times. The world's order naturally imposes itself on that reformist approach, but this latter actually imposes very little on the world's order. The ethical demand is trapped inside legal elaboration alone (with its formalism and technicality), and is reduced to the formulation of *fiqh*, and timid judgments (*fatwâ*), formally conservative and often marginal. The inspiration of the ethical demand that, moved by faithfulness to conscience, questions the world's order and human practices in the name of respect for nature and for men, in the name of justice and coherence, seems to have lost its energy or to have simply disappeared from a reformism that keeps adapting and eventually ends up acknowledging the very terms pointing to its own disqualification.

The second point of disagreement is fundamental, both in its assumptions and in its consequences. Because, all things considered, the limits of the contemporary elaboration of *fiqh* I have just described reveal a true problem—an objective impediment—to the renewal of contemporary Islamic thought. At a time when science and scientific techniques are becoming increasingly complex, one is struck by the natural failure of scholars who specialized in texts (*fuqahâ, 'ulamâ' an-nusûs*) to attain full knowledge and mastery of the sciences concerned with humankind, societies, and the Universe. It is clearly this failure that drives *fuqahâ'* to their attitude of reactive resistance and protection, which is, after all, understandable under the circumstances. Yet, it is clear that the demand for better implemented, more effective ethics—as far as respecting the dignity of nature and of humankind is concerned, for instance—requires fuller mastery of the areas of knowledge and of the human environment in contemporary societies. Leaving the responsibility for developing law and ethics in the hands of text scholars, of *fuqahâ* alone, is not only contradictory, but it also necessarily entails shortcomings and discrepancies that the increasing complexity of scientific and practical expertises cannot fail to bring to light, as is indeed the case today. This observation is now so obvious that it entails, by induction, that we should not only question the practice of *fiqh* but also the nature of its fundamentals and the categorization of its sources.

As suggested earlier, it is at the level of the fundamentals of *usûl al-fiqh* that questions must be raised: was the classical tradition right when it restricted the sources of law to the texts alone (and to the modalities of their interpretation), or should we question this restriction nowadays precisely *because* it causes us to reach limits that no longer produce more than formal or marginal ethical coherence? Should we, or should we not, consider the world, nature, and the human and exact sciences, as sources of law? This is an essential issue, for a reform that all at once wants to remain faithful to its values, adapt to the world but also transform it, cannot be effective unless it integrates all of those fields at the very source of its reflection. This would amount to saying that the texts are not the only sources of law and that we should question this traditional tenet, that has been wrongly taken for granted. This point will be examined in the third part of this book.

The last point of disagreement is, as can be easily understood, the direct consequence of the first two: reflecting on the status of ethics and questioning the sources of its elaboration inevitably bear on how authority over the production and implementation of applied law and ethics is determined. If these latter are to inspire all the areas of human behavior, and if knowledge of the environment and of the sciences is indispensable, then it is impossible that text specialists alone should remain in charge both of faithfulness to Islamic teachings and ethics and of authority over them. The women and men who have studied the experimental and human sciences and who are attentive to the issue of ethics in the use and practice of their function must absolutely be integrated into the debates about the formulation and implementation of ethical principles in the contemporary world. The matter at hand is not, of course, to deal with the tenets of the faith (*'aqîdah*) or the fundamental commands directly linked to ritual practice (*al-usûl* and *al-'ibadât*), but with the broader implementation of Islamic ethics in the fields of human action. In that respect, the need is urgent to widen the circle of expertise and call on context specialists (*'ulamâ al-wâqi'*) and no longer only text specialists (*'ulamâ an-nusûs*) to formulate judgments, stages, and action strategies according to the requirements and modalities of moral faithfulness and coherence in modern times (by taking into account the specificities of every society). The issue of authority is a central one and it will also be further developed in the third part of this book.

Indeed, something "radical" does exist about the reform I call for. The very idea of returning to the dimension of "transformation" instead of just "adaptation" to the requirements of the modern world demonstrates an intellectual and ethical posture that is both clear and demanding. Many in the West, Muslims or non-Muslims alike, expect Muslims to adapt to the modern world, to modernity, to modernism, to postmodernism, to progress, to democracy, and to the sciences. Besides the fact that those general and generous appeals mix up spheres of totally different natures (ideology, science, and political models), it often appears that what is expected of the Muslim world in general, and of Muslims in particular, is that they should adapt, catch up with advanced societies, and integrate their achievements. In effect, this means developing enough awareness and critical debates about themselves (their relation to scriptural sources, their interpretations, etc.) to enable them to attain modernity through self-criticism (or more precisely, to attain a criticism-free modernity). While the first part of the statement is laudable (nurturing critical awareness and self-criticism), the second is far less so in its assumptions and consequences. Islam and Muslims are expected to adapt and not to contribute and propose their own answers. A deep and constructive "criticism of modernity," or of "postmodernity," does not seem to be within Muslims' scope; at most, it would be thought to reveal their wish to find pretexts to reject it, or simply, more insidiously, their attempt to "Islamize" it. Some Muslim thinkers have integrated such postulates and keep trying to show how "progressive" they are by constantly "adapting," which, in the end, amounts to wholesale "intellectual assimilation" to the terms of the debate as stated by many Western elites. They thus confuse necessary self-criticism and the surrender of intelligence to the decrees of the prevailing order.

Between the self-enclosure of some *fuqahâ* (with *fatwâ*, which adapt out of necessity and subsequently confirm the existing order) and the self-dilution of some thinkers (through a self-critical approach that sometimes extends to denying oneself and one's own ability to suggest alternatives), there is another way that both disrupts a tradition made so sclerotic by fear that it has become ossified and criticizes the all-out surrender that is often motivated by the same fear, the same lack of self-confidence. Muslims need a new, more coherent balance, as well as new, more stimulating energy, to enable them to contribute and propose their own answers in today's and tomorrow's world.

At the close of these initial reflections, it is now clear that the reform we intend questions the established geography of the fundamentals of Islamic *usûl al-fiqh* as well as the limited—and sometimes counter-productive—implementations of contemporary *tajdîd* and *islâh*. It is an appeal to reconsidering the sources through their necessary reconciliation with the world, its evolution, and human knowledge. Thus reconciling conscience with science is imperative. Does this imply, however, that this reform will produce uniform interpretations and readings? That it will be blindly modern and modernist? This is far from certain, and some scholars or thinkers might indeed choose "tradition" or "some traditions," as sophisticated criticisms—and resistances stemming from mature thought—opposed to some excesses of a postmodernism perceived as rootless and soulless. In the order of political ethics, the same diversity of approaches will be present with as broad a range of differences as those, in the Christian Universe of reference, between the liberation theologians one finds active at the grassroots in some countries in South America and the Christian democrats involved in the political arena in Western societies. Thinking out ethics and its implementation does not mean one has finally circumscribed and determined the ideological framework, political affiliations, and economic aspirations of the protagonists involved, and the same conclusion will certainly be true in the Muslim world. There will have to be debate areas, there will be disagreements—for the first time so explicitly within the reformist camp—but the contemporary Muslim conscience has to transform this turmoil of converging or contradictory ideas into an energy of debate, renewal, and creativity that produces faithfulness as well as serene coherence at the heart of our modern age and its challenges.

II

~

Classical Approaches of the Fundamentals of Law and Jurisprudence (*Usûl al-Fiqh*)

As I said in the first section, the main challenge for contemporary Muslim conscience lies in the categorization and geography of the fundamentals and sources of Islamic *usûl al-fiqh*. This by no means implies underrating the importance of working on the relevance and interpretation of reference texts (Quran and *ahâdîth*) or the centrality of a renewed approach of *fiqh* applied to the new circumstances of life.[1] Yet as I pointed out earlier, such work (when it is not associated with thorough reflection and reassessment at the level of primary sources) approaches limits I think it has now reached.

Hence, I must focus on the fundamentals of law and jurisprudence, their historical elaboration, and then their categorization in terms of classical norms of reference. In the Prophet's time, Revelation was being elaborated through time and circumstances and the Messenger was its first interpreter and its first practitioner. The revealed text both provided direct answers to needs and events and at the same time established an orientation, a Way (the initial meaning of *ash-sharî'ah*[2]) to follow through history, beyond the singular history that gave it birth and meaning. After the Prophet's death, the Companions (*as-sahâbah*) who had lived close to the Revelation and in immediate contact with the Prophet, drew on his example (his Sunnah) to interpret and implement the verses. Their methodology was based on imitation of the Prophet or analogical reasoning made easier by their living during the same period and in the same environment.

The next generation of Muslims (*at-tâbi'ûn*) basically followed the same method. Even when they lived in different cities, they drew on the Prophet's example and strove to remain faithful to him in substance, form, and spirit. They did not feel the need to refer to a precise methodology or draw up specific categories: once again, proximity in time and similar environments made for a faithfulness that they scarcely questioned. However, as time went by, things changed and greater distance resulted in varied approaches, causing fears for the essence of the message and for coherence in its implementation. Increasing numbers of scholars were preoccupied by the multiplication of interpretations and of proposed implementations that might, instead of the originally accepted diversity, lead to chaos as to acknowledged norms.

3

Imam ash-Shâfi'î:
The Deductive Approach

Tensions and Confusions

In this context of fears and concerns about how to protect the Islamic tradition, Muhammad ibn Idrîs ash-Shâfi'î (died 204/820)[1] proceeded to an initial categorization of Islamic sources and did so in several stages. His personal history and the debates in which he was involved are especially enlightening about his motivations and on the substance of his legal thought and output. Ash-Shâfi'î was probably born in Gaza, Palestine, in 150/767.[2] He arrived in Mecca when he was about ten years old and lived there with his mother in great poverty. At that time, the two main centers of Islamic legal thought were Iraq (with the cities of Kûfah and Basrah) and Hijâz (with the cities of Mecca and Medina). Iraqi scholars, influenced by Abu Hanîfah (died 150/767), were known to follow the school of opinion (*ahl ar-ra'y*),[3] whereas those of Hijâz, under the authority of imam Mâlik ibn Anas followed the school of tradition (*ahl al-hadîth*). Living in the very birthplace of Islam—in Medina and Mecca—the Hijâz scholars saw themselves as safeguards against what they considered as excess on the part of the scholars of Iraq (or of more distant peripheral areas) who, they felt, made immoderate use of analogical reasoning (*qiyâs*) or of autonomous critical reasoning from and beyond the texts (*ijtihâd*). Thus, Mâlik ibn Anas insisted on the superiority of the Quran over any other legal source, followed immediately by the Prophet's tradition and that of his Companions living in Medina or in Mecca. Mâlik, who was critical of the Hanafî school jurists whom he deemed too neglectful of tradition,[4] put important stress on the methodological requirement of following the Prophet's example and the practices of the Companions who were necessarily better apt to understand and interpret the meaning of legal verses and to implement them faithfully.[5]

Ash-Shâfi'î was Mâlik ibn Anas's pupil for ten years in Medina (probably between 170/787 and 179/796). He studied his master's key work, *al-Muwatta'*, and came to know it by heart. He followed in his master's footsteps and soon took a stand as the guardian of tradition against the advocates of opinion and of a critical approach. When Mâlik died, ash-Shâfi'î left Medina for Iraq, the very center of the *ahl ar-ra'y* whom he had opposed from Hijâz. In Baghdad, he became acquainted with one of Abû Hanîfah's most famous followers, Muhammad ibn al-Hassan ash-Shaybânî (died 189/805): a sharp, intense debate started between the two men. Ash-Shâfi'î criticized Abû Hanîfah's approach and that of ash-Shaybânî and their followers, and the followers complained. Ash-Shâfi'î was soon pressured to leave Iraq by those opponents and the rejection he encountered. It was probably during that first stay in Iraq that he wrote the first version of his book commonly known as *ar-Risâla fî usûl al-fiqh*:[6] ash-Shâfi'î felt the need to answer his critics by laying out a framework, rules, and a methodology of how the Quran and Prophetic traditions should be understood and interpreted. He knew that differences in views originated earlier in the process than legal opinions themselves, and were directly linked to the way fundamental texts were approached to extract rulings and practices (*istinbât al-ahkâm wal-qawâ'id*). Responding to the advocates of opinion, he drew up the primary principles of the fundamentals of Islamic *usûl al-fiqh*; in doing so, he was heavily influenced by the debates and controversies of his time. As a disciple of Mâlik resisting the criticisms of the advocates of the Hanafî school, ash-Shâfi'î determined the primary sources of Islamic law in an attempt to establish a clear framework. However, the years he had spent with

the advocates of opinion—who leaned heavily on analogical reasoning and critical reading of scriptural sources[7]—were to have a
crucial impact on the evolution of Imam ash-Shâfi'î's thought: later,
when he settled in Egypt, he reconsidered his positions and wrote
a second version of the *Risâla* (which is the only one that has come
down to us complete).

After that initial confrontational encounter in Iraq, ash-Shâfi'î
did leave Iraq and went back to Mecca for a few years. There, he
met Ahmad ibn Hanbal (died 241/855), who was to become his
pupil, and with whom he was soon to differ. His stay in Iraq already
seemed to have had some effect on Imâm ash-Shâfi'î, who, according to Ibn Abî Hâtim ar-Râzî, seemed to have become less strict
about almost exclusive references to the texts and tradition.[8] He left
Mecca again to return to Baghdad where he stayed for four years.
In 198/814, the Caliph al-Ma'mûn established his rule in Baghdad,
and he decided to make the doctrine of the rationalist Mu'tazilî
school the official doctrine. The pressure, then the rapid repression
inflicted on those Muslim scholars who disagreed with the rationalist approach, seem to explain why ash-Shâfi'î's left for Egypt. There
he settled and remained until he died. The second version of the
Risâla was therefore written in Cairo: it seems to be the new work of
a scholar intent—amid the surrounding tensions and confusion—on
setting up clear principles about how to approach texts and providing his contemporaries with a methodology that took into account
the wide range of views he had encountered during his life. Imâm
ash-Shâfi'î indeed stands out as a prominent figure in the geography and chronology of legal schools: as Mâlik's pupil, ash-Shaybanî's
contemporary and Ahmad ibn Hanbal's teacher, he was best suited
to perform a kind of synthesis that was not merely the reaction of
one trend of thought (*ahl ul-hadîth*) against the other (*ahl ar-ra'y*).
His second work is more "inclusive" even though it clearly bears the
influence of the atmosphere of the time, with its unending tensions
and the scholar's fear of seeing new interpretations emerge in total
disregard for the objective requirements of the text or of the Prophet's example. In the realm of legal studies, then, ash-Shâfi'î strove to
fulfill the increasingly obvious need for a general framework, or synthesis, enabling legal scholars to remain faithful to primary sources
and to harmonize their works without refusing the natural diversity
of their legal approaches.

Deducing from the Sources: Methodology and Hierarchy

Imâm ash-Shâfi'î had defined Islamic law and jurisprudence (*fiqh*) synthetically, and as centuries went by that definition was to prevail and become a reference for specialists over and above the differences between legal schools. *Fiqh* was, according to him, "knowledge of the [revealed] rules of [Islamic] law [related to human action] and extracted from the evidence in specific [scriptural] sources."[9] From the outset, following the example set by the Prophet and his Companions, Muslims strove to "extract" from the scriptural sources of the Quran and Prophetic traditions (*Sunnah*) laws and rulings enabling them to regulate their actions in their respective societies, first in Medina, then in Hijâz, and finally throughout the rapidly expanding Muslim world. The exercise was natural, necessary, and somewhat imperative for Muslims, who wanted to remain faithful to the Revelation while facing new environments and new realities and cultures.

We saw earlier that the Prophet had, when sending his companion Mu'âdh ibn Jabal to Yemen, stressed the need and spirit of this continuous effort of legal elaboration. Therefore, the Companions, and later scholars, found no difficulty in recognizing the need for that critical work of legal elaboration and they undertook it almost naturally. What caught ash-Shâfi'î's interest in the course of his travels and of the many debates he was involved in (whether with Mâlik and the Malikî, with the Hanafî, or with Ahmad ibn Hanbal himself) was the process rather than the actual production of law and jurisprudence. Like the other parties, he was not opposed to the principle of extracting (*istinbât*) rules through critical reading (which he considered to be part of the practice of *fiqh*) but he identified a growing problem in the absence of extraction principles, of a clear methodology as to how scriptural sources themselves should be read. He was convinced of the need for critical readings in the field of *fiqh*, and the debates with opposing scholars convinced him that laying out a framework, fundamentals (*usûl*)—that is, a methodology and rules—beforehand was a necessity. He set out to provide a methodology regulating the extraction of rules, determining typologies and the different levels of semantic expression, as well as a categorization of rules and injunctions taking into account their mode of exposition and their substance. This represented the birth of a new and foundational science:

usûl al-fiqh, the fundamentals of law and jurisprudence, and ash-Shâfi'î's seminal work stands out as a turning point in the history of Islamic law.

Ash-Shafi'î proceeds by returning to the initial scriptural sources, the Quran and Prophetic traditions (Sunnah) and establishing categories among the sources themselves, then within the respective sources, distinguishing the different levels of enunciation as well as taking into account such elements as scope and clarity in the wording of rulings. As early on as the second chapter of his *Risâla*,[10] he focuses on the concept of *"bayân"* (which can literally mean "explanation," of "the substance of what it conveyed" as well as "clarification of the substance of what is conveyed") and points out that "the term is generic and can have several meanings."[11] He starts by drawing up an initial categorization, identifying five levels of clarification, referring both to the varying importance of the injunctions and to the specificity of their sources (Quran alone, Quran and Sunnah, or Sunnah alone). Without going into details, which would divert us from the issue at hand, ash-Shâfi'î's intentions are clear from the beginning: he sets out to deduce a framework, a reading grid, from scriptural sources (while distinguishing their nature—Quran and Prophetic traditions—as well as the importance and the decisive character of the statement of rulings) to be able to suggest a kind of typology of the orders of law, which is indeed sketched in the following chapter and that focuses on the different levels of Islamic legal knowledge.

The approach adopted is hence clearly deductive: it first of all focuses on the fundamental texts—without giving attention to the specific productions of law and jurisprudence—and draws up the first basic categories as to the modalities of text reading. It was in the chapter dealing with the Quran itself that ash-Shâfi'î proposed an innovative approach that was later to be praised by the scholars of all legal schools, because it established distinctions both in modes of expression (general or specific) and in the substance of statements (explicit or implicit). Such an approach was apt to outline a methodology relying on a twofold distinction as to enunciation levels and the nature (and often the cause) of the utterance itself. Ash-Shâfi'î first of all distinguishes the general and the specific in the Quranic text; then he identifies subcategories in the first sort (the general) referring to the context of enunciation, or to the implicit character of the meaning, or to the need to relate to the Prophetic tradition (Sunnah) to understand it. For each of those categories, he refers to verses and proves the validity of his approach by detailing the various possible types of interpretation those verses can be given. He completes those reflections with a study of the need to rely on the Prophetic tradition (thus clarifying his position amid the debates that opposed the *ahl al-hadîth* and the *ahl ar-ra'y*) and of the modalities of its use in relation to the primary source, the Quran.[12]

The general framework and the basic typology were thus established, and this enabled ash-Shâfi'î to carry on what he had undertaken to do: extracting and ranking principles. Amid the sharp debates of his time, in the face of criticism, keen to provide a synthesis about the fundamentals of law and jurisprudence, ash-Shâfi'î mainly focused on the two fundamental scriptural sources about which a clear consensus existed. He gave less attention to discussing secondary sources such as *ijmâ'* (consensus) and *qiyâs* (analogical reasoning). His approach is coherent and admittedly logical, since only after drawing up the methodology and establishing typologies and enunciation categories can it be possible to deal with the question of unprecedented situations about which the texts say nothing. Although from the outset, as we have seen, the Prophet's Companions and the *fuqahâ'* (jurists) accepted the principle of interpreting scriptural sources and resorting to critical and autonomous reasoning (should such sources be unavailable), proposing to establish a framework and methodology—beforehand—for the exercise of critical interpretation could not but be a sensitive issue and a particularly perilous undertaking, since it entailed establishing the framework of legitimacy and of legal authority beyond the universally accepted authority of the texts.

Texts, Contexts, and Secondary Sources
(Ijtihâd, Ijmâ', Qiyâs)

We have seen that ash-Shâfi'î's primary aim was to establish a framework and methodology in approaching texts, which were the main object of his study. In the course of this analysis, I have also noted that he often referred to the "context" when this was necessary or simply when it shed light on the meaning of the texts at hand. Thus, some verses are linked to specific stories, for instance when a particular situation is mentioned. Ash-Shâfi'î quotes the verse: *"Ask them about the town standing close by the sea..."*[13] and points out that the mention of the inhabitants who "transgressed in the matter of the Sabbath" after that verse gives a contextual clue to understand that the initial reference to "the town standing close by the sea" is actually about its inhabitants. In this case, various elements in the text determine an enunciation context that makes it possible to extract the actual meaning of one or several elements in the text at hand. Ash-Shâfi'î also establishes the same principle for Prophetic traditions: texts, enunciation contexts, but also specific human situations, can shed a new light on some texts that are open to interpretation (*zannî*), and the human context is thus explicitly or implicitly called on in the interpretation process.

The specificity of secondary sources lies in the fact that the very justification of their existence is linked to the new social and cultural environment that makes it necessary to draw up laws in addition to what is present in the initial scriptural sources. Moving from Medina to Yemen, for instance, or encountering sharper cultural differences, or the mere evolution of history, compels scholars to read the texts critically "in the light of the human context" to remain faithful to the texts and their spirit when integrating and coping with the new reality. Ash-Shâfi'î's approach of the notion of *ijmâ'* had evolved dramatically. Initially, under Mâlik's influence, he restricted its scope to the scholars of Medina or of Hijâz, but in his last book, *ar-Risâla*, he insisted *ijmâ'* should extend to the community as a whole. This opening could however, paradoxically, amount to restricting the possibility for scholars to resort to consensus, for indeed consensus of the entire community is impossible in practice and could only be achieved over the basic, founding principles of Islam (*al-usûl*) about which consensus exists as a matter of course and would, therefore, be tautological and useless.

That actually rather restrictive outlook is confirmed when one considers ash-Shâfi'î's caution as regards autonomous critical reasoning (*ijtihâd*), which he all but reduces to analogical reasoning (*qiyâs*). It should be kept in mind that ash-Shâfi'î's initial intention was to defend the texts' primacy and to provide a reading grid that would ensure faithfulness to their substance. His insisting on analogical reasoning exactly fits with this undertaking: indeed, the environment challenges the scholar's interpretation of the texts, but he must return to the text itself, determine the effective cause (*'illah*) of the revealed ruling from its enunciation context (or its human context), and carry on his reflection to adapt that ruling to the new environment or situation. Thus, the scholar's critical reasoning is controlled and protected: the texts make it possible to think out the new reality mainly "by analogy" to a previous ruling: the framework of the text stands out as the reference and the norm. Ash-Shâfi'î is cautious and his account of those fundamental issues remains very brief. It remains, nevertheless, that he acknowledged the need for *ijtihâd* after initially considering that the context could not—in one way or another[14]—be called on to understand scriptural sources. His deductive approach has the advantage of clarifying categories and making the scholars' field of investigation considerably more secure. The methodology and extraction principles were indeed established by determining the fundamental sources of law: the Quran, the Prophetic traditions, *ijmâ'* in the broader meaning of community consensus, and *ijtihâd* in the more restricted meaning of *qiyâs*.[15]

The religious, political—and historical—environment around ash-Shâfi'î enables us to understand his priorities and the nature of his approach. By returning to the fundamentals of *usûl al-fiqh*, he restores the Quran and, especially, the Prophetic tradition, to the core of the debates. The deductive method that guides him through his venture systematically puts forward the centrality of the texts and clarifies enunciation categories. This is indeed, as we have said, a reading grid making for a faithful extraction (*istinbât*) of Islamic principles, rules, and rulings. The human context is everywhere present—and necessary—in the explanation of the method, but it remains a secondary reference. In any case, the context is less a reference than a clarification, a means of revelation, and often a mirror. Scholars or jurists, specialized in the study of texts, analyze it insofar as it sheds light on an aspect of the text or questions the text (as well as its silences) in a specific way. The environment is not one of the sources of the fundamentals of law, but all the textual fundamentals relate to the social, human, and historical context whether to act on it, to explain it, or to direct the implementation of principles and rulings.

4

The Hanafî School:
The Inductive Approach

Imam Abû Hanîfah (died 150/767) was born in Kûfa (probably in the year 80/699); he was one of the most eminent scholars in the Iraqi legal tradition and, therefore, among the advocates of opinion (*ahl ar-ra'y*).[1] Abû Hanîfah himself did not write about his own thought, methods, and conclusions: what we know of his methodology and practices has mainly come down to us through his pupils—such as, in particular, Abû Yûsuf, Muhammad ibn al-Hassan ash-Shaybânî, and Zafar ibn Hudhayl. Nothing certain is known about how he wrote and composed his famous collection of Prophetic traditions (*ahâdîth*), *al-Musnad*, but it seems that, essentially, his pupils compiled the book, which he then reviewed, under his authority following the chapter order of classical *fiqh* works. Abû Hanîfah was at first a trader (a lifelong occupation); he gradually became interested in the learned circles of his native town, Kûfâ, where debates and disputes over issues of *fiqh*, philosophy (*kalâm*), belief (*'aqîdah*), or politics were sharp and frequent. He studied numerous subjects such as *kalâm* (philosophy) and *tafsîr* (Quran exegesis); he then focused more specifically on *fiqh* and studied under the authority of an Iraqi scholar of his time, Hammâd Abû Sulaymân. Later, he met scholars belonging to different traditions (various Shi'î trends) and legal schools (Mâlikî, Awzâ'î, Thawrî) as well as Companions of the Prophet, in particular during his stays in or journeys to Mecca.

Abû Hanîfah: A Period, a Life, a Method

Imam Abû Hanîfah lived in an earlier age than ash-Shâfi'î and did not face the same challenges. While the former carried on the legal elaboration of the Prophet's Companions and that of the following generation (at-tâbi'ûn) in a city where intellectual activity was a century-old tradition, the latter—with his work ar-Risâla—worked on clarification, synthesis, and normative refocusing in the face of the excesses and legal disagreements that were increasingly numerous at the time. Kûfa's scholars included Shiites (Ja'far as-Sâdiq was to be one of Abû Hanîfah's teachers), Zaydî, Khârijî, Mu'tazilî, and other trends or sects: Abû Hanîfah did not hesitate to argue and debate with them. He even went to Basrah to debate the opinions of the advocates of various sects, and even of the Dahrites, who were atheist materialists. Those debates and journeys went on throughout his life. His six-year stay in Mecca enabled him to meet some Companions of the Prophet, the new generation (at-tâbi'ûn), and imams Mâlik and al-Awzâ'î, among other scholars, as well as to get acquainted with the thought of the advocates of tradition (ahl al-hadîth). A long way from Hijâz, with a limited number of Prophetic traditions available to him, Abû Hanîfah was to seek knowledge from the greatest possible number of sources and draw up his own methodology, which his pupils' commitment later turned into an acknowledged and respected legal school (madhhab). Abû Hanîfah's time, unlike ash-Shâfi'î's, was mainly involved in legal work that the location itself made necessary: far away from Mecca and Medina, new solutions to new challenges had to be found.

In his city, Abû Hanîfah rubbed shoulders with Greeks, Indians, Persians, and Arabs, and their sundry cultures came in addition to the many different trends of thought just mentioned. Those features were to exert obvious influence on his thought, as, indeed, was his constant involvement in trade. His legal thought was directly confronted with the reality of customs, trading, and financial practices and the difficulty, if not the impossibility, of failing to take into account the interests of the people. His reading of the texts is therefore naturally impregnated with the requirements of reality and of people's daily life. Those requirements make it necessary for him to question scriptural sources when they are open to interpretation (*zannî*) or simply have nothing to say on the subject: he must find answers that remain faithful to the texts while solving the problems of his time. Abû Hanîfah identifies three secondary sources that he combines with (or with which he supplements) the three main sources acknowledged at his time (Quran, Sunnah and *ijmâ'*). He thus reinforces and gives a place of honor to the practice of analogical reasoning (*qiyâs*), while relying on the principle of *istihsân* (legal preference established by a scholar while taking public interest into account) and integrating reference to custom (*'urf*) into legal elaboration. The common feature of those secondary sources is to take into account, all at once, the environment, new situations, cultures, and, of course, the interest of societies and people. Thus, the texts remain the primary reference but the human and social context must be taken into account to nurture legal elaboration: reading the texts while attempting to extract the finalities of enunciation (as the *ahl ar-ra'y* strove to do) made for a more natural integration of the context as those texts were implemented in a new environment.

As we have seen, Abû Hanîfah did not write any synthesis of his own thought and methodology. It was through his pupils that the bulk of his production as well as information about his method came down to us. He used to gather his students, present a case and let them study it, debate over it, and state their opinions. Only then would he step in and expound his own opinion on the issue. Moreover, unlike Imam Mâlik, as we shall see, he did not hesitate to devise hypothetical situations and to extrapolate, prompting his students to formulate potential answers. Such hypothetical juridical elaboration (*fiqh taqdîrî*)[2] is interesting insofar as the scholar questions the text while imagining the possibilities of reality (or even of the future): he thus continuously compels himself to seek the justification, the effective cause (*'illah*) of commands or prohibitions to remain as faithful as possible to it whatever the environment or human situation. Abû Hanîfah was interested in *fiqh* and never thought out—or clearly stated—categories for extracting rulings from primary scriptural sources. His production in the field of *fiqh*, as transmitted by his pupils, soon focused on the practical aspect, the ramifications of law (*furû'*), and detailed secondary questions. His method, insisting on confronting human realities, naturally led him to produce detailed, pragmatic answers. These answers were to serve as a basis to elaborate the inductive method of Hanafî scholars.

The Practice of Induction: Identifying Theoretical Fundamentals from Practical Legal Responses

The previous short account of Abû Hanîfah's experience and output is highly relevant to the present study. One can clearly perceive that the legal scholar, the *faqîh*, is faced with the realities of his society and of the human beings around him; he seeks concrete solutions in the light of the texts but also takes into account the requirements of the place, of customs, and of the common good. In the process, he naturally seeks to identify the *'illah* of the commands and prohibitions stated in scriptural sources, in order, after this has been established, to lay out rules or suggest legal opinions (*fatâwâ*), which will remain faithful to the objective of the injunction (as revealed by the aforesaid *'illah*) beyond the letter of the text (or its "silence"). The surrounding reality's presence is everywhere to be felt in Abû Hanîfah's undertaking, and it must be noted that the school of the advocates of opinion (*ahl ar-ra'y*) having flourished in Iraq rather than in Hijâz is by no means coincidental. Naturally enjoying less direct access to the Prophetic traditions, and living in a society that was quite different from that of the cities of Medina and Mecca, those scholars were compelled to face the requirements of the context, its complexity, and new questions, at the very time when they were trying to implement the rulings stated in the text. With Abû Hanîfah, we are still in the early stages of the production of this applied law: questioning, a critical approach—occasionally courage and daring—and continuous, confident creativity accompany the scholar, the jurist, who does not hesitate to press deeply into the discussion of practical details, or even, as we have seen, to imagine hypothetical situations.

About half a century later, ash-Shâfi'î was already in a different situation. Although, in his work as a legal scholar, a *faqîh*, he did not

hesitate to summon the same critical spirit, courage, and inventive-
ness as his predecessor Abû Hanîfah, he nevertheless perceived the
first signs of excess in the use of secondary sources—opinion, legal
preference based on the common good (*istihsân*), custom, and even
inordinate use of analogical reasoning (*qiyâs*)—at the expense of the
texts' central status as primary references. This led him to return to
the texts and decide, as we have seen, to suggest a reading grid, a
ruling (*ahkâm*) extraction methodology with its categories, principles, and tenets. He was intent on drawing up a framework to ward
off deviation in the field of *fiqh*. It must be noted that Abû Hanîfah
himself had been faced with sharp criticism of his methods: he was
accused of neglecting the Sunnah (Prophetic traditions) in favor of
analogical reasoning (*qiyâs*) and of making immoderate use of his
own opinion when determining legal preference (*istihsân*). Facing
public authorities as well as debating with other scholars, he repeatedly had to respond to such accusations and to insist on the essential
status of Prophetic traditions in his thought and in his *fatâwâ*.[3] He
once said: "What comes from the Messenger of God, peace be upon
him, we accept with our mind and heart, by my father and mother,
we cannot oppose it. What comes from the Companions, we choose
from. As for what comes from other sources, well, they are human
beings as we are."[4]

Beyond ash-Shâfi'î's encounter with one of Abû Hanîfah's
pupils, ash-Shaybânî (as already mentioned) and the disagreements
between them, the elaboration of the fundamentals of law (*usûl
al-fiqh*) as set forth by ash-Shâfi'î turned into a real challenge for
the advocates of the Hanafî school. For how could they explain the
conclusions reached by Abû Hanîfah and his most prolific pupils?
How indeed could they explain the disagreements within their own
school (since the pupil Abû Yûsuf repeatedly mentioned his differences of opinion with his master)? How could the bulk of the
Hanafî legal output—which closely followed reality and was therefore highly detailed—be integrated with the methodology and,
going forward, the almost *a priori* categories laid out by ash-Shâfi'î?
Abû Hanîfah's advocates were therefore to adopt a different attitude
from ash-Shâfi'î's in their approach to texts and to the fundamentals of law: instead of questioning—or restricting—the production and practical output of *fiqh* by imposing a frame of reference
beforehand, they reconstructed such a frame of reference from

their scholars' conclusions and legal opinions: they proceeded by induction to "reach up" to the motives and effective causes ('*ilal*, plural of '*illah*) of the scholars' opinions in order, in the process, to identify the '*ilal* that explain textual rulings (as understood by their scholars). This thus enabled them to identify a number of extraction rules (*qawâ'id al-istinbât*) specific to their school as well as lay out a general methodology and categorization based on the scholars' customary practice.

This inductive work is interesting but it is also naturally rich with the experience of law applied to the realities of the world that characterized Abû Hanîfah and his advocates. The impressive legal output of Hanafî *fuqahâ* is well known, with such famous works as Abû Yûsuf's *Kitâb al-Athâr* or *Kitâb al-Kharaj*, or ash-Shaybânî's *al-Mabsût* (sometimes called *al-Asl—The Primary Principle*—on account of its importance), *al-Jâmi' as-Saghîr* or *al-Jâmi' al-Kabîr*. But the synthesis of Hanafî thought in the field of the fundamentals of *usûl al-fiqh* especially appears in the works of Abû al-Hassan Ali ibn Muhammad al-Bazdawî (died 483/1089), also known as "Fakhr al-Islâm" (the pride of Islam). His major work on the question, *Kanz al-Wusûl ilâ Ma'rifat al-Usûl* (sometimes simply referred to as *al-Usûl*),[5] sets forth the Hanafî school's principles and methodology concerning the fundamentals of law (*usûl*) resulting from lengthy inductive work (carried out by Bazdawî himself but also by earlier Hanafî scholars). In the light of this major work, as well as taking into account Abû Hanîfah's own sayings (as reported here and there),[6] one can identify the sources on which the Hanafî school relies to extract rulings. They are seven: the Quran, the Sunnah (Prophetic traditions), sayings of the Companions, *ijmâ'* (consensus), *qiyâs* (analogical reasoning), *istihsân* (legal preference), and *al-'urf* (custom).

The inductive method that reconstructs the sequences of dialectical reasoning (text-context), starting from legal answers and working its way up towards the codification of theoretical fundamentals, clearly differs from ash-Shâfi'î's inductive method on at least two levels: the modalities and nature of reasoning from *fatâwâ* on which realities have already exerted considerable influence—if not a decisive influence as in the case of *istihsân*—and, of course, how to identify the sources of the fundamentals of law (*usûl al-fiqh*).

Rationality, Methodology, and Sources

Hanafî scholars, who tried *a posteriori* to understand the logic and coherence of the methodology Abû Hanîfah had laid out—without ever setting it forth explicitly—first had to compare his conclusions, his answers, and sometimes his own revisions or corrections of some of his legal opinions. It was impossible for them to refer only to verses and Prophetic traditions, and therefore, in their attempt to extract the effective causes of the interpretations, they had to look into the texts' relations in terms of specific contexts, for that justified the various legal opinions stated. From the beginning, the analysis they undertook was based on dialectical reasoning between text and context, since those two dimensions were already present, as a matter of course, in the practical legal answer that was their starting point. The exercise therefore consisted in drawing logical links between the causes and consequences of a human legal opinion on the one hand, and on the other, one or several revealed texts or Prophetic traditions relevant to the issue. This work of logical and dialectical correspondence was meant to shed light on what had been understood of the explicit and implicit intent of scriptural sources. One can see here that reality, the social and human environment, sheds light—by induction—on the modalities of interpretation of the text and makes it possible, in a two-stage process, to extract not only the effective cause of the mere legal opinion but also the effective cause (*al-'illah*) of the texts themselves. Rationality, dialectical reasoning, and identification of the effective cause of a ruling (*hukm*) shape the Universe of the scholars seeking the fundamentals of law and permanently compel them to take into account not only the enunciation context—as with ash-Shâfi'î—but also the human and social contexts as a whole.

Hanafî scholars were gradually, like Bazdawî, to lay out the framework of a methodology that, while it had not been explicitly set forth by Abû Hanîfah himself, was nevertheless the reading grid underlying the bulk of his output. The context's constant presence made dialectical reasoning and critical argumentation necessities, as we have seen, and Ibn Khaldûn was later to point out how decisive Bazdawî's contribution had been in this field. That methodology, which was initially practiced naturally and informally, made it possible when theorized to work back to the fundamentals of law (*usûl*), to categorize them, but also, in particular, to identify the sources that accompanied the inductive work. When ash-Shâfi'î had undertaken his deductive work starting from scriptural sources, he had clearly stated not only that the latter were central to the process, but also that they were to have priority over any other consideration. Thus, even when the text says nothing, critical, autonomous reasoning (*ijtihâd*) is possible, in the restrictive sense of analogical reasoning (*qiyâs*)—or possibly of *istihsân* (legal preference)[7]—which takes the scholar back to the logic and the effective cause ('*illah*) determined by the text itself. Abû Hanîfah and the scholars of the Hanafî school of course accepted the central status of the Quran and Prophetic traditions[8] and in this sense, as we have said, the criticisms Abû Hanîfah encountered for neglecting the Sunnah are unjustified, all the more so when one considers the high importance he—and his pupils after him—granted to the opinions of the Prophet's Companions. However, what clearly appears in the Hanafî school's *a posteriori* identification of the sources of Islamic law is a series of secondary sources that clearly took into account the relation to the social and human context.

When scriptural sources say nothing about a particular issue, Abû Hanîfah recognizes the binding character of *ijmâ*'—which he defines as the consensus of the Companions and of law scholars in general—which appears as the first (collective) form of the exercise of *ijtihâd*. Analogical reasoning (*al-qiyâs*) is of course central to the Hanafî school's methodology, and "hypothetical fiqh" (*al-fiqh at-taqdîrî*) constantly relies on analogy while examining more and more numerous and complex situations. Unlike ash-Shâfi'î, Abû Hanîfah never considered *istihsân* as a mere extension of *qiyâs* (which should indeed have restricted its use) but rather, along with Imam Mâlik,[9] as a self-sufficient reference and tool. Indeed, *istihsân*'s role for Abû Hanîfah is almost the opposite of its restricted position in ash-Shâfi'î's categorization: he does not restrict *istihsân* through *qiyâs* but on the contrary resorts to *istihsân* (literally, legal *preference*) to avoid a strict and literal implementation of analogical reasoning in contradiction with the objectives of the Revelation, which are primarily to protect people's integrity and belongings while making their lives easier. One can see that in practice, without denying the necessary relation to texts, *istihsân* appears as a secondary source that—by definition—takes into account the social and human context. The same applies, of course, to the seventh source mentioned: *al-'urf*, custom, which by definition establishes a relation to the environment: this latter is taken into account to shed light on the reading of scriptural sources, guide the concrete implementation of rulings, and, finally, bring into the field of legality positive (or inherently good) customary practices about which the texts say nothing. This additionally requires scholars to understand the society in which they live when formulating laws.

Abû Hanîfah's work was earlier than ash-Shâfi'î's; the will to clarify and restrict appeared *a posteriori* when it seemed that excesses were increasing and that some people were taking too much liberty with the binding and normative character of the texts. Historically closer to the source, Abû Hanîfah has a naturally more confident approach and tries to extend the experience of the first community of believers as to faithfully implementing rulings, keeping to the spirit of the texts (to make life easier for human beings) and giving pragmatic answers. His own experience of men was always called on during his legal elaboration, in particular in the field of trade: a number of rules or exonerations set forth by Abû Hanîfah (for example, paying *zakât*—the purifying social tax—in cash rather than in kind, or less burdensome rules when trading in non-Muslim countries) were clearly influenced by consideration for the social environment or even for people's customs and habits. Such flexibility in a large number of fields is also found in the work of his contemporary Imam Mâlik, with his detailed exploration of *al-masâlih al-mursalah* (public-interest issues that are not mentioned in the texts) or his resorting to *istihsân* to regulate an overrestrictive or counterproductive exercise of analogical reasoning: in both cases, one can see that the context is largely taken into account. It is, indeed, still considered as a secondary source, but its role is fundamental and implicitly or explicitly plays a regulating part either in the reading or in the implementation of texts. The point is always to identify the motive, the effective cause (*al-'illah*) of a command or prohibition to extract the intention (*niyyah*), the objective (*qasd*), or the wise purpose (*hikmah*) behind the said injunctions. Without such a process, it becomes impossible to implement rulings (*ahkâm*) or to state *fatâwâ* in a new environment without running the twofold risk of either literal implementation betraying the spirit or immersion in social reality causing to neglect the letter.

The deductive method, like the inductive method, made it possible in the course of time to establish the primary sources of Islamic law and jurisprudence. The issue at stake was knowing how to handle the reference texts in new contexts and throughout human history. The preoccupation was, and is still, trying to remain faithful to the Quran and Prophetic traditions: early scholars naturally sought solutions for their time, but it was also necessary to lay out a framework, norms, and a methodology. What emerges from this long codifying process is that initially, early scholars opened out toward the world, society, habits, and customs as natural spaces that were to be taken into account in the lawmaking process; then, with the passing of decades—and with territorial expansion and often excessive extrapolation—scholars refocused on texts and stressed their precedence over any other consideration. However, at no point did this historical movement prevent legal production nor, especially, consideration of the texts' effective causes and objectives. This preoccupation is inherently linked to the early works of *fuqahâ*. Later scholars, more interested in the fundamentals of law (*usûliyyûn*), were to rely on the bulk of the heritage left by the *fuqahâ* and legal schools to strive to put forward a new reading grid and methodology derived from the higher objectives of Islamic law. This is almost a third age of the sciences of fundamentals (*usûl al-fiqh*) and this school's contribution was to have a crucial impact, particularly by imposing a new way of approaching and considering the relationships among the law, its objectives, and the human and social context.

5

The School of *Maqâsid*:
The Higher Objectives of Law

While studying the respective contributions of the Hanafî school or that of ash-Shâfi'î, one can note that whether in the practice of *fiqh* itself (law and jurisprudence) or in the deductive or inductive codification of *usûl al-fiqh* (the fundamentals of law) earlier in the process, questions about the reasons for a ruling and explicit or implicit references to the effective cause of a command or prohibition (*'illah*) are present everywhere. Indeed, analogical reasoning (*qiyâs*) or legal preference (*istihsân*) is only possible after the cause has been identified in the primary scriptural source: this makes it possible to extract the principle (*al-asl*) that alone enables scholars to transfer the legal reasoning involved to other human situations with similar stakes (*al-furû'*, plural of *al-far'*). More generally, the same applies to the sphere of *masâlih mursalah* (public interest issues about which the texts say nothing) established very early on by Imam Mâlik (died 179/796), which requires scholars, when no text is available, to produce laws in line with the extension and logic of scriptural sources: such an undertaking is impossible without previously extracting the implicit or explicit intents in reference texts.[1] Thus, as can be seen, early *fuqahâ'*—and *usûliyyûn* after them—constantly had to refer to the cause (*sabab*), effective cause ('*illah*), intention (*niyyah*), objective (*qasd*), or sometimes wise purpose (*hikmah*) justifying or underlying a command, permission, or prohibition (*hukm*) to be able to state new legal opinions (*fatâwâ*) or lay out a methodology including principles for ruling extraction (*istinbât al-ahkâm ash-shar'iyyah*). Looking into this was a practical necessity as part of the scholars' relation to the texts, either to implement those texts in reality or to compose a reading grid that could control and guide this practice of implementing rulings in new realities. Whether for *fuqahâ'* or *usûliyyûn*, for the deductive or the inductive method, the objectives of rulings (*maqâsid al-ahkâm*) extracted in this manner were therefore necessarily circumscribed; practical necessity required that light should thus be shed, one after the other, on each and every one of the rulings established by scriptural sources.

The insight of some scholars specializing in the fundamentals of law (*al-usûliyyûn*) was to devise a more general approach, stepping back from the piecemeal examination of the effective causes ('*ilal*) or the explicit or implicit intents of individual rulings (*al-adillah at-tafsîliyyah*) to try to pinpoint the objectives motivating the bulk of the corpus of rulings (*al-ahkâm at-tashrî'iyyah*) found in scriptural sources. The point was thus to attempt to extract and classify the "higher objectives of law" (*maqâsid ash-sharî'ah*) and thereby constitute a kind of general philosophy of Islamic law. As we shall see, the early scholars who formulated some of those higher objectives by no means had the intention, nor even the intuition, of founding a new *usûl* school; they simply meant, by developing a holistic approach, to establish the fundamental coherence of the whole corpus of *ahkâm* to clarify the stakes in the practice of *fiqh*. This original approach was nevertheless to have important consequences not only in the way texts were handled by the *usûliyyûn* but also in the practical exercise of the *fuqahâ'* who had to state legal opinions (*fatâwâ*) in new contexts. By operating a synthesis of the deductive and inductive contributions before them and by determining the higher objectives of the texts, the scholars of what was to become the "school of the higher objectives" (*madrasat al-maqâsid*) not only established a new categorization of priorities about objectives and rules, but as we shall see, they especially, and paradoxically, opened the way to a necessary and more structured integration of the human and social environment in the practical implementation of law.

A School Comes into Existence:
From al-Juwaynî (Died 478/1085)
to ash-Shâtibî (Died 790/1388)

We have seen how Imam ash-Shâfi'î (died 204/820) outlined the new science of the fundamentals of *usûl al-fiqh*. None of the later studies in this field could overlook ash-Shâfi'î's seminal work and crucial contribution on the issue. For centuries, and to the present, he established a framework and an approach that was unanimously acknowledged, although it was debated over, discussed, and sometimes challenged: indeed, disputes over the identification of primary and secondary sources—beyond the unanimity over the Quran and Sunnah—have never stopped. The influence of Imam ash-Shâfi'î's school has been, and remains, transversal, and its impact has affected all schools of Islamic law and thought. Ash-Shâfi'î had opened a new way and set forth a methodology and rules that all later scholars, whether they specialized in fundamentals (*usûliyyûn*) or in implementing law and jurisprudence (*fuqahâ'*), were to benefit from by integrating them or by debating about them.

Almost two hundred and fifty years later, a scholar from the Shafi'î school initiated an original reflection about the fundamentals of Islamic law (*usûl al-fiqh*). He indeed relied on ash-Shâfi'î's works, but he kept insisting on some aspects about which his master had remained cautious for he felt they could allow excess in subverting the texts: the Lawgiver's intention, and the effective cause (*'illah*) of commands and prohibitions beyond mere analogical reasoning (*qiyâs*) acknowledged by ash-Shâfi'î. Abû al-Ma'âlî al-Juwaynî (died 478/1085), also known as "the imam of the two sanctuaries" (*imam al-haramayn*)—who was, incidentally, Abû Hâmid al-Ghazâlî's (died 505/1111) master—drew up a new categorization in his seminal work *al-Burhân fî Usûl al-Fiqh*:[2] indeed, he seems to have been the first to establish a categorization of rulings according to what could be perceived of the divine Lawgiver's intent—and the effective causes (*'ilal*) of the rulings—and not only about those rulings' letter and substance. Thus, he suggested to start by classifying them vertically according to their degree of importance and priority (from the most important to the secondary), identifying five different levels.[3] To this classification, he added a horizontal categorization distinguishing the goal sought by the rulings (religion, human life, chastity, etc.).[4] Al-Juwaynî was thus the first to set out a methodology that stood back from Islamic law and jurisprudence and their practical implementation: by starting from the intention and effective cause underlying each ruling, he tried to identify the divine Lawgiver's higher intent as it could be extracted when considering the bulk of the rulings and the Revelation as a whole. Many scholars before him had referred to intentions and effective causes and had, as we have seen, had the insight that such dimensions had to be taken into account, but nobody had so far suggested such a systematic and coherent categorization of *ahkâm* (rulings) according to the higher principles underlying them.

Abû Hâmid al-Ghazâlî, al-Juwaynî's pupil, took up the task and attempted to clarify such categories and the principles they could include. Although he came from the Shafi'î school, al-Ghazâlî returned to the notion of *istihsân* that Imam ash-Shâfi'î had, as we have seen, restricted so drastically so as to divest it of any substance of its own other than the mere exercise of analogical reasoning (*qiyâs*). In his major work about the fundamentals of law, *al-Mustasfâ min 'Ilm al-Usûl*,[5] al-Ghazâlî clearly supported the opinion of Mâlik and his school about *al-masâlih al-mursalah* (public interest issues about which the texts say nothing) and *al-istislâh* (reasoning that, in the absence of relevant texts, it relies on public interest). He thus says:

> In its essential significance, (*al-maslahah*) is a term that means seeking something useful (*manfa'ah*) or warding off something harmful (*madarrah*). But this is not what we mean, because seeking what is useful and preventing harm are objectives (*maqâsid*) sought by creation, and the good (*salah*) in the creation of mankind consists in achieving those *maqâsid*. What we mean by *maslahah* is preserving the objective (*maqsûd*) of the Law (*shar'*) that consists in five ordered things: preserving religion (*dîn*), life (*nafs*), reason (*'aql*), progeny (*nasl*), and property (*amwâl*). What ensures the preservation of those five principles (*usûl*) is *maslahah*; what goes against their preservation is *mafsadah*, and preventing it is *maslahah*.[6]

More clearly than his master, al-Ghazâlî drew up five categories that were to become the source for all later scholars. Shihâb ad-Dîn al-Qarâfî (died 684/1285),[7] Najm ad-Dîn at-Tûfî (died 716/1386), and Tâj ad-Dîn ibn as-Subkî (died 771/1369)[8] added honor (*al-'ird*) to the five main objectives or principles—other scholars sometimes accepted this, but sometimes rejected it—but it can be stated without hesitation that the general framework laid out by Abû Hâmid al-Ghazâlî served as the starting point of reflection in the early stages of the "school of objectives" (*madrasat al-maqâsid*) up to the time of ash-Shâtibî. To this should be added the vertical categorization that al-Juwaynî had at first established on five levels, and that al-Ghazâlî then synthesized by distinguishing among three groups of objectives according to their importance and priority: *ad-darûriyyât* (the five main objectives), *al-hajiyyât* (the objectives linked to complementary needs), and *at-tahsiniyyât* or *kamâliyyât* (secondary objectives linked to embellishing or perfecting). Thus al-Ghazâlî's work—and particularly, in this field, his book *al-Mustasfâ min 'Ilm al-Usûl*—is seminal in the birth of a new approach to the fundamentals of *usûl al-fiqh*: after al-Juwaynî, he set off a process seeking to determine a philosophy of Islamic law, advancing from the mere reading of rulings, which aimed to identify *a priori* a fundamental reference to which the scholar (*al-faqîh*) would have to refer and on which he would have to rely *a posteriori* to implement the law while constantly keeping in mind the order of the objectives to be preserved. Those objectives being thus determined, beyond the letter of the texts, they require legal scholars to integrate the human and social context into their reflections as to the concrete and practical implementation of rulings, for indeed the recurrent question al-Ghazâlî's ongoing reading grid entails is how, at a given time and/or in a given context, one can remain faithful to the objectives of scriptural sources when implementing legal rulings (*al-fiqh*) in the field of social affairs and interpersonal relations (*al-mu'âmalât*).[9]

Two particularly important points must be noted concerning this discussion about the fundamentals of law and their evolution in the "school of objectives": the first is its transversal character, since this reflection over "higher objectives," although it seems to originate with Shafi'î scholars, was to be integrated and/or debated about in one way or another by all the Islamic legal schools. Hanafî, Mâlikî, Hanbalî scholars (such as Tâj ad-Dîn ibn at-Tûfî), and even the more critical Dhahirî, were often to accept the theoretical prerequisites of this objective-based reading or adopt a critical stance (but without rejecting the approach altogether). The second point that must be stressed here pertains to al-Ghazâlî's (and his master's) return to the sources and his reintegrating the principles stated by the first Medina school (*ahl al-Madînah*) and especially, of course, Imam Mâlik ibn Anas (died 179/796). Indeed, such dimensions as the reference to *al-masâlih al-mursalah* (public interest issues about which the texts say nothing)—when determining objectives (*maqâsid*) and public and individual interest (*masâlih*)—as well as the specific modalities of the Mâlikî reading of texts seeking to identify their intent (*niyyah*) and objective (*maqsûd*), bring the theoretical framework of law fundamentals set forth by Shafi'î scholar al-Ghazâlî closer to the Mâlikî school's concrete implementation of rules. In Medina, 'Umar—the Prophet's father-in-law, close Companion, and later the second Caliph—the Companions, and later Mâlik (who synthesized the fundamentals of the thought and practices around him in his seminal work *al-Muwattâ'*), implemented Quranic rulings while constantly taking into account—in social affairs (*mu'âmalât*)—the texts' objectives as well as people's interest. Their knowledge of scriptural sources as well as of their natural human and social environment enabled them to be often highly flexible concerning permissions, which remain foremost in human affairs as stated in the famous rule: "the primary principle in anything [linked to social and interpersonal affairs] is permission." This can particularly be seen, as was the case with Abû Hanîfah, in all that concerns agriculture, trade, and customary practices, which Mâlik integrates into his reading of objectives and intentions. Even the principle of *sadd adh-dharâ'i'* (forbidding what can potentially lead to the unlawful or harmful), which was occasionally to lead to excessive prohibition in its later implementation, was initially set forth with a prospective outlook seeking to determine what could lead to transgression, extending from bad intentions and harmful objectives. This strict precaution as to the ways leading to the unlawful was originally clearly counterbalanced by confidence and flexibility concerning what is permitted (*mubâh*) and lawful (*halâl*).

It is interesting here to note this return to the origin of practices operated by later Shafi'î scholars. As I have said, ash-Shâfi'î had drawn up a very clear framework to avoid and ward off the excesses some scholars of his time had fallen into, and he had therefore been particularly strict about secondary sources and their use. Later, the scholars specializing in fundamentals of the law revisited those fundamentals and tried to rediscover and revive the spirit, methodology, and tools that had enabled Abû Hanîfah and Mâlik ibn Anas to not only be faithful to the texts but also particularly confident and flexible in human and social environments whose culture, customs, and practices in various fields they knew from within. Paradoxically, it was in early times, in the outlines sketched by the first school of Medina Companions, then in Mâlik's legal elaborations, that the scholars of the school of objectives were to find (again) an objective-related reading of the texts that was altogether dynamic, more flexible, freer, and always oriented toward a dialectic relation to the context.

Ash-Shâtibî: Integrating the Deductive and Inductive Legal Approaches into a Global Inductive Outlook

Abû Ishâq ash-Shâtibî was, it seems, born in Granada where he almost always remained.[10] Studies about him, essentially based on what his pupils said of him,[11] mention no important stay abroad and suggest that his life was marked by the religious and intellectual environment in which he was immersed since childhood. Ash-Shâtibî was trained in the Malikî school and most of his masters in Granada were known to be strict advocates of that school of thought, for instance, Ibn al-Fakhkhâr al-Bîrî and especially Mufti Abû Sa'îd ibn Lubb (with whom ash-Shâtibî was later to disagree strongly over the issue of beliefs—al-'aqîdah). Considering what was already mentioned about the Medina tradition and the Malikî school, ash-Shâtibî's coming from the latter does not seem coincidental, since his whole work was to be influenced by the tools laid out by the Companions, the subsequent generation (at-tâbi'ûn), and, of course, Imam Mâlik. He indeed returns to this while taking into account, or even integrating into his approach, all the works and methodologies produced in the meantime by scholars from the other schools—Shafi'î, Hanafî, Hanbalî, Zâhirî (with Ibn Hazm, died 456/1064), and the various Shî'î schools. As-Shâtibi's role in drawing up a new theory about the fundamentals of law (usûl al-fiqh), based on extracting and categorizing "the shari'ah's higher objectives," is unanimously acknowledged nowadays: he took up al-Ghazalî's reflections and completed, detailed, and fixed the methodological groundwork of a school that would henceforth be able to claim such a status, having its own philosophy of law, legitimate reading modalities (for texts as well as contexts), and its own outlook on how to deal with legal issues in practice. It should be added here that I by no means suggest there had been no interesting scholar, no major contribution in this field, during the two centuries between al-Ghazâlî and ash-Shâtibî: such works as those of ar-Râzî (died 606/1209), al-Baydâwî (died 685/1286), Ibn as-Subkî (died 771/1369), at-Tûfî (died 716/1316), and Ibn Taymiyyah (died 728/1327)—to mention only a few famous scholars—are rich and important. However, ash-Shâtibî's work does operate a major turning point in the approach to the fundamentals of law, with a theory and methodology that transcend legal schools while integrating the various tools those schools have provided (in particular the deductive and inductive approaches already mentioned).

Ash-Shâtibî's intention was not initially to establish a new school, but to return to the sources and revive the original spirit—based on rigor, faithfulness, and confidence—which animated early Medina scholars at the time of their practical legal elaboration. His will to "return to the source," to remain faithful, and to clarify, is confirmed by his first major work *al-I'tisâm*[12] ("seeking refuge, protection") in which he attacked all the innovations and deviations (*bida'*, sing. *bid'ah*) that he could see were more and more numerous in the field of the Islamic creed (*al-'aqîdah*). He did not hesitate to oppose his former masters and defend firm stances over *'aqîdah*-related issues, in particular concerning religious practices, certain Sufi trends, and local customs (regarding prayer, invocations, saints, etc.). His critical attitude was to cause him to have many enemies, whether among the political authorities or other scholars, but he unwaveringly kept to his commitment and clarified his thinking and his opposition to innovations by writing *al-I'tisâm*. This attachment to faithfulness, rigor, and "returning to the source" in the field of *'aqîdah* (belief), where scriptural sources must be the only reliable reference, was associated with the same will to return to initial practices in the field of "social affairs and interpersonal relations" (*mu'âmalât*). While "being faithful" to the sources and following the example of the Prophet and the Companions meant being strict and uncompromising in the fields of belief and worship (*al-'aqîdah wal-'ibadât*), this attitude also gave rise to necessary reconciliation with the methods initiated by the predecessors (*as-salaf as-sâlih*) based on knowledge of the texts and of the environment, on the divine Lawgiver's intent, on awareness of people's interests, and mostly on confidence as to the interpretative latitude scholars could enjoy.[13]

It is in the second volume of his book *al-Muwâfaqât fî Usûl ash-Sharîah*, throughout the section entitled *Kitâb al-Maqâsid* (the book of objectives),[14] that ash-Shâtibî sets forth the principles of his methodology in full detail. What strikes the reader from the beginning is the first section title and the account that follows. Indeed, ash-Shâtibî immediately distinguishes two types of objectives: those determined by "the divine Lawgiver" (*maqâsid ash-Shâri'*) and those stemming from "[accountable] human beings" (*maqâsid al-mukallaf*). This seemingly anodyne typology immediately places the text between two intentions (or goals) that the law scholar must try to "read," extract, understand, and, in the end, try to harmonize while implementing the law as well as when orienting human beings' understanding and behavior. Central to this approach is the primary general principle on which the teaching of *maqâsid* school relies: all the commands and prohibitions stated by the divine Lawgiver and established by the Prophet aim to promote good and to benefit human beings and to protect them from evil, from harm, and from subsequent suffering. This principle sheds light on how texts should be read and understood and produces a methodology based on the induction (that is, indeed, already found, on a different scale, in the work of ash-Shâfi'î, Abû Hanîfah, Mâlik, and other earlier scholars) of intentions and effective causes (the *'ilal* as a whole) that will necessarily appear as positive to "accountable human beings" (*al-mukallafûn*) after they have identified and understood them. There should therefore be natural intellectual acceptance of the meaning of well-understood rulings, and this should be completed with spiritual exercise orienting the individual's heart and intention toward answering the call of the divine and thus completing the harmony of the two types of objectives.[15] Thus, one can see that, even before drawing up a categorization of higher objectives, ash-Shâtibî establishes a dialectical relationship between the intentions of the divine and those of human beings, necessarily going through the twofold mediation of the divine text and human context.

When dealing with the divine Lawgiver's objectives and proposing vertical[16] and horizontal[17] categorization of orders, ash-Shâtibî does not add anything specific to what we have already found with the teachings of al-Juwaynî and more precisely with al-Ghazâlî. What is enlightening is rather his reflection on the consequences of this categorization: what matters, in the end, is to uncover a scale of priorities and also the links through which some rulings depend on others. Clearly, essential objectives (*ad-darûrât*) must be protected first, before complementary objectives (*hajiyyât*) or those aiming at embellishment (*tahsiniyyât*): if the text enables us to establish this fundamental typology, it is the human and social environment, the context, which will require us to determine when essentials are endangered; whether a complementary or embellishing objective should be compromised to protect a higher objective; and finally, whether a process can be planned in stages, and if so, in what way, and so forth. Moreover, examination of texts cannot be carried out unless public interest (*masâlih an-nâs*) is taken into account, since ultimately, all these categories are only determined to serve that higher objective set up by the divine Lawgiver. Here again, ash-Shâtibî sets forth a categorization of human interests distinguishing "primary [basic] interests" (*al-masâlih al-asliyyah*) from "secondary interests [those that follow]" (*al-masâlih at-tâba'iyyah*), and they symmetrically correspond to the objectives set up by the Lawgiver, since the former are linked to protecting the five categories (religion, human life, progeny, property, and intellect) that are required of human beings, while the *al-masâlih at-tâba'iyyah* correspond to the secondary objectives that include all that has to do with their well-being and happiness.[18]

In the analysis concluding this section, ash-Shâtibî deals with an essential question (*By what means can the divine Lawgiver's intent be known?*) and settles on an intermediate position between the literalism of Zâhirî and the very open interpretations of Bâtinites (who keep looking beyond the text itself for the hidden—*bâtin*—meaning of its phrasing). Most scholars, ash-Shâtibî recalls, have opted for close and thorough consideration of the text in its form and substance without neglecting to identify and extract the causes and effective causes (*'ilâl*) of the rulings at hand (*ahkâm*). This twofold approach, this twofold perspective, will make it possible to achieve an exhaustive, in-depth understanding of the divine Lawgiver's text and of His intentions. Ash-Shâtibî then carries on his categorization work and sets forth the order and stages to follow in dealing with and understanding revealed rulings: first of all, explicitly stated commands and prohibitions must be listed; next, their effective causes and objectives (*'ilal*) must be identified; then, secondary effective causes and objectives; finally, consideration should be brought to the silences of scriptural sources over new issues (whether those had appeared at the time of the Revelation) that legal scholars are faced with in their new environment. Here, ash-Shâtibî simply integrates the deductive and inductive approaches we have already studied in ash-Shâfi'î's work and within the Hanafî school, but his fixing higher objectives *a priori*—earlier than the actual reading of the texts—sheds specific light on this rule-extracting process and imposes a general inductive approach in the light of the said higher objectives. His categorization by order of priority (from explicit texts to silences in the texts) already detailed makes it possible to guide, and thereby protect, the process of legal extraction, while higher objectives—determined according to the divine Lawgiver's intent—give the whole process its meaning and orientation. To this end, the social and human environment cannot but be taken into account in all circumstances, whether to state a ruling or a legal opinion (*fatwâ*) or to devise its practical implementation through the twofold prism of faithfulness to the causes and the explicit (or not) wording of texts on the one hand, and, on the other, protecting the interests of people at a specific time, and in a specific environment. Legal scholars must therefore read, infer, and understand texts in the light of the intentions of the divine Lawgiver, who moreover requires that they should always take into account the situation and people's well-understood interest. Only with a twofold thorough knowledge of texts and contexts can they complete this undertaking involving a triple mediation: between the text and its effective causes, among the text, its effective causes, and silences, and finally among the text, its effective causes, and silences on the one hand, and the social and human environments on the other.

This multidimensional dialectical approach is presented as a middle way that strives to remain faithful both to texts and to intentions: as can be seen, ash-Shâtibî's strict, clear-cut approach regarding rulings related to belief (*'aqîdah*) and worship (*'ibadât*) is associated with a methodology that is indeed strict, but essentially confident, in the field of interpersonal relations and social affairs (*mu'âmalât*). Taking human interests into account, alleviating the legal burden, and simplifying the system of rules must be constant preoccupations when considering and implementing scriptural sources. The inclusion of "the divine Lawgiver's silence" (*sukût ash-Shâri'*)[19] into his classification is not something new, but here—within the global inductive approach—it takes on particular importance. Without saying so explicitly, ash-Shâtibî's methodology reconciles scholars with the original confidence shared by the Prophet's Companions, the people of Medina, and Mâlik himself, because they moved more freely between the meaning of texts and their own excellent and intimate knowledge of their human context. More broadly, and more essentially, it sheds renewed (*mujaddid*) light on the Prophetic tradition (*hadîth*) that states: "God has set some limits, so do not transgress them; He has commanded some commands, so do not ignore them; He has made some things unlawful, so do not commit them. He has also kept silent (*sakata*) about some matters as a mercy toward you, not because He has forgotten them, so do not ask about them."[20] The divine Lawgiver's silence is a mercy, a grace offered to human beings so as not to make their burden too heavy, but it is also a positive and trustful recognition of their human and intellectual ability to devise their own ways of being faithful to the message through time and the variety of places. Here silence eases conscience and summons the intellect.

Higher Objectives of Law and Human and Social Contexts

Ash-Shâtibî's contribution is immeasurable in the field of the study of the fundamentals of Islamic *usûl al-fiqh*. He clearly did not invent everything, as we have seen, through the approach through the "higher objectives" of law, but his work of synthesis, categorization, and clarification laid the groundwork for a complete, autonomous methodology that was to renew the modalities of reading and implementing scriptural sources through History and the different human environments thoroughly. Three specific orders linked to this renewal that can be identified are particularly relevant to the present discussion.

The first order has to do with the qualification of objectives and higher principles (essential, linked to complementary needs, or having to do with embellishment): more outspokenly than anyone before him, ash-Shâtibî stresses their universal character, transcend-ing all religions. Al-Ghazâlî had pointed out their higher transver-sal character (across all religions) but ash-Shâtibî forcefully claims that no religion or previously revealed text fails to mention those higher objectives explicitly or implicitly, nor states a norm that contradicts them.[21] The all-encompassing principle of those higher objectives being to promote good and ward off evil and harm, those objectives cannot but be universal and shared by all in one way or another. Thus, the inductive work of reason has made it possible—through its essential mediation—to identify a series of higher objec-tives, to categorize them, and to determine the core of common universals for all human beings. Thus, protecting religion, human life, family relations, property, and the intellect (ash-Shâtibî also, at various points in his analysis, includes the notion of *al-'irdh*, honor, as a sixth category), constitutes, according to him, a set of objectives common to all religions and therefore transcending them to make up the framework through which all revealed texts—and especially the Quran, of course—must be grasped. Unlike the deductive and induc-tive methods already presented, which were produced by scholars who were primarily law and jurisprudence specialists (*fuqahâ*) inter-ested in practical issues and answers, ash-Shâtibî first of all induces the higher, universal objectives from the scriptural sources them-selves, and only then does he tackle practical issues in the light of the injunctions and orientations determined by those higher objectives: this influences the way texts are understood and also, as we shall see, the practice of autonomous and critical reasoning in *ijtihâd*.

Those higher, universal objectives, with their three separate lev-els, shed particular light on texts, rulings (*ahkâm*), and their practi-cal implementation: it is impossible, in the light of higher objectives, to consider texts apart from their relation to the context of their practical implementation, since this implementation must, in all cir-cumstances, remain faithful to the principles of protecting good and warding off harm in the various categories mentioned. The environ-ment, the individual or the group's situation, habits, and customs, the intentions of the people involved, must certainly be taken into account as part of the process of giving the law, stating *fatâwâ*, and implementing them. This is so true that ash-Shâtibî points out, even more precisely than earlier scholars, that although an action may be deemed permissible (*mubâh*), recommended (*mustahab*), lawful (*halâl*), objectionable (*makrûh*), or even unlawful (*harâm*) in itself,[22] its status can change according to the context in which it is considered and judged. The same also applies, indeed, to the order of priorities among elements that in themselves belong either to essential objectives (*ad-darûrât*), or to complementary needs (*al-hajiyyât*), or to embellishments (*at-tahsiniyyât*)—in the same manner, those can be inverted and so move from one category to another according to context. The methodology thus established beforehand from a general outlook and universal objectives—set forth inductively through reason—requires rules to be implemented in the light of those objectives and compels scholars to operate constant critical (rational) and dialectic to-and-fro movements between the texts and their effective causes on the one hand, and among the context, human beings, their practices, and their intentions on the other. Literalism (*at-tatbîq al-harfî*) and blind imitation of forerunners (*at-taqlîd*) are thereby made impossible and the range of possibilities for rationality and reason-based statement of rulings (*ahkâm*) and *fatâwâ* is henceforth far broader, beyond strict analogical reasoning (*qiyâs*) or legal preference (*istihsân*), which are restricted to very limited situations in the implementation of *fiqh*. The point is to be faithful to the higher, universal objectives of scriptural sources and no longer only to the wording of a specific ruling: ash-Shâtibî's methodology has transformed, and sometimes inverted, perspectives.

His very reading of scriptural sources is, in this respect, most original, and it leads us to the second order in the aforementioned renewal. To ash-Shâtibî, the Meccan revelation period (610–622) is crucial because the verses revealed during this initial temporal sequence established the higher, universal objectives of Islamic law and jurisprudence. Thus, such principles as protecting religion, and human life, as well as the elements of the two categories of complementary needs and embellishment, had already been stated during the first years of the Prophetic mission and all the later verses revealed in Medina (between 622 and 632) bringing greater detail and more concrete implementation are only the rendering and illustration of the meaning of those objectives and principles in the Medina context.[23] Thus, there is already a specific temporality and a clearly determined relation to context that must be taken into account when dealing with scriptural sources themselves, and indeed that inductive legal work can only be performed coherently and in depth by taking such objective data into account. Moreover, one should keep in mind another order of priority that has to do with the Quran's relation to the Prophetic tradition (Sunnah): the revealed text comes first; it determines major principles and sometimes states a number of details, while the Sunnah's function is to detail, clarify, and illustrate, and thereby it occupies a secondary position.[24] Reaffirming this—classical and acknowledged—subordinate relation of the Sunnah to the Quran, at this stage and in this manner, is crucially important: in effect, it amounts to liberating the Quran from the specific contextual interpretation offered by the Medina period alone. Indeed, this latter illustrates the meaning of legal rulings and determines a particular mode of interpretation, but it cannot close off the Quran and the divine Lawgiver's higher, universal objectives into a particular, historically dated, and quite specific implementation. This twofold process of classification within the basic Islamic corpus itself (Mecca/Medina period, Quran/Sunnah) once again makes it possible to lay out a framework and priorities ahead of any ruling extraction or implementation work. Furthermore, ash-Shâtibî grants particular importance to the social and human context in the inductive process and in understanding higher objectives, because scholars must constantly ask themselves this question: if the divine Lawgiver wanted such and such a principle (or such and such a ruling) to be implemented, in such and such a way, in such and such an environment, how can the primary objective of that principle (or ruling) be established inductively, beyond that specific environment, so that it can be of use to other human beings living in another age and other societies?

It is clearly the same preoccupation with context, with reaching beyond it and reconsidering it in the light of higher objectives, which orients ash-Shâtibî's analysis when he deals with the rulings defining the duties and obligations of accountable beings (*al-ahkâm at-taklî-fiyyah*).[25] He begins by looking into the category of the permissible (*al-mubâh*) and presents a long analysis of the relationship between actions and the intentions that motivate them and give them their moral qualification. This latter, therefore, requires another simple inductive process that necessitates that individuals' motivations should be understood, and the category of the "permissible" (*mubâh*) opens a vast field in which the Lawgiver allows full scope to human freedom and enables everyone to live according to her or his nature, habits, and customs so long as she or he does not overstep the limits of the unlawful stated in the texts. What matters then will be the person's intentions and motivations. By making this clear, ash-Shâtibî takes a stance in the debate that has opposed two great trends of thought (beyond the scope of legal schools): against those who think that the range of permitted things should be restricted (or that the faithful should be invited to avoid them), for fear of falling into the unlawful, ash-Shâtibî is intent on protecting the vast field of what is morally indeterminate, and he sees no justification to restricting its use. On the contrary, according to the same inductive mode, he determines some characteristics of the higher objectives that can be extracted from the field of the permissible in the relation to human-kind, societies, customs, and more generally to individual and col-lective interests (al-masâlih). Here again, the approach through the "naturally permissible" also requires us to consider the social and human context immediately to understand the meaning and nature of divine silence in this matter.

The whole discussion over autonomous critical reasoning (ijti-hâd), which has to do with our third order of considerations, bears the influence of the previous analyses: whether texts are available or not, human reason is constantly summoned to discover causal links, the different relations of induced objectives to visible consequences, potential spheres of analogy, and the dialectical relationships of texts to the various contexts. This process as a whole therefore occurs mid-way between the recognition of higher, universal objectives (induced and established beforehand) and the requirements of the concrete implementation of law and jurisprudence, ultimately, at a given time and in a specific environment. The practice of ijtihâd consequently requires thorough knowledge of higher, universal objectives, of scriptural sources, and of extraction rules, as well as of the interests of groups and individuals. In contrast with the long lists of condi-tions stipulated by earlier scholars, ash-Shâtibî synthesizes them into two broad categories and says: "the degree of ijtihâd is reached when two qualities are present: 1. thorough understanding of the objectives (maqâsid) of the sharî'ah; 2. real proficiency in the vari-ous deduction and extraction (istinbât) methods, rooted in knowl-edge and understanding."[26] As can be seen, what matters, whether in analyzing revealed texts or in dealing with situations where scrip-tural sources are silent, is sound knowledge of the objectives of law and jurisprudence: this condition comes first because it determines the modalities for extracting rulings and their effective causes from texts, which come in second position here, and it requires scholars to integrate all the parameters linked to the interest of societies and people when no text is available, in the light of the context (*al-masâ-lih al-mursalah*). The philosophy of law produced by the methodology of higher objectives is original, and it infuses concepts with new substance and meaning. The formula *"maqâsid ash-sharî'ah"* clearly refers to the etymology of the word *sharî'ah* ("a way, a path, leading to a [water] source") mentioned in the first section: it is "a Way" with its source (the divine Lawgiver) and its higher, universal objectives (*al-maqâsid*) to which men must, through their history and in their various societies, strive to remain faithful when concretely elaborating *fiqh*, whether scriptural sources are vocal or silent. *Ijtihâd* is therefore the indispensable tool and field of expression of human reason; it is both faithful and autonomous, since it makes it possible to establish all the dialectical relations (induction, deduction, analogical reasoning, etc.) necessary to remain faithful to the Way (*maqâsid ash-sharî'ah*) through human history. This approach also sheds fresh light on rules, rulings or laws per se: literal implementation is actually impossible (apart from most worship-related rulings) and they must constantly be placed in perspective from the standpoint of the Way's higher objectives that must at all times determine the modalities of their possible implementation (even for the most explicit texts). This is how one should understand the Caliph 'Umar's decision to suspend the implementation of punishments for poor thieves in times of famine: literal implementation of the punishment would have run against the higher objective of justice since poor thieves would have been twice victimized. Hence, the Way's objectives clearly orient and determine the implementation of rules and laws beyond their literal expression in reference texts: thus putting them in perspective in the light of the objectives is the *sine qua non* condition of faithfulness.

It is indeed impossible, in the school of higher objectives (*madrasat al-maqâsid*), not to take the social and human environment into account. Not only does it shed light on fundamental texts, but only by knowing it accurately can one remain faithful to the divine Lawgiver's intent. It is therefore important to include it from the very beginning of the legal elaboration process to deal adequately with new situations about which the text says nothing. As Ahmad ar-Raysûnî aptly points out: "Hence, by means of thorough acquaintance with the rulings and objectives of the Law, awareness of the conditions and requirements of the Muslim nation, careful investigation and rational assessment, it becomes possible to identify unrestricted interests (about which the texts have remained silent, *masâlih mursalah*) and to arrange them in the proper order of priority."[27] "Awareness of the conditions and requirements of the Muslim nation" is indeed everywhere present in the elaboration of ash-Shâtibî's methodology, and this requires closer consideration. One can see, after the synthetic analysis of his thought, that ash-Shâtibî was able to lay out particularly significant categories as to the *sharî'ah*'s higher, universal objectives. In the process, he kept referring to human and social contexts, whether to identify higher objectives *a priori* or to devise an implementation of the rules that remained faithful to them *a posteriori*. One can therefore understand how important sound knowledge of the human context is. The first question that we are faced with today is whether the school of *al-maqâsid*, to the time of ash-Shâtibî, went through all the possibilities as to extracting higher, universal objectives, or whether the challenges of our own time might require us to review the list of five or six basic categories (religion, human life, progeny, reason, property, and sometimes honor) and add other universal higher objectives. For indeed, as ar-Raysûnî points out in his extensive analyses of ash-Shâtibî's thought, the categorization of those objectives remains the fruit of induction carried out by human reason. The second question is no less essential—perhaps it is even more so: it is whether the human social environment has received sufficient attention in the elaboration of Islamic *fiqh*. Indeed, what appears—albeit still implicitly—in the works of *maqâsid* school scholars is that the social and human environment operates as a potential source of law insofar as the scholar (*al-usûlî*) must constantly take it into account to understand a ruling, think out its implementation, or state a legal opinion (*fatwâ*) when no text is available. However, stressing the importance of awareness and thorough knowledge of the context is one thing, while it is quite another matter to give it its true place and grant the environment the same work of categorization and ranking of priorities. In the next chapter, I propose a new geography of the sources of Islamic law and jurisprudence. Before that, it seems necessary to draw up a kind of halfway assessment after this presentation of the various classical schools of the fundamentals of *usûl al-fiqh*.

6

A Synthesis

My analysis of ash-Shâfi'î's work (died 204/820) has shown how central his contribution has been and is in the field of the fundamentals of Islamic *usûl al-fiqh*. He was the first to sense that before elaborating and practicing *fiqh*, a framework must be established and a reading grid and methodology must be supplied to deal with scriptural sources. He therefore drew up rules, identified the relations between texts and enunciation contexts, and established relations with the social and human environment to be able to define norms to extract the effective causes (*'ilal*) of rulings. Starting from this work, he then determined the scope and limits of analogical reasoning (*qiyâs*) and, restrictively, of the use of legal preference (*istihsân*). In the third century after Hijrah (ninth century) ash-Shâfi'î who was Mâlik's pupil, contemporary with Abû Hanîfah's two main pupils Abû Yûsuf and ash-Shaybânî, and Ibn Hanbal's master, was at the center of the most heated and passionate legal debates. He realized that more and more scholars or schools seemed to take liberties with the texts in the name of very free analogical reasoning (*qiyâs*), of vaguely verified consensus (*ijmâ'*), or of more or less justified *istihsân*. He therefore decided to lay out a strict framework so that the very fundamentals of Islamic *fiqh* would not be lost or dissolved as a result of the increasing liberties scholars and political authorities were taking with scriptural sources. He returned to the founding texts and deductively established a methodology intended to set up a framework and prevent excessive legal elaboration.

Hanafî scholars did not have such a methodology established beforehand but they could rely on the whole corpus of legal opinions (*fatâwâ*) stated by Abû Hanîfah (died 150/767) and his pupils. They used them as a starting point to try to reconstruct their masters' various reasoning processes to identify the logic underlying their thought and the modalities of legal ruling extraction. This inductive method, although it came after ash-Shâfi'î's deductive method, caused them to return to a practice that was historically closer to that of the Prophet and his Companions. In the tradition of the people of opinion (*ahl ar-ra'y*), Abû Hanîfah had never hesitated to interpret situations, resort to *qiyâs*, or even project hypothetical situations (*fiqh taqdîrî*). The most notable feature of his approach to *fatâwâ* is his constantly taking into account the environment, human realities, and customary practices that he and his pupils integrate into their stating of the law (as the Companions naturally did in Medina, in an environment they knew perfectly). Abû Hanîfah, summoning up *istihsân* to prevent a restrictive implementation of *qiyâs*—contrary to ash-Shâfi'î's position—left a vast field open for the practice of critical and autonomous reasoning (*ijtihâd*) based on his trust in his own understanding of the texts as well as in his knowledge of his society: this is particularly explicit in the field of trade, which he took part in professionally.

In the eighth century after Hijrah, ash-Shâtibî (died 730/1388)—after al-Juwaynî, al-Ghazâlî, and many others—revived and amplified the inspiration that had nurtured the founder (or reference scholar) of the legal school that prevailed in Granada at the time. Imam Mâlik ibn Anas (died 179/796) had lived in Medina and was even closer to the Companions and the following generation (*tâbi'ûn*) than Abû Hanîfah had been in terms of chronology. His strictness in the field of belief (*'aqîdah*) and worship rules (*'ibadât*) was associated with a confident approach to new situations about which no specific text had been revealed (*masâlih mursalah*). Mâlik never hesitated to look for the effective causes of commands and prohibitions (*'ilal*, to analyze intentions beyond the literal meaning of texts and sayings and to take into account the interest of society and individuals when no text was available about an issue (*istislâh*): for him the field left open to interpretation, to the exercise of autonomous critical reasoning (*ijtihâd*), was in proportion to the tools available to the law scholar (*faqîh*). Over five hundred years later, ash-Shâtibî, using the same tools and performing a synthesis of numerous earlier works (by scholars from all legal schools), suggested an approach based on the higher objectives of law and jurisprudence (*maqâsid ash-sharî'ah*) that, by its very nature, compelled scholars to return, because of the method's own requirements, to the natural attitude of the first Companions and the first jurisprudence specialists (*fuqahâ'*). The point was to think out the implementation of law and rulings according to the higher, universal objectives that entailed both the phrasing of the texts *and* the human and social contexts (*al-wâqi'*) should be taken into account. We have seen how ash-Shâtibî insisted on the process of extracting effective causes (*'ilal*) in inducing higher objectives, so that the latter could then orient the work of *fuqahâ'* in implementing rulings. The omnipresence of *ijtihâd*—both to understand and to implement texts—takes us back to the Companions' attitude and to the very meaning of the answer most naturally expressed by Mu'âdh ibn Jabal replying to the Prophet's questions. In Yemen, in a new context, an effort of autonomous critical reasoning had to be performed (when no text from the Quran or Sunnah was available) to find the correct legal answer respecting the objective, spirit, and letter of the message.

On closer study, it emerges that the further one goes back in time, the closer one gets to the Prophet and his Companions, the more one feels that scholars, less worried by their contemporaries' potential excesses, trusted their ability to understand the meaning of texts and the modalities of their implementation in their environment. What mainly determined the Companions' and early scholars' approach was their perfect knowledge of their society from within. Their natural attitude toward the texts implicitly presupposes such knowledge of the surrounding environment, enabling them to establish links, to devise adaptations, to "read" the text differently. This knowledge was endogenous and was so taken for granted that it did not compete with the knowledge that was seen as needing to be acquired, and thus exogenous (i.e., that of scriptural sources). One cannot find any articulate reference to knowledge of the environment, except as an adjunct to knowledge of the texts. Even so, any serious study of the legal scholars' works, especially such early scholars as Mâlik or Abû Hanîfah, shows their competence in terms of the texts and the nature of the secondary sources (*istihsân, istislâh, 'urf,* etc.) that they resort to; these primarily result from an implicit element in their dealing with texts that is their knowledge of their society or of the field of activity in which they state the law. The higher objectives school would not indeed constitute an original contribution if it did not include awareness of the social and human context in the description of its methodology itself, as we have seen. The question that now faces us once again is whether scholars have gone far enough in integrating the context into the elaboration of law and jurisprudence. Should not knowledge of the context, which was at first natural (for the Companions and early scholars) and then required as an implicit or indirect secondary reference (by the methodologies of the fundamentals of *usûl al-fiqh*), acquire a new status, since its knowledge has grown so complex and now requires so many and difficult parameters to be taken into account? And if so, should we not reconsider the position of the human and social environments in the geography of the sources of Islamic law and jurisprudence? Those are the questions I shall deal with in the next section of this book.

III

❧

For a New Geography of the Sources of Law and Jurisprudence (*Usûl al-Fiqh*)

I have shown in the first section of this work those limits I think have been reached by focusing essentially on the concrete implementation of *fiqh*. The whole contemporary output of legal rulings (*fatâwâ*) is necessary insofar as it enables Muslims to face the immediate challenges of their time. It remains, nevertheless, that those rulings promote and maintain an *adaptation reform* by creating, at the heart of the modern age, restricted spaces built inside or next to the system or the global order where Muslim ethics are protected, but fail to exert any particular influence on that order itself, either on the level of fundamental theoretical criticism, or of actual resistance, or of transformation practices. Those pockets of *ethical* (*halâl*) *activities* indeed sometimes result from constructions legitimated by a casuistic approach that—relying on Arabic and Islamic terminology and on frequently petty formal readjustments—addresses techniques rather than substance, apparent means more than higher ends, in just about every field, from the question of education to economics, from the status of women to scientific, social, or cultural challenges. Contemporary Islamic ethics has become defensive, passive, behind the times, and isolated, and it by no means corresponds to the requirements of a religious and humanist conscience that ought, in keeping with its ideals, produce a *visionary, committed, open ethics* that questions the world, its order, its achievements, and its lapses and then devises and proposes concrete modalities to transform it.

As we have seen, the problem lies, I think, further along than the current issues related to *fiqh*. Neither does the problem lie in the need for *ijtihâd*. What is at stake is the very nature of the exercise of critical autonomous reasoning, and we must imperatively ask ourselves about its object, its latitude, and the qualification of the women and men who can, and must, perform it today. Before such questioning can occur, there is the necessary first question of identifying the primary sources that legitimate the exercise of contemporary *ijtihâd*: can we rely on the classical traditions of the fundamentals of law? Should we consider other sources, or should we simply devise new tools? Rather like ash-Shâfi'î in the ninth century or ash-Shâtibî in the fourteenth, we are faced with the critical fundamental question of our relation to scriptural sources, so much does the world around us question our faithfulness, our coherence, and, ultimately, the meaning of our being in the world. We have seen in the second section that the classical traditions of the fundamentals of law and jurisprudence have always approached the founding texts with the deepest respect and devotion and that, while reference to the historical and social environment was always present, it mainly served to shed light on the meaning of the texts or how they should be implemented. The Universe, the social and human context, has never been considered as a *self-standing* source of law and of its production. It is this status, this qualitative differentiation in authority—between the text and the context—that to my mind is a problem today. Early scholars were intimately familiar with the environments in which and for which they made the laws, and this is why they were so confident, creative, and pragmatic. The world has grown more complex, local practices are connected to the global order, all the spheres of human action are interdependent and interconnected, and it is impossible for scholars today to grasp this complexity with the same confidence as early scholars. On the contrary, because the difficulty is so apparent, fear has set in and produced a timid reactive legal thought, afraid of what it no longer controls, acting as the guardian of beleaguered references. Only through better knowledge of the world, its complexity, and the deep stakes of the present and future, can Muslim scholars (*ulamâ'*) regain the confidence—and accompanying creativity—that will enable them to outline a contemporary applied Islamic ethics, based on justifications other than necessity (*darûrah*) and need (*hâjah*). This requires acknowledging that the world, its laws, and areas of specialized knowledge not only shed light on scriptural sources but also constitute a source of law of their own. This is what I shall be discussing next, and it must be stressed that such a position has deep implications for the fundamentals of law and of contemporary Islamic thought.

7

Determining the Sources of Islamic Law and Jurisprudence

We have seen in the previous section that the further one goes back in time—and the closer one gets to the Companions or the scholars who met them or knew the next generation (*at-tâbi'ûn*)—the more one feels that the texts were indeed approached with thoroughness but also with confidence as to their interpretation as well as their implementation. It has become clear that what made this possible and most natural was of course the chronological proximity of the revelation of scriptural sources but most importantly the intimate acquaintance early interpreters of the texts had of their own context and society, of the areas of knowledge that were mastered at the time, as well as of the customs and practices that were commonly recognized. The constant to-and-fro movement between the objectives stated in the texts and the intentions and habits of surrounding populations was natural, obvious, and so did not require any particular effort. In early societies on the Arabian peninsula, the social and human context was in itself a source of law that was so fully integrated by interpreters of texts that they only had to refer to it implicitly, without any particular insistence, to be understood. The scholars who came after them, as guardians and interpreters of the texts, mainly concentrated on the texts as sources of law, because it seemed to them that this very human context, becoming more varied and complex, was beginning to endanger faithfulness to the texts due to increasingly free interpretations resulting from many concurrent factors (poor knowledge of Arabic, distortion in the meaning of verses, falsification of *ahâdîth*, new human realities requiring an *ijtihâd* perceived as excessive or unjustified, etc.). It seemed imperative, as we have seen, to impose a framework, a reading grid, and a methodology.

What nevertheless got lost in the process of this necessary historical exercise was the imperative awareness of the human and social context as a source of Islamic law and jurisprudence (and as an inescapable reference in the process of its implementation). What for early scholars (who did not refer to any methodology built *a posteriori*) had been naturally integrated became, as this methodology was elaborated through history, a secondary element, at best a reference that might or ought to be taken into account, but no longer, at any rate, a source clearly perceived as such by interpreting scholars. This distinguishing and ranking process (texts are the source of law, the human context is a secondary reference) was naturally amplified by the fact that it was becoming first increasingly difficult, then outright impossible, for scholars specialized in texts, *fuqahâ'*, to master the whole range of knowledge gathered over time in their respective societies. It has indeed become impossible to be both a specialist in scriptural sources and perfectly acquainted with all the scientific, economic, and social knowledge of one's time: what was originally natural and integrated in the same person gradually became distinct, complex, and distributed among the minds of the social body immersed in history. Where scholars used to strive for complementarity and harmony, tensions and conflicts between areas of knowledge were more and more present, and attempts at defining a hierarchy of course had to do with the essential issue of authority and power, beyond the natural need to set up a framework through which to approach texts. We should therefore go back to the beginning and ask ourselves what scriptural sources ultimately tell us about the role of the Universe, creation, and the human and social contexts in the elaboration of law and jurisprudence. In other words, what light does knowledge about texts shed on knowledge about human contexts? What does the atemporal Revelation teach us about how we should deal with the temporality of history? Such questions are essential and lie at the core of the present analysis.

The Two Revelations: The Universe, the Text, and Signs

It should be remembered that the early revelations in the Quran (generally the last surahs of the text in its final form) constantly refer to the created Universe, to the elements in Nature, and to the "signs" that pervade it. From the outset, the revealed text establishes a link between the written Revelation, knowledge, and the surrounding Universe, as three dimensions testifying to God's presence. The first verses revealed are explicit: *"Read in the name of your Lord [*Rabb-Educator*] Who created—created man out of a clinging clot. Read, [for] your Lord is Most Bountiful, He who taught by means of the Pen, taught man that which he knew not."*[1]

Those verses point out the fact that God has created humans and that He has taught them "by means of the Pen," which directly refers to the Revelation of the Book—to book learning—that begins with those words.[2] The other surahs and verses that were rapidly added to those constantly involved the Universe and the elements as evidence of God's presence:

> *"All that is in the Heavens and on Earth declares the praises and glory of God. To Him belongs dominion, to Him belongs praise. He has power over all things."*
>
> *"I swear by the planets that recede, go straight or hide; and the night as it dissipates; and the dawn as it breathes away the darkness, that this [Quran] is the word of a noble messenger."*
>
> *"Glorify the name of your Lord the Most High, who has created and given order and proportion, who has measured and granted guidance, who has brought out pastures and then made them swarthy stubble."*[3]

Those verses were among the first to be revealed and they all appeal to the Universe as a witness of the Creator's presence—both on the spiritual level and as the material expression of His natural order. In surah *Pilgrimage (al-Hajj)*, the link between those two dimensions is quite explicit: *"Do they not travel through the land, so that their hearts may learn wisdom [understand] and that their ears may learn to hear? Truly it is not the eyes that are blind, but the hearts that are in their breasts."*[4]

The Universe is a space that speaks to the mind and heart and reveals the meaning of Creation. If the heart cannot reason and understand, then the eyes can no longer see, they become blind and cannot "read" the world anymore. In five very brief verses, *The Most Gracious* (*ar-Rahmân*) surah gathers the essence of the message and links all those dimensions: *"The Most Gracious! It is He Who has taught the Quran. He has created man. He has taught him an intelligent speech. The sun and the moon follow courses exactly computed. And the stars and the trees bow in adoration."*[5]

The written Revelation is a teaching (*'allama, ta'lîm*) that reminds humankind of the blessings surrounding its creation: the Most Gracious has given the Revelation, knowledge, and speech and humans must learn to see and grasp, with the physical eye of their intellect, the precise order of Nature, as well as to understand the elements' prayer with the spiritual eye of their hearts. This is confirmed by another verse establishing an implicit correspondence between the two orders of the Revelation and the Universe: *"In the creation of the Heavens and the Earth, and the alternation of night and day, there are indeed signs* (âyât) *for all those endowed with insight."*[6]

The Heavens and the Earth, night and day, space and time, testify to the presence and infinite generosity of the One who has laid out the Universe like an open book pervaded with "signs" offered to people's minds and hearts. The notion of "signs" (*âyât*, sing. *ayah*) is essential and from the very beginning it establishes a correspondence between orders. What has been translated as "verses" in European languages—on the basis of the "verses" in Biblical versification—has quite a different meaning in Arabic. The exact translation, which is most significant here, is "sign," which means that the revealed text is made up of "signs" exactly as the surrounding Creation is a Universe of signs that must be grasped, understood, and interpreted. Signs tell of meaning...and the signs in the Universe therefore reveal that the latter is fraught with meaning. One finds this even in Abû Hâmid al-Ghazâlî's profound reflections about the "outspread book" (*al-kitâb al-manshûr*), the Book of the Universe, which is the theological as well as physical mirror of the Quran, the "written book" (*al-kitâb al-mastûr*). This theme was common in early renaissance European literature and gradually changed the outlook of the world, which was seen as a space to be deciphered, interpreted, and understood: a horizon open to reason, learning, and science.

This correspondence between the two books is everywhere present in the Quran, which keeps referring to the signs in one or the other of these orders and invites human intelligence to understand the revealed text as well as created Nature. The two Universes address and echo each other and reveal to mankind that the Creation, the life of people, and history are fraught with meaning: those are clearly two "Revelations" that must imperatively be received, read, interpreted, and understood in their inherent complementarity. The heart, nurtured by faith, must be able to observe signs, reason must strive to understand the natural order, extract its meaning, and identify finalities. Interpreting the Universe, like interpreting the text, requires the heart's light to grasp the meaning, the "why" of things. Both the Universe and the text only reveal their order, structure, and meaning—as to the "how" of things—through the complementary mediation of human reason; this latter, relying on thorough analysis, must try to harmonize and unite the order of the "why" and that of the "how."

Early scholars had noticed, when trying to determine the higher objectives of the revealed text, that its intent was ultimately to promote good for humans and to protect them from harm and evil. All that is said about the creation of the Universe exactly answers the same higher objectives: the Universe is a gift, the aim of its creation is good, and the essential, and *natural*, finalities of Nature are what is good for and benefits human beings. That is what many verses in the Quran recall: *"They ask you [the Messenger] what it lawful [permitted] to them* (uhilla lahum). *Say: all things good and pure* (at-tayyibât) *are lawful to you. (...) This day, all things good and pure are made lawful to you."*[7]

The lawful naturally corresponds to what is good and Nature offers itself as the essential and primary space of what is good and right, pleasant, and permitted. Even the next verse, although more specific, directs human beings' consciences toward associating what is "good and natural" with what is "lawful and permitted": *"O you people! Eat from what is on earth, lawful and good!..."*[8]

Those verses and many others are what led jurists to consider Nature and its order with a basically positive outlook and to formulate the legal maxim that "the primary principle is permission" (al-asl fî-l-ashiyâ' al-ibâha) concerning the relationship to Nature, interpersonal relations, and social affairs. The vocabulary used expresses this confidence in the natural, both in the relationship to the Universe and in the natural dispositions of human beings. Thus, the lawful (*halâl*) is constantly associated with the good (*tayyib*) and the lawful and permissible (*mubâh*) refers the conscience to collective human inclination: *al-ma'rûf* (from the root *'a-ra-fa*), which literally means "acknowledged as good by society," is the Quranic concept that refers to what is good, permissible, and lawful, thus more generally covering the two categories of *halâl* and *mubâh* (but also the intermediate categories of the disliked permissible—*makrûh*—or the recommended permissible—*mustahab*).

This open, positive outlook on the world—as well, indeed, as on human nature in general[9]—is important because, from the outset, it qualifies the Book of the Universe, its Revelations, its different orders, and the way it should be considered or interacted with. Just as ash-Shâtibî had made it clear concerning the Quran (with its founding principles revealed in Mecca, then simply implemented and respected in the specific context of Medina), one can say that all of the first verses quoted in relation to the book of the world, the created Revelation, direct the conscience toward an order that impresses itself on people and is a *sign* of the Creator's presence. By understanding with their hearts and analyzing with their reason, people discover—it is revealed to them—that the goals of the created Universe are as close to their hopes as the order of the "good and profitable" for them and their future (in that the lawful corresponds to what is naturally pleasant and useful to them). There is thus no feeling of guilt, simply a relationship of conscience and responsibility: recognizing the good, being thankful, and acting accordingly, consistently. From the first Mecca *âyât* to the last *âyât* revealed in Medina that is quoted above (surah 5), the Universe presents itself as a book that reveals and a space that welcomes confidently, generously, and harmoniously. Humankind must, through the ethics of their actions in the world, try to remain faithful to what they have received in the very nature of their being in the world. One should therefore act faithfully and not forget to be thankful: *"Eat from what God has granted you, lawful and good, and be grateful for God's favours, if it is He whom you serve."*[10]

This outlook on the world and this constant thankfulness of the conscience and being ultimately say everything about this Revelation, this first Book, and the second Revelation then illuminates, reveals more explicitly, and echoes with a reminder (*tudhakkir*) of the meaning of signs and of objectives.

The Immutable and the Changing

We have seen that the Universe, just like the written Revelation, needs to be approached with the eyes and intelligence of the heart and of the mind. It is important to remember that we are in the order of a message revealed to the believing conscience, which is called on to seek not only to recognize and get closer to the One but also to understand His intents and strive to remain faithful to them. The message addressing the heart meets with the universal natural quest for meaning that is so set in human beings, the Quran calls *al-fitra*:[11] beyond the self, the materiality of the world and the realities of time, it is this natural longing for the transcendent, whether intimate or metaphysical, which is expressed in the question "why?" The revealed text actually encounters and welcomes this human quest—this essential need for meaning—and thus liberates human intelligence and invites it to seek, observe, analyze, interpret, and understand. The written Revelation calls on the mind to set out on a quest as well, freely, with all the resources of its intelligence, and to study the Revelation spread out in front of its eyes, the Universe, which will reveal its secrets and truths, and confirm the essence of the message. The two Revelations will echo each other and be unveiled to each other through this union of the two horizons: at the heart of this basically confident approach, the order of the "how" will harmoniously encounter the order of the "why" and reason will confirm faith. As I said elsewhere responding to Pascal's formula "the heart has reasons that reason does not know": here, the heart has reasons that reason will recognize.[12]

This is not, however, a teleological approach where the world's supposed goals would confirm, *a posteriori*, the existence of divine intents. The revealed Book neither stifles nor directs the mind, it liberates it at the heart of the Universe: the world speaks by itself, autonomously, and it is human intelligence's task to understand its language, its vocabulary, its semantics, its rules, its grammar, and its order. The written Revelation is not a science book, but it calls on the human mind to engage all its critical, analytical, and scientific potential in its quest for knowledge. Nothing is less present in the Quran than the fear or rejection of knowledge, whether sacred or profane, and this is what early scholars or scientists had felt and understood perfectly when they engaged in all the fields of learning (from philosophy to the exact and experimental sciences), confident that the absolute freedom of their reason in those fields in no way hampered the reasons and the essence of faith.

The revealed text does not impede human reason: on the contrary, it opens manifold, diverse horizons for the exercise of an autonomous active rationality. Several levels of discourse can be perceived throughout the text, referring either to the natural order or to the specificities of human societies, but always calling on human intelligence to observe and understand. It thus emerges that in the order of the Universe as well as in that of the revealed text, some laws are universal and definitive laws and some others are contextual, changing, and immersed in history: here again, the two orders echo one another. Very early on, as we have seen, the Quran referred to the natural order and, at first, to what is immediately visible to believers' eyes: the sky, the earth, the sun, the moon, the stars, trees, water, springs, vegetation, the desert, animals, and the rest of it. The intellect is thereby invited to observe and study those elements but also to become aware that some definitive, universal natural laws exist: thus *"The sun and the moon follow courses exactly computed"*; we are made to notice that they both *"float along, each in its rounded course"* and that *"it is not permitted to the Sun to catch up [to] the Moon, nor can the Night outstrip the Day: each floats along in its own orbit."* [13]

Celestial bodies require human reason to understand and study Nature and its order. If, for the heart, the Universe is already filled with signs, these will only be really accessible to the intelligence after it has observed the order, after it has studied its complexity and coherence. Myriad Quranic *âyât* refer to this natural order and call on the human mind to observe and think. After associating the principle of life with water, since *"we made from water every living thing,"* the Revelation reminds human beings of the universal reality of death: *"Every human being shall have a taste of death."* [14] Broadening the horizon beyond its temporality, the observation of the Universe must enable humans to grasp its laws as well as its cycles. Thus, the encounter between rainwater and the earth generates diversity and protects life:

> *And in the earth are neighbouring tracts, gardens of vines and fields sown with corn, and palm-trees growing out of single*

roots or otherwise: watered with the same water, yet some of them we make more excellent than others to eat. Verily in these things there are Signs for those who understand!" [15]

One and the same water gives rise to rich diverse vegetation that ensures the survival of living species: *"Do they not see that we drive rain to parched soil, and therewith produce crops, providing food for their cattle and themselves? Do they not see it?"* [16]

Still, human intelligence should observe and become aware of the universal—biological, physical, and historical—principle of cycles through the alternation, mentioned above, of night and day, of death and life, of draught and rain. Calling on the human conscience, at first through the intelligence of desert peoples, the Revelation repeatedly returns to that image of the cycle through that of the dead earth: *"And among His Signs [is this]: you see the earth humble [because of drought]; but when We send down rain to it, it is stirred to life and yields increase."* [17]

What human beings can observe around them of natural and universal laws is confirmed in their own beings and within the human groups around them. Thus: *"It is He who has created you from dust, then from a sperm-drop, then from a clinging clot; then does He get you out as a child: then lets you grow and reach your age of full strength; then lets you become old,—though some of you die before."* [18]

Together with the common immutable human condition reflected in the stages of life and the inevitable death of everyone, one should however observe—as a law of nature—the diversity of beings and forms: *"And among His signs is the creation of the heavens and the earth, and the variations in your languages and your colours: in that indeed there are signs for those who deeply know."* [19]

Those colors, those languages convey something about the fate of peoples in their qualities and specificities. For although all humans always come from the same source, *"a male and a female,"* they have been made *"into nations and tribes"* [20] and must therefore cope with such diversity and differences. This corresponds to a definitive law, just like the diversity in vegetation previously mentioned.

As can be seen explicitly, the written Revelation refers the human conscience to a profound observation of the Universe around it and invites it to ponder over its natural and universal laws. Thus, while the written text contains *signs*—verses—that clearly and explicitly refer to definitive principles (essentially, but not only, belief—*al-'aqîdah*—and ritual practices—*al-'ibadât*), the Universe also reveals to the observer its natural, universal laws (*as-sunan al-kawniyyah*) that are no less clear, explicit, and definitive. In the language of textual specialists, one could say that they are *qat'iyyah*, clear, definitive, and offer little room for interpretation about their essence.[21] On this first level, the two Revelations echo and mirror each other: the Universe, like the text, has its principles, its laws, and its grammar. Human intelligence must observe these principles and laws and extract their logic and categories in order, necessarily, to take them into account both in its rational approach to Nature and in its management of societies.

There is in the book of the world another level of discourse that does not concern natural laws but diverse and changing human realities in the course of history. We have just read the Quranic reference to diversity in colors, languages, peoples, and societies; this principle of natural difference is completed by that of the established diversity of religions and beliefs: *"To each [human community] among you We have prescribed a Way and a Teaching [a praxis]. Had God so willed, He would have made you a single community, but [His Plan is] to test you by what He gave you. So vie with one another in good works."*[22]

This objective reality, willed by the Creator, has immediate consequences on the attitude human beings must adopt: *"Had your Lord so willed, all the people on earth would have believed. Will you then compel* (tukrihu) *mankind, against their will, to believe?"*[23]

Beyond the principle of tolerance, presented as a choice offered human beings, the principle of diversity, established beforehand, requires human conscience to *respect* the natural order by ordering it to live with and approach differences with great acumen. That is confirmed by the fundamental principle, stated as a superior and universal general law, of respect for freedom of conscience: *"No compulsion in religion."*[24]

The written Revelation abounds in stories about human communities that differed in their cultures, their customs, their dwellings, their social and political systems and also, therefore, their beliefs. Running through the history of humankind, the history of prophecies highlights the twofold reality of diversity and permanence. Some people worship celestial bodies, others worship statues; some dig their dwellings out of rock, others live in ephemeral tents; some are nomads, others are stationary; some have a woman for Queen (governing through consultation) while others bend to the harsh rule of a God-King (exerting cruel, arbitrary power). Diversity is everywhere present within those human communities and analyzing human and social contexts is often a necessity to understand the meaning of the teachings conveyed by the various stories.

We are here in the realm of transient cultural, social, and political realities that correspond to the manifold choices of human communities and never remain fixed and definitive. The rule here is that there *is* no single rule, no natural law standardizing the historical fates, cultural systems, social fabrics, or collective psychology of human communities. It is up to the observer to try to extract the specificities of each society or population, establish relations between historical contexts and human choices, and then analyze and interpret behaviors in the light of those different parameters. The point is to grasp the fundamentals on which those communities build themselves and explain their daily practices. This is part of the Universe of the human sciences that, from social and political science to individual and social psychology, attempt to study human diversity and, when possible, to infer potential constants, common principles underlying the apparent natural disparity of human behavior. In the realm of the study of the written Revelation, we encounter some signs (*âyât*), which are speculative, open to interpretation, *az-zanniyât*. The Universe, like the revealed Book, is filled with realities, *signs*, that offer themselves to human interpretations: unlike definitive natural laws, the principles of physics, chemistry, or biology, which are the specific fields of study of the exact and experimental sciences, what humans must study here is what is varied, and changing at the heart of cultures and societies, and they must attempt to understand and give a meaning and coherent orientation to the way those realities are handled.

The revealed Book already lays out some of the primary principles that should be inferred within the study of the social sciences. For instance, there are indeed constants when one observes the attitude of the rich and powerful when they are faced with threats to their privileges, and, conversely, in the attitude of poorer people striving for social and political freedom. The essential link that exists between established customs, the fear of what is strange and new on the one hand, and the relationship to power on the other, is another constant present in all the narrations of the revealed Book describing the reaction of authorities and populations to those who seem to threaten the old order: *"Have you come to us to turn us away from the ways we found our fathers following, in order that you and your brother may have greatness in the land? But we shall not believe in you!"*[25]

One could thus identify a large number of such constants that ultimately establish the principles commanding human action throughout history and indeed determine its cyclic character, the same happening again, however different the periods. The observer and "reader" of the book of the world must study those realities, interpret them, and strive as best he or she can to establish laws and rules of the observable behavior of individuals and human communities. This is what the Revelation refers to when it mentions "God's way" (*sunnat Allah*: literally, *"God's tradition"*) expressing the constants of history, which are repeated and verified in a variety of ages and contexts and thus constitute principles that can be deduced or inferred according to the circumstances: *"Such was the tradition [law, constant practice] of God* (sunnat Allah) *among those who lived before you. You will find no change in the tradition [law, constant practice] of God."*[26]

Behind the apparent diversity, if not disorder, of human affairs, then, there are constants and definitive principles that make it possible, at the source, to establish a reading grid for the world, a methodology, and explanatory categories. Beyond our perception, human history answers an internal logic and this is what Ibn Khaldûn established in his work *al-Muqaddimah* (*Introduction, Prolegomena*) when he stated the principle of the phases and cycles in civilizations. The Quran frequently repeats this truth that similar recurring patterns emerge behind history's apparent lack of logic and harmony that makes it seem to lie beyond the scope of a scientific approach: *"such days [of greatness and decline] we give to men [and societies] by turns."*[27] The task of human intelligence is to read the world's reality, to grasp its meaning and infer its grammar: *"There have been examples [traditions, constant practices]* (sunan, *sing.* sunnah) *in former generations: travel through the earth and behold...."*[28]

This work of inference follows exactly the same logic as what we have seen with the scholars of fundamentals (*al-usûliyyûn*), from ash-Shâfi'î to ash-Shâtibî, about establishing links between texts, expressive contexts, and, more broadly, social and human environments: the search for the effective cause (al-'illah), the explanatory principle of an observation, a *sign* from the real endowed with meaning; all this actually echoes the research carried out in the human sciences about observing constants in the behavior of men and societies. This is indeed the order of *zanniyyât*, of signs and realities that do not refer to the exact sciences and are offered to human intelligence, which must observe them, analyze them, establish meaningful relationships, and induce particular laws and the constant character of certain principles.

In the Universe, then, one can find definitive elements beyond the changing (natural laws and physical principles—*as-sunan al-kawniyyah*) as well as definitive elements at the core of the changing (the constants of history—*sunan Allah*), exactly in the same way as there exist definitive transhistorical rules within the revealed text (belief and practice) and constant effective causes (*'ilal*) (that can be inferred) behind the interpretative latitude offered by speculative (*zannî*) *âyât*: the two Revelations require the intelligence to distinguish those two categories and carry out important analytical work in each of the two areas, in particular, to reach appropriate understanding both of the Universe and its order and of human beings and their diversity in space and time.

In the study of mutability, the Quran is not the only fundamental textual reference. As we have seen, it primarily deals with general principles, while it is mainly in the Sunnah, the Prophetic traditions, that the diversity of cultures, customs, and social realities through space and time is very directly emphasized. As scholars unanimously noted, it is through those texts that the implementation of general rules materializes in detail. In this respect, the Prophetic experience is highly significant: in the different realities of Mecca and Medina, Islamic principles and practices were to remain the same but the relationship to the surrounding culture, local customs, and social practices had to change.[29] Many Prophetic traditions explicitly or implicitly mention the cultural differences between the two cities, which required the scholars of the fundamentals of law (*usûliyyûn*) as well as those of law and jurisprudence (*fuqahâ'*) to take into account people's common good (*masâlih an-nâs*) and customs (*'urf*) when using analogical reasoning (*qiyâs*) and, more broadly, implementing legal preference (*istihsân*). The change from a trading society to a more agricultural one, from a public space from which women were mostly absent to a cultural universe where they enjoyed considerable status, along with very different attitudes to celebration, art, and aesthetics, were to have considerable influence on the understanding both of immutable religious principles and of changing social realities. When the Prophet stressed a cultural feature specific to the dwellers of Medina (*Ansâr*) when he told his wife, as a wedding was being celebrated: "O 'Aïshah, is there not anything there to entertain them? The *Ansâr* enjoy entertainment"; when, at another time, he asked, "Have you sent any singer with her [the bride]? The *Ansâr* are people with some taste"; or when his own wife 'Aïshah commended, "Blessed be the *Ansâr* women [what excellent women they were], modesty did not prevent them from seeking knowledge [in religious affairs],"[30] all this means that the implementation of rulings must be accompanied by a process of analysis, observation, and inference about contingent social and cultural realities. It is from such a study, working from concrete and visible realities to the rules underlying them, which will make it possible to establish a coherent methodology for dealing with the human fact and managing the questions raised by a given society at a specific time in history.[31] This is again the methodological preoccupation we had encountered with scholars in their approach to texts.

To be exhaustive, at the close of this analysis, it is important to recall another dimension that I alluded to earlier without really insisting on the teachings to be drawn from it. For the fact that the two Books, the two Revelations, address both the mind and the heart is essential, beyond the mere process of observation, analysis, and inference that makes it possible to understand the Book and the Universe. For a believing conscience, what matters is not just to understand facts—although this in itself is essential—but also to understand the intents, meaning, and finality of the world's order and of the substance of the revealed message where, ultimately, the two Revelations meet. Meditation of the heart and spirit must be allied to reflection of the mind: to this the Quran invites the human beings who receive it: *"Do they not ponder on the Quran? Had it been from any other than God, they would surely have found in it much inconsistency."*[32]

It also says: *"Do they not ponder on the Quran? Or is it that there are locks upon their hearts?"*[33] This spiritual and intellectual meditation about the Revelation is an invitation to recognize the presence of the divine, the truthfulness of the message, and the fate of human beings. The same outlook, the same meditation, is set for people as a parable about the book of the world when the "deposit of faith" encounters the signs of nature: *"We did indeed offer the trust [of faith]* (al-amânah) *to the Heavens and the Earth and the mountains, but they refused to undertake it and were afraid of it...."*[34]

Even more explicitly, the two Revelations meet through the mediation of the mountains that would—as a massive, imposing element of the real—be torn asunder in front of the message's spiritual power: *"Had We sent down this Quran on a mountain, verily, you would have seen it humble itself and cleave asunder in awe of God."*[35]

The two orders, mirroring each other as to the study of definitive and changing laws and principles, unite and harmonize at the level of the essence and meaning of creation and of life. Here, the believing conscience finds a Way (*ash-sharî'ah*), a direction (*hudâ*), the meaning of a free and therefore responsible destiny. A person must go to the end of her or his mind's potentialities, to the bottom of the heart's spiritual resources, remembering that the mind needs the heart as much as the heart needs the mind and that the higher reconciliation of orders is achieved in deep intelligent meditation that grasps meaning and reaches toward the divine. This ultimate stage in the mirror approach is of course essential in the order of faith while it sometimes remains absent in a purely rationalistic scientific approach. The two orders are not opposed, each of them completes the other, gives it meaning and perfects the path of knowledge by reconciling the "why" and the "how," thus enlightening the mind and appeasing the heart. This union, this spiritualization, is not, however, devoid of teachings, which indeed determine the nature and importance of human responsibility before the laws extracted from the two Revelations—some of which are *qat'iyyât* (clear and definitive) while the others are *zanniyât* (open to interpretation)—to which a person must strive to remain faithful. Since preserving meaning is so essential and respecting objectives is so imperative, this means pondering on the book's commands and protecting the order of the Universe. The ethical conscience naturally projects itself into the science of Nature and it is this essential teaching that is expressed in the Prophet's brief, but dense formula stating: "Take care of the earth, it is your mother" and his qualifying its *naturally* sacred essence when he said, "The whole earth is [set for me as] place of prostration (of worship, literally *a mosque*) and [a space of] purity."[36] The profane and the sacred meet because the message blends the spiritual and the natural and thereby requires harmonizing the ethics that orients and the rationale that describes.

8

The Context (*al-Wâqi'*) as a Source of Law

We saw in the second section that the scholars of fundamentals (*usûliyyûn*) as well as those of law and jurisprudence (*fuqahâ'*) naturally focused according to the available corpus of texts and that they set out to determine a typology of sources, a reading and extraction methodology, a categorization of approaches, and an ultimate order of principles, maxims, and rules providing the elaboration of law with a clear framework and some coherence. At each stage, in each of the spheres delimited in the course of their theoretical elaborations, the human and social contexts (*al-wâqi'*) are mentioned as a necessary reference and an inescapable dimension that must be taken into account in the implementation of law. It remains that, for the jurists (*'ulamâ'*) specialized in texts, context mainly serves to shed additional light and act as a help—or sometimes a tool—in understanding the fundamental texts, which remain the sole sources of law and jurisprudence. Never indeed is the Universe, the unfurled Revelation, considered in its own right as an autonomous complementary source of law and its elaboration.

Today, it has indeed become impossible to rely on a knowledge of contexts naturally integrated by text scholars, because social and

scientific knowledge has grown so vast that it can no longer be mastered and assimilated without highly specific specialization in one
particular field of the exact, experimental, or social sciences. Can
reference to the social and human context—about which the amount
of knowledge available has grown so extensively—remain so secondary? Must the gap between the two orders of knowledge, texts and
contexts widen? Such a situation, as we have seen, places contemporary Muslim jurists in a strictly reactive and protective posture:
since they no longer master the specialized fields of expertise that
explain the world's realities, it has become impossible for them to
look forward, to foresee what is real or even to orient its present
or future evolution. It is simply no longer enough to follow evolution, a step behind as far as mastery is concerned, because this offers
no other possibility than constant adaptation to new realities that
impose themselves because they necessarily overstep the knowledge
gathered by text scholars.

Even so, when returning to scriptural sources themselves, one
realizes that they give another image of the Universe and grant
it quite another status. These are indeed—as I mentioned in the
previous chapter—general, universal principles, which are given
little detailed elaboration, but this does bear out what all law fundamentals scholars noted when they sought to grasp the nature of
Quranic teachings. Whether the written Revelation refers to itself,
to the Universe, or to behavioral rules, it always sets general principles: laying out an initial framework, determining higher universal
objectives, and making it possible to outline the Way of faithfulness
(*ash-sharî'ah*) through history. But still, everything in the Quran
suggests that the unfurled Revelation, the book of the world, should
be considered with the same importance, the same spiritual depth,
and the same analytical and rational thoroughness as dealing with
scriptural sources requires. I must thus, by referring step by step
to what was said earlier about nature, go on to produce the same
work of analysis, typology, and categorization of orders for the Universe and the social and human context (*al-wâqi'*) as was developed
for texts. Like a revelation of its own—conveying universal laws,
constant principles, specific rules, and indeterminate areas—the
Universe must be considered as an autonomous and complementary source of legal elaboration. This is what I shall attempt to do
in the following chapters, thereby making it possible to assess the

meaning and consequences of such a statement (if I carry it to its logical end). I must therefore pause to look into the typology and organization of context (*al-wâqi'*)-related knowledge.

Mirror Readings: Categorization and Hierarchy

In the light of what was covered in the previous chapter, I can elaborate a categorization of knowledge related to understanding the world. It is quickly perceptible, however, that the typology presented corresponds—without getting into the often confused debates over "epistemological typologies"—to what we know in the field of contemporary sciences with an initial distinction between the empirical sciences (natural sciences and social sciences) and the logical and formal sciences (mathematics, logic, etc.). What I said in the previous chapter about the different levels of expression regarding the book of the world and its rules naturally confirms this. What is of interest to us does not lie in the originality of the proposed categories but rather in the qualification of the rules extracted in each of the various spheres of scientific knowledge.

Before studying the typology of those fields of knowledge, it is important at this point to recall an *a priori* principle revealed by the texts as to the way the Universe, its order, and its diversity should be approached. Indeed, just as the fundamental, higher objective of the Revelation as a whole is to promote what is good and profitable for human beings (and consequently also protect them from all that can harm them), the Universe itself and its laws are presented as a gift and a positive space for humankind, determined for its good, its welfare, and its intellectual and physical improvement.

> *It is God who created the heavens and the earth, who sent down water from the sky, and with it brought out fruit for your sustenance. It is He who subjected* (sakhkhara) *the ships for you that they may sail through the sea by His Command; and He also subjected the rivers for you. And He subjected for you the sun and the moon, both diligently pursuing their courses. And He subjected for you the night and the day.*[1]

This initial positive outlook, associated with the invitation to the human conscience to remember and be thankful, is of foremost importance. It affects all the areas of human knowledge about the created Universe: a Universe that is both a gift and a "sign" fraught with meaning and its Creator, as we have seen, keeps inviting "those who are endowed with insight" to observe, study, and analyze it in all its dimensions. As I said, the knowledge gathered through such an undertaking can only confirm—in the logic of the Quranic text— the "meaning of the sign" and therefore it can never put faith at risk. Not only is "strictly scientific" knowledge not considered inferior to allegedly "strictly religious" knowledge; it becomes interesting, positive, as it focuses on an object, Nature, which is no less positive and friendly. The fears of Blaise Pascal who thought it fit to "write against those who delve too deep into science," or the reflections of Friedrich Nietzsche describing science as set, by definition and by nature, "against the fortress of faith," are unfounded: here the quest for scientific knowledge is a companion to faith and is qualified as fundamentally positive in its object and objectives. This is what the Quran expresses when it first of all mentions the order and colors of Nature:

> *Do you not see that God sends down water from the sky? With it we then bring out produce of various colours. And in the mountains are tracts of white and red, of various shades of colour, and black intense in hue. And so men and beasts and cattle are of different colours....*[2]

And then it goes on to add: *"Only those among his servants who have knowledge truly fear God."*[3]

Here, the reference to those "who have knowledge" (*ulamâ*) is thus generic and includes all those who have some learning, whether about the Universe or about the text. Indeed, even before tackling the typology of sciences and their qualification in the order of law, it is important to consider the basically positive light in which scriptural sources, and therefore the believing conscience, view such subjects when entering the autonomous Universe of the sciences.

The first level, as we have seen, is that of the sciences of Nature, which aims to study the phenomena of the Universe. Here, the Universe is to be observed to understand its laws and *how* it works. Many of the laws extracted, or of the principles identified, are definitive and universal and impress themselves on people at any time and in any place. In truth, the universal and definitive character of some of those principles will never be absolutely established (as is revealed by new discoveries and, more fundamentally, by the theory of relativity or quantum physics) and is relative to the interaction of different phenomena; it remains, however, that many laws and principles are established as universal (i.e., universal natural laws) and definitive. In the order of the world, and mirroring the qualifications of the definitive rules established by text scholars, those laws are *qat'iyyah*, in that they clearly and finally impress themselves on human intelligence and belong to the *sunan al-kawniyyah* (laws of the Universe). Any action in the world that failed to take such laws into account or to respect them would act against the order and meaning of the displayed Revelation, certain principles of which impose themselves on human intelligence. In the order of the treatment of texts, determining the definitive, undeniable essentiality of the principle of prayer (deduced from *qat'î* principles) corresponds to identifying definitive, undeniable laws and principles (e.g., law of gravity), in the order of Nature (deduced from *qat'î* principles). Consequently, it is important to study and know such laws and to take them into account in all circumstances, and the revealed Book, which aims to give ethical orientation to the action of humankind in history, cannot be understood and respected if the laws of the book of the world are not similarly recognized and respected.

The experimental sciences (chemistry, physics, biology, and, more broadly, the various medical disciplines) observe reality, establish causal relationships, and go on to deduce and induce laws and rules verified by experimentation. Some of those laws are established, universal, and definitive (e.g., how matter or the human body functions), while others remain relative to the state of human knowledge at the time and are liable to evolve or become more precise as time goes by. It remains, nevertheless, that those laws and principles extracted and established by human rationality—after a long process of observation and experimentation—naturally impress themselves on human intelligence as definitive and universal: as far as their categorization is concerned, then, they also belong to the order of the *qat'î* (clear, definitive, undeniable principles) already mentioned. No particular moral connotation is associated with those laws and principles as such, apart from the need to remember, from the outset, that the higher objective of the whole Universe and of its laws is the good and welfare of humankind. The practice and instruments of science are therefore not subject either in and of themselves, nor as tools, to a specific moral qualification. This qualification is present from the outset, as we have seen, in its object (the—induced—reason for the Universe) and, further on, in its objectives (acquiring knowledge, granting human beings better protection, promoting their good, pondering Nature, etc.).

Things are somewhat different in the context of the human and social sciences (e.g., philosophy, anthropology, political science, psychology, history, ethnology, economics), which are not exact empirical sciences. Here, phenomena are diverse, fluctuating, and subject to manifold, contradictory interpretations. When studying humans in their environment and time, we are no longer dealing with facts but with intentions, individual and group psychology, different value systems, cultures that do not answer to precise laws or to a single universal principle of causality. In social sciences, two operations must nonetheless be distinguished, again mirroring what we had seen about the treatment of scriptural sources. First, in the course of their studies of behaviors and societies, specialists in human sciences had to develop an inductive approach that enabled them, from the realities and patterns observed in the field or in history, to work upward and identify a principle accounting for a constant that explained individual and/or collective behavior. The diversity of behaviors can be explained through a series of constant principles that can be identified in a given society or can, more broadly, operate transversally in all human societies whatever their cultures or specificities. This type of reading of reality corresponds to the other reading that law scholars performed on speculative (*zannî*) texts, for which they tried to extract an effective cause behind the statement or statements inductively to establish logic and coherence at the heart of that diversity. Social scientists try to do the same in their field of study and attempt in the process to identify universal principles (or general principles, for a given society) explaining human behavior. The latter's universality is a moot point and has led to endless debates (over the scientific or unscientific character of discoveries in the various fields of the social sciences), but it remains that there are indeed a number of laws or principles regulating or explaining social and human behavior, which specialists or protagonists in the various societies must take into account. Thus, the constants in the various legislative models, relations to power, domination structures, the relationship to politics, the historical behaviors of the rich and the poor, and symbolic expressions, match logical patterns and causality principles that may be verified even though those are not exact and scientifically definitive. The laws underlying the diversity of phenomena remain operative and universal and in this respect they are similar to the *qat'î* category as to their qualification. One cannot, in the social sciences, deny or overlook the presence of constants explaining human behavior patterns, even though, once again, a large interpretative margin remains.

The second operation is of quite a different nature since it consists in observing, analyzing, and understanding the diversity of societies and cultures, of systems and values, in their immediate, historical factuality. No law immediately imposes itself here and the field of observation is open to scientific, cultural, aesthetic, or even ideological interpretation: one can detect no underlying natural laws, no certain uniformity behind the undeniable materiality of diversity among people. Here, human intelligence must observe, understand, and interpret without any preestablished reading grid, immersed in the manifold, contradictory diversity of human societies with their histories, their cultures, their memories, and their behavior. Critical reason is left to itself, *autonomous* in the strictest possible sense, for it is confronted with the most open, the most speculative, and the least definite of realities. The Book of the Universe and the social sciences that unfold there open the doors of the *zannî* that requires human reason to perform a constant *ijtihâd* (autonomous critical approach) to identify enduring or/and changing causality principles, the various relationships to cultures and/or customs, symbolical and/or imaginary projections, and the like. A vast field thus opens for the exercise of human rationality, and it is by no means less important because it contains less certain knowledge than the exact or experimental sciences: on the contrary, it is because of the need to be in direct contact with the lived reality and with human behavior (in its diversity in worldly time) that specific attention must be paid to the social sciences as a whole. What they teach us about humankind, about indeterminate elements in groups and in human behavior, in value systems and in cultures—although this is *zannî* (open to interpretation) or rather *all the more so* because it is *zannî*—is essential to any intellectual exercise striving to remain faithful to the ethical meaning of the revealed Book. It is indeed in this field of the *zannî* that jurists elaborated the main part of their reflections: at the heart of diversity, of the nonorganic, the seemingly unorganized, they tried—by deduction as well as by inference—to suggest ways of respecting faithfulness to the global, and invariably positive, message of scriptural sources. The social sciences, the many specializations in the observation and understanding of reality, play the same part and it would be unthinkable—and quite illogical and absurd—to cut oneself off from those fields of knowledge because they offer nothing "certain" or because behaviors, or even "moral categories," appear there as indeterminate or contradictory. This is what can be heard today—explicitly or implicitly—among the *usûliyyûn* or *fuqahâ'*: they naturally admit, by the force of laws and things, that they must take into account the undisputed knowledge reached by the exact and experimental sciences, but they stay far away from studies and research in the social sciences, which seem quite secondary to them; they only usually refer to them as a circumstantial add-on (to give a social or economic phenomenon circumstantial explanation), but never as a constant—and mirrorlike—source of legal reflection. It is as if the complexity of this human reality, devoid of any definite order or rule, opened such a vast range of indeterminacy that faithfulness to the texts and to the Way could be endangered, so that it became necessary to seek protection from it or disregard it during the extraction of laws and rulings from the scriptural sources. This attitude of fear or mistrust of the social sciences and the *zannî* category (open to interpretation and therefore to the exercise of autonomous critical reasoning) in the realm of human reality is in contradiction to the original confidence mentioned earlier. The first Companions, as well as early scholars, confident, as we said, in the Revelation's global message and intimately familiar with their natural environment, never refrained from including the latter in their legal elaborations. In a Universe that has grown so complex, and equipped with increasingly specialized text-related knowledge (but inevitably, less and less in touch with the environment), scriptural scholars have preferred to set limits on the influence of the sciences—the social sciences in particular—either with the noble aim of preserving religion or, more selfishly, to preserve the field of their own authority against areas of knowledge they could no longer master.

Adequacy and Harmonization

The above analysis nevertheless shows that it is possible—and I think imperative—to undertake a global approach to the two Revelations (the text and the Universe), setting them face to face and constantly seeking complementarity. This does not mean confusing orders or imposing values and methodologies that do not actually belong to one or the other of the fields of knowledge involved. Thus I by no means suggest that the exact, experimental, or social sciences should be subjected to an initial "ethical reading grid" that would influence their methods of analysis or orient their conclusions formulated in the name of "correspondence" (or of agreement[4]) with the norms stated in the fundamental scriptural sources: each field of knowledge necessarily lays out its own method, rules, and analysis and experimentation norms autonomously according to its area of study.[5] Using complementary approaches cannot mean confusing orders, and just as text scholars must imperatively—as they have been doing from the beginning—establish norm extraction principles and rules from the texts and their specialization, it is no less necessary to leave it to scientists, as competent authorities, to determine just as autonomously their respective methods, their norms, and their applications as far as their own field of study is concerned.

What is at hand here is quite another matter. It is to determine the preestablished principles of a holistic approach that alone, I think, can enable the Muslim conscience to revive faithfulness to the founding texts and restore creative confidence with regard to contemporary science and knowledge. It is to base faithfulness on a twofold understanding (of the texts and of the Universe) and, faced with the growing complexity of knowledge, to give ourselves the means to refer to the whole range of expertise to delineate the outline and conditions of a solid ethical authority apt to orient the reform process. The sciences should neither be held down nor feared, but instead fully and equally integrated into the production of contemporary applied ethics, as we shall see later. The preceding pages have unveiled the outline of this holistic approach that keeps calling on the conscience to observe human realities in parallel, while it protects the sciences' autonomy: the texts that express meaning and the Universe that expresses the reality are suffused with laws, principles, and realities that are sometimes universal, definitive, and final (*qat'î*) and other times circumstantial and relative (*zannî*); those two horizons need one another, for each of them can only be grasped in relation to the other so as to establish a knowledge that explains and an ethics that shows the way, an applied ethics of science and knowledge. It is the responsibility of critical and autonomous human rationality to deduce and induce laws, principles, and norms and to establish correspondences between the various spheres of knowledge: it must grasp the latter in their various relationships to their field of study, which imposes itself on them, and without being put off by their multiplicity and complexity. The human conscience must welcome this complexity, and in its light it must identify and recognize the variety of skills and grant itself the means to harmonize them. Simple though it may seem, this recognition of rationality requires a fundamental reconsideration of the classical categorization of the sources of law.

The issue is complex and habits are set deep: indeed, the old categorization of the sciences, which has come down to us from the Middle Ages and remains effective in "Islamic sciences" departments throughout the world, reveals the nature of the problem and the complexity of the paradoxes. All the fields that had to do with the study of scriptural sources have been termed "Islamic sciences," and it has always been clear—and explicitly acknowledged—in the sphere of reference to religion and ethics that text scholars were the sole and primary "guardians" of the essential sciences and of faithfulness. The other sciences, those that were not termed "Islamic," were considered as secondary in the order of faithfulness and thus, consequently, in the hierarchy of knowledge useful to believers (*'ilm nâfi'*). This categorization is a problem, as we have seen, in that it is impossible to be faithful to Islamic ethics applied to the whole range of sciences without possessing a large mastery of those disciplines. The distinction between the "Islamic sciences" and other sciences is not only inoperative, it is also counter-productive and, in the long run, dangerous. Unless one simply aims to qualify the sciences according to their object (the "Islamic sciences" being, in this case, those that deal with "Islamic" reference texts[6]), it seems problematic to qualify fields of knowledge in such a restrictive manner: inductively extracting rules for interpretation and understanding from a "body of texts" is no more "Islamic" or "sacred" than identifying a principle in the functioning of the human body. There is nothing "Islamic in itself" in the rational study of a text or of a human environment unless, once again, one has decided *a priori* that some functions of human intelligence are more "Islamic" or by essence more "important" than others.[7] The different "text sciences" that have been termed "Islamic" or "sacred" as opposed to the "other" sciences (of the context in its wider sense) have indeed gained in "religious authority" what they have effectively—and paradoxically—lost in terms of efficacy on reality. They have literally moved away from reality, and despite the slogans about the "holistic character" of the "Islamic sciences" and the "global character" of the implementation of Islamic ethics, it is becoming clear today that the "Islamic or sacred sciences"—which hold a (real or symbolic) position of authority over all other sciences—have in effect become marginalized, that they often lag behind all the other areas of knowledge and fail to take the lead.

What was legitimate in earlier times, because of the state of science, must now be reconsidered unless we accept, in the field of Islamic thought, to endorse a permanent break between the sources of law on the one hand and the various fields of human knowledge on the other. What matters in the different text or context sciences is the demanding process of adapting the methodology to the field of study and extracting laws and principles that make it possible to understand and grasp them. This involves the intelligence, the autonomous critical mind that observes, categorizes, and attempts to analyze and understand the two Books, the two Revelations, that it is faced with. This painstaking process, ruled only by the field of study and the intelligence that examines it, has nothing "Islamic" about it from an intellectual viewpoint and it requires of scholars specific critical skills.[8] It is, however, on the other two levels that the harmonization of fields of knowledge is to operate: the sciences of religious texts (*'ulûm an-nusûs as-dîniyyah*)—and no longer "the Islamic sciences"—as well as the sciences of social and human environments, while they require of scholars truly scientific thoroughness when elaborating and dealing with their respective knowledge, by no means prevent them from combining this with a twofold spiritual and ethical perspective on the meaning of the real. The heart's meditation about the origin, meaning, and higher objectives of the texts and contexts, as well as the conscience's formulation of ethical limits to human action in the Universe and toward humankind—those are the attitudes that underlie the "Islamic" dimension of the scientific approach and of ethical choices. It is not a matter of superficially "making science and knowledge Islamic," but rather, essentially and deeply, of establishing an *Islamic conscience* of objectives and an *Islamic ethics* related to human behavior and the qualitative use of knowledge.

This is a colossal undertaking that involves reconsidering the old categories established by scholars and unquestioningly accepted by Muslims. Going forward, this primarily means reconsidering what the scholars of fundamentals, regardless of the school to which they belonged, from ash-Shâfi'î to ash-Shâtibî, categorized as sources of law. If there are actually two Books, two Revelations, which respectively have their own universal laws and their own circumstantial and historical laws; if understanding texts and contexts requires extracting those laws through an autonomous critical study based on the object studied; and if the believing conscience must meditate about final objectives and ethics in the light of the two Books and of all areas of knowledge, then the Universe and the sciences related to it must imperatively be considered as objective, indispensable sources of Islamic law and jurisprudence. We cannot maintain the classical categorization that, through an outdated viewpoint on the state of science and knowledge, maintains preeminence and authority relationships that stand in the way of the reform that is required today.

9

The Growing Complexity
of the Real

Having stipulated that the Universe—as a "Book" and a "Revelation"—
and social and human contexts, in their geography and historicity,
are full-fledged sources of Islamic law and jurisprudence is not
enough to reach the proposed goal. Besides, *ulamâ'* (whether *usûliyyûn* or *fuqahâ'*) would have no difficulty in admitting this principle;
they would even hasten to add that context has always been taken
into account by text specialists, in one way or another. What matters
most is not only clarifying the meaning of this re-balancing between
texts (*an-nusûs*) and context (*al-wâqi'*), but in essence also drawing all the consequences of that thesis in the light of contemporary
knowledge, whether in approaching texts or in dealing with scientific
and human knowledge, and indeed, more broadly, in implementing
Islamic ethics.

Contemporary *ulamâ'* are right to claim that, as I have pointed
out several times in this work, the world, history, and the environment have always been integrated into their analyses of texts. In early
times, this awareness was at its most natural because scholars were
intimately familiar with the environment for which they set the laws
(many were also expert scientists, physicians, and philosophers);

then, as time went by, they did not hesitate to call on specialists (*mutakhassisûn, khubarâ'*) of this or that scientific field, who were asked to inform them about the state of knowledge in their fields or answer questions. All *fuqahâ'* councils worldwide have gathered opinions of scientists or specialists who can inform them about specific fields of expertise; this is naturally more systematically done in the experimental sciences. Those experts represent their field of study, answer questions, sometimes provide an opinion or advice; then the council of *ulamâ'* specializes in the study of scriptural sources—with the help of the information provided by the scientists, but most often meeting on their own—formulate a ruling or legal opinion (a *fatwâ*) about a specific issue. In very rare councils (or on rare occasions) scientists, text specialists, and experts in a given scientific field (related to the human context at large) sit down together to determine the outline of an applied ethics in a particular area of knowledge. This kind of work has probably been carried out most dynamically and efficiently in the fields of medicine and astronomy, but this is an exception rather than the rule.

Yet reflection about the nature of knowledge in modern times requires me to question both the framework and the methodologies used in the councils and circles of contemporary Islamic legislation. I see that knowledge is growing extraordinarily more complex, and that a deep-set revolution is occurring in human potentialities, and yet nothing seems to be changing in the production of Islamic ethics in the light of such upheavals. This reality, as I said, produces a much more far-reaching problem later on, in defining the sources of law and consequently, as we shall see below, in establishing *spheres of authority* in the development of ethics. We must, however, take a closer look at the evolution of the sciences to reach a clearer view of what this is going to entail as far as dealing with texts and establishing an Islamic ethics is concerned.

The Evolution of the Sciences

The amount of knowledge accumulated during the past four centuries and especially, of course, during the twentieth century, is truly astounding. This scientific revolution has had consequences for the whole range of human behavior and more generally on the evolution of societies. People have grown better able to grasp reality, but at the same time this reality itself has grown more complex and has revealed myriad topics that still remain to be observed and discovered. From astrophysics to neuroscience, all scientific research points to the same conclusion: we have acquired extraordinarily extensive and complex new knowledge, but what remains to be studied and understood is immeasurably vaster. This upheaval has naturally required scientists to become more and more specialized in the different fields of knowledge and in highly specific areas within each field: all the exact, experimental, or social sciences without exception have undergone a growing extension and compartmentalization of their object of study as the available amount of knowledge has increased.

It is therefore impossible, as I said, for a text specialist (*'âlim*) to be able to assimilate the whole range of those sciences, not even an *ulamâ'* council might suffice, since those fields of knowledge largely exceed their own area of expertise. Even when these experts councils must today set forth the law in a local context, for a society or culture they know from within (like the *ulamâ'* of former times), the world and all areas of knowledge have become so interconnected, the situations so intricate and complex, that it is impossible for them to rely only on naturally acquired knowledge to be in full and adequate understanding of their time and place, however "local" these might initially seem. From the most technologically advanced societies to those that experience the direst realities of economic underdevelopment—from North to South, from East to West—realities echo one another and areas of knowledge communicate: it becomes impossible to isolate situations and to put forth legal opinions (*fatâwâ*) and ethical answers, unless by perpetuating a long-outdated perception of the real.

It is, of course, in the field of experimental sciences that the knowledge acquired necessarily confronts *fuqahâ'* with fundamental, explicit questions. The knowledge acquired in physics, chemistry, biology, neuroscience, or medicine, for instance, has enabled scientists to reach a better understanding of the organization of matter, or the functioning of living beings—of the brain and the human body, for example. We are indeed faced with a reality that is becoming increasingly complex, one that requires human intelligence to expand its knowledge and establish an approach that is both holistic

and specialized, if the desire is to think and develop an applied ethics that is up to date with knowledge about the subjects at hand.
Fuqahâ' have easily admitted that the amount and complexity of the
knowledge acquired in the contemporary experimental sciences out-
stripped their own capacities and skills, and that it was necessary for
them to rely on scientists to adapt their legal rulings as needed. All
that is known today about DNA, cells, living tissue, and embryos, as
well as the functioning of the brain and clinical death definitions, for
instance, has immediate consequences on the legal rulings that must
be developed whether about general situations or more limited cases:
from genetic engineering, to cloning, organ donation, abortion, or
euthanasia, it is impossible to issue a legal ruling or opinion (*fatwâ*)
without taking into account the state of contemporary knowledge.
The question that remains, and to which I shall return below, is how
to integrate, or rather how better to integrate, scientists into the production of thought and the implementation of ethics in our times.

The Universe of the social sciences is just as complex: whether
in anthropology, psychology, economics, or other disciplines, one is
faced with the same growing complexity and accumulation of increasingly specialized and precise knowledge. We have seen that, with
those subjects being less "exact," less able to be "verified" by scientific
experimentation, *fuqahâ'* quickly considered them as "secondary"
and, therefore, as less imperatively requiring them to be integrated
into the formulation of legal rulings. It indeed seemed useful to rely
on expert research, on thinkers' reflections, or on working hypoth-
eses, but this consultation was never so important, nor was its binding character so clearly felt, as has been the case for the experimental
sciences. This distant—if not wary—relationship with the social sciences remains the rule today and consultations remain marginal and
superficial.

The bulk of the production and theories of the social sciences
(e.g., sociology) has been largely ignored by Islamic scholars as they
elaborate their legal rulings (although these function in and for social
and historical contexts about which thorough research has been conducted). Inferential studies about social dynamics that try to extract
basic principles and constant causality relationships in the changes
in constituted human groups are of very little interest to *fuqahâ'* who
go on pronouncing the law without considering those fields of study
that they deem "too approximate." Similarly, the different branches

of applied psychology are but scantily referred to: in addition to the often global, simplifying, and simplistic rejection of psychoanalysis (reduced to a biased analysis of Freud's work alone), one can perceive that the different theories elaborated in applied psychology, from cognitivism to behaviorism, or more broadly, cross-cultural psychology, are not taken into consideration. Moreover, it can also be noted that this research as a whole is neglected, along with its fields of application, whether clinical psychology, social psychology, education psychology, legal psychology, or the various types of psychotherapies and studies in neuropsychology and psychopedagogy. Those are indeed not "exact" and definitive sciences, but those different fields do provide perspectives that are important to know and that seem necessary to integrate into the elaboration of ethical norms orienting individual and collective human behavior.

The same observation can be made in the order of the economic sciences. Indeed, *fuqahâ'* or Muslim economists have carried out—sometimes very thorough—research about the contemporary economy and its complexity, but it remains that one cannot but notice the huge gap between the *fatâwâ* stated by *fuqahâ'* in this field and the concrete practices that can be observed in the Universe of the global, national, or even the local economy. The very idea that there could be an "Islamic economy" (I shall return to this point later) is misleading if not dishonest: for after all, what is truly "Islamic" in this economy—its tools, its methods, its norms, its goals? One can everywhere observe a lack of mastery of the complexity of the various fields of the contemporary economy, of the global interdependence relations at the heart of the global market (between African or Asian peasants and Western buyers; between the various stock exchanges of Wall Street or the city of London, the speculations and commercial relations within societies and in the city streets of developing nations); a lack of awareness of the fluctuating dynamics inherent to the global market economy (that is out of step essentially with a strictly structural and normative legal approach, which is currently thought outdated). The economic sciences have grown more complex just as their object of study has, and it is impossible to outline "an applied Islamic ethics in economics" without relying on contemporary expertise and research, unless one reduces economic activity to the use of a few tools without going to the trouble of thinking through the philosophy and objectives of human behavior in that field. Unfortunately this is what can be observed, and the dysfunction comes from the answers offered by successive *fuqahâ'*, in the light of the elements made available to them by their (mainly Muslim) economist advisors: a partial (and often biased) accounting of the complex workings of the contemporary economy, an obsession with tools and norms leading to ends that are dangerously overlooked, and finally—according to most practitioners—structural, marginal, and often cosmetic answers to questions about the global economic order.

Text scholars (*'ulamâ' an-nusûs*) must necessarily integrate the evolution of the experimental and social sciences—that are all ways of understanding, reading, and interpreting the Book of the Universe—into their research and the production of legal rulings in the fields at hand. One can no longer be content with providing formal answers, focusing only on the structural—and almost technical—framework within which *fuqahâ'* have got into the habit of operating, since the amount of knowledge in the experimental and social sciences overstepped them, they naturally responded by declaring themselves the protectors of ethics against the "excesses" of the sciences. This response is, of course, understandable, humanly and historically, but it has led to restricting ethical elaboration to a timid, reactive, defensive posture in virtually all scientific fields. The original confidence, which was characterized by an ethics that mastered the sciences and carried a vision of purposes and objectives, has given way to a reflection about texts that is wary of the evolution of social and human contexts and, instead of providing a vision for the future, is content with laying out—with little effort—the ethical framework of an *adaptation* to the requirements of the present. While the textual scholars might shoulder most of the responsibility for this, scholars of the context—clinical scientists and social scientists—and the Muslim general public are not entirely blameless either. Like the jurists, these scholars focus on their particular field of knowledge and lack religious education beyond the basics so that they too often compartmentalize their lives and knowledge. They seem to have internalized the notion that their knowledge being outside of the "Islamic sciences" is thus irrelevant to Islamic legal deliberation and reform. They wait to be invited as experts rather than demanding a place of full participation at the table of deliberation. The Muslim public also fails its role to demand more of scholars of text and context and often seems to be content with adaptive tactics that comfort them rather than acting as agents of transformation in a world that constantly challenges the global ethics of their faith.

The Prerequisites of a
Transformational Reform

I have already mentioned in the first section the difference I draw between adaptation reform and transformation reform. With this reflection about the Book of the Universe and the sciences as a whole (exact, experimental, and social), we are touching the heart of the matter. As I said, *usûliyyûn* as well as *fuqahâ'* have over decades and centuries repeatedly said that the environment as a whole, as well as the specificity of human and social contexts, must be taken into account when elaborating rulings (*ahkâm*) and issuing legal opinions (*fatâwâ*). And indeed, they continue to refer to social realities, to customs (*'urf*), and to the people's common interest (*masâlih*). However, a gap has gradually appeared between their immediate and natural knowledge of the societies for which they articulated the law and the complexity of those societies' organizations, the interaction and interdependence of the various areas of human activity (private, public, work, leisure, etc.), their relation to other societies, and of course the huge amounts of scientific knowledge acquired. That gap, which is so evident in contemporary Islamic thought, has, as I said, put scholars in an essentially reactive and protective position: the reform of Islamic thought—that is in effect accepted—has now been understood as a means of preserving essentials while being content with acknowledging the need to *adapt* to the realities of a world and of amounts of knowledge the complexity of which increasingly elude us. Even so, we have seen why adaptation alone cannot be satisfactory since it reduces faithfulness to the message and ethics to a process that is always considered *a posteriori*, aiming to protect "ethical areas" or "practices" within a global system that no vision directs, that no one acts to transform at the source, and that eventually imposes itself on human intelligence and human conscience.

Giving ourselves the means for a transformation reform, a visionary ethics that accompanies and integrates the evolution of knowledge, requires us to rethink the classical apparatus of the fundamentals of law and jurisprudence at their source. The first prerequisite consists in clearly establishing that those sources are not simply scriptural but also the Book of the Universe and with it, all the sciences that strive to understand it better and improve human beings' actions and conditions in their various spheres and in their specific social contexts. Thus, the classification that was content with drawing up a list of the sources of law (Quran, Sunnah, *ijmâ', qiyâs, 'urf, istihsân, istis-lâh*, etc.) and with focusing almost entirely on relating to the texts (the reference to custom and common interest is primarily considered as a support to aid understanding the texts), must, I think, be revised and reconsidered in the light of contemporary realities. From a strictly theoretical, and fundamental, viewpoint, we have seen that the Universe imposes itself on the human intelligence as a book, with its rules, laws, principles, semantics, grammar, and signs, and that, in effect, as the Revelation itself repeatedly suggests, it is imperative to approach the two Books in parallel and complementarily.

The evolution of the experimental and social sciences similarly compels us to perform this fundamental rebalancing and to clearly acknowledge natural and universal laws and the constant or circumstantial principles of human action in history as full-fledged sources of Islamic law and jurisprudence (*usûl al-fiqh*). As such, then, they must be included in ongoing ethical reflection, and the men and women who are specialists in these various sciences must take an active part in formulating ethical norms in their own field. What had so far been accepted as an implicit approach, often as a possible supplement, —awareness of the natural, social, and human context (*al-wâqi'*)— here becomes an imperative requirement in legal and ethical structures in the contemporary world. The point is then to clearly place the two Books, the two Revelations, the text, and the Universe on the same level—as sources of law—and consequently, to integrate the different universes of the sciences and their various areas of knowledge and specialities into the formulation of legal rulings about very specific scientific, social, or economic issues. It is this confident integration of all the sciences, of the knowledge acquired, and this better mastery (of texts—so far exclusively called "Islamic"—as well as of Nature and contexts—implicitly, and strangely, considered as "non Islamic"), which will enable contemporary Islamic thought to formulate a vision for the future, to work out goals from the substance of scientific knowledge (and not only from its tools and techniques), and thereby, ultimately, to outline the stages of a wide-ranging transformation reform in the name of applied ethics.

This entails—and this is the second prerequisite—that text scholars (*'ulamâ' an-nusûs*) as well as context scholars (*'ulamâ' al-wâqi'*) should participate on an equal footing in elaborating ethical norms in the different fields of knowledge. Even though the fundamentals of belief (*'aqîdah*) and worship (*'ibadât*) obviously remain the prerogative of the *fuqahâ'* insofar as they are exclusively determined by the texts, this is not so for social, economic, and scientific issues for which an ethical reflection is only possible by relying on the knowledge of specialists, while respecting the autonomy of their practice and of their scientific methodologies when taking their expertise into account. I shall later be discussing the practical consequences of such an approach, but it can now be said that we consider it to be the only one that will allow contemporary Islamic thought to free itself from its reactive, defensive attitude in its relationship to knowledge and the sciences, primarily owing to the fact that from the outset, a lack of balance had been accepted when establishing the sources of law: thus established, those sources came to impose an ethical framework that was always "outpaced" (systematically *adapting*) because of imposed needs (*hajât*) or inescapable imperatives (*darûrât*).

The third condition that must be mentioned is, of course, linked to the direct consequences of the growing complexity of the sciences and of knowledge already discussed. While it is imperative to rely on the specialization and expertise of scientists, whether women or men, in their respective fields, it will also be necessary to require of textual scientists that they have a twofold specialization. To classical learning in the fundamental texts, their higher and specific objectives, and the finality of rulings, an effective specialization should be added in one field of human activity or another. Whether in the experimental sciences, in medicine, in economics, in psychology, or in art and culture, the holistic approach must be allied with a specialized ethical approach to respond appropriately to today's challenges but also to elaborate a prospective, creative body of thought. The specialization of *fuqahâ'* clearly appears to be the condition required for applied ethics to be efficient in the various fields just mentioned.

Thus, it is not enough to admit that reform or renewal (*tajdîd*) is an integral part of the exercise of legal thought. This principle must certainly be associated with a thorough reflection about the sources of law, their geography, and their status in the elaboration of norms and ethical finalities. My proposal for the general system—including the natural and universal laws that are the sources of law, integrating scientists into the formulation of ethical norms, and *fuqahâ'* acquiring specialized scientific knowledge, however simple it may seem, is nevertheless fraught with consequences for any approach to the fundamentals of law (*al-usûl*) and the concrete implementation of norms (*al-fiqh*). Clearly, when reconsidering the nature and status of the sources, this approach also questions the spheres of authority and powers of the scholars and scientists interested in those matters. Beyond general reflection, and the philosophy of law and of ethics that motivates it, resistance to this radical reform—in the geography of law as well as in its methodology—is bound to appear at the center of *usûliyyûn* and *fuqahâ'* circles who have so far represented authority and guarded faithfulness to Islamic norms. It has always been so—this reaction is natural and in itself quite understandable; it is moreover respectable when it expresses wariness and actual concern about the potential deviations in scientific practices or about the unrestricted acceptance of all types of social behavior. In my opinion, the approach to the fundamentals of law must be reformed for exactly opposite reasons: acquiring better mastery of human knowledge, deeper awareness of what is at stake, a capacity to anticipate and transform reality *in order to* harmonize the definitive objectives of ethics and human behavior in history.

Shifting the Center of Gravity of Religious and Legal Authority

As I said in the first section of this book, we have reached limits that prevent contemporary Islamic thought from moving forward and thus in facing the challenges of our time as it should. The first insight of scholars and thinkers consisted, in the late nineteenth and early twentieth centuries, in distinguishing between definitive universal principles inspired by the texts that constituted the *sharî'ah*, and their concrete implementation in the different geographical and historical contexts, that pertained to *fiqh*. This distinction between *sharî'ah*, that is, of divine origin, and *fiqh*, which is associated with the open and relative activity of human intelligence, has been and remains fundamental since it makes it possible to distinguish between the recognition and respect of higher revealed principles on the one hand, and their understanding, expression, and implementation at a given moment in human history on the other. In the sphere of *fiqh*, and specifically in the vast field of social affairs (*mu'âmalât*), it therefore became coherent and legitimate to analyze and discuss a historical heritage composed of interpretations, established rules, or legal opinions that were produced by human intelligence in striving to face the challenges of its time amid the diversity of societies. Islamic thought thereby gave itself the means to become reconciled with the practice of autonomous critical reasoning (*ijtihâd*) not only to evaluate the interpretations of the past but also, and especially, to suggest new perspectives and produce legal rulings adapted to the challenges of the present and future.

Thus, reformist thought again grew very dynamically throughout the twentieth century and one must admit that Islamic thought has evolved considerably. *Fuqahâ'* and thinkers have not hesitated to delve into the legacy of the past and revive approaches and philosophies of law that had been too long neglected despite offering a stimulating framework for the renewal of legal elaboration. They often worked in association with the three classical schools already mentioned: both ash-Shâfi'î's clarifying framework and the Hanafî's flexible inductive method have often been integrated into the seminal methodology of the higher objectives school of which ash-Shâtibî is historically the primary representative. Throughout Muslim-majority societies, from Pakistan to Indonesia, from Egypt to Saudi Arabia, from Algeria to Morocco, including African societies and Muslim communities of people now settled in the West, new reflections have emerged about a number of scientific discoveries, about medical ethics, economics, politics, power, gender studies, culture, interreligious dialogue, and civil society in general. In the area of Islamic law and jurisprudence, of *fiqh*, things have been moving along and it would be unfair to deny the existence of those developments and the realistic originality of some standpoints. It nevertheless remains, as I said, that the keywords of those developments are "necessity" (*ad-darûrah*) and "need" (*al-hâjah*) that convey the idea that *fuqahâ'* are compelled—under the pressure of reality—to decree *fatâwâ*, enabling Muslims to *adapt* to new realities while preserving a minimum level of ethics (whether in their activities themselves or through the techniques used).

We have therefore also reached the limits of the prospects opened by the distinction between *sharî'ah* and *fiqh* in contemporary Islamic legal thought. The process of "adaptation reform" that has made it possible to reconsider in a positive way some issues and responses of our time no longer offers *fuqahâ'*, and more generally Muslim societies and communities throughout the world, the means to respond to the major challenges that contemporary science and knowledge represent—unless we continue to be content with remaining followers and reducing ethical reflection to an exercise that consists in assigning ever-shrinking boundaries to the protected area of values and morals at the heart of a time or of societies we have given up trying to act on and transform (to prevent their possible deviations). *Fiqh* must, of course, continue to be dynamic and open to *ijtihâd*, but this dynamism must also, at the source, be enriched with other skills, other scientific authorities, and be able to perform a radical reform through the equal, holistic integration of all areas of knowledge, thereby establishing a new relationship to the world, to the sciences, and to societies.

The new geography of the sources of law that I suggest clearly and deliberately entails *shifting the center of gravity of religious and legal authority* in contemporary Muslim societies and communities. We can no longer leave it to scholarly circles and text specialists to determine norms (about scientific, social, economic, or cultural issues) while they only have relative or superficial, second-hand knowledge of complex, profound, and often interconnected issues. If we are to elaborate a vision for the present and future and have the ambition to establish the principles of a living applied ethics able to transform the world by establishing goals that are both realistic and visionary, it is urgent for us to integrate and harmonize the different sciences and all the areas of human knowledge and make them truly interdependent and complementary. To my mind, only by adopting a holistic approach going onward with the recognition and respect of highly specialized expertise can a global, coherent, and liberating reformist thought appear.

The traditional distinction between "the Islamic or sacred sciences" (dealing with the study of scriptural sources) and other sciences (implicitly "less" or "not Islamic") has produced an authority relationship about the elaboration of norms and ethics in favor of text specialists (*usûliyyûn* and *fuqahâ'*) although nothing basic legitimates nor justifies such a privilege. It is rather the opposite, for all that has been said about the room for interpretation offered by the fundamental texts, their silence, and the necessary dialectic relationship to the social and human context, clearly argues for a complete integration of all areas of human, historical, and circumstantial knowledge, when considering the written Revelation that aims to orient human action.

Clearly then, my point is not to discuss the authority of one scholar (*faqîh*) or another belonging to one trend of thought or another,[1] but indeed the authority of *fuqahâ'* in general. We shall see in the next chapter how the new geography, and its consequences for spheres of authority, can take concrete shape in Muslim societies and communities, and particularly in the circles specializing in *fiqh* and ethics. I can just note for the time being that this critical approach about the sources of law, the objectives of its elaboration from the two Books, the spheres of scientific and ethical authority, has and will go on having numerous consequences in different fields and on different levels. Not only should normative, legal, and ethical answers be different—and more in touch with the reality—but the involvement of Muslim societies and communities should be more far-reaching, more concrete, in elaborating rules and strategies to promote an efficient, operative applied ethics. This will, of course, be done through scientists and thinkers, but as we said, no practical skill should be disqualified for cooperative work in this field. Women's analysis of all issues and particularly—but not exclusively—the issue of their being, their status, and their role; writers and artists' views on cultural issues; contractors, bankers, and traders about financial, economic, and social issues—all must be able to feel involved in the reflection about the issues raised by their own concrete participation in a specific issue or in a specific field. Those practical elaborations are examined in the final section of this work.

10

Elaborating an Applied
Islamic Ethics

The new geography of the sources of *usûl al-fiqh* that I wish for, and which seems so imperative today in view of the challenges that Muslims are facing, requires serious reconsideration about the source of legal elaboration and will, as we have seen, produce crucial consequences. First of all, fundamental rebalancing is needed concerning the identification and respective status of the sources of law: the absolute preeminence the texts had received in the elaboration of law and the exclusive authority granted to text specialists (*usûli-yyûn* and *fuqahâ'*) have resulted in a situation of extreme discrepancy between the fields of knowledge—and in effect, a rift—even though Islam is thought to need a holistic approach. "Islamic sciences" scholars (text scholars) live in autarchy, well removed from research in the exact, experimental, and social sciences; they make do with scanty information, with research-based conclusions, to issue legal rulings about realities and contexts that are inevitably more complex than they can understand. The danger of "science without conscience," of uncontrolled excess, of an obsession with scientific performance and profitable productivity of course exists; its reality and consequences must not be understated, but this cannot justify the disjunction and discrepancy that can be observed today between the productions of *usûliyyûn* and *fuqahâ'* and the state of knowledge reached by scientists who specialize in the experimental and social sciences.

After I determined that the sources of *usûl al-fiqh* should include the two Books, the text, and the Universe on an equal footing, it becomes necessary to think through and reconsider the list of principles and higher aims that can be deduced from the two Revelations made available to human intelligence. In both cases, as I said, the primary and *a priori* importance of the Creation as well as of divine Messages through history is to preserve what is good, beneficial, and useful to the human race and to protect it from what is evil and harmful. On that basis and in the light of this first principle, text and context scholars must work together to draw out and construct the higher objectives and aims that must provide ethical orientation for their respective thoughts and productions, first within their own field of specialization, then by joining their reflections with those of others. Only through such a global approach can different areas of knowledge truly be reconciled, by stipulating higher universal principles in the future and protecting the sciences' autonomy (concerning their methodologies, research, and subject matter in the process). It appears clear that the five or six higher principles laid out by the objectives school (*madrasat al-maqâsid*) already mentioned above will not be sufficient. Many scholars had already challenged the restricted character of this list (this point will be developed later on in this book), but it is evident that the present state of our knowledge—in both the experimental and social sciences—requires us to reconsider the number and nature of those "higher objectives" and most probably to state them more precisely through concrete reference to the applied sciences.

Those fundamental reflections—increasingly to be produced jointly—establish the framework, the reading grid, that makes for a holistic approach and a calmer understanding of the Universe of the sciences, of *all* the sciences. Most important, they make it possible to avoid terming some sciences "Islamic" and others "non-Islamic," and to be critical of what appears to be the other side of this same shortcoming and of this same reductive approach—that is, the emergence of such debatable qualifications as "Islamic medicine," "Islamic economics," "Islamic finance," "Islamic psychology," and "Islamic pedagogy." One can understand the intent and meaning of this attempt to recolonize the Universe of knowledge through an inflated use of the term "Islamic," but it is clear that the process is purely formal, that the real problem has not been tackled. Most important, this is not a good way of solving the problem of the dichotomy and discrepancy between the different Universes of knowledge. Indeed, adding the adjective "Islamic" to all the "other" sciences—those that are not "text sciences"—will not help in harmonizing approaches or establishing a coherence among norms, ethics, and the experimental and social sciences. As I said, the text sciences are no more "Islamic" than the sciences of the Universe, and there is no more an "Islamic medicine" than an "Islamic astrophysics" or an "Islamic economics": can there be an "Islamic" way of operating on hearts or brains surgically or an "Islamic" method to understanding the law of supply and demand? Such terms may be comforting but they are mostly misleading: the methods, techniques, and scientific methodologies established to understand and analyze an object of study and realize how it functions are by no means inherently "Islamic"; they must meet the requirements of the indicated object of study and they must therefore remain free and autonomous about the rational frameworks and techniques chosen by scientists to comprehend their field of investigation. What is "Islamic" are the ethics, the norms, and the goals that are to orient—and limit—the use of the knowledge acquired. Thus there are, properly speaking, no "Islamic sciences," nor "Islamic medicine," nor "Islamic economics," but "Islamic ethics" assists in the treatment of texts, study of the human body, or in the conduct of commercial affairs. To avoid being misled by formulations that connect without harmonizing, it is imperative to distinguish ethical goals from scientific methods, not to *divorce* them but to *unite*—to reunite—them as we should, in an approach that integrates higher objectives and scientific techniques while avoiding the dangerous and counterproductive confusion of the religious, ethical, and scientific orders.

Islamic faith, which nurtures and legitimates Islamic ethics for the believing conscience, of course establishes *a priori causes*, called *postulates* in philosophical terminology, at the origin of the texts and of the Universe, and this determines an outlook on the real and endows the relationship to the two Books with meaning and outcomes, which are also considered *a priori*. Practitioners of all the sciences and in all areas of knowledge think of themselves in terms of *qualitative goals* and not only of *quantitative accumulations.* This is obvious, but faith, that is, a vision of the heart that points to a meaning in the use of reason, cannot overreach its prerogatives and cause the putative reality to say what it does *not* say nor the opposite of what it says. Thus, faith sets down as a truth an undeniable postulate insofar as it is concerned, that the text has been revealed, but it cannot prevent reason from considering the texts in terms of what they are, with their meanings, morphology, grammar, and semantics, in relation to their twofold enunciation relationship, both intertextual and in dialectic relation to the social and human context. This was indeed acknowledged by text scholars from the outset, when they distinguished in their consequences that which is imposed on reason after it has been understood (*al-'aqîdah* and *al-'ibâdât*) and what requires of reason a continued elaboration (*al-mu'âmalât*). The same is true with respect to the sciences of Nature, the experimental or social sciences. The truth, or the undisputed postulate, of the

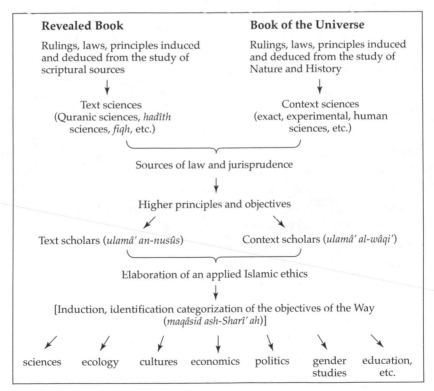

Figure 10.1

"created Universe" cannot justify imposing limits or specific scientific methods to comprehend this creation. The ethical reference may sometimes determine that some areas of knowledge or some techniques are useless, if not dangerous; it may then suggest or impose a limit to research, not in the name of what they are in and of themselves, but out of fear about their use, of the consequences of excess, or of madness in terms of higher goals, (e.g., genetic manipulations).

In this chapter, we are going to look into the concrete consequences of this new "landscape" and thus also outline an approach—implying practical decisions—that can lead to the elaboration of an applied Islamic ethics in the various fields of knowledge. Before going into detail about this subject, figure 10.1 is a visual presentation of the elements already discussed, to clarify the new geography aforementioned.

Text Scholars (Ulamâ' an-Nusûs) and Context Scholars (Ulamâ' al-Wâqi')

The first direct consequence of this new approach and of this new geography of the fundamentals of Islamic law and jurisprudence (*usûl al-fiqh*) is linked, as I said, to the question of authority and legitimacy since extratextual sources have been integrated. I mentioned earlier a shift in the center of gravity of authority in the field of the elaboration of law and ethics, since the balance must be restored between the objects of study (the text and the Universe) and the sciences connected with them. This means that those specialists (scientists or experts) with the best mastery of contemporary scientific knowledge within their specialities and the research techniques related to them must be integrated into the circles of text scholars during their debates and deliberations to formulate legal rulings, the *fatâwâ* about specific issues.

Text scholars who practice *ijtihâd* (*mujtahidûn, fuqahâ'*) in various national or international circles established throughout the world (in Saudi Arabia, Cairo, Damascus, Tehran, Qum, Kuwait, Amman, Djakarta, but also in Washington, Dublin, and other cities) have always admitted that it was imperative for them to be informed and accompanied in their reflections by scientists or doctors who could provide precise information about the state of knowledge or the potential consequences of some particular technique or scientific practice. Moreover, what is accepted in the experimental and medical sciences, because of the precise nature of the expertise involved, has no parallel in the social sciences where such consultations are rare, if not virtually absent. Economists, lawyers, experts, sociologists, or political scientists are often considered as "intellectuals" (*muthaqqafûn*), as "thinkers" (*mufakkirûn*), and sometimes as specialists (*mutakhassisûn*): all those qualifications implicitly fall short of acknowledging the skills of such experts and recognizing their areas of expertise as "sciences," and all the more so in considering them as "scientists." This implicit hierarchy—that is yet so explicit in effect—has the twofold function of clearly defining where "Islamic authority" should reside and, consequently, who can legitimately state opinions and express themselves in the fields of law and ethics.

This begins by acknowledging them as *ulamâ'*, a status established by the Quran itself, as we have seen, as extending beyond the sphere of the knowledge of texts to include that of Nature and the social and human environment. We should therefore recognize that there are not only *ulamâ' an-nusûs*, scholars specializing in texts, but also *ulamâ' al-wâqi*, context scholars. The integration of *ulamâ' al-wâqi'* into *fiqh* councils has become imperative and should make it possible to broaden the horizons of *ulamâ' an-nusûs* so that scientific stakes can be perceived both globally and historically. Applied *fiqh* is a field of legal elaboration that can, when separated from the world and its complexities, come to a standstill or turn into thought-establishing atemporal—or rather ahistorical—categories (lawful/unlawful, allowed/forbidden) that shape our thinking and to which what is real is reduced. Any coherent thought, however, aiming at reforming today's world must devise a dynamic *fiqh*, taking into account the time factor, intellectual and social dynamics, and dialectic tensions between higher objectives, universal principles, and historical models: such a *fiqh* should certainly not rigidify normative categories for fear of scientific, social, and human complexities that elude it. Law and jurisprudence related to human and social affairs (*fiqh al-mu'âmalât*) must set higher objectives and aims and establish the framework of an ethics that determines the stages of mastery and transformation, a *fiqh* that foresees and foretells from the present state of scientific knowledge, which it integrates and uses (and not that which it fears and avoids, that eventually becomes isolated and adapted). Context scholars, specialists in the sciences of Nature, in the experimental and social sciences alone are able to achieve such a global, controlled, and confident (or at least, less wary) outlook about the sciences, societies, and the world: their presence in *fatâwâ* councils and committees (when they address issues that do concern them) is apt to cause a radical change in approaches, to revolutionize them by making possible the integration of scientific knowledge, historical projection, and the elaboration of an applied ethics that can anticipate and orient because it is in harmony with the knowledge of its time.

It is urgent to devise *equal-representation, egalitarian, and specialized* research and *fatwâ* committees that are able to ally three essential requirements: global understanding of the two Books' higher goals, awareness of the higher objectives and goals in their field of study (the texts or writings in a particular scientific field), and first-hand specialized knowledge in the said subject (*fuqahâ'* specializing in texts related to medicine, economics, and other fields—according to the committee in question—being naturally associated with scientists dealing with the same fields). These would not be mere consultations, but work carried out together, with equal proficiency and legitimacy, so as, in the name of the higher aims, to provide ourselves the means to grasp reality in its complexity and manage to transform it for the better. Confidence and skill must be allied with a prospective approach at the heart of all areas of knowledge, so that the "Islamic sciences," text sciences, are no longer presented as a sort of beleaguered territory that stiffens and freezes, despite the accumulation of formal reforms and structural adaptations, to avoid being taken over or disappearing altogether.

Fatwâ and ethics committees with a broad, global vision and strict, specialized and up-to-date scientific skills—this is what can enable contemporary Islamic thought to become reconciled with the essence of its message and the meaning of its conclusions. Although *fuqahâ'* should by definition be Muslim scholars, nothing opposes recruiting non-Muslim context scholars in those committees, provided their skills are well known and they can contribute to enriching the reflection both in the scientific field in question and in the applied ethics that must be produced. Declaring that they respect the *a priori* goals of Islam's message might be a condition but, indeed, this condition itself might prove unnecessary since scientists who join such applied ethics committees—whether Islamic or not—are already *a priori* preoccupied with allying the universal objectives of respecting human dignity and Nature with contemporary outcomes and scientific practices. Moreover, even a scientist who does not show any interest in ethics but stands out by his expertise in the field involved should not be disqualified out of hand. Those options, which make it possible to call on the whole range of scientific skills both nationally and internationally, should remain open and flexible to answer the numerous, circumstantial needs of societies and non-Muslim and Muslim communities throughout the world.

Reconsidering Islamic Ethics and Its Higher Objectives

We saw in the second section that the first Companions, and then early scholars, had already performed natural deduction and inference from the texts, from the latter's intrinsic enunciation levels, and always in the light of their own social and human context. The first law schools, which grew up around scholars such as Mâlik ibn Anas or Abû Hanîfah, were distinguished by their custom of referring to sources and tools (*masâlih al-mursalah, istihsân, 'urf*) and by highly contextual legal elaborations that revealed both thorough knowledge of the texts and constant awareness of the social environment and of the practices and interest of human societies. Their approach was indeed both holistic and pragmatic: the two Books' *a priori* higher objectives and outcomes were not doubted and were intuitively integrated into the subsequent normative process. They constantly aimed to preserve humankind's good and to ward off what was bad and harmful to them while respecting the divine message and easing their burden in daily life and in history.[1]

Ash-Shâfi'î's deductive work, then the inferential work of Abû Hanîfah's pupils, then the slow elaboration and historical maturation of the *maqâsid* school from al-Juwaynî to ash-Shâtibî, continuing on to the present, aimed to establish an initiatory framework and determine the higher goals to orient the reflection of law scholars (*fuqahâ'*) even as they faced the difficulties, complexity, and evolution of reality. The *a posteriori* inferential work on the texts was to lead to the establishment of an *a priori* normative and ethical reading grid in terms of acting on the real. We have seen why this approach seemed imperative, first to ash-Shâfi'î, then to all law fundamentals scholars (*usûliyyûn*) after him—whatever their school—because pressure from reality, from social and human contexts, caused them to fear that the texts' orientations and prescriptions might be pushed aside, then betrayed. Any serious study of Muslim ethics and law cannot fail to integrate this vast and rich historical heritage into its reflections and proposals, taking into account scholars' past fears but also trying to identify the direct or indirect consequences of their approaches in history: potential limitations in the higher outcomes inferred from law by referring to the texts only; confirmed separation between text sciences and Universe-related sciences; as well as a defensive position in terms of the message's eternity and universality before the evolution and movements of history and societies.

Thus, elaborating an applied Islamic ethics is not only an intellectual exercise in establishing a general orientation or setting out norms about the possibilities or limits of human action. Earlier on in the process than this exercise itself, attention should be paid to the way in which the Islamic tradition has thought out (or should think out today) its relationship to the texts and to the Universe, about the philosophy of the sciences deduced from that relationship, and about the meaning to be given to human action in history. Should we simply protect ourselves and prevent things from getting worse, basically maintaining a wary relationship with human history, or should we reform and transform—as far as is humanly possible—while integrating the whole range of knowledge acquired by people? Those two approaches, here presented in a simple, or simplified, manner, will have obvious consequences on the elaboration of an ethics applied to modern times. What matters, therefore, is, before any practical attempt at formulating, to carry out again this task of working out higher objectives (*al-maqâsid ad-darûriyyah*) from the two Revelations and what was said about them, to reconsider and, if necessary, to redefine the nature and number of those objectives. What we know of the Universe and what the diversity and evolution of human societies have taught us must henceforth be integrated into the formulation of higher goals with good judgment and confidence.

Many contemporary scholars have called for such a renewal and insist that it is imperative. Mohammad Hashim Kamali, for instance, tries to open interesting prospects in his recent works. He indeed stresses that very early on, scholars—like Taqî ad-Dîn ibn Taymiyyah (died 1328)—had suggested that the five or six higher objectives were not sufficient to account for the orientation of the texts in the light of human contexts, nor even in the order of faith. For example, Ibn Taymiyyah had added to the list of higher objectives respecting contracts, honoring neighbors' rights, and, on the level of the relationship to the hereafter, love of God, sincerity, faithfulness, and so on.[2] Kamali adds his voice to that of several other scholars he mentions, such as "Muhammad 'Abîd al-Jâbirî, Ahmad ar-Raysûnî, Yûsuf al-Qardâwî and others," arguing that the formerly established list of higher objectives should be extended (we can add here the precious work of Muhammad At-Tâhir Ibn 'Ashûr[3]). In his seminal *Freedom of Expression in Islam*, Kamali observes that scholars' natural tendency about rulings handed down (*ahkâm*) has been to insist on duties and prohibitions rather than on rights and freedoms: his work is an attempt at approaching the subject from another standpoint (of modifying the paradigm underlying the reading of the texts) and identifying which rights are protected in the higher objectives (*maqâsid ash-sharî'ah*).[4] He clearly states in his introduction that this approach is carried out in the light of the questions ever present in contemporary societies.[5] Interestingly, he points out what al-Juwaynî and others had incidentally shown when stating the textual evidence (*adillah*) justifying the categorization of higher objectives—that those latter had essentially been established in terms of the rulings punishing transgressions (*al-hudûd*): reflection on the effective causes of the punishments (*hudûd*, sing. *hadd*) for such offenses as murder, consumption of alcohol, adultery, and other transgressions, enabled them, through *a posteriori*, positive reasoning, to determine what was to be protected and defined as a higher objective.[6] Ahmad ar-Raysûnî develops similar ideas, although his are more directly linked to ash-Shâtibî's works. He argues that the list of objectives should be reconsidered and he too integrates a spiritual dimension regarding behavior (*al-kuliyyât al-khuluqiyyah*)—a kind of ethics of the heart—into the contents of higher objectives.[7] One can thus sense, from the work of early scholars who established the higher objectives to that of contemporary scholars who express the necessity for fundamental reconsideration and broadening the approach, that classical methodologies and their instruments are reaching their limits as they stumble across contemporary challenges and questionings.

As I said, my inclination is that adding objectives to the existing list is not enough, but that we should reconsider their source, their origin, and thereby their categorization and formulation. The two Books, read and understood in parallel, on the basis of a fundamental rebalancing and a new landscape, should enable us to present higher objectives in an original—and always open—way, involving, most importantly, a new, more specialized, and more pragmatic relationship to reality.

An Applied Ethics of Being, of the Heart, and of the Experimental and Social Sciences

It is on the basis of the two Books, then, and of course taking into account the evolution of our knowledge in the two fields of study (text sciences and the sciences of the Universe), that it appears necessary to set on inferring, identifying, and categorizing the higher objectives and aims of the Way (*maqâsid ash-Sharîʿah*) and thereby determining the theoretical and practical outline of an applied contemporary ethics.

It should first of all be pointed out that there are a few problems with the very contents of the classical list of five or six objectives first drawn out by al-Juwaynî (died 478/1085), as we have seen, then taken up and confirmed by later scholars up to the present day, of course, through the mediation of ash-Shâtibî (died 790/1388). One can understand the initial intention to stress the fact that the primary function of the written Revelation is by definition to protect religion, faith, and the requirements about worship and behavior related to them. This search for a hierarchy, at the core of a list of objectives drawn up mainly with the effective causes (*ilal*) of the sanctions (*hudûd*) in mind,[8] indicating what was to be protected in priority, nevertheless has two unfortunate and, ultimately, negative consequences. Willingly or not, by including *ad-dîn* in a series of higher objectives—also including the integrity of body (*nafs*) and mind (*ʿaql*) etc.—it implicitly reduces the notion of *dîn* and identifies it only to the pillars of faith (*'aqîdah*) and of Islam (*'ibadât*) that should there-fore be protected. The second consequence, directly stemming from the first, is that such an approach stands in the way of a global and coherent vision of applied Islamic ethics understood—at each level and in each of its categories—as a process of normative elaboration faithful to the Way, to faith, and to the meaning of the conception of life and death as a whole (that is the original meaning of the notion of *dîn* as we shall see).

In the light of those initial considerations, I prefer to suggest an identification of aims and higher objectives as situated on two dif-ferent axes: a vertical axis that enables us to identify and distinguish objectives according to their global or more specific character; and a horizontal axis that offers the possibility of establishing a separate list of objectives for each level established on the vertical scale. Thus, at the top of the hierarchy of higher goals one would find two objec-tives inferred from what was already said above about the two Books, their meaning, and their objectives. Recognizing that we are before two Revelations, coming from one Creator (*at-Tawhîd*), and that He expects us to recognize Him, to have faith in Him, and to strive to remain faithful to His teachings, He establishes through the essence of this approach the contents of the primary objective I am trying to identify here. The idea that humankind is placed in a sort of "debt" (*dayn*) of gratitude and faithfulness to the One is the etymological and profound meaning of the concept of *dîn* just mentioned, and it comes from the same verb root. This *dayn* requires us to strive to live up to our faith, trying to remain faithful to the conception conveyed by the two Revelations about life and death (*dîn*) while following the Way (*ash-sharî'ah*). Thus, it is not only a matter of protecting the pillars of faith or ritual but also establishing a holistic approach that makes it clear, on the basis of the recognition of *Tawhîd*, that the nat-ural and primary function of ethical elaboration—in its totality and on all levels, from the relationship to Nature to medical practice—is to remain faithful to this existential recognition of a debt (*dayn—dîn*) and act on it coherently. This global dimension is revealed by the following verse that associates *ad-dîn* with *al-fitrah* (natural attrac-tion for what lies beyond sensory perception, for the transcendent): "*So set your face truly* [be faithful] *to the religious conception of life and death, as a sincere monotheist.* [This is] *the natural attraction in which God has* [naturally] *created mankind.*"[9]

But turning to the One and considering this "debt" does not merely consist of recognizing that the Creator is and has created the Universe and humankind; we have seen that, from text sciences to the sciences of the Universe, it can be deduced that everything has been devised for the good of humankind and to protect it from what is bad and harmful. Therefore, what qualifies the creation as a whole, more so than the objectives and ends established by the two Books, is the preeminence of the protection of the common good and interest (*al-maslahah*) for humans as indeed for the creation itself. It might be argued that the broad definition of *ad-dîn* includes the notion of *al-maslahah*—which could be justified from the standpoint of Ibn Hazm's positions, for instance—but such a distinction makes it possible to bring to light a relationship of causality and orientation, a higher goal and connection: the objective of protecting *ad-dîn*, in the aforementioned wider sense, establishes the framework for recognizing the One, while the objective of promoting and protecting the common good and interest (*al-maslahah*) of humankind (and the Creation) determines the meaning of the Way and thereby the orientation of the whole normative and ethical apparatus that is to be pondered.

The most important purpose and objective of the Way, then, is the protection both of *ad-dîn*—in the sense of a conception of life and death stemming from recognition of the One and of the Way— and of *al-maslahah*—in the sense of the common good and interest of humankind and of the Universe. The greater objectives that lie on the next level—they of course stem from a reading of the two Books based of contemporary knowledge—also pertain to ethical elaboration as a whole but they at the same time include categories that will be directly linked to distinguishing fields of study. Even before getting down to the specifications of human action, one might identify, very soon, three fundamental objectives: respecting and protecting Life (*hayâh*), Nature (*khalq, tabî'ah*), and Peace (*salâm*). If one can assert that protecting the global Islamic conception of life and death (*ad-dîn*) and the common good and interest of humankind and Creation (*al-maslahah*) are the two essential perspectives of ethical elaboration as a whole, one can say that protecting/promoting Life, Nature, and Peace are its founding pillars. The whole of the Islamic message, through verses, the Prophet's (or the Prophets') practices and the recognition of the Universe as a sign and a gift, refers to those three essential, *a priori* goals. The list of verses and Prophetic traditions that could be quoted to support the legitimacy of this choice would be far too long to present in this book, but recall the verse that associates killing one man to killing all mankind, the Quranic injunction not to corrupt God's creation, or all the Prophetic traditions (*ahâdîth*) demanding respect of Nature.[10] The call for Peace is inscribed in the very root of the word "islâm," with of course the notion of *salâm*: *islâm* means "entering (giving oneself wholly away to) God's Peace" (*idkhulû fis-silm kâffâ*).[11] The only purpose of *jihâd*, of intimate or collective resistance against the oppression of one's own instincts or other people's would-be aggression, must indeed be the search for peace, never the aim for tension, conflict, or war.[12]

After people are equipped with the essential perspective (promoting/protecting *the global conception of life and death* and *the common good and interest*) and have identified the founding pillars of ethical elaboration (promoting/protecting Life, Nature, and Peace), one can move on to write the list of higher objectives that are more directly linked to humankind's being and action, both as an individual and as a member of society. At this point the list gets longer, but most important, it is still not definitive. New scientific knowledge, shaping a new outlook on human beings or Nature, might lead us to extend that list, since this must always remain a dialectical elaboration: starting first from what the texts say about higher objectives, then from what social and human contexts reveal (and sometimes impose), we must return to the texts with a renewed, deeper understanding about the meaning and implementation of the aforesaid rulings. The historical context, but also the risks and dangers of our own time, enable us to have a better understanding of some Quranic injunctions and to insist on some goals that may have appeared secondary, if not completely useless, in more traditional societies. On this third level, then, and before getting into narrower categories, the list of objectives could read as follows: promoting and protecting Dignity (of humankind, living species, and Nature[13]), Welfare, Knowledge, Creativity, Autonomy, Development, Equality, Freedom, Justice, Fraternity, Love, Solidarity, and Diversity. By reading the two Books in parallel, the reasons for this classification can be better understood: those are higher objectives stipulated by the texts, sometimes either more or less explicitly, but whose essential and primary character is made clear by history and the evolution of societies. The Quran clearly stipulates that dignity is part of human-kind's essence: *"We have indeed honoured [given dignity to] human beings"* and that the latter should strive to preserve it with all the abilities and means made available to him by the Creator, while always seeking good through ease and welfare rather than useless difficulty: *"He [God] has imposed no hardship [difficulty] on you in religion."*[14] The Prophet also said: "Make [things] easy, do not make them difficult! Spread good news [that causes joy], not bad news [that causes fear and rejection]!"[15] For such welfare to be achieved, all human faculties must be allowed to develop: reason and imagination must be fulfilled through knowledge and learning, through imagination and creativity (those are both objectives to be achieved and rights to be respected). The Infinitely Good has taught humankind the Quran and He *"has taught them intelligent speech* (al-bayân)*"* and its art: "God is Beautiful and He loves beauty,"[16] the Prophet reminded us. Humans being responsible before God, and therefore necessarily autonomous among their fellow humans, since *"No bearer of burdens can bear the burden of another,"* society must guarantee development (individual and collective), equality, and justice while accepting diversity. However, laws are not sufficient to regulate human relations: *"God commands justice,"* indeed, but also *"excellence* (al-ihsân) *and solidarity towards one's kin"*[17] that suggests a tendency of the heart to reach beyond the law through the meaning of brotherhood, solidarity, and love beyond a potential obsession with the norm. Contemporary times compel us to return to the texts and extract objectives that may have appeared secondary in the past. Elaborating an ethics that is not built according to potential punishments but, more fundamentally, on the basis of higher objectives to be achieved by the action of time, societies, and cultures requires the horizon of higher objectives to be broadened in its range of implementation while becoming more specific about the subjects to be considered. Those thirteen objectives of the Way trace the path along which a contemporary ethical elaboration that is both normative and practical must be developed. Their presence and necessity can be perceived in all the fields of human action. To repeat, text learning and contemporary knowledge related to historical, social, and human contexts enable us to identify the outline and essential principles of Islamic ethics in terms of knowledge to be integrated, assets to be preserved, risks to be prevented, and horizons to be explored. History and the evolution of contexts reveal certain hidden horizons in the meaning of texts and enable us to rethink priorities not only in their universality but also according to the circumstances: the relationship between the immutable and the mutable remains the rule in elaborating applied ethics.

Those first three general, inclusive levels—in terms of identifying higher objectives—must be completed with three other levels that comprise so many distinct categories. Long ago, some scholars—such as Ibn Taymiyyah—considering the five or six classical goals of the objectives school, had already criticized the lack of objectives related to the heart's life, to spirituality, or even to the relationship to death and the hereafter. More recently, others (e.g., al-Qardâwî, ar-Raysûnî, Kamali) pointed out that contemporary challenges, especially of a social nature, required those principles to be developed so as to include the collective and social dimensions in some fashion. On closer study, I certainly think an even clearer and more systematic categorization and classification of objectives must be carried out. One should indeed distinguish the inner being alone, the individual being, the being in the group and in the world, and for those categories, draw up a specific list of higher goals apt to smooth the way toward the elaboration of Islamic ethics.

There are clearly in the texts, as indeed in the relationship to the Creation, higher objectives pertaining to the inner being: the spiritual, intimate dimension of the heart that absolutely must be encouraged and protected. There is plainly an "ethics of the heart" whose horizons must be determined in the light of all the sources of the Way. Here, we can identify the objectives of Education (of the heart and mind), Conscience (of being and responsibility), Sincerity, Contemplation, Balance (intimate and personal stability), and Humility. Thus bringing to light the objectives of the Way in terms of the heart's life and of the inner being is essential and it indeed stands, for the believing conscience, as the reference granting the whole ethical apparatus its legitimacy. Stating, for instance, that any person has the right to an Education who shapes a responsible Conscience amounts—when integrating the principle of Autonomy stated earlier on—to recognizing and protecting the rights of men but also those of women and children who must be considered in their being and autonomy and not merely in their social function. This issue is further discussed in the last section of my book dealing with practical cases—and in particular those related to gender issues—but it is important to note here that elaborating an ethics related to the inner being, promoting balance among the heart, mind, and body, is likely to entail fundamental consequences for religious discourse and social policies.

It is on the level of the individual being, of the human being's ethics, that four of the five (or six) classical higher objectives established by scholars and already mentioned above will be found to lie. I think, however, that they should be developed not only in the light of scriptural sources but also of contemporary knowledge and related ethical requirements. At this level, we thus find promoting and protecting Physical Integrity, Health, Subsistence, Intelligence, Progeny, Work, Belongings, Contracts, and our Neighborhoods. Those nine objectives are essential and enable us to approach the individual person, her or his responsibilities and rights, in a wider sense while also taking into account contemporary realities and challenges. An applied ethics pertaining to the human being cannot but take into account those dimensions that the sources of law point to and to which reason and human practices must remain faithful.

While the third category, the group, is often absent from the reflections of *usûliyyûn* and *fuqahâ'* about law's higher objectives and principles, it is nonetheless fundamental both in the light of the texts and when considering contemporary issues. As stated in another context, rebalancing the sources from the outset enables us to approach this field in a new, and I think more *complete*, manner. We should integrate the objectives related to societies and human groups, with regard to whom it is essential to promote and protect the Rule of law, Independence (self-determination), Deliberation, Pluralism, Evolution, Cultures, Religions, and Memories (heritage). The texts and the contemporary world, through the study of history and of the social sciences, require us to identify the higher goals that must direct visions of society both independently and in *inter*-national relations. The world's evolution, the effects of globalization on the economy, in the means of communication, in culture, as well as postmodernist philosophical thought, are some of the many phenomena that call on us to think inductively and draw up an ethics of groups, nations, and cultures at the heart of the history of humankind. We are faced with difficult, complex issues that require fundamental reflection, if only to devise a contemporary ethics that promotes and protects pluralism and the independence of nations, religions, and cultures in the light of the statement-injunction of the Revelation establishing diversity (in societies, religions, and groups) and the balance of (independent) forces as conditions for peace and the respect of common good among human beings: *"And had God not checked one set of people by means of another, the earth would indeed be full of mischief."*[18]

This recognition of the diversity of nations and of the necessary balance of their powers, which in itself supposes them to be independent as conditions for the future of humankind and its survival, is covered in many teachings that posit a host of practical requirements that must be studied and reformulated for contemporary times. We can see here that the scope of autonomous critical reasoning broadens as it gets more complex: not only is it imperative to think over and deepen an *ijtihâd* in texts, but we should also produce studies and elaborate strategies in harmony with the environment, an *ijtihâd* applied to sociohistorical contexts (taking into account natural laws and the constants of history at the same time as developing a creative and practical vision of human possibilities for the future). Equal-representation ethical committees must be the places where the union of the two *ijtihâd*, in texts and in individual human and wider social contexts, must be thought through in a concrete, realistic, and

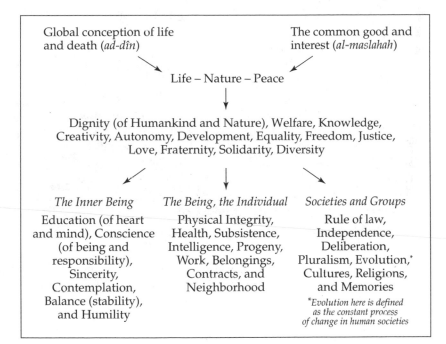

Figure 10.2

pragmatic manner, on all levels and in all the categories of contemporary Islamic ethics that have been clarified in this section. This triple dimension of applied *ijtihâd* could be rendered as shown in figure 10.2.

This approach should be the rule in all the fields mentioned and should take into account the different levels and categories of Islamic ethics that could be presented as shown in figure 10.3.

As I have explained, the primary principles are the higher objectives of protecting the global conception of life and death as well as the common good and interest of humankind and the Universe. At the second level, three other objectives are added: Life, Nature, and Peace, which all in all transcend and include everything that is developed later on in terms of ethics applied to humankind and its action. The twelve founding objectives, added to those goals more closely linked to the ethics of the heart, of the individual, and of societies, enable us to produce a global, and thereby holistic, vision of contemporary Islamic ethics integrating the whole range of knowledge, both about the texts and about the Universe.

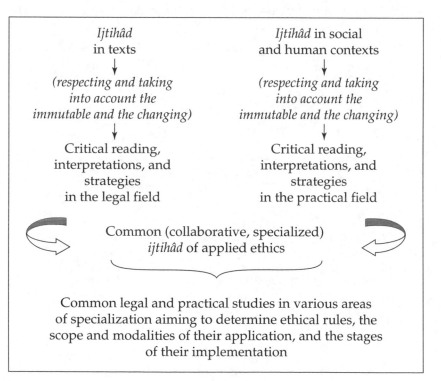

Figure 10.3

Islamizing Modernity
or Modernizing Islam?

The entire discussion about the fundamentals of Islamic law and jurisprudence undertaken in this section, and more particularly the previous reflections about ethics, throws light on the partial, biased, and indeed oversimplified and simplifying nature of the criticisms to which I have been subject to for wanting to "Islamize modernity" rather than "modernizing Islam." Some thinkers, historians, or sociologists felt uneasy faced with an Islamic thought that they recognized was reformist (but which did not reach the conclusions they hoped for, that is to say a sort of an Islamic thought that blindly embraced contemporary "liberalism"—from *liberal* social thought to the *liberal* economy—without daring to voice a critical position), which was an assertion put forward by the French historian Dominique Avron. He claims that my project was far from being reformist and that it simply consisted of giving Islam and Muslims new means of dealing with modernity.[19] This was, in brief, a power struggle prompted by a reconquest ideology.

Yet this assessment of my research reveals more about its authors than about my work. Indeed, why should the will to remain faithful to one's religious tradition and to the ethical principles it has developed betray a resolve to "Islamize modernity," unless it is postulated *a priori* that "modernity" does not consist of trying to live within one's time but that it should only be understood as the Western way–implicitly regarded as the only really *modern*, not to say universal, way––of facing the present. Not only is this double reduction (modernity is Western and only the West produces the universal) groundless philosophically, historically, and scientifically, its binary character (the "West" versus "the others"; "modernity" versus "tradition") is also deeply ideological, particularly arrogant, and, in the long run, dangerous. It amounts to saying that any attempt by a non-Western religion or civilization (and, of course, especially Islam that currently threatens "from within") to find its own answers according to its own terms of reference and ethics to contemporary challenges means refusing universals and resisting "modernity" by shrewdly trying to colonize it, to *Islamize* it.

This approach goes a long way toward unveiling the outlook some people in the West have on their own civilization. For them, along with economic, scientific, and technological domination, "the West" owns the exclusive monopoly for expressing universals and, in the same way, holds the keys to "modernity" (which is never really defined but always perceived in its expression as centered on western values). However, universals are never the monopoly of one civilization and can only be the expression of values shared and nurtured by the historical experiences and varied expressions of many societies, religions, and cultures. The applied Islamic ethics I propose here most definitely have a universal role for the contemporary Muslim conscience, but this latter cannot express it by arbitrarily excluding all other expressions of the universal. Besides, "Western civilization" is merely a construct, just like "Islamic civilization": neither of them is monolithic, both were mutually cross-fertilized and there is—and has long been—some Islam in the West and some West in Islam. The new generations of Muslims in the West will only be reinforcing this reality in the future.

The will to remain faithful to a religious tradition, to values, and to an ethics at the heart of modern times, certainly does not mean refusing to live in accord with one's time. It is indeed exactly the opposite: rethinking a tradition—that is anything but a *static* reality to appear a caricature opposed to the ongoing *movement* of "modernity"—while giving oneself the means to give meaning and outcomes to the means (intellectual and technological) produced by "modernity" reveals a will to devise a faithfulness that is considered impossible without a continued process of *re*-formation, of reform. This is what all my research has tried to produce over the past twenty years, with the conviction that the critical approach to "western modernity"—from within the West itself—can only be salutary for Western civilization itself because it questions its objectives and opens the horizons of a fundamental, pluralistic critical debate. As can be seen, I am far from wishing to "Islamize modernity" and my objective is much more transparent and coherent—although it is particularly difficult—since it is to give ourselves the means to remain faithful to a religious tradition at the heart of the modern era while opening a dialogue about values and purposes, whether specific or universal, shared between civilizations. This is the profound meaning of this work of elaborating Islamic ethics that I have undertaken here. It does not consist in refusing "modernity" nor in resisting the West (which is a construct that does not exist) but rather in striving to promote a global Islamic ethics aiming to regulate human action: such ethics can only be nurtured by the input of all the world's civilizations, and it must certainly contribute to an open and pluralistic reflection.

As I said, the criticisms I have been subject to reveal more about their authors than about my thought. Those debates nevertheless teach us that the crux of the matter is not really the question of values themselves but rather the state of mind with which one engages in debates about civilizations, traditions, and modernity. Before commencing those discussions, one should establish three intellectual dispositions: humility, for no civilization or religion holds the exclusive monopoly of universals nor of "good modernity"; respect for what "the other" is, believes, and can bring to the construct of common universals (both in terms of contribution and of constructive criticism); and finally, concern about coherence in the formulation of the values and objectives of ethics and their concrete implementation in daily life, which means developing a self-critical spirit along with an objective outlook on others, avoiding, for instance, comparing "our ideals" with "their practices." *Humility* (associated with self-doubt), *respect* (allied to a positive outlook on others), and finally *coherence* (concretely expressed in a constant critical self-assessment) are the three prerequisite conditions that seem necessary to apprehend one's own and others' Universes of reference in an open, critical, and constructive way. I felt it important to spend a moment over those considerations at this point in our reflection, so deeply have some studies misrepresented my intentions and distorted the very meaning of my undertaking, because of an obsession with the binary relationship between "tradition" and "modernity" or the fantasized opposition of "Islam" and "the West," in a caricatured relationship of otherness or, most often, of confrontation, distrust, and power.

More ethics in science, politics, and economics at the heart of the modern era does not mean refusing "modernity" but calling for the dignity of humankind in history. Unless some of the thinkers of that "West" eventually come to think about their own being and domination without any reference to values or ethics—arrogantly, disrespectfully, and indeed inconsistently—this would mean the end of "the West," for such an intellectual disposition can only contain the seed of its own disappearance from history. My approach, perceived as a threat and a refusal of "the West" by the most superficial and biased analyses, is nurtured by exactly opposite intentions, stipulating that survival will depend on our capacity to outline a global, joint, universal applied ethics, with the collaboration of all civilizations, including Islam. "Reforming Islam" is a meaningless formula; what matters is to know what Muslims—reforming their understanding—can contribute, without dogmatism and in collaboration with other traditions, to the ethical reform of the contemporary world.

Faithfulness, Mastery, and Transformation

This reform is indeed deeply "radical" since it entails reconsidering the sources of the fundamentals of law and jurisprudence, rebalancing them, and necessarily shifting the center of gravity of authority in Islam. However, it springs from a no less fundamental desire to be faithful, and it would be wrong and contradictory to consider it as nothing but a way of projecting an *a posteriori* ethical apparatus on the scientific Universe with the declared or tacit intention of taking hold of it. That has nothing to do with it, and indeed I have taken a stand against such an approach—an ill-arranged (and belated) union of ethics and science—from the beginning of this study.

The primary principle I have formulated, that of the presence of the Divine, of His oneness (*tawhîd*), and His communication with the human Universe through two Books, two Revelations—the text and the Universe—in effect establishes a relationship to meaning and purpose. Faithfulness to this Universe of reference implies that ethics comes before scientific and/or technical acts and considers them from the standpoint of quality and not merely quantity and performance. It must be recalled that faithfulness to the two Books and their signs leads to the will to be faithful to their primary and higher objectives. It must also be added that there is nothing new about this conception of faithfulness: one could even say that it relates to the very old tradition of the "advocates of faithful renewal" (*al-mujaddidûn*) in the fields of law, intellectual production, and the sciences.

What is at stake here is more precisely devising the means that will make it possible thus to reconcile objectives, meaning, and the sciences, and later in the process, produce the conceptual and historical tools necessary to face all the concrete, structural, and technical consequences about humankind's relationship to knowledge. In this sense, one cannot leave out the stage in this initial, holistic vision that places people in their relationship to the divine, that offers them the tools for intellectual and scientific autonomy (while recognizing their natural aspiration to performance), but that, most important, constantly calls on their consciences to evaluate the meaning, objectives, and moral quality of their (social, scientific, and cultural) commitments in history.

At the core of modern times, accompanying scientific progress and state-of-the-art new techniques, my point is indeed to insist on the goals and qualitative dimension of knowledge and research. Distinguishing the order of conscience from that of science does not mean divorcing them, but on the contrary requires giving deep consideration to the terms of their union, accepting their respective autonomy while highlighting their complementarity. The technologically most advanced societies inform us everyday that it is impossible to produce an effective ethical reference—a framework of objectives—unless the Universe of the sciences is approached, understood, and mastered seriously and expertly. Scientists, doctors, and economists are too often led to smile at the proposals suggested by religious representatives, philosophers, or ethicists, because they see such people as oversimplified, naive, or out of step with the state of research in their field of specialization. This discrepancy, this gap, between holistic thought about objectives and specialized mastery of the complexity of techniques and means in effect gives rise to an outright rupture. Scientists move fast, very fast, opening up a horizon of possibilities as promising as they may sometimes be threatening, and ethicists—clerics, philosophers, or ecologists—follow them as best they can without ever having the means to anticipate or prevent. An applied ethics in the sciences can only be effective if it requires itself to master these sciences and techniques: in other words, there can be no ethics of purpose without a mastery of knowledge and means. This must materialize—both through their composition and through their methods of investigation—in the circles where the threefold dimension of contemporary *ijtihâd* mentioned earlier is thought out, where applied ethics is discussed, and where circumstantial legal rulings (*fatâwâ*) are formulated. What we should do, as I said, is reconsider old categories based on the traditional distinction between the "Islamic" sciences and the "other" sciences and rethink the paradigm underlying their geography and their respective status. This operation does not consist—I insist—in submitting to the imposed order of quantity, productivity (or productivism), and scientific performance, but rather in giving us the means required for their ethical, humanistic mastery.

Associating conscience and science, ethics and techniques, faith and reason, at the source of reflection and research, is the only means to think over the reform (on the basis of Islam's references) and transformation of the world and of our societies for the better. Utopian, illusionary, often naive religious, philosophical, and ethical thought, which makes scientists smile—is no solution because it is paradoxical and often counterproductive. It elaborates ethical, qualitative ideals remote from the World and from societies and ends up accepting, in daily life, the practical, quantitative consequences of the experimental and human sciences. Reform would then be nothing but a mere adaptation that in effect confirms the defeat of ethics. Religious and philosophical traditions, and Islam is no exception in this respect, are out of step, marginalized, and they would seem to have finally accepted thinking about themselves as on the margin of history's scientific march. The potential ecological catastrophes compel humankind to think about objectives for it is obliged to devise the means of its survival: it must henceforth transform things rather than merely adapt them. What the Book, the written Revelation, called for in its essence and principle, the Book of the Universe now compels us to do because of natural catastrophes and other forms of sheer necessity: thinking out objectives, undertaking reforms, imposing fundamental transformations without which we are on the road to ruin. Our responsibility is infinite and involves all areas of knowledge and all specialists: awareness of our finitude, which ecological catastrophes and climatic upheavals remind us of, has opened up a debate about purpose. Today, adaptation means getting lost and dying, and only a radical, multidimensional reform determining the terms of the transformation can guarantee the survival of humankind and the Universe. Natural necessity has called on the human conscience, Muslims and non-Muslims alike: we must learn again how to read the two Books, qualitatively and ethically.

An Ethics of Liberation: A Force
of Resistance and Proposal

After a quarter of a century spent in studying the production of great
Muslim scholars through history as well as classical and contemporary Islamic thought, trying to understand and assess in the best and
most precise way the respective contributions of the literalist, traditionalist, reformist, rationalist, Sufi schools and the religious, social,
or political approaches of ancient or modern Islamic and/or Islamist
movements, visiting, living, and working with Muslim communities
East and West, I am still haunted by the same question: how can we
explain the deadlocks, the always real but so often aborted renewal,
the crisis running through the contemporary Muslim conscience
as well as Muslim societies and communities the world over? The
problem is profound and the causes are many, of course, but everything is as if—when returning to the sources—one came across
obstacles accumulated in the course of history, which could sometimes be explained through the fears of Muslim scholars or thinkers,
sometimes through power conflicts, sometimes through insufficient
knowledge of the world and of its composite societies. This is no real
paradox; it's as if there were a complacency about the solutions to be
promoted, sometimes, finally, through the reduction of Islam's message to a set of norms supposed to be sufficient to answer fundamental questions about meaning.

Our perception, after so many years, is that it is urgent for contemporary Islamic thought—beyond the usual discourse about the
global and coherent character of the message (which, of course, I by
no means dispute)—to be reconciled with the stated global character
of the message by imposing on itself a holistic approach that takes
its conditions and consequences to their logical end. This means
for jurists as well as thinkers, scientists, and other parties involved
to approach the texts and the Universe as two Books echoing one
another, imposing rules and principles of which some are definitive
while others are changing, constantly calling on the human mind
and heart and inviting them to think, to understand, and especially,
to give themselves the means—through the evolution of history and
the diversity of societies—to remain faithful to the higher objectives
stipulated by the two Revelations. Thus, the texts and the social and
human contexts will again become the inescapable sources of ethics,

law, and jurisprudence and impose, on whomever seeks to be faithful to Islam's message as a whole, a substantial broadening of the range of knowledge and the integration of all the areas of learning into the production of applied ethics. In brief, sources must be reconsidered, areas of knowledge must be rebalanced, means must be redefined, and authority relationships must be reorganized in terms of the legitimacy of intellectual, legal, and ethical production: in other words, both our understanding and our methods must be radically reformed so that we can free ourselves from the restraints of preconceived ideas.

I have repeated many times, in my previous books, that contemporary Islamic thought (the problem appeared long ago) is shot through by fear of everything that seems to it to be imposed from outside, and particularly of course by the dominant "Western civilization." Although rejection is not always present, one can constantly observe suspicion and a defensive attitude toward the other's values, practices, and culture, whether a potential threat or just a stranger. The reform I call for is difficult because undertaking it requires a state of "self-confidence" that is precisely and cruelly lacking today at the core of Muslim societies and, more specifically, among its jurists and thinkers. For decades, the Muslim world has been producing thought either as an almost blind imitation or on that of rigid, exclusivist defensiveness...it has rarely shown autonomy, creativity, and contribution. The first liberation therefore consists in breaking this unhealthy vicious circle by restoring the requirement of mastering all the diverse areas of knowledge, wherever they come from, and instilling confidence about acquiring the means to be faithful to the message, not "against others" but "for ourselves." We must reconcile ourselves with the world to be better reconciled with ourselves.

To this end, it is imperative to protect ourselves against the elitist temptations that result in those continued adaptation reforms already mentioned when the territories of "Islamic" knowledge and "legal" competence are determined. We must also free ourselves from that. If the list and categories of the objectives of applied Islamic ethics are indeed such as I already suggested (without being by any means immutable nor final), it is imperative to adopt a fundamentally inclusive approach toward all areas of knowledge, all scientists, but also all the knowledge and practices accumulated by societies and communities themselves. For it is impossible to understand and grasp the "common good and interest" (*al-maslahah*) if one considers the Islamic references separately from the practical knowledge and skills of women and men. Transformation—contribution, creativity—reforms will only be achieved in practice if the whole range of skills is integrated into the process, and particularly those that are not obvious at the heart of the practices, the life (sometimes the survival) and creativity of ordinary women and men, in their daily lives. Indeed, the requirements and conditions of the knowledge necessary to approach, understand, and interpret the texts must be recognized (this obvious scientific fact must be stressed here), but other skills should be added when dealing with the experimental and human sciences and finally, as I have just said, with the practices—and questionings and soul-searching—of Muslims in their daily lives. This accumulated knowledge must enable us to reach better understanding of the theoretical deadlocks, the practical inconsistencies, not to say the processes of enclosing, alienation, or domination both inside Islamic frames of reference and within social, economic, and political dynamics. This confident, inclusive approach can, as we shall see in the ensuing section through the study of a few practical cases, set off interesting reforms and new approaches, and, most important, constitute a force of resistance not by taking a defensive stance but, on the contrary, by being a force of contribution and proposal in the face of our era's profound challenges.

In the course of my different lectures or encounters with Muslims throughout the world, the same question comes up again and again. Who has the power to start those reforms? Who can make things move from within? People often expect a benevolent scholar or thinker who will come along and toss aside old readings as well as old, outdated practices. This reminds us of the Prophetic tradition quoted earlier, referring to that someone who will come, every hundred years, to enable the Muslim community to "renew its religion." What is sometimes misunderstood is that the *hadîth*'s use of the Arabic noun "*man*" can mean one person or a group: this expectation of a "singular" or "charismatic" leader has often had counterproductive effects in the history of Islamic thought, as if the presence of such a "leader," "scholar," or "thinker" stripped the whole community of its responsibilities and indeed of their abilities. Even more seriously, this reveals a very partial reading of the *hadîth* itself, which not only insists on the person or persons who will accompany this renewal process, but also on the factor of time. Between two renewals, the reference to a "hundred years" expresses the notion of evolution, phases, crises, which Islamic thought and Muslim societies will necessarily undergo. Appreciating those "hundred years," understanding those phases, analyzing those crises, is everyone's responsibility, according to her or his respective abilities and commitment. Renewals should not be awaited, they should be planned and prepared for.

Muslims are now going through a difficult, complex, and profound transition period, whose reality and effects can be felt on the intellectual level as well as on the scientific, social, and political levels. Faith, numbers, and motivation are present, but what is sometimes lacking are depth, spirit, and energy: it is as if thought were imprisoned, narrow, uneasy, alienated. This is precisely what we need: determined commitment, *jihâd*, for the freedom to question tradition *faithfully*, to reconsider practices and to challenge the established (and protected) scholarly powers as well as their authority critically. This also means going far enough—to the logical end of the conditions and consequences of reform as I said above—in the analysis of our relationship to knowledge, of authority and power relationships, of interpersonal relations (between social classes, men, and women), of cultural constructs, regarding what prevents Islamic thought from evolving, from liberating itself, from facing the challenges of modern times. We should again become subjects of history, and act as a proposal force, present and creative although not exclusive, in the concert of intelligence, societies, cultures, religions, philosophies, and civilizations. Being subjects of history means, paradoxically, becoming reconciled with humility: standing on the margin of progress and knowledge, one can indeed nurture the arrogance of "knowing" beyond complexity and of holding the ready-made alternative, ready for use since it is of divine origin. Not only is such an attitude dangerous, it is also nurtured by a deeply simplifying, and all in all inconsistent, spiritual, and intellectual attitude: beyond the words of faith that expresses itself in history, one senses a tendency to place oneself on the level of divine time, in its purity, far away from the tensions and temptations of the present time, societies, and humankind. Simplifications—of religious and/or rationalistic origin—have the peculiar characteristic of allying apparently paradoxical, and yet ever so frequent, intellectual and social attitudes: intellectually deficient analyses associated with humanly most arrogant judgments. Unsurprisingly, indeed, the intellect, the object of history and of its own alienation, is often the most dogmatic.

A liberation based on confidence, in ourselves and our means, along with the capacity to integrate into our own development the whole range of knowledge through a revisited geography of the sciences, relying on the entire diversity of skills (and those of the whole community)—this to me is a priority when the multidimensionality of contemporary Islamic ethics is to be thought out. Becoming subjects again also means thinking of ourselves as responsible actors in history's evolutions and stages, at the heart of transitions and crises, as agents of renewal and reform. Taking its place in time and societies, directly in touch with the complexity of knowledge and of social, economic, and human processes, the contemporary Muslim conscience will then be better equipped to achieve another union— without any paradox in the order of faith or of reasonable rationality: that of respect for obvious complexity and humility as to what one understands and proposes.

IV

~

Case Studies

The theoretical framework outlined in the first three sections of this work enables me to approach some issues from a new, or at any rate critical, standpoint. Most important, it invites me to open new ways of investigation in fields where Islamic thought seems to be stalling, becoming fearful, defensive, and self-withdrawn. The terminology exposed and clarified in the first section, along with the rebalancing of the sources of law—taking into account social and human contexts and the sciences—calls on us to think about reform not only in terms of theoretical references but also in relation to situations that touch on the daily lives of Muslim men and women and so require very practical answers.

We have seen that in some fields the relationship between text sciences and context sciences has been established more easily and naturally than in others, due to the nature of those sciences. Thus, in medicine, 'ulamâ' councils have been set up to integrate physicians and their skills: they do not hesitate to issue legal rulings (*fatâwâ*) in keeping with contemporary knowledge. They also take into account the complexities of reality when establishing coherent links between the state of knowledge and the goals to be preserved in the light of contexts in which and for which the law is to be articulated. This is a difficult exercise, but *fuqahâ'* have turned to it as a result of both scientific and practical necessity. It is certainly in medicine that the newest, most appropriate, but also boldest answers, have been devised and formulated by legal councils; I shall begin with those issues to better understand the spirit and methods in which this research and the formulation of concrete proposals were carried out.[1]

I shall then turn to other fields, moving from culture, art, gender issues, and ecology to economic, political, and philosophical issues for which I think the rebalancing I have suggested would have direct consequences on the *fatâwâ* issued. By no means am I going to draw up a list of final rulings, since what I suggest is a new methodology that precisely aims to enable *fuqahâ'* and scientists to work together on specialized, new, open reflection together, and formulate adequate opinions. This section includes reflections involving introductory, holistic, but nevertheless very practical approaches, in delicate, but urgent areas. Both text and context scientists specialized in their various fields of expertise will then need to examine things further in the light of the ethical objectives already suggested (possibly adding others), and suggest modes of reform, stages, strategies with their scientific instruments (together with an educational process) to enable today's Muslims to live in faithfulness to the Way. It is important to reconcile ourselves with the essence of the "Islamic tradition" that, contrary to what is commonly thought, is not frozen into permanent immobility: the essence of "tradition" is the continued movement in history that requires of the human conscience a need to recognize higher aims and strive to remain faithful with heart, mind, and body. In this sense, "tradition"—God's, the Prophet's, as well indeed as that of all spiritualities and all religions—is defined much less in relation to the sources and roots of the past (to which it is reduced when it is depicted of a kind of caricature set up as a contrast to "modernity") than by the means it gives itself to remain faithful to future goals. Applied ethics is thus the method a religious, spiritual, or philosophical *tradition* gives itself to think out its *modernity*, and this is what I would like to start looking into—in a practical way—in this final section. It will be up to text and context scholars to carry out a host of thorough, specialized reflections in their respective fields and issue the legal rulings necessary to their time and place.

11

Islamic Ethics and Medical Sciences

Islamic scriptural sources, whether Quran or *ahâdîth*, are redolent with references to the human body and to health and hygiene in general. From chapters explaining the conditions and goals of ritual purification (*at-tahârah*) to others dealing with bodily care or illnesses, in virtually every page *fuqahâ'*—some of whom were also considered medical specialists in their own time—refer to what would today be called "medical ethics." At the source, there is, of course—explicitly or implicitly—a direct relation to the goals inferred from the message. Following the order I suggested above, one could say that the aim has always been—in the light of *the Islamic conception of life and death*[1] (*ad-dîn*) and of *people's common good and interest* (*al-maslahah*), to protect the *life, dignity, and welfare* of humankind by protecting their *conscience* and their personal *stability* (on the level of their intimate being) as well as their *personal integrity* and *health* (on the individual level).[2] So many Quranic verses and traditions refer to those dimensions that of course they cannot all be quoted here, but I will mention those texts that make it possible to sketch the outline of medical ethics.

At the source of the whole discussion about medicine, the Quran presents itself as a Revelation that integrates *health* (as the expression of *al-maslahah*) into the very essence of *ad-dîn*. For the Quran is in itself *"a guide and a remedy [a balm, a cure, that restores health]* (shifâ') *for those who believe."*[3] This dimension of inner health, the heart's health, is essential when one seeks to understand the essence and meaning of life for believers: it is indeed to fight all the ailments of the heart (from denying the One to hypertrophy of the ego, arrogance, lying, etc.)[4] and strive to protect one's heart to come back to God, beyond death, with a "healthy heart," calm, at peace, balanced, in good "spiritual health." This is also what the Quran reveals when it tells us that there will come *"a day when neither wealth nor children will be of any use, but for who returns to God with a sound* [i.e., healthy, balanced, peaceful] (salîm) *heart."*[5] The root of the word *salîm*, *sa-la-ma*, is the same as that of the word *salâm* and here it refers to health and welfare, as well as tranquility and inner spiritual peace.

The Revelation is a remedy and it calls on believing consciences to strive with all their might—to undertake an intimate *jihâd* of the inner being (*jihad an-nafs*)—to preserve their inner health and reach higher well-being. In all the texts, one can find the same requirements, the need for this same quest for health for the human body. God has entrusted humans with the responsibility of being the vicegerents of Life and of the Earth: *"Then We made you vicegerents on Earth"*[6] and in this sense they are its guardians. The Prophet reminded us that each human being is a guardian and that "each is responsible for what they guard [will be questioned about the quality of their guardianship]."[7] We have been given life, and anyone who saves a human being's life is *"as if they had saved all mankind."*[8] The Creator has also given us our bodies to care for and keep fit and we must remember that, the Prophet said, "Your body has rights over you."[9] Those rights include protecting life, as we have seen, but also all that pertains to health care, hygiene, welfare, and therefore "health" in its broadest sense, naturally enough. This is what the Prophet referred to when he told a Companion: "Ask God for health, for nobody receives anything better than good health."[10]

Human beings are the guardians of their own bodies and they must respect and cherish them, keeping in mind their debt (*dayn*) toward He whom they come from and to whom they are one day to return.[11] Respecting and protecting one's body implies seeking all the means to cure it, for as the Prophet said, "There is no disease for which God has not provided a cure."[12] We must therefore study, extend our learning, and develop all the ways to cure illness, to restore health, and to enable humankind, through history, to equip itself with the means to answer the requirements of the Creator who commanded it to care for its body as well as its heart. In this respect, new scientific discoveries—providing new means that are not always mastered, the astounding amount of medical knowledge gathered about the functioning of the human body, and the appearance of previously unknown diseases require *fuqahâ'* as well as physicians to provide new, detailed answers in the light of the goals already mentioned (whatever the circumstances *life, dignity, welfare, conscience, personal stability, physical integrity,* and *health* must be protected).

The point is not to define the outline of an "Islamic medicine" purported to be different from "Western medicine," as argued by as prominent a medical doctor as Dr. Ahmed al-Kadi.[13] What clearly stands out here is the fundamental link that exists between establishing the objectives of Islamic ethics relative to the health of the heart and body, and how medicine is practiced, and how limits are determined in difficult situations (serious diseases, end of life, or general bioethics issues). Medical knowledge and the instruments available as well as social and human contexts compel us to devise a most efficient Islamic ethics relative to medicine. It is in this field that *fuqahâ'* have necessarily had to collaborate with medical specialists, and it must be admitted that they have often shown initiative and genuine pragmatism.

The Medical Code of Ethics

The idea that medical practice must be associated with a code of behavior for physicians themselves is anything but new. The famous Hippocratic Oath that established a moral framework for a physician's attitude toward his masters or teachers, his patients, and their relatives, insisting on fair treatment and the obligation of confidentiality, dates back to the fourth century BCE. This oath remains the standard point of reference in the medical profession and even though it has been repeatedly revised, amended, or updated, its substance remains the same and lays out the principles of the medical code of ethics. In the ninth century CE, Ishâq ibn Alî Ruhâwî in his book on the *Practical Ethics of the Physician* (*Adab at-tabîb*)[14]—the first work entirely devoted to the subject—draws up a very long list of rules that, according to him, physicians must follow while practicing medicine. It includes elements from the Hippocratic Oath as well as a number of broader considerations (the physician's general behavior, his attitude toward his field of expertise) and other quite specific points (how to examine the body to provide a diagnosis, the approach to providing medications). Those reflections belong to a very old tradition associating the practice of medicine with an ethical reference that requires physicians to treat their patients with dignity, respect, and fairness. To this day, most medical students recite a revised or updated form of the Hippocratic Oath at the completion of their studies.

Referring to the medical code of ethics happened early in the Muslim world and it has never ceased to occupy physicians' reflections. The framework established by Hippocrates—like its many later versions[15]—created no problem as far as medical practice itself was concerned, but it did give rise to reservations regarding the references it included (initially, ancient gods) or those it did not include (no reference to a Creator or a religious framework, while it aims to orient a behavior and not to define a science). During the first *International Conference on Islamic Medicine* that was held in Kuwait in January 1981, under the auspices of the Islamic Organisation for Medical Sciences (IOMS), Muslim physicians and *fuqahâ'* first debated then issued an important document henceforth known as the Code of Islamic Medical Ethics.[16] The initial reference to the Creator places the document within the Islamic Universe of reference: the oath as a whole is, however, universal in scope and the Muslim physician's code of ethics includes no differentiation based on religion, gender, or social class. The terms of the oath are explicit:

> *"I swear by God ... The Great*
> *To regard God in carrying out my profession*
> *To protect human life in all stages and under all circumstances,*
> *doing my utmost to rescue it from death, malady, pain and*
> *anxiety*
> *To keep people's dignity, cover their privacies and lock up their*
> *secrets*

To be, all the way, an instrument of God's mercy, extending my
medical care to near and far, virtuous and sinner and friend
and enemy
To strive in the pursuit of knowledge and harnessing it for the
benefit but not the harm of Mankind
To revere my teacher, teach my junior, and be brother to
members of the Medical Profession joined in piety and charity
To live my Faith in private and in public, avoiding whatever
blemishes me in the eyes of God, His apostle and my fellow
Faithful.
And may God be witness to this Oath." [17]

A physician may, in his attitude and action, be personally motivated by an Islamic ethics, but this should by no means affect the way in which he practices his calling and treats his patients. The approach of Muslim physicians fully agrees with the substance of all the landmark oaths in the history of medicine. In this respect, indeed, they revive the spirit that always motivated the Prophet and the early community of believers about caring for the sick and the conditions involved in doing so. Beyond the rules of decency and social decorum, treating diseases, wounds, and pain requires specific interventions and behavior answering the imperative of curing and saving lives. In the course of therapy, patients have no religion, social status, or gender, and the only dimension that must motivate a physician's commitment is the sacred character of the patient's *life* and the protection of his or her *welfare*.

Thus, on battlefields, in the Medina period and in the Prophet's presence, women used to care for wounded men without anyone's objecting. Later, scholars codified the rules specific to medical treatment and Hanbalî scholar Ibn Qudâmah al-Maqdisî (died 620/1223) stated, in his comparative *fiqh* work *al-Mughnî fî-l-Fiqh*,[18] that a man may without any constraint physically examine a woman for diagnostic purposes (and vice versa) so long as the treatment requires it. Legal schools have since adopted the same position virtually unanimously, insisting on need and/or necessity: if no physician of the same gender is available (for both men and women) or has the necessary skills, if the treatment requires it, or if the social context imposes it. Those legal rulings and opinions (*fatâwâ*) are worked out in the light of the specific requirements of medicine, which aims to cure patients and to save lives. The first of those requirements is of course for the physician to master his subject matter. The Prophet had already said: "Whoever gives medical treatment without knowing medicine will be held accountable [for their act and its results]."[19] As well as mastering their art, physicians must abide by a strict code of ethics requiring them to respect their profession, the patient, and the patient's family, and to make no distinction when they are called on to cure someone or save a *life*. The *Islamic Code of Medical Ethics* may indeed spring from the Islamic Universe of reference but it is implemented in the sphere of common, shared, and universal ethics. In its daily practice—treating pain and facing conditions dangerous to life—medical science has never ceased to call on *fuqahâ'* to read the texts from the standpoint of the universals shared by all humankind. There have indeed been here and there tensions between *fuqahâ'* and physicians, some *fuqahâ'* being sometimes tempted to restrain available medical modalities (for instance about kinds of treatment or about organ donation and transplantation by or for a non-Muslim) in the name of a restrictive reading of Islamic rules. Physicians then had to step in to recall the ethical code of their art, which imposed open, inclusive ethics rather than narrow, exclusive, and, ultimately, illegitimate norms.

Fuqahâ' *and Physicians*

Works by early *fuqahâ'* contain many references to medical practice because a number of verses of the Quran but more particularly Prophetic traditions (*ahâdîth*) deal directly or indirectly with the issue of health. I have already quoted a few (concerning the sacred character of life, the need to look for cures, the physician's competence, responsibility as to one's body, hygiene) and this corpus as a whole has led text scholars to establish categories of rules and conditions concerning medical treatment: following the physician's code of ethics just mentioned, encouraging experimental sciences, integrating new knowledge, mastering instruments and techniques, as well as knowing the limits of medical practice are all issues that were tackled at a very early stage in the works of *fuqahâ'*. As a matter of fact, it was not unusual during the Middle Ages for a text scholar to be proficient in different areas of knowledge and to speak competently in two specialized fields, like the famous Ibn Sîna (died 428/1038).

For centuries, legal rulings were issued on the basis of general medical knowledge; areas for consultation between jurists and physicians seemed neither a necessity nor a hindrance. The astounding accumulation of medical knowledge, the mastery of new, highly sophisticated tools, and physicians' new powers in the treatment of life as such, of the human body and about keeping it in a "survival state," are among the many new phenomena that have compelled *fuqahâ'* and physicians to try to improve the organization of consultation and the conditions in which legal rulings (*fatâwâ*) relative to tricky cases and restricted situations are clarified. Thus, original initiatives have sprung up in the medical field during the past fifty years: formal and informal committees have been convened throughout the Islamic world, bringing together text scholars and physicians, often with the aim of keeping *fuqahâ'* informed about the evolution of knowledge and thus enabling them to issue legal rulings with full knowledge of the facts. In 1981, in Kuwait, the IOMS was created to enable text scholars and scientists specialized in medical questions, men and women (even though the latter were a small minority), to debate the medical knowledge acquired as well as the legal rulings issued in the past and those that must be formulated in the light of contemporary knowledge. Tremendous work has been carried out and numerous publications have accompanied this consultation process (in particular, the voluminous and exacting proceedings of the papers and debates in the seminars).[20] On reading those documents, one can clearly see that the papers by *fuqahâ'* (presented in specific sections entitled *Fiqh papers*) establish general frameworks and see that the concrete implementation of Islamic references is carried out on the basis of physicians' accurate, specialized knowledge. Jurists directly questioned physicians about the state of knowledge on a given issue. This is the case, for instance, regarding the issue of the determination of clinical death: in his lecture about laws and the *sharî'ah*, Dr. Muhammad Abd al-Jawâd Muhammad expounded all the—sometimes contradictory—theories formulated to this day about the exact determination of death and added—as to the decision—"it is up to them [physicians] to decide and we are waiting for such a decision."[21] Not only are fields of expertise recognized, but their relationship, in terms of the legal decisions to be formulated to cover a series of situations related to them (medical treatment, pro-longed artificial life support, stopping machinery, organ donation), is considered in complementary, critical fashion, as is shown by the debates following each presentation.

As early as the 1960s, numerous associations bringing together Muslim physicians were created—in the United States, in Europe, but also in South Africa, and throughout Muslim-majority countries—and they deal with issues of ethics and bioethics. Formal joint orga-nizations bringing together *fuqahâ'* and physicians are less common but they do exist, whether on a permanent basis, like the IOMS, or on an ad hoc basis. They discuss the latest discoveries, sensitive issues, and, of course, the various legal rulings (*fatâwâ*) issued to deal with those situations. The medical sciences have built up such a vast amount of knowledge and physicians now possess so much potential power and use such sophisticated instruments that it seemed urgent to bring areas of expertise together and make decisions adapted to current needs. It is no longer simply a matter of thinking through the physician's code of ethics (which, of course, remains a highly impor-tant measure in the working out of medical ethics) but also the objec-tives, rules, and limits that must inform the practice of his speciality. Medical ethics and bioethics issues are numerous, complex, and cumulative, since progress makes them more numerous and more difficult on a daily basis: it was unthinkable—for such crucial life-and-death issues—to allow uncertainty about areas of expertise and, especially, about the requirements of collaboration and complemen-tarity. Text scholars easily admitted that it was impossible for them to deal with the complexity of contemporary medical sciences that requires more and more specific specialization within the profession itself. Things have gone a long way in this field, although it must be said that a lot remains to be done—first of all, of course, by formally establishing more institutionalized, specialized joint committees and centers for consultation and research, both nationally and interna-tionally. This requires considerable financial and human investment, but the importance of the goal considered—protecting life, curing diseases—makes it necessary to organize this field of shared knowl-edge and skills even more.

The latest evolutions in medical knowledge and practices the world over compel us to add other dimensions to the current discussion. Indeed, medicine is not practiced in a neutral Universe devoid of any ideological or economic considerations. It is clear today that medical ethics must integrate elements of clarification—and sometimes resistance—regarding different forms of pressure, particularly political and economic. Thus, specialists from other fields of expertise must also join in the debates about some tricky issues such as organ donation and sale in developing countries (from both living and dead donors); accelerated treatment in the determination of clinical death in rich countries (because the machines used are expensive or because of a pressing need for organs); the treatment of prisoners sentenced to death, of their bodies and their organs (in some Arab countries or in China, for instance); the relationship of physicians and their skills to the practice of torture (in so many Arab countries but also in the West and in Israel); issues related to the treatment of AIDS patients who require support procedures more than moral judgments about their sexual practices, and other such issues. The list is very long indeed but one can see that the point here is to integrate the ethical decision—related to strictly medical issues—within wider social, economic, and human contexts, which also requires calling on the expertise of other specialists acquainted with real-life, day-to-day situations. We shall be seeing later why and how this should be achieved today.

Contraception and Abortion

It has often been suggested that all religions hold the same theoretical and practical position about contraception and abortion, amounting to common rejection if not condemnation. The study of texts, however, and the analysis of legal rulings (*fatâwâ*) throughout the history of Islamic legal thought up to the time of promulgation of contemporary positions on the questions, show that the range of possibilities is far wider than is generally suggested. Since early times, through the inherent nature of their methods that defined Islam more as a religion based on ritual than rigid orthodoxy, *fuqahâ'* have managed to be pragmatic and integrate new medical knowledge into the formulation of their *fatâwâ*. It should indeed be noted that regarding those two major issues (but also for a majority of medical issues), jurists were naturally compelled—sometimes without even clearly codifying or categorizing the objectives they pursued—to refine their understanding of the five (or six) finalities that had been traditionally established in the "higher objectives school" (*madrasah al-maqâsid*) mentioned previously. It is clear that *fuqahâ'*, like physicians, have integrated the higher principles of *dignity* (here *physical integrity*), *welfare* (in this case, contemporary ethicists and philosophers would speak of the "good life" principle, that is, address quality-of-life issues), of *autonomy* and *personal development*, to which must be added the specific finalities of *conscience* and *stability* (for the inner being), *respect* for the family, all with the general aim of protecting the person's *health*. Those are some of the higher objectives that I have tried to present and categorize more clearly in my previous section, and that physicians are daily confronted with in the practice of their calling.

The issue of contraception is particularly interesting because it immediately opens vast fields of investigation about understanding the higher objectives of the Way (*maqâsid ash-sharî'ah*). Indeed, the first goal of sexual relations was very early identified as the legitimate means for a women and men who are married to each other to have children. As in the Christian tradition, the endpoint of the act of copulation should therefore be procreation and any attempt to stop this natural process determined by God should be forbidden (*harâm*) or at least strongly objected to (*makrûh*). Some legal schools (*madhâhib*), or more precisely some scholars from various legal schools or from the literalist *salafî* trend, share that opinion and continue to oppose all contraceptive methods except in case of extreme necessity. Yet, very early on, some *fuqahâ'* relied on a number of texts that allowed other interpretations and left room for a less rigid attitude about this issue in the name of a different understanding of the purpose of sexuality itself.

Questioned by his Companions about natural contraception as practiced at the time (*al-'azl*, coitus interruptus), the Prophet allowed its practice and declared it neither *harâm* nor objectionable (*makrûh*). An authenticated Prophetic tradition reports through Jâbir: "We used to resort to coitus interruptus (*'azl*) while the Quran was being revealed."[22] In another version: "We used to resort to coitus interruptus (*'azl*) in the Prophet's lifetime and he did not forbid it."[23] Indeed, as Ibn Hajar al-'Asqalânî mentions in his famous commentary of the *ahâdîth* compiled by al-Bukhârî, *Fath al-Bârî fî Sharh Sahîh al-Bukhârî,*[24] some scholars such as Ibn Hazm considered that those Prophetic traditions had been abrogated, but the vast majority of scholars acknowledged them as valid, although they added that this practice required the woman's consent. They were referring to a saying reported from Umar ibn al-Khattâb stating that "the Prophet had forbidden the practice of coitus interruptus with a free woman unless her consent had been obtained." Most scholars understood this condition to be linked to respect for a woman's right to have children as a result of sexual intercourse. Very early on, however, some *fuqahâ'* induced that sexuality itself had another purpose and stipulated that this also meant respecting the woman's right to pleasure. Ja'far as-Sâdiq (died 148/765), who was Abû Hanîfah's and Mâlik ibn Anas's teacher, refers to women's right to pleasure, and so do many scholars from the Malikî and Hanbalî schools:[25] the purpose of the sexual act is therefore clearly understood, beyond procreation, as the fulfilment of a need involving both women's and men's right to pleasure. This interpretation is confirmed by a famous *hadîth* in which the Prophet associates lawful sexual intercourse with a pious act, with charity (*sadaqah*). The association of desire and pleasure with spiritual and religious recognition at first surprised his Companions: "In your sexual intercourse with your wives, he said one day, there is an act of charity." His Companions reacted in surprise: "Messenger of God, when one of us fulfils his [sexual] desire, he also gets a reward for it?" Muhammad answered: "Tell me, if one of you had had unlawful intercourse, would he not have committed a sin? This is why when he has lawful intercourse he is rewarded for it."[26]

This understanding has important consequences on the attitude towards contraception itself. Although a minority of scholars forbid it, a significant number see it as a *makrûh* while others consider it to be simply permitted (*mubâh*). In the twelfth century, Abû Hâmid al-Ghazâlî already went very far in his work *Ihyâ' 'Ulûm ad-Dîn*, in considering that the practice of contraception is permitted and that a woman may resort to it even in a situation in which her main motive is to preserve her beauty. Thus, on a personal level, the parents' personal situation, their income, the number of children, the social environment, or any other reason can justify the couple's resorting to natural contraception, after conscious choice and consultation, but also, as analogical reasoning (*qiyâs*) stipulates, to any other contraceptive device while making sure to avoid all the secondary negative effects this could have on one of the spouses' health.

Such an understanding of the higher goals of human life and of sexuality, which must, beyond mere procreation, allow for the individual's intimate and spiritual fulfilment by achieving her or his desires, balance and stability, personal welfare (and that of the spouse and other family members), psychological and physical health enabled some *fuqahâ'* to develop an open, coherent outlook on contemporary problems. Thus, the issue of family planning in poorer societies has not always been received unfavorably by most Muslim religious authorities not only because contraception is not forbidden in Islam but also because the matters in question also involved issues of *social development*, children's *education*, and family *welfare*. Many contemporary scholars, acting on the basis of reports from physicians, nongovernmental and quasi-nongovernmental organizations, and social workers, have acknowledged family planning programs to be lawful. Opposition was often voiced to resist what was perceived as dictates from the rich West compelling the South's poor to have fewer children while refusing to be critical of the dominant economic order that maintains indecent privileges and prevents a fair sharing of wealth (which would enable the poor to provide for their children). The best example of those tensions (and misunderstandings) was the International Conference on Population and Development held in Cairo in 1994. The refusal of Muslim-majority countries to tackle the issue of family planning, and therefore of contraception, has often been presented as the expression of a new alliance of religions (especially those "inevitably" opposed to contraception, like the Roman Catholic Church). Yet, although some scholars did have restrictive views on the issue, the substance of the debate was quite different and had to do with relations between peoples in the Northern and Southern Hemispheres. The view seemed to be forcibly put forward that the primary cause of underdevelopment was that the poor had too many children, and not that Northern countries were reluctant to share the wealth. During the conference, contrary to what was reported by most Western media, Iran and many Sunni scholars worldwide were not opposed to the principle and philosophy of family planning as such, but rather to its presentation and promotion as the only answer to the issue of controlling the world's overpopulation, without any critical or self-critical consideration from industrialized countries about the economic order they force on the world and the ensuing poverty.

Very early on, scholars distinguished between contraception and abortion, which could be construed to mean intervening in the baby's life and was therefore linked to the question of "causing death." Abû Hâmid al-Ghazâlî, as early as the twelfth century, made a distinction by allowing contraception and forbidding murder of a fetus (abortion). In debates about abortion, the standpoints of *fuqahâ'* can be classified according to two general positions that have crucial consequences on their approach to the issue. For one group, naturally integrating the debates and standpoints present in earlier religions and especially those of the Roman Catholic tradition, abortion amounts to disposing of a human being's life and is therefore forbidden unless the mother's life is at risk. Life is to be protected, as the Revelation recalls, and scholars have understood this injunction to extend to any attempt on life such as abortion: *"Do not kill your children for fear of want: We shall provide sustenance for them as well as for you. Killing them would be a great sin."*[27]

This is the general principle position adopted by *fuqahâ'*, but it is far from being the only Islamic position firmly developed by the Sunni or Shi'î legal traditions. The primary principle indeed consists for all *fuqahâ'* since this involves tampering with the principle of life (or getting ever so near to it) in establishing the unlawful (*harâm*) character of disposing of human life and the noncommendable, or even objectionable (*makrûh*), character of being obliged to resort to that procedure. This outlook indeed reflects the experience of all the women who had to undergo (and the verb is quite telling here) abortion (or who claim the right to resort to it): abortion is always a painful, noncommendable experience in itself, and the right to resort to it never implies seeking a pleasure but rather admitting to having to take an often difficult, painful decision out of one's free choice.

Beyond this principle, scholars from all legal schools rely on other texts—in particular Prophetic traditions—to temper the initial prohibition. The reference *hadîth* on this issue is that which mentions the moment when the soul or spirit is sent into the embryo so that the flesh, the mere material body, is transformed into a human being (*nafs*: the body inhabited by the soul): "The conception of each one of you in his mother's womb is accomplished in forty days, then he becomes a clinging clot (*'alaqah*) for the same time, then a lump of flesh (*mudghah*) for the same time. Then an angel is sent to blow life spirit (*ar-rûh*) into him."[28] Other Prophetic traditions confirm the terms of this *hadîth* or add variants:[29] this has led some *fuqahâ'* (a majority of Hanafî along with a minority of scholars from each of the other schools) to state that abortion was permitted during the first hundred and twenty days for, the soul being absent, the embryo could not yet be considered as a human being. Very diverse and sometimes contradictory positions were formulated by scholars in the course of history: they debated over the very principle of abortion, the time of the intervention (the only consensus is over abortion being forbidden beyond a hundred and twenty days, or even forty-two days when considering the *hadîth* reported by Muslim), and finally the conditions required. What emerges, then, is that there is no formal, undisputed prohibition of abortion as most Muslims or Islamic studies researchers seem to believe. Existing opinions are far more numerous and less clear-cut than that, and recent discoveries, along with the possibility of keeping very premature babies alive after only twelve weeks' gestation, have compelled and continue to compel scholars to refine their positions on the subject. Physicians with up-to-date knowledge of medical progress have alerted *fuqahâ'* about the need to clarify things as to the seventeen-week period (a hundred and twenty days) and its consequences.

One must admit that the platforms bringing together *fuqahâ'* and medical specialists have led to remarkable developments about abortion. Of course, some scholars (from all the different schools but especially Malikî and some *salafî* literalists) do refuse to tackle the issue, but the majority accepts that it may be considered and that such situations must be dealt with on an individual basis. The primary principle of prohibition is often recalled (because abortion is a very serious matter and its excessive use is very real today, especially when abortion is considered as merely another method of contraception), but *fuqahâ'* committees, sometimes in direct association with physicians, have in effect allowed abortion after rape, when prenatal tests revealed the child to have irreversible physical and mental deficiencies, and in cases of involuntary or accidental pregnancies, especially when the family situation or the social context could prevent the family's and/or the child's fulfillment in life. They have, of course, always placed the woman and man face to face with their consciences and required prompt intervention. Some scholars, especially from the Hanafî school, admitted very early on that the decision primarily concerned the woman and that she could resort to abortion without her husband's consent.[30] It is clear that the rule remains to avoid the procedure since abortion is never "commendable," but that the intervention can be considered when protecting a person's *health, development, autonomy, welfare, education,* or *dignity.* Those are the higher goals that were identified and classified in the previous section, and they are implicitly present in all the debates between *fuqahâ'* and physicians: it is the latter who can, through their expertise, say how and at what point, considering the present state of medical knowledge, objectives and ethics could be lost, betrayed, or transgressed on. In medicine, physicians are therefore the primary guardians of the imperative balance between applied ethics and the legal rulings that *fuqahâ'* call on the faithful to respect. *Fuqahâ',* faced with the very nature of the object of study, which deals with life and health, and the extent of the knowledge they could not possibly master, have acknowledged the limits of their competence in this field and the need for constant balanced and dynamic collaboration. This is the attitude that has led to the progress that can be observed today.

Facing Death: Euthanasia and Organ Transplantation

Reading numerous reports produced by the different legal consultation committees and proceedings of the various seminars or conferences about euthanasia confirms what was said at the beginning of this chapter: *fuqahâ'* and physicians have made considerable progress in working together to produce proposals for applied Islamic ethics adapted to the medical knowledge of their time. Trying to remain faithful to the higher goals of the Islamic message regarding the relationship to life and death, text scholars and physicians have developed particularly well-supported and sophisticated opinions and legal rulings, appropriate to deal with situations on a case-by-case basis.

The aim has always been, in the light of the requirements of the *Islamic conception of life and death* (*ad-dîn*), and of *humankind's al-maslahah,* to protect first *life* then *personal integrity* and *dignity,* while preserving *conscience, autonomy, balance, development,* and *welfare* as best as possible. Yet there are situations in which human beings, because of an accident, illness, or simply because they are at the end of their lives, express the wish to stop living or must accept news of impending death while experiencing psychological pressure and/or physical suffering. Confronted with death, with the wish to go or the undoubted need to prepare for it, physicians—and ethicists—have determined various kinds of situations: euthanasia cases fall into several groups, each of which requires specific discussion. To formulate a legal ruling *(fatwâ)* on the practice of direct or indirect, active or passive euthanasia (there are also other categories such as those related to relative states of consciousness and "voluntary" vs. "involuntary" cases), *fuqahâ'* must know the specific details of situations, the latitude available to physicians, and the (concrete, potential, or even hypothetical) consequences of such or such action. Only physicians, with their knowledge, skills, and experience, can shed appropriate light on how to deal with such issues. As can easily be seen, contemporary Islamic thought has evolved considerably on those issues and has provided highly interesting answers.

The Revelation is explicit as to the question of the value of life, its sanctity, and the prohibition of suicide:

> *"And do not take human life—which God has made*
> *sacred—except for justice."*[31]
> *"Do not kill yourselves: for verily God has been most merciful*
> *[infinitely good] to you."*[32]

In the light of this message, assisted suicide or direct active euthanasia that consists of giving medication (with the intention to cause death) to patients who may or may not be at the end of their lives has been determined as strictly forbidden. *Fuqahâ'* have called on physicians, for those particular cases, to seek the means to provide psychological, spiritual, and human support. In situations involving intense physical suffering, physicians are called on to provide all care necessary to reduce pain and thereby enable patients to enjoy minimal comfort. In the order of the higher goals of Islam's message, suffering must be treated and palliated by all lawful means (suffering is not thought to be intrinsically or spiritually saving). There are indeed Prophetic traditions *(ahâdîth)* that mention the spiritually purifying function of illness and of the attendant suffering, but the point is mainly to insist on the increased awareness and introspection that result from it, requiring human beings to return to God with patience and trust. When the Prophet says: "The Muslim's situation is most surprising: all that happens to him is good for him; if some good befalls him, he thanks God and that is good for him, and if some evil [illness, pain] befalls him, he bears it patiently and that is good for him,"[33] he gives pain a spiritual meaning and thereby offers believers a kind of implicit psychological support, but he does not make of suffering itself a necessary and/or welcome experience in faith.

This is why *fuqahâ'* have naturally addressed the issue of indirect active euthanasia, which involves treating end-of-life patients who may be suffering intensely. A terminally ill patient can—after the lack of possible recovery has been confirmed by doctors—be administered morphine to reduce suffering; however, morphine can indirectly accelerate the process leading to death. This situation, which frequently occurs in hospitals, has been declared lawful by *fuqahâ'*. The aim is not to cause death intentionally but above all to ease suffering for a woman or a man in an irreversible situation involving morbidity. Death may indeed come sooner than it would have if things had been left to pursue a natural course, but the main intention was to ease pain and consider the patient's *welfare* in the final moments of life.

Situations involving passive euthanasia initially compelled text scholars to consider a matter of principle about medical treatment. Is a human being, whatever his or her illness may be, morally obliged to seek treatment? The Prophetic tradition transmitted by Ibn 'Abbâs, reporting the dialogue between the Prophet and al-Jâriyyah, who suffered from fits of epilepsy, has been a key reference on the issue for *fuqahâ'*. Al-Jâriyyah asked the Prophet to invoke God for her, and he answered: "'Either you choose to bear this patiently and you will have paradise, or if you prefer I shall invoke God for you so that He may cure you.' She answered: 'I shall be patient but [during my fits] I get uncovered; invoke God so that I do not.' And the Prophet invoked God so that she did not get uncovered."[34]

The majority opinion is that it is recommended (*mustahab*) to seek treatment, but that it is not compulsory (some Shâfi'î and Hanbalî *fuqahâ'*, however, think, on the basis of the Quran and of other traditions, that seeking treatment is an obligation, *wâjib*).[35] This majority opinion has a direct bearing on the issue of direct and indirect passive euthanasia. Ceasing to take a medication and accepting the natural, and therefore lethal, consequences, of that choice or, at a certain stage in the irreversibility of the disease or comatose state, stopping the machine that keeps a human being alive are conditions that *fuqahâ'* have examined, declaring such decisions lawful (*halâl*). The free choice of the individual or that of the patient's family members to let the disease follow its natural course and/or to discontinue artificial life support, ultimately belongs to those it affects directly, with the advice and support of medical staff. The higher ends of protecting *dignity* and *welfare* are assessed in light of the irreversible character of the disease: at the end of life, or being kept alive mechanically, it is up to the patient or patient's family to choose (like al-Jâriyyah) either to use all the curative means available or to accept the decree of fate.

Moreover, it is society's responsibility, and that of hospitals and doctors, to provide adequate support for patients and to help them face divine decree in such extreme situations, without artificially prolonging life but providing palliative care aiming to protect the aforementioned higher goals during the final hours of life. When assessing reports of the different scholarly committees or the proceedings of the many seminars or conferences on those fundamental issues, one can realize that *fuqahâ'* and physicians have fortunately gone very far in their analyses and proposals about management of borderline situations with, for example, discussions about euthanasia, genetic manipulations, or the different types of cloning. The output of these reports is impressive; the resulting proposals are interesting and very often attuned to contemporary medical concerns. Such progress is welcome. Yet it remains true that such reflection does not always entail the implications of the medical knowledge acquired in a given society to their logical extent: once again, medical knowledge and medical practice do not stem from a neutral Universe that does not interact with the social, political, or economic environment. The ethical reflection worldwide about support to the dying and about the need for human and financial investment in care that preserves the *dignity* of human beings at the end of their lives makes it necessary to broaden the scope of the debate and question the political choices pertaining to health care and medicine in both rich and poor societies. It is not enough to think about ethics in a specialized, efficient manner; it must also be influenced by a global, critical vision. Professional ethics about medical devices and practices may come perilously close to being "technicist ethics" if it loses touch with considerations about the meaning of the political and economic choices in which it is rooted. This reduction is dangerous because it can lead to the ethical reflection as it is linked to use of specialized techniques and practices being subsumed into a political and economic order whose agents avoid questioning their own choices and attendant consequences. Joint *fuqahâ'* and physician committees rarely go that far, unfortunately.

The different legal standpoints about organ transplantation beautifully illustrate these reductive processes and show how incomplete the ethical reflection remains. *Fuqahâ'* generally admit, in the name of the principle of the priority of *life* over *death*, that organ donation is lawful: from a (consenting) living person, if it is imperative and does not endanger the donor's life; from a deceased person (with prior consent, or the consent of relatives') as soon as death is verified. *Fuqahâ'* and physicians have long debated different aspects of the question: how death is determined, what organs can be transplanted, whether organs may be sold or bought, and the donor's personal qualifications (origin, religion). The answers have been developed and have grown more detailed over the past twenty years, leading to a more precise vision of Islamic ethics on this point. Thus, it clearly comes out that

- the criteria for determining brain death are fixed by physicians on the basis of current knowledge about the subject (and verified in practice by neurosurgeons through use of various clinical tests: electroencephalograms, reaction to stimuli, reflexes).
- donating all organs (except for the genitals) has been considered lawful, regardless of the social status or religion of the donor or recipient.
- any trading is rejected as a rule, buying or selling organs being declared unlawful (even though a small minority of *fuqahâ'* have nevertheless accepted the idea of the circumstantial necessity of buying, or even of selling, when the donor's life is not endangered).

These are the general principles that have been decreed about blood donation and organ transplantation: there is no major disagreement among *fuqahâ'* and physicians. Ethical reflection keeps to those general positions and carries on its reflection about the wide breadth of medical practice on the basis of the knowledge acquired in the fields of specialization linked to organ transplantation proper: types of organs, tissues, techniques, etc. Once again, one can only observe that the approach, however sophisticated, remains partial if it is assessed in the light of real and potential practices in hospitals today. Economic and material matters—directly or indirectly forced on physicians—can seriously and dangerously influence medical decisions nowadays. A selective approach to the criteria determining (brain and/or heart) death; failing (often voluntarily and selfishly) to take into account newer holistic approaches regarding the human body's life (and therefore death); considering the cost of equipment needed to support or artificially support life; pressure about the need for organs for the living, who are seen as more "useful" and lucrative than the dead—all those dimensions require fundamental reflection at the source, for which simply declaring the principle of organ transplantation lawful is not enough. An ethical principle that seeks to preserve *life* on the medical and technical level can, as is so often the case on a daily basis, be misused, alienated, and betrayed within a system in which the motivations of its use are linked to budgetary pressure and economic interests.

Numerous initiatives have sprung up the world over to resist such contradictions. Christian ethics specialists, and the Pope himself in 2006, have asked for the criteria determining human death to be refined. Ethicists speak out against hasty organ transplantation increasingly used in the world's most technically advanced hospitals and question the technological, reductive medical approaches to determination of clinical death.[36] A publicity campaign was launched in Switzerland in autumn 2007, demanding that the physicians who determined a patient's death should be different from those who were to perform organ transplantations, to avoid deviations and any temptation to accelerate decisions about making organs "available for use" more quickly.[37] Contemporary Muslim ethical reflection has not responded to such debates: it is urgent to say and repeat that this specialist approach—although most necessary, as we have seen—cannot be separated from the global ethical approach that takes all parameters into account, and particularly the social and economic systems of which such practices are part, and thus can betray the principle of human *dignity* in whose very name the reflection had been initiated.

AIDS

Debates about the medical treatment of AIDS are another topic in which one can observe a sort of confusion and standpoints that do not fit into the global framework of AIDS treatment, especially the concrete, day-to-day situations that must be faced. Physicians and social workers are confronted with matters of conscience in which they often find no clear answers from *fuqahâ'* or physicians specializing in ethical issues.

The first answer about how AIDS should be faced has always been, for Muslim text scholars and physicians, to repeat the moral principles of sexual behavior in Islam as a preventive measure. Such rules governing sexual intercourse within marriage only, faithfulness, the prohibition of homosexuality, and abstinence are pointed out in all the texts and conferences dealing with the issue of AIDS, which is seen as a disease almost exclusively resulting from inadequate and/or deviant sexual behavior (which is not true). The disease's negative moral qualification is what has led some *fuqahâ'*—and even some joint legal councils—to this day to insist on this negative dimension, although this is by no means the only cause of transmission. Women, men, and children have been infected through mere blood transfusions, dirty hypodermic needles, or sexual intercourse within marriage with a spouse infected by HIV or born with it because the mother herself was infected. All these data should of course lead to changing the terms of the debate, but even if this was not so, a principle of the medical code of ethics to which Muslim physicians and believers in general must adhere should be insisted on: whatever the patient's religion, color, or gender, and whatever the behavior or moral transgressions that may have resulted in their having AIDS or any other disease, physicians are not permitted to pass judgments: their duty is to provide treatment without discrimination, thus respecting the ethical goals of their medical calling. Therefore, one should never raise the question of the "moral (or immoral) why" of the behavior that resulted in a patient's illness, but only that of "how in practice" they can be enabled to survive and live with dignity.

Reminding society and people at high risk about moral principles and their spiritual outcomes is necessary and helpful in terms of prevention, but it cannot resolve everyday situations. Once the disease has been diagnosed and one considers the actual day-to-day behavior of women and men—leaving aside questions of guilt or blame—appropriate social, economic, and ethical measures must be taken to fight the disease. Above all, HIV-infected patients should not be the objects of accusations and made to feel guilty, so that they are compelled to become invisible, to constantly lie, to hide from their families, their society, and their community (or be rejected by them).[38] I have met ever so many women and men in the West, in Africa, and in Mauritius, who were compelled to lie or simply felt rejected by their spiritual community and their society because they had contracted AIDS. What is said (and what is left unsaid) often shows completely inappropriate disrespect, and *fuqahâ'* and physician committees must become more visible and more vocal on such matters. In terms of such sensitive and extensive issues as AIDS, medical ethics cannot be seen as on the fringes of civil society: to continue to do so would be adding injustice to suffering; this contradicts all the objectives of the Way I have mentioned. Society must go further and dare to tackle the position of AIDS patients in contemporary societies: we cannot accept the employment, housing, and societal discriminations that stigmatize the sick and marginalize them all the more. The reflection must integrate those essential dimensions.

In practice, *fuqahâ'* and physicians have never opposed medical treatment for AIDS patients. On the contrary, their commitment on this point has always been clear. What remains incomplete, however, is the reflection that must lead them to answer the questions of the women and men working in the field. In the streets of Africa, Europe, the United States, or Asia, the virus spreads among injecting drug users because of lack of hygiene and needle swapping, as well as through unprotected sexual intercourse and in situations involving prostitutes. The ethical question is quite clear: must distributing clean needles or providing condoms be banned in the name of Islamic principles, since their use does not answer Islamic moral criteria, or must controlled distribution of needles and condoms be officially organized, thus choosing the lesser of two evils (that is, behavior seen as immoral, or the spread of the disease, which in some places soon leads to death). It looks as though Islamic legal councils, composed of jurists and physicians, focusing on incantatory reminders linked to prevention and acceptance of necessary treatment, did not pay attention or refused to speak out clearly on those essential issues: fighting AIDS and its spread requires a global approach as well as bold and coherent ethical decisions. Many social workers and some physicians have provided a practical answer to day-to-day conditions and started distributing needles and condoms themselves. Some have questioned *'ulamâ'* and *fuqahâ'* without actually getting a clear answer about the matter.[39]

The higher objectives of the Way, which require people to protect the individual's *life, dignity, integrity, personal development, health,* and *inner balance*, call on jurists and physicians to consider the issue universally and to come up with practical answers. The rules or maxims of fundamentals (*qawâ'id usûliyyah, sing. qâ'idah*) stipulating that one must choose the lesser of two evils (*akhaf ad-dararayn*) and that necessity makes what is forbidden permissible (*ad-darûrât tubîh al-ma'zurât*) should be appropriately resorted to so as to enable physicians and social workers to go about their work confidently and more openly and efficiently. Controlled needle exchanges (among injecting drug users) or taking into account the actual sexual behavior of individuals (in drug addicts, prostitution, or in general mores) are necessities of our time. Accompanying this action with adequate training about preventive measures—in terms of awareness, personal responsibility, or/and spiritual reminders—is imperative so that the operation does not turn into legitimizing all kinds of behavior, but this approach cannot replace hands-on realism. The ethical goals of medicine cannot remain blind to what causes the disease in the first place, unless we aim to produce an Islamic ethics that remains ideal and pure but thereby half blind and inoperative.

Another dimension must be added to fighting the spread of AIDS, and this once again has to do with integrating the debate about the economic order imposed on today's world. What is medical discourse—and the accompanying ethics—worth if nothing is said about the injustice about the availability or unavailability of medication in the world? While patients survive and live on in rich Western countries because they have access to highly active antiretroviral therapy (HAART), millions of children, women, and men die in Africa and in poorer societies because multinational drug companies produce and sell medications at unacceptably high prices. Worse still, they prevent poorer countries from getting access to the same drugs in their much cheaper generic versions out of economic motives. Those policies cause millions to die each year, and no legal council is heard to speak out clearly, although the issue surely has to do with ethics and the practice of medicine in contemporary times. Again, it is not enough to promote a normative, technical, formal management of medical practices without considering what, in some way or other, tends to prevent achieving higher objectives and goals. To this end, as I said, spaces for reflection and legal elaboration must be open to medical specialists but also to social workers and other women and men working in allied fields of health care. The latter must also make themselves heard and avoid adopting a passive attitude often allied to critical and/or complaining discourse about the failure to provide answers or the *'ulamâ's* inability to meet the challenges of our time. In the end, this attitude associated with evading responsibility fails to help anybody and is certainly not apt to change the order of things.

This long discussion about medical ethics has at least proved two theses: nothing, in the Islamic Universe of reference, opposes the emergence of new, dynamic, up-to-date discussion, as we have seen for some sensitive issues. *Fuqahâ'* and physicians have often proceeded hand in hand and developed appropriate, reasonable answers about faithfulness to ethical outcomes. It has appeared, however, that as it grew more specialized, reflection sometimes became technical and formal, losing touch with the complexity of the world and of day-to-day realities. It is as if, while gaining effective specificity, legal councils had lost ground in terms of global vision and social, political, and economic considerations. As if, once again, medicine—whose specific complexity has been acknowledged—was practiced abstracted from the complexity of societies and economic issues. As if, indeed, this had no bearing on medical ethics proper. Yet this is anything but true, and we must carry on the reflection in the medical field to become aware of the heavy demands imposed by the objectives of the Way as they were presented in the previous section. Taking into account *the Islamic conception of life and death (ad-dîn)* without ever overlooking *the common interest of people and societies (al-maslahah)* is an extraordinary challenge that demands much more than we are doing today.

12

Culture and the Arts

The question of culture is central to debates concerning Islam today. Although it must be reiterated that Islam is primarily "a religion" and not "a culture," one should immediately add that religion never finds expression outside a culture and that, conversely, a culture never takes shape without deferring to the majority values and religious practices of the social group that constitutes it. There are, therefore, no religiously neutral cultures, nor any culture-free religions. Any religion is always born—and interpreted—within a given culture and in return the religion keeps nurturing and fashioning the culture of the social community within which it is lived and thought. Those inevitable and complex links make it difficult to define—whether in the relationship to texts or in religious practice—what belongs to religion proper and what instead pertains to the cultural dimension. Even so, the nature of contemporary challenges and the re-examination of the rich Islamic legal tradition (its fundamentals—*usûl*—as well as its implementation—*fiqh*) require us to investigate the issue more closely and try to determine a theoretical framework and clearer principles regarding the relationship between religion and culture.

We may for instance begin by trying to identify which texts in religious teachings will, while of course initially finding expression within a given culture, transcend the cultural framework of the original social group through principles and objectives (stipulated in those texts). Religion cannot find expression without culture but not all of religion can be reduced to culture. Scriptural sources establish a truth and transcendent values; the faithful of that religion necessarily believe them to be universal. What would be fundamentally reductive and dangerous, as far as understanding scriptural sources is concerned, would be to reduce the meaning and substance of the text revealed for everyone—beyond a given time and geographical and cultural space—to give in to the interpretation of some readers who would monopolize interpretation in the name of their own proximity to the original culture. Many contemporary *salafi* literalist movements generate such reductionism without always being aware of it, since their very methodology for approaching texts makes it difficult to distinguish between religious practice and its cultural expression.[1] For many scholars of that school, cultural diversity and evolution are akin to unacceptable religious innovations (*bida'*, plur. of *bid'ah*). The problem here does not simply lie in text-reading modalities but rather in the relation established between religious principles (whose contents and importance ought to be determined) and their historical expression within a given culture. This begins with language: Arabic is the single reference language of the Quran and Islam, but the Arab culture of the Arabian Peninsula is not the sole culture of Islam. Reducing one to the other is wrong and has consequences for the understanding and practice of religion across time and societies.

It is therefore important to try to distinguish religious principles from their cultural garb: the process is sometimes easy (for anything involved with creed and with worship proper), but things may become more complex and require more specialized, sophisticated interpretation to point out what the text actually says, what is open to interpretation in the text itself, what is linked to the interpreting scholar's culture, what is immutable, what is changing, and other issues. The challenge is a major one, but it is inescapable: if Islam is indeed a universal religion, it must provide its faithful with the means to approach the diversity of cultures appropriately. Concretely, this means the diversity of collective mindscapes, ways of life, social models, imaginations, tastes, and aesthetic and artistic expressions. Common principles—here Islamic ethics—must *a fortiori* provide a clear frame of reference enabling people involved to act and interact confidently within their own cultural Universe, both on the level of simple day-to-day details and on that of artistic creativity.

Religion and Culture

One should start at the beginning and try to classify the nature of the relations the Islamic religion has, from the outset, maintained with the culture in which it was born and took shape. This issue is essential to determine the nature of the relationships Muslims must maintain with "other," "non Arab" cultures. It is anything but new, since Muslims living in Africa or Asia very early on had to determine how they were to relate both with the universal religion and with the "original culture": such distinctions were made almost naturally in the course of history, respecting the principles of religious practice that integrated within surrounding cultures (accepted de facto). Islam's universality, which was also termed "Islamic civilization," was achieved through this union between the unity of principles and the diversity of cultures. What is new today has to do with the effects of globalization and the emergence of an increasingly global dominant culture. Even if one wanted to discuss the facts, one cannot deny the reality of perceptions among the populations and elites of non-Western countries: Western culture seems to have settled everywhere and imposes itself through the globalization of media and means of communication. Everywhere, one can observe the same phenomenon of attraction-repulsion that is common to psychological situations nurtured by a feeling of self-dispossession: while instinct and desire attract us to an object, our intelligence and conscience cause us to hate what excites and sometimes intoxicates us. Muslim-majority communities and societies are rife with such contradictory tensions, which sometimes come close to nurturing almost schizophrenic attitudes and discourse toward the "West" that people are as eager to imitate as to condemn.

Faced with this increasingly uniform global culture, one might be greatly tempted to react by proposing the alternative of another equally uniform worldwide culture.[2] This tendency has emerged in the contemporary *salafî* literalist trend or in some traditionalist trends— such as *tablighî* movements—and has gained an audience the world over, despite representing a minority. The methodology that those trends have always used in relating to texts—assimilating religious practice to its (supposedly) original cultural expression—paradoxically, but after all quite logically, enables them to face the challenge of the West's cultural domination by promoting the return to an original culture that is also perceived as universal. To them, therefore, the aim should be not only to respect the principles of religious practice, but to live, dress, and interact with the human and social environment as we suppose the inhabitants of Mecca and Medina must have done in the light of the texts that have come down to us. This globalization- exportation of a very local culture is fundamentally questionable, but it stands out by providing immediate, simple, and very clear answers to those who feel torn and lost between their spiritual aspirations, their instinctive attraction, and their intellectual repulsion. It rep- resents a simple—and often oversimplified—response to a complex and often painful experience.

The issue here is to identify what in religious teachings is univer- sal and how these concepts require us to tackle diversity in general and, as far as the present discussion is concerned, the diversity of cultures. We have already seen that the Quran's message stipulates, as a primary, higher principle, the Creator's will to establish diversity among humankind, summoning the latter to respect it. This is pre- cisely the meaning of the verse: *"Had God so willed, He would have made you a single community...."*[3] Regarding cultural diversity, one should turn to the Messenger's practice to reach a better understand- ing of how he dealt with differences within the first community of believers. The Quran indeed lays down broad principles, but it is dif- ficult to define a more precise orientation than (essentially positive) diversity having been established and willed by God among people and societies. The Prophet's experience tells us much more than that indeed: not only did the Prophet welcome the ideas and practices suggested by his Companions from different backgrounds and cul- tures (Arab, Persian, African) when they did not oppose (or directly involve) a religious injunction, but it must be added that he himself had to experience exile and to come to terms in Medina with a cul- ture that was different from Mecca's.

The Companions who went into exile because of repression in Mecca (*al-Muhâjirûn*) had to learn to distinguish what concerned only their religion and what were instead rather more cultural features: the people of Medina, the Helpers (*al-Ansâr*) were indeed to share with them the principles of their common religion, but they nevertheless maintained specific cultural traits that the Prophet not only did not ask them to change, but also that he treated with thoughtfulness and respect. This can be seen in many situations involving customs, individual relations, and public modes of expression: respecting the *Ansâr's* taste for art and singing, or women's role in society (they were far more evident in Medina than in Mecca).[4] The Prophet was constantly bent on integrating customs and habits and respecting tastes and aspirations. From the outset, then, the universality of Islamic principles, between Mecca and Medina, never meant standardizing cultures but on the contrary integrating them while respecting the common principles of faith and religious practices (*al-'aqîdah*, *al-'îbadât*) and the valuable variety of human and social experiences.

This was not easy for the first Meccan Muslims who must have thought, like 'Umar ibn al-Khattâb, that it amounted to harming Islam, by failing to implement its rules, if not by perverting it. The Prophet's answers, often his silences, were so many signs and messages indicating that he acknowledged those cultural features and behaviors (this was often the case, as we said, regarding women's presence and role in society) and that he did not object. The exiles, *al-Muhâjirûn*, therefore had to make an imperative but difficult effort to distinguish between Islam's universal principles and the tensions that the experience of exile necessarily led to regarding their original culture: they clearly had to strive to distinguish between religion and culture. But there was more to it than that: not only did they have to separate religious principles from customs, they also (on occasion) had to be able to be critical of their own culture. The attitude of Medina women had shed light on some Meccan cultural traits that had to be reconsidered and about which self-criticism was required. The experience of exile, and therefore of cultural diversity, in fact had this twofold positive consequence: imposing a distinction between what was actually religious and what pertained to culture, but also allowing a critical outlook on their own customs and habits, which might so far have seemed unquestionable because they were so natural. Indeed the religious reference can and must act as a critical mirror of cultural habits: the religious message's universality, to be fully achieved, must not only integrate the diversity of customs but also establish a set of principles making it possible to reform behavior seen as culturally normal (or accepted because it is natural and widespread) that must nevertheless be subjected to serious ethical assessment. This applies to all collective temptations, within Muslim societies and communities, to admit almost normalized discriminatory or racist attitudes toward a given group—whether "Blacks" for some, or for others "Turks," "Pakistanis," "converts," or other groups: other religions or civilizations, toward women, for instance. This was often true in the Prophet's lifetime as well, regarding seemingly trifling yet significant situations. On one occasion, for instance, the Prophet kissed his grandson in front of a Bedouin. The latter told him: "I have ten children and I have never kissed any of them." The Messenger answered: "He who does not spread mercy will not find mercy [with God and Men]."[5] Thus it is not simply a matter of relying on religious injunctions to draw up constructive criticism of cultural habits but also, as is the case here, of immersing oneself in spiritual teachings and appealing to the heart to make mind-sets change from within.

The universality of Islam's message therefore constantly relies on this twofold movement that consists, on the one hand, in integrating cultural specificities so long as they do not contradict a religion's formal injunctions, and, on the other hand, in allowing for critical assessment of the surrounding cultural reference. This assessment must be carried out through a twofold lens: that of religious teachings proper, which fashion a disposition of mind and heart, which must lead to constantly reassessing questionable or biased customs, and that of the enriching encounter with other cultures, which can point out the flaws of the former society. Such study and reflection require thorough specialized analysis about the constitutive elements of the various cultures, their sources, relation to one another, meaning, and possible evolution. The prescriptive approach is never sufficient for this concerns codes, meaning, and both collective and individual psychology: social scientists and social workers can contribute very usefully to formulating the objectives of an ethics that takes realities into account while critically and constructively orienting cultural facts. An extreme but highly significant case sheds light on the nature of the work that must be carried out: it is not enough, for instance, to state that female genital mutilation is not an Islamic injunction, that it is "cultural" and that it must be stopped. We should also understand what it represents in some societies—for Muslims and non-Muslims alike—and equip ourselves with the means to change mind-sets progressively, from within, so that people not only abide by the legal ban (and do not evade it clandestinely) but fundamentally agree with the principles and objectives of the process. Denunciation is not enough: it must be accompanied by educational action not only taking into account the cultural aspirations of societies and communities but also teaching people to set aside any practices that do not respect human beings' *integrity, dignity,* and *rights.*[6] What was said earlier of women's right to pleasure is essential and it is important to elaborate a global approach including all those aspects. All the skills available—those of *fuqahâ'*, anthropologists, ethnologists, psychologists, physicians, as well as social workers—must be enlisted to accomplish this effort.

Literalist versus "Cultural" Reading

Today's Muslims are faced with two major problems that lie at the heart of many sensitive debates about culture, women, economics, and politics. Two modes of text interpretation complete and confirm each other: giving texts a strictly literalist reading, and reading them through the lens of this or that cultural context. The first type of reading operates through *reducing* the global message by insisting on some verses or Prophetic traditions without taking into account other scriptural references (or their chronology), while the other type proceeds through *projection*, imparting to the text a cultural garb that results in legitimizing or prohibiting practices that *a priori* are not mentioned in the texts. It should first be said that the diversity of interpretations must be respected, unless, of course, they run against an established Islamic injunction or a recognized higher objective: thus it is by no means possible, in the light of the global message and its means, to justify child labor, violence toward women, forced marriages, honor crimes (i.e., revenge), or female genital mutilation. In this sense, there are limits to accepting interpretations: the texts say something and establish a minimum reference framework that cannot be twisted to support just any interpretation, in one way or the other (restriction or permissiveness). In terms of this diversity, those literalist, traditionalist, conservative, or "culturalist" readings, however, must not prevent us from opening a critical—and, of course, constructive—debate about their potential consequences. For indeed, while such readings must be understood and justified as free choice for oneself or one's group—as was the case among the Prophet's Companions—it remains true that they lead to excess by reducing or restricting the message or in judgments that shun (*takfîrî*) other interpretations seen as too liberal or somehow outside the scope of Islam.[7]

In debates about some practices among Muslims, a cultural reference is often—and almost exclusively—blamed. Yet, I have been repeating for twenty years that the problem is not merely cultural but that it has to do with the interpretation of texts and particularly with the most literalist and traditionalist interpretations. This consideration is hardly new and it can be found in all the debates that opposed renewal *'ulamâ'* (*al-mujaddidûn*) to those they called imitators (*al-muqallidûn*).[8] The criticisms were clear: the former reproached the latter for simply repeating what some scholars had said and elaborated for their own time, keeping to a literal reading of the texts or sacralizing, as it were, earlier merely human opinions. According to the *mujaddidûn*, the study of social mores required a continuous effort at rereading, contextualizing, and adapting the implementation of injunctions in the light of the texts' global meaning, depending on the nature of the environment and of the time period. This is how they understood the meaning of *ijtihâd*. That debate is still ongoing: the issue is indeed religion and the nature of the texts' position in terms of their relationship to the surrounding culture. This dimension must certainly be taken very seriously; contemporary debates about latitudes in text interpretations must not be minimized. I have repeatedly stated that discussing the status of the Quran—however appealing it may be to some academic and interreligious circles in the West—will have little effect on the Islamic world and Muslims, since recognizing the Quran as "the revealed word of God" is one of the pillars of faith (*rukn min arkân al-îmân*).[9] What will really have a decisive effect lies in the nature of the proposed readings, the religious legitimacy of the interpreters, and the horizons opened by those interpretations—and by the accompanying autonomous critical reasoning (*ijtihâd*). Such interpretations, produced from within, defended and argued in the light, and in full respect, of the texts, will alone be able to rival the "immediate" acceptance of literalist readings, which prevail because of the legitimacy enjoyed by the *'ulamâ'* who promote them and the simple clarity of the interpretations and rulings they decree. One should insist on the chronology and evolution of the Revelations, the different texts related to a given issue, the hierarchy of sources, authenticity, and the Prophet's attitude in specific situations (since he is considered as a model for all Muslims). Text scholars, women and men, must offer their particular contributions.

Yet we also need an external as well as critical outlook on the process of reading and interpretation. Having studied the Islamic legal tradition from its beginnings to the present, in the three fields of Quran commentary (*tafsîr*), the fundamentals of law and jurisprudence (*usûl al-fiqh*), and law and jurisprudence (*fiqh*), I am convinced that no scholar has ever approached the texts without being, in one way or another, influenced by the culture in which she or he lived. Indeed, this influence was not conclusive in some fields such as, in particular, the fundamentals of faith and worship, but it remains important to try to understand how this influence of culture may have operated on more secondary, and sometimes highly sensitive, issues. The remarks about women by Imam Abû Ja'far at-Tabarî (died 923) in one of the earliest established commentaries of the Quran— as well as those by Abû Hâmid al-Ghazâlî (died 1111), Fakhr ad-Dîn ar-Râzî (died 1210), or Abû 'Abd Allah al-Qurtubî (died 1273), to mention only the most famous—as well as the observations, but also indeed the silences, of great scholars about social relations, women, art, and taste, all clearly bear the influence of their surroundings and times. It is important to do a thorough critical analysis of those influences on respective interpretations but also, at the source, on how texts are read and subsequently understood and categorized. This will make it possible to identify more precisely the nature of historical cultural projections and therefore the possibilities of new reinterpretations.

It is often, of course, in issues related to interpersonal relations, the public space, women (who are discussed in the next chapter), education, aesthetics, and artistic expression that the cultural referent has had considerable, and sometimes harmful, influence.

A thorough rereading must be carried out, but it will be all the more efficient if, once again, it calls on different specialized skills. Women and men coming from the various fields of the social sciences, speaking about a given environment from within, can help *fuqahâ'* relate more critically to the inherited legal tradition by enabling them to understand more thoroughly the cultural systems within which and for which they decree the law. This entails comprehending power relations, the relationship to language, modes of expression and communication, generational relations and/or gaps, knowledge and behavior transmission modalities, male-female relations, group relations, collective psychology, even "rites of passage," established or not, which remain present even in the most modern societies. Without straying too far into some construct derived from the social sciences that could interfere with the relationship to the texts, we must develop a thorough knowledge of the social and cultural environment to regain hold of their meaning and goals through a new reading that does not deny its relation to the cultural environment, which actually gives it meaning. The message's universality resides precisely in this ability to accept inevitable cultural projections, claiming the right to move past earlier concepts to allow a necessary reappropriation by present ones without ever betraying the immutable fundamentals of the religious message and its ethics. This is the true meaning of tradition: there is no universality without diversity, and no faithfulness without motion.

Cultures, Expression, and Symbols

The cultural question must therefore be taken very seriously, not only about the mediation it naturally sets off in the interpretation of texts, but also about what those texts say about their own existence, meaning, and richness. As I pointed out in the previous section, the Creator's will to establish manifold languages and skin colors, in a variety of nations, tribes, and religions, is presented in scriptural sources as the source of mutual enrichment, peace through balanced forces, and an appeal to work toward good deeds through high-mindedness, coherence, and contribution to humankind's universal heritage. But there are universal conditions that require understanding and respecting the higher outcomes just mentioned: societies and human groups must, relying on the *rule of law, independence,* and internal *pluralism* (and *deliberation* structures), make sure to remain faithful to their own natural *evolution, culture*(s), and *memory* or *heritage.* The universality of Islamic ethics thus necessarily implies respecting those higher objectives that give meaning (without ever being restrictive) to national histories, cultural specificities, common roots, and collective memories. The twofold critical work that is required today about the relationship between "religion" and "culture" now stands out clearly: first, those cultural features that have sometimes reduced, oriented, if not altogether distorted the meaning of the texts must be identified; then, we must return to higher goals and the interpretative freedom allowed by scriptural sources, thus equipping ourselves with the means to encourage creativity and fresh, original cultural expressions. In other words, a double effort is needed: on the one hand, resisting the exclusive, uniform appropriation of the texts' initial meaning by the original Eastern culture, and, on the other, resisting the homogenization imposed by Western culture, which leaves no room either for other traditional expressions or any viable idea of "cultural ethics."[10]

This is a huge, crucial challenge. Modernism, the cult of progress, technology, and productivity clearly go in tandem with impoverishment of the souls of nations and peoples. East and West, women, men, and teenagers, increasingly induced to live at a fast pace, to preserve their youth indefinitely, and to focus on the future, gradually lose touch with their personal memories and with the meaning of roots and history. They engage in putative "clashes of civilization" while they hardly know any more what a tradition or a civilization is, or the meaning of origins and of their ever-shifting identities. Devoid of confidence, they experience self-doubt, fear other people, so that the clash is now often between minimal, superficial "perceptions" rather than "civilizations." Muslims the world over fall prey to such confusion and dangerous reductions: spirituality confused with emotive reactivity; obsession with norms without any consideration of meaning; schizophrenic attitude toward the dominant culture (both rejection and attraction) without proposing any alternative creativity; all these are symptoms of the ills that affect Muslim-majority societies and Muslims elsewhere in the contemporary world. The series of *fatâwâ* issued by various *fiqh* committees throughout the world daily reveal that problems are not given in-depth treatment and that cultural issues are often either understated or wrongly assessed and misunderstood.

If Islam is universal and if, as I said, it is imperative, when elaborating the different dimensions of its ethics, to integrate the diversity of cultures, their languages, their modes of consumption, their means of expression, and their symbols, it is becoming urgent to reconsider very thoroughly the relationship of Islamic discourse and points of reference to cultures in societies around the world. Resisting the danger of the twofold standardization previously mentioned means, according to the rule that states that "the principle in everything is permission," that the various cultures must be studied from within to identify the roots of their traditions, their distinctive nature, and their creativity, while helping them survive and encouraging their expression. This should extend from daily consumption (local foods and beverages) and fashion, to language, architecture, music, and all forms of artistic expression. Against the culture of "fast food," drinks, and music that are Americanized both in taste and spirit, we should promote and support the cultural expressions that relate differently to time, being, meaning, and goals...ranging from Chinese tea to local gastronomy from Africa but also from European countries or regions of the United States, or American provinces.[11] This is again twofold resistance since, as can be seen, protecting the diversity of cultures implies refusing to submit to a global economy that imposes certain tastes and fashions, a global aesthetics that is now standardized for all.[12]

This deeper, more intimate relationship to national and local cultures is necessary for Muslims the world over. It not only enables them to enrich the modes of expression of their inner being and aspirations, but also to understand more fully the richness of human communities (according to the Quran's phrase, *"that you may know each other"*[13]) and contribute to the creativity of each of them by integrating them into their own self-expression in a voluntary but always constructively critical way. Concretely, this means remaining faithful to higher principles and ethical objectives, wherever one may be, while developing a curiosity and creativity that make it possible to integrate aesthetic models and artistic expressions from all cultures and backgrounds. For instance, "Islamic" music and songs do not have to remain "oriental," nor do mosques have to be built in imitation of what was done "over there," in the countries of origin. The concept of faithfulness to Islam's principles is being impoverished through the damaging standardization of all social, cultural, artistic, and even political models the world over. This imperils any ethical Universe of reference when what is normative becomes more important than what is reasoned and this reductive process leads to the loss of the ability to understand that a variety of ways of life and approaches to meaning are possible while respecting those same norms. Left to themselves, in an attitude that can only be defensive about the global culture that is being forced on societies, *fuqahâ'* are unable to open new, original, creative perspectives in the worlds of culture and the arts. Here again, there is a dire need for broader skills closely involved in such fields, and for the ability to devise a renewal that can resist the twofold standardization, seeking the means to mobilize the intelligence and creativity of populations, artists, and architects to come up with "something else," rich and varied alternatives, and encouraging traditional expressions as well as original initiatives while respecting—as a higher principle of their ethics—all the world's cultures and their essential *diversity*.

Cultures include symbols and just as there are no societies without cultures, there are no societies without symbols. The idea of a culturally neutral public space is not only absurd, it can also turn out to be dangerous because of the amount of secular dogmatism that would be necessary even to consider it concretely. Religious and cultural symbols tell of societies' roots and soul, and it is important never to minimize those dimensions of collective psychology.[14] Neither is it wise to hide behind other people's symbols and become invisible, but to recognize this element and find the means to express one's faithfulness to Islam's ethical principles while integrating the symbols of the culture in which one lives, in the West or in the East. As time goes by, a two-way influence will naturally set in, but it is important to show respect for the cultural motives, modes of expression, and symbols a culture has developed over its history, crises, and evolutions. Here again, respecting the higher aspirations of Islamic ethics requires additional creativity rather than isolation and confinement within exclusively "oriental" expressions and aesthetics. Once more, *fuqahâ'* are in great need of historians, architects, and artists.

The Entertainment Culture

The culture of entertainment and "play" has taken on considerable importance in our lives. The young immediately come to mind, but in effect, all societies and all age groups are affected in the same manner. This is what Umberto Eco calls the "carnivalization of life," which he describes in apt, humorous terms.[15] Entertainment is indeed an important dimension of life, but it should constitute "a pause" between two more important things: its function is primarily to give rest to the mind, heart, and being, to *divert* them in Pascal's usage, so as to enable people to return to more important things, to their responsibilities regarding life, society, work, justice, and death. This is exactly the meaning the Prophet of Islam had given it when he had been questioned by his Companion Handhalah who, on the contrary, saw in entertainment evidence of his hypocritical disposition before God (since it led him to forget). The Prophet answered him: "By He who holds my soul in His hands, if you were able to remain in the [spiritual] state in which you are in my company and in permanent remembrance of God, angels would shake hands with you in your beds and along paths. But it is not so, Handhalah, there is a time for this [devotion, remembrance] and a time for that [rest, distraction, entertainment]."[16] Perversion, as defined by Eco, and as we witness it daily, sets in when—for reasons of economic profit—everything is turned into play, into entertainment, and the scale of meaning and values fades away. A double challenge must be faced here: determining the place of entertainment and play in our lives, and thereby considering their meaning and goals. When everything becomes dangerously entertaining, from politics as show business to reality shows, from the domination of "sports events" to televised charity marathons, establishing an ethics of entertainment is necessary.

It should first of all be recognized that, for the young as well as for adults, entertainment is a necessity of life and that the standpoints of some literalist scholars or rigorist trends are untenable and absurd. They seem to want to force on us a kind of daily life devoid of entertainment, without reading, without imagination, without music…without even spiritual rest. This cannot be and does not correspond to Islam's teachings. We hear that music has become the universal language of young people, that the images on television and in films agitate the minds of people the world over, that great sports events have become the ritual gatherings of modern times...and we should act as if this had no impact on the minds, hearts, and daily lives of believers wishing to live in harmony with certain principles and a life ethics?! The question is not to know whether we should entertain ourselves, but what the meaning, form, and nature of that entertainment should be.

What is at stake are the *welfare, balance,* and sound *development* of the children, teenagers, men, and women of our time, both North and South. In this sense, entertainment and play must represent "pauses" of a sort at the heart of more serious intellectual, social, and political preoccupations, but they should by no means promote values contrary to the higher goals and general ethics I have mentioned. This is why recreational activities and their management within human societies must be considered in the light of philosophical and ethical issues, and the problem is not all that trivial: what is the meaning of entertainment and play? Why do we enjoy recreation and what objectives or role do we wish to assign the concept of play within the society? Is the objective self-forgetfulness, giving full range to all the expressions of human instincts (the natural attraction for physical appearance, money, and sex) or is it an "invitation to travel," which stirs the heart, mind, and imagination while edifying, soothing, and appeasing them with amusements that strive to be human and remain "humanizing" and healthy? The point is not, as in "the carnivalization of life," to promote continuous play and an endless quest for entertainment that dominates everything else, which acts like a drug and transforms us into slaves addicted to our sensations and emotions. It should be the opposite: devising entertainment that makes human beings balanced, independent, and freer. This means that it is important to think about the nature of the proposed activities, their organization in time (day, night, time of the week) and space (the home, the faith community, society at large) and of course the ages and evolution of individual people and their personalities. Muslim societies and communities are so afraid of the effect of alienating entertainment that they produce amusements and games that are either packed with religious references (and thereby no longer provide actual, necessary recreation) or childish (as if to enjoy recreation as a Muslim, one must refuse to become an adult or pretend never to have become one...).

Women and men who possess this inclination and skill ought therefore to be invited to show more creativity, to integrate modern techniques of communication, to specialize in that Universe, and to show discriminating professionalism. To find the means to encourage children, teenagers, and adults to return to reading (according to age, tales, novels, essays); to express and convey their own imagination; to become involved with texts, literature, poetry, drama, and other forms of literature. To nurture their taste for art, painting, or music, which open up inner prospects and nurture a curious and calm outlook on the world. To produce and integrate playful activities for various age groups and to enable children to become interested in all sorts of subjects, in human beings, animals, history, psychology, forms of physical expression, sports, and so many other activities. Muslims today are lost between trends of thought that forbid everything (and that make life arid and/or intolerable) and the realities of a carnival of life that alienates them (which they claim to reject but which they end up becoming involved with or simply imitating). Yet, we should become reconciled with the essence and meaning of creativity, which is so necessary today to resist the global culture that produces this new imperialism of entertainment and play, which nobody controls any more and whose driving force is the financial profit amassed by its producers.

Twofold critical work is needed here: first, the specialization and professionalism of the artists and designers of that culture of entertainment will enable them to produce something new through the use of state-of-the-art technology and methods. Alternative productions will only prevail over the dominant trends in entertainment if they can bear comparison in terms of design and production values. It is also important to be able to distinguish, among recent productions, those works and products that stand out because of their sense of ethics and respect for human dignity. Thus, the range of choice in recreational activities, experiences, books, and other works of art can be broadened and organized according to age groups and locations. The other challenge is to educate the general public, to get them to enjoy edifying recreational activities, literature, painting, that is, to comprehend the higher values inherent in play and entertainment. Resisting the alienating, standardized global culture requires training critical minds and good taste. The young must be taught to put a value on their own imaginations, to consider their own inclinations, and to analyze the activities available to them. We should fashion a conscience that is, as far as possible, aware of the meaning and objectives of both physical and cultural "consumption": this means equipping it with the means to resist the imperialism of play and entertainment, the carnivalization of life, and soulless consumerism. Learning to manage one's need to forget is never easy, and the contemporary Muslim conscience often has only normative reflections about the duty not to be led astray. Contemporary Islamic thought simply does not know how to manage entertainment and play. This is serious, for we know how deeply valued entertainment is to the human conscience. It is what food is to the body: a vital need without which it will eventually waste away or deny its existence. This is the collective responsibility (*fard kifâyah*) of the whole spiritual community.

The Arts: Goals and Ethics

One of the most important dimensions of culture is, of course, that represented by imagination, collective mindscapes, and art in all its expressions. Islam does not totally separate art from ethics, but no Islamic teaching can justify that, in the name of ethics, art should be muzzled, stifled, and ultimately banished as poets were banished from the ideal city, in Plato's *Republic*. A number of *'ulamâ'* have argued, on the basis of partial, biased readings of the Quran or of Prophetic traditions (*ahâdîth*), that Islam opposed poetry, painting, or music. Those opinions exist and I have already discussed them elsewhere, but thorough study of the Prophet's life, of the Companions,' and of the history of Islamic civilization has convinced us that nothing opposes artistic expression in Islam. On the contrary;[17] faced with the standardization of global culture and of its artistic expressions, it is urgent to give this issue serious, in-depth consideration and to stop maintaining a strictly defensive position from the standpoint of normative values. It is as if, through a peculiar shift in perspective, the basic rule had been perverted as far as art was concerned: here, "the primary principle in all things" seems to be prohibition (*harâm*). This perspective is wrong and requires us to recover the original confidence and creativity to offer "something else" to the Muslims of our time. However, we must not indulge in naïve smugness about such issues: literature, painting, music, and movies do not wield marginal influence on societies, minds, and shared popular culture. Those are very powerful instruments, both necessary to human beings' development and potentially destructive to their ethical references. The world of imagination is that of suggestion, possible transgression, humor, and satire and sometimes provocation: the arts in the West have integrated those dimensions without linking them to ethics, sometimes even in opposition to ethics, to give meaning to autonomous, free, Promethean art. The philosophical comments of Nietzsche (from his first work *The Birth of Tragedy*), Dostoevsky, Camus, or Sartre about art and literature confirm that ethical issues (and sometimes, their unconditional rejection) have long been grasped and understood in the Western conscience.[18] This artistic process (of liberation, possible transgression, and provocative play) is—when measured against the world's various societies—the exception rather than the rule in the arts and aesthetics that cultures have produced. It is because of the West's economic power and technological domination that all the other civilizations and cultural traditions are confronted with those major issues linked to the essence and "identity" of their arts, to the meaning and objectives of artistic expression, from painting and architecture to poetry, music, movies, and other art forms. Most of them were unprepared to face this domination and were not really ready to surrender.

The Islamic Universe of reference is no exception, and like some African, South American, or Asian artists—for instance, those in China or in India—it is imperative to ask ourselves about the meaning of art, the objectives invested in it, and the prospects it is offered in Muslim societies and communities the world over. There is no denying that reflection about such issues is shamefully weak and dangerously superficial. The responsibility does not rest with *fuqahâ'* alone, for one cannot but admit that Muslim writers and artists have often been the first to desert the field of this fundamental reflection. Some writers, musicians, or filmmakers reproach *fuqahâ'* for their lack of courage or creativity in the field of artistic ethics and argue that they merely imitate (*taqlîd*) early scholars by reproducing their restrictive legal rulings (*fatâwâ*). However, one cannot deny that too many artists in turn *imitate* (*taqlîd*) the dominant culture's artistic expressions without serious fundamental reflection or actual creativity. Some, who want to show an ethical preoccupation, an "Islamic intent," add a few Islamic references here and there, words in Arabic, a touch of spiritual emotion, and too hastily consider that they are contributing to the emergence of what they call "Islamic art." All this is a bit thin, oversimplified, and above all dangerous.[19]

Fundamental reflection is also necessary about the meaning of imagination in our lives, the essential role of creativity in inner balance, and also the presence of literature, music, and art in general in our daily lives. The point is to be, to tell, to express ourselves and to build up our *intimate and collective development*: all those goals involve the higher objectives of Islamic ethics as discussed here. We must revive the deep tradition that integrates the cultural element (*al-'urf*) and neglects none of its productions or of the artistic expressions that are naturally related to it. At a time when global culture imposes itself on other cultures, when tastes—fashioned by massive economic interests—seem to become dangerously standardized (not through the transcendent appeal to shared imagination but rather, mostly, through exciting our common instincts), it is imperative to think through and elicit another relationship to art in particular, and to the culture of entertainment in general. Each society has an artistic tradition that tells of its relationship to imagination, space, time, love, needs, desires, hope, and death. We should take time to revisit those horizons, to honor the writers and artists of those manifold traditions, and to try to revive, in some way or other, all the works that have, in their own style and within their cultural Universe of reference, expressed humankind's *dignity* (*al-karâma*), quest for meaning and love, self-respect, sufferings, happiness, and nobler aspirations. We must revive with depth and confidence the diversity of human imaginations that have tried to express humankind's common quest for meaning, its need to express the doubts of reason, the wounds of its heart, and the hopes of its being. The Merciful (*ar-Rahmân*) has indeed taught the Way of the Quran (*"'allama al-Qur'ân"*) but He has also given to us the power to express (*"'allamahu al-bayân"*[20]). Our daily lives constantly show us that this power springs from a deep-seated need, inherently linked to human nature. By giving us this power to express (*al-bayân*), the One grants us the means to achieve and fulfill ourselves through words, images, music, and all the other arts that enable us to convey, suggest, accompany, nurture, discover, and protect our intimate Universe, our emotions, our souls.

Faith needs art. And everywhere, in all cultures and civilizations, from the oldest to the most modern, the arts have always expressed and conveyed humankind's common aspiration to remain upstanding, to try to understand, and to tell the meaning of their lives, of their sufferings, of their loves, and of their deaths. Those works are invaluably rich and the various societies' cultural heritages must be studied from within. All that a culture produces is not always satisfactory from an artistic or ethical standpoint and it is important to adopt a critical approach that manages to be both inclusive and selective. Innumerable works produced by non-Muslim cultures and artists by no means contradict Islam's ethical goals: those varied forms of art, literature, or music must, in the name of the universality of principles, be integrated into the shared cultural and artistic heritage of societies and, more generally, of humankind.

Some contemporary artists will no doubt be horrified by such a statement, yet it must be said and repeated: there *are* higher ethical goals in art, as in any other human activity. It would be impossible here to draw up a complete list of all the higher objectives related to the arts (or that the latter might fulfill) but some preoccupations already mentioned in this discussion can be singled out. Preserving the *common good*, *dignity*, and *welfare* is, of course, essential, as is the importance of *dignity*, *creativity*, and *diversity*. In addition to celebrating those higher goals, it should be possible to discuss tensions, doubts, grief, and suffering, not to nurture them morbidly but to come to terms with them in a quest for *balance, peace, contemplation*, and *sincerity* that can never be fully achieved. The Universe of art is a Universe of questions rather than answers, and it should not be reduced to conveying only religious answers. Artistic expression precedes such answers and the accompanying norms: it seeks to reach and convey the essence of emotion and meaning, and any attempt seeking to reduce it to a strictly religious or Islamic message would naturally leave people unsatisfied. Art asks questions, faith supplies answers: it is important for faith to allow the heart a space where it can express with *freedom* and *dignity* its simple, human, painful questions, which may not always be beautiful but are never absolutely ugly. Moreover, as I said, faith needs it, for such an experience enables it to gain depth, substance, and intensity.

Those reflections have a concrete effect on the way we understand what "Islamic art" is today. In the past, speaking of "Islamic art" mainly referred to a certain taste, to inspirations, forms, specific motives, and to an often Eastern way of conveying and expressing emotions and meaning. Today, "Islamic" works and songs are mainly works whose substance is religious because the references or themes are, or have to be, "Islamic." To resist the globalization of a culture that is increasingly motivated by economic profit, shared instinctive drives, and the human interest in money, physical appearance, and sex, Muslim artists often respond with works uniformly nurtured by the same Islamic references and consequently with the same clear-cut, final answers. It is as if people no longer understood the essence of art, which, along with the quest for beauty, allows us to tell of the need simply to express feelings, doubts, our heart, everyday sorrows, the joys and tears of adolescence or of fathers and mothers, old age, solitude, hope, and so many other things. Those aspirations must be taken very seriously because they are meaningful in themselves, above and beyond the religious and philosophical quest for meaning. Islamic "art" cannot be reduced to a series of answers and religious motives expressed more or less beautifully and more or less professionally (and too often, childishly), or to a more or less elaborate reminder of principles that must be respected and norms that must not be transgressed on. Here, perhaps more than anywhere else, a renewed surge of deep *creativity* is required.

The Alternative

The conclusions of *fuqahâ'* and specialists on this issue are still very weak and, in terms of some of the arts, totally absent. Our societies have changed, global culture reaches into the living rooms of even the poorest homes the world over, and fashions have increasingly standardized, formatted, and sometimes depleted mindscapes, imaginations, and hopes. In more developed societies, rifts set in between the artistic Universes of the elite who strive to preserve traditions, a memory, a meaning, and the people who are increasingly supplied with art based on entertainment and instant enjoyment. "Popular" culture produces huge financial profit, especially through music and films that have become the "predominant arts" of our times; this does not mean that this is where the greatest creativity or originality is displayed. On the contrary, literature, painting, and more generally the so-called classical arts go through crises related to identity and meaning. People today read less, and very differently, since mass audience television became one of the main purveyors of "good books"; the so-called classical arts are torn between remaining an elite culture and taking the risk of being popularized and thereby vitiated. Those issues are indeed anything but new, but the context of globalization makes their urgency and depth stand out all the more clearly. Young people the world over speak of "music" and think of themselves through the images of world cinema, and nothing in contemporary Islamic thought seems to supply the means to provide in-depth, expert consideration about the substance and mechanisms of culture and the arts in the daily lives of women, men, and young people.

As I said, after the fundamental objectives of Islamic ethics have been determined, the world's cultures and their particular artistic productions should be considered with an open, critical, and always inclusive outlook. We should welcome and integrate as our own all the artistic works—from music and architecture to cinema, literature, and drama—that express humankind's nobility and essence in its quest for meaning, its questionings, its emotions, its sufferings, and its joys. We must certainly neither promote censorship nor restrict writers' and artists' freedom of expression, but rather call on the consciences and hearts of the women and men who encounter these works to seek dignity and high-mindedness, and expression that inspires rather than stirring up the most regressive impulses—to respect and accept questions, doubts, and sorrows and hail the artistic talent of those who try to convey them. Accordingly, it is important to work up an outline of an in-depth critical artistic education: learning the meaning of the artistic act itself, learning about art history, schools of thought, historical viewpoints, and debates helps fashion minds, nurture tastes, and offer a freedom of choice that can resist the pressure of contemporary global culture. Being intellectually—and spiritually—devoid of any notions about art history (and the questions that run through it) entails risking being subsumed by an art of mass instinct, with ready-made aspirations and answers that do not seem so dogmatic simply because the majority, in this global culture, naturally seem to share them. Important specialized work is required here, performed in the light of the aforementioned higher goals, and relying on knowledge of past and contemporary works. This requires studying classical theories, the theses of art for art's sake or functional art (such as the *Bauhaus* program as taught by Kandinsky), as well as the claims of the various schools of modern and contemporary art. It also requires learning about the meticulous work of anthropologists and ethnologists in their studies of cultural arts and artistic cultures. Culture and art cannot be ignored: women and men of faith must be given the means to understand and receive them more coherently, without betraying themselves but also without becoming artistically blind and deaf.

This means encouraging the cultural and artistic creativity of Muslims themselves. If Islam's message calls on us to understand the meaning of life and to respect people's *common good* by celebrating *life, peace, dignity, welfare, justice, equality, conscience, sincerity, contemplation, memories,* and *cultures,* then the Universe of artistic expression is opened wide to everybody's creativity. What is at stake is not to produce "Islamic" songs that only speak of such "Islamic" motives as God, the Prophet, respecting parents and norms, and similar things; it is to express through art the feelings and experiences that are part of humankind's hearts and daily lives, with talent and art. I repeat, speaking about childhood, fears, tensions, desires, love, friendship, wounds, separations, hopes, and death in an intimate, natural, universal way *is* "Islamic" and it is not necessary to add specific references linked to a Universe of norms, such as verses, *ahâdîth,* or Arabic words to give the impression that the work or product has been "Islamized." Such an attitude reveals a deep lack of self-confidence in the forms of culture and art in general. Obsessed by the fear of transgressing norms, people no longer know how to simply talk about *meaning*; they find it difficult to convey the most natural emotions and share life experiences that transcend religious belonging, although those give norms their true meaning.

What must characterize contemporary art nurtured by Islamic ethics is its capacity to speak about everything, the universal inner self, aspirations and contradictions, good and evil, quest and betrayal, with nobility, sincerity, and warmth. Art should be reconciled with the true freedom of saying everything while inviting the heart and mind to transcend the worst degradation. We must certainly not produce a "moral" art setting up an idyllic, untruthful image of reality and daily life: what is needed is "truthful" art, which dares express the realities of life, in their specificity as well as their universality, and which invites us to look things in the face, to learn to tell of ourselves sincerely while summoning us to transcend ourselves in respect, friendship, solidarity, and love. The point is not, either, to imitate the popular productions of global culture and copy their rhythms or their methods of production while "Islamizing" them. It is urgent to invest time and thought in the now central area of culture and the arts, to devise an alternative that is altogether original, appealing, and faithful to the ethical outcomes. Not all women, men, and young people in societies the world over are blindly drawn to popular mass culture, music, and movies devoid of soul and of significant creativity: everywhere, people are looking for artistic expressions that are beautiful, inventive, noble, and inspiring, and this is what must be encouraged today. What is needed is "ethical art" whose ethical dimension does not lie in being artificial and moralizing but in resisting the pressure of money, of show business, of meaningless tastes that have been preprogrammed, standardized, reduced to their crudest expression. The tendency of some contemporary artists to associate morals with *hypocrisy* leads them to associate artistic *honesty* with works that include the most vulgar and bestial expressions: everything to them is and could become possible, even emphasizing what is worst and turning the unveiled human *being* into a humiliated *object* to be shown. Reconciling art with imagination, music with spirit, literature with the inner self, painting with a spiritual quest—such are the prospects of an in-depth reflection about culture and the arts in our time. This requires more than a normative and totally inadequate debate about the limits of the lawful (*halâl*) and the unlawful (*harâm*) in music, television, and the movies. Indeed, the issue of norms must be considered but it can only be out of touch—or somehow schizophrenic—if it is not integrated into the issue of the meaning and goals of art in modern times. All interested artists, in all types of artistic expression, should be invited to share in this reflection. They should strive to give birth to professional, appealing, new, universal productions, avoiding the two dangers that seem to threaten Muslims: on the one hand, imitating popular culture while "Islamizing" products of the Americanization or Westernization of cultures, and, on the other hand, confining themselves to Islamic productions that reduce artistic and aesthetic substance to the mere repetition of appropriate affective and behavioral "norms" that ultimately only address those who are already convinced.

13

Women: Traditions and Liberation

The approach presented throughout this study involves important consequences for a variety of different fields, as we have seen. By suggesting to rebalance the sources of Islamic law and jurisprudence (*usûl al-fiqh*) and integrate all scientific competencies into debates about ethics and contemporary legal processes, it obviously upsets some preconceptions and questions certain boundaries of religious legitimacy and power. The aim, as I said, is to recapture the message's coherence but also to find a way to face the challenges of modern times while remaining faithful to principles and founding objectives.

It may well be over the women's issue that tensions, contradictions, and concerns are most frequent and complex. This involves human relationships, deep-seated representation, and relationship logic that, beyond scriptural sources themselves, have to do with age-old cultural and social heritages that remain deeply ingrained and highly sensitive. Speaking about women in any human group means interfering with the groundwork of social structures, of cultural symbolisms, of gender roles, of the position of the family unit, and of authority and power relationships. It also means speaking about human beings, their freedom, their autonomy, and their individual, spiritual, and social aspirations. Discourse about women reveals collective mind-sets, confidence and fear, the protective strength of what is said and the unsaid, and the deep-rooted foundations of social structures and their role. This is no simple matter: complex, interdependent issues are involved, and focusing on one dimension rather than another can sometimes lead to excess and distortion in both criticisms and claims. But debate is necessary.

In recent years, debate in the West, and subsequently in Muslim-majority countries, has focused on the more visible aspects of the "status of women in Islam." This is indeed an essential issue, but reducing it to a passionate, oversimplified debate about a list of "problem practices" led to evading the heart of the matter. The issue of "Muslim women" is being bandied about today as if it characterized the irreconcilable relationship between Islam and the West, the opposition between a Universe of submission and another holding the promise of freedom, with, of course, the leitmotiv of the contrast between patriarchal traditions and Western modernity said to be an increasingly feminine viewpoint. Then the list of discriminations related to dress, polygamy, violence, inheritance, and other issues is repeated again and again. Aside from the fact that the substance of the claims presented here is open to debate (while of course, the nature of the discriminations Muslim women may face today must not be understated), it seems imperative to broaden the scope of the debate and return to the sources and fundamentals of representations and discourses.

Many Muslim women and men have already started this essential work on the contents of scriptural sources, how they should be read and interpreted, and how they relate to surrounding cultures and social structures. Such studies must be carried out, although two main pitfalls must be avoided. On the one hand, one must beware of focusing too much on some sensitive issues having to do with text interpretation while neglecting a more comprehensive approach that would link texts, the social environment, and the logics that in this latter case legitimate specific readings and sometimes result in inducing false religious truisms. On the other hand, one must avoid thinking about this process of critical reconsideration only in terms of the West, no matter whether this latter is praised or rejected. Clearly, the internal debate in the light of scriptural sources must be thought through and started from within, and it cannot simply and naturally identify with, or be assimilated with categories introduced by women and feminists in Western societies.[1] It would, however, be wrong and inconsistent to reject the reflections produced by the long and intense debates and confrontations in modern societies about the issue of womanhood, of women's autonomy, their sexuality, their roles (in the family, in society, or economically and politically), as well as logics of power and processes of alienation. Starting from a divine Revelation, some questions are bound to be highly specific and must be tackled as such, but one should also study all possible interactions between early interpreters, their cultural environment, and social structures.[2] The feminine equation includes several factors and requires that certain standpoints be taken from the beginning, even before starting to discuss the nature of the research and proposed solutions. Regarding the issue of women, I think it will not be enough to rely on a few bold legal opinions— opening the way to new prospects—to further the cause of women in any fundamental way. In this field, seeking justice, ending discriminations, and promoting reform require us, as a priority, to reassess the framework and methodology that have been determined in order to understand and remain faithful to scriptural sources through history and in different sociocultural environments: later in the process, this implies integrating the latter into the reflection and understanding how male-female relations and the distribution of roles and power operate. This also means carrying such reflection to its logical extent by giving thorough consideration to the alienation situations in which women, instead of being subjects, become the objects of men's or society's representations; this includes studying the perverted logics through which some demands have backfired and caused women to move from one form of alienation to another. Many women, among them feminists, have dealt with those developments and sometimes those paradoxes, and their reflections should be read and studied.[3] They shed light on possibly converging views about sociopolitical and cultural issues and emphasize essential differences as related to oneself, to the being, to others, and consequently to freedom.

Early Readings, Early Interpreters

Initially, Quranic verses used only the masculine plural form to refer to the women and men in the new faith community. For years, "believers" (*al-mu'minûn*), and "the truthful" (*as-sâdiqûn*), either referred specifically to men or to the men and women who constituted the Prophet's first Companions. Once, a woman (or several, according to the different traditions) asked the Prophet why women were not explicitly mentioned in the revealed message. The Book—which, while revealing a universal message, also included responses to the questions asked by the Men around the Prophet—was later to mention women and men distinctly, as in the verse:

> *For Muslim men and women, for believing men and women,*
> *for devout men and women, for true men and women, for pa-*
> *tient men and women, for God-conscious men and women, for*
> *men and women who give in charity, for men and women who*
> *fast, for men and women who guard their chastity, for men*
> *and women who remember God, for them God has prepared*
> *forgiveness and a great reward.*[4]

This evolution of the message is part of divine pedagogy in the process of revelation carried out over twenty-three years:[5] the faithful are thus led to evolve in their understanding of things and critically reconsider some of their cultural or social practices. The status of women, who were sometimes killed at birth because of the shame they might bring, was to be reformed in stages, as verses were revealed. It thus appeared more and more clearly that the Quran's message and the Prophet's attitude were apt to free women from the cultural shackles of Arab tribes and clans and from the practices of the time. The Creator addresses women as being on an equal footing with men, their status as beings and believers is the same as men's, and the requirements of worship are absolutely identical. They are partners on the spiritual path, in which support and protection are needed: "*They are your garments as you are their garments.*"[6] "*Love and mercy [kindness]*"[7] are the heart's resources that make life together possible: love to combine qualities, mercy to overlook failings and weaknesses. Exile from Mecca to Medina also played a major part, as I said, in the evolution of mind-sets among Muslims: women in Medina were more evident, more involved, bolder and more assertive, and they surprised the Prophet's Meccan wife, the learned Aishah, who said: "Blessed be (what excellent women were) the *Ansâr* women, whom modesty did not prevent from seeking instruction [in religious affairs].[8] The Medina period helped sort out religious principles from Meccan Arab customs and bring about changes in women's status: the reform movement was thus started and accompanied by the Revelations, by social experiments, and, of course, by the Prophet's attitude as the example the Companions were to follow.

The different verses were therefore to be read and interpreted in the light of that movement, and early readings and interpretations of revealed texts were to be viewed in the ideal mirror of the Prophet's behavior. Accordingly, highly original interpretations regarding women, their status, and their rights appeared very early on.[9] The inner reform movement was perceived, understood, and commented on from the first centuries, during which the text sciences was established, but it remains true that early readers were mainly men who read the Revelation through the double prism of their gender and of the culture in which they necessarily lived.

The Companions and early 'ulamâ' could not but read the text in the light of their own situation, viewpoint, and context. While the Book spoke about women, their being and their heart, *fuqahâ'* set out to determine their duties and their rights according to the various functions society imparted them. Women were therefore "daughters," "sisters," "wives," or "mothers"; the legal and religious discourse about women was built on those categories. It is indeed difficult for a man, and what is more a jurist, to approach the issue of women primarily as beings in their integrity and autonomy: whatever the internal process initiated by the different revelations or historical experiences, such an approach inevitably orients and restricts the reading and interpretation of texts. Their concern was to impart a function to women, to draw up a list of rights and duties. A closer reading of the texts, however, shows that the purpose of the inner evolution just mentioned, revisiting women's status step by step, is in fact to bring the believing conscience to perceive women through their being, beyond their different social functions. This inductive movement toward the primacy of being naturally involves an effect on the issue of social status; this, however, implies allowing full scope to the interpretation process and accepting all its consequences.

Early 'ulamâ' obviously could not undertake this task. As men, they could hardly do more than determine women's functions. As actors in a given culture, they could not transcend that culture. In addition to being subject to their gender, they were necessarily also products of their culture. Yet, in the light of the higher goals we noted, of the individual's *dignity, integrity, autonomy, development, education, intelligence, welfare, health,* and *inner balance* (to mention only the most essential), one can realize that a number of rules inferentially establish an explicit status for women as beings. Their spiritual quest is recognized as part of their being and development like men's, and education is an imperative requirement: "Seeking knowledge is an obligation for every Muslim man or woman."[10] Women's recognized autonomy is outlined in their having the right to acquire property and goods and manage them as soon as they reach maturity without having to answer to anybody (neither their parents nor their husbands), as well as their keeping their own family name when they marry. On a more personal level, the recognition, as we have seen, of their right to sexual pleasure, of their choices regarding marriage, divorce,[11] contraception, and abortion establishes, both in practice and in the purposes of the Islamic message, the groundwork of elaborate discourse about women as beings, their status, their autonomy, and their legitimate aspirations, before beginning any discourse about their rights within the limits of their families and social functions.

Text scholars were remote from such considerations when they undertook the first legal deciphering. Interested in the legal framework, they mainly focused on function. They were also influenced by culture, which fashions gender relations and the conception of the natural status of women in traditional Eastern, Arab (or Persian or Asian), and patriarchal societies. Reading the early commentaries proposed by such great scholars as at-Tabarî, ar-Râzî, or al-Qurtubî clearly shows that they were indeed immersed in a specific culture and that their comments about women—their role as well as how they should be treated—stem as much, if not more, from cultural projection as from normative critical reading. This latter might, in the light of the Revelation's evolution over twenty-three years, of the Prophet's attitude and of the objectives that have been worked out, have continued to propose liberating paths for women if early interpreters had not confined themselves to formal literality, or to stipulating rights and duties only, or to accepting customs. Men, the texts' early readers and interpreters, felt no need for that, while women, who were directly affected by social realities and possible distortions of the texts, were absent from that legal elaboration. Mâlik ibn Anas and Abû Hanîfah were able to make daring comments regarding their environment, particularly in fields whose practices they knew from within such as clan relations or trade, but it was impossible for them to do the same in terms of women's issues, precisely because they were not women and they could not understand from within how the latter experienced interpersonal relations and integrated social dynamics.

Relating to Texts

Accordingly, we should indeed return to the texts and the modalities of their reading and interpretation in the light of the environments in which they were revealed. Islamic legal thinking about women is certainly the field that has suffered most from the two phenomena already mentioned: literalist *reduction* and cultural *projection*. We have seen that the Revelations, accompanied by the Prophet's example, represented a divine pedagogy that consisted, over twenty-three years and according to historical circumstances, in changing early Muslims' mind-sets and leading them to consider the issue of women differently. A study exclusively focusing on the texts, their substance, comparison, and chronology, such as that of scholar 'Abd al-Halîm Abû Shuqqah, *Tahrîr al-mar'ah fî 'asr ar-Risâlah* (*Women's liberation in the age of Revelation*),[12] shows that this is a continued process of liberation that is accounted for by the message's global vision and by the objectives (*maqâsid*) inferred from the process. Therefore, in addition to reading the texts, one should examine the cultural environment of the time and understand what these texts refer to and which issues are involved in what they say. It appears that in virtually all the fields of women's being and activity in societies, text sequences not only state injunctions but also open prospects that can only be extracted through a holistic, goal-oriented approach. Whether about the relationship to God, to faith, or to the mosque; about necessary education and autonomy, for oneself and toward others; about relating to the body, sexuality, marriage and divorce; about relating to work, money, politics, or even war, one can observe that the Quran and Prophetic traditions take highly innovative positions, which are also very open about their understanding of and dialectical involvement in social environments. The issue, then, is no longer only to know what the texts say about women, but rather to understand what was promoted, defended, and prescribed concerning women's being and power, in relation to the environment of the time. The relationship between texts and contexts must be studied, and this will enable us to extract principles and objectives. Texts do not speak by themselves, and teachings are both synchronic and diachronic: the relation to time is crucial, the relation to the context is imperative. A literalist reading cannot account for those evolution dynamics and their tense relation to time and environments. Specializing in the contents of texts alone, as is required of *fuqahâ'* as a priority, is likely to restrict both the substance of the message and its higher objectives.

Because some existing texts are sometimes read and interpreted without considering chronology and context, it becomes impossible for some *'ulamâ'* to dare express clear legal opinions in the light of higher objectives. They should, for instance, speak out on the fact that keeping women illiterate and forbidding them to work, reach financial autonomy, or play a social and economic role, as well as such practices as female genital mutilation, forced marriages, the denial of divorce, or restraint against domestic violence, are absolutely contrary to Islam's message as shown through its evolution (over twenty-three years) and the Prophet's own attitude. However, that is not all: such clear positions must be completed with studies about the different social dynamics or the management of real or figurative powers between women and men, shedding light on the complex situations in which (in the name of religion itself or of its rejection) rights can be lost, discrimination can set in, or some forms of alienation may replace others. Women are the first victims of those reductions of rights in the substance of texts, and of the obstacles that lie deep within social structures; that is why they should train in the study of texts, acquire the tools to interpret them, and complete the understanding of principles with thorough reflection about environments and the logics of discrimination or alienation.[13] Such issues as the right to work, polygamy, divorce, or inheritance cannot be approached only through the study of what the texts allow or do not allow. The approach can only be holistic and elaborated in the light of higher ends; otherwise, the very essence of the ruling (*hukm*) may be betrayed. What can be the meaning, in an environment where unlimited polygamy was the rule, of verses and Prophetic traditions that drastically restrict polygamy and add such demanding conditions that some scholars—in particular of the Hanbalî school—could claim that this requires the first wife's prior consent and that she can oppose it in her marriage contract? What is the higher objective of monogamy and of this restrictive toleration of polygamy? The full scope of the message, from texts to the context of their expression and their objectives, must be grasped as an entity. A literalist, strictly legal reading produced by men cannot, by definition, take up this challenge and meet its requirements. Women are necessary here, both to the text reading process and to the study of the social contexts in which they live.

Solid training in the social sciences can help women, together with men, carry out thorough, constructive critical work about the cultural *projections* worked out—sometimes most unwittingly—by *usûliyyûn* and *fuqahâ'* in their interpretations of the texts. What sometimes favored open and flexible interpretations related, as we have seen, to people's *common good and interest* (*al-maslahah*) may, in the case of women, have had exactly opposite consequences: when taking into account the often static customary practices of the societies for which law scholars issued rulings, and by which they naturally were often influenced, it became natural to issue restrictive, sometimes partial and biased interpretations of the texts, because of the influence of cultural context on the reading itself. The texts' higher, universal ends were then restricted by the closed prospects of cultural singularity, which drew on the latitudes offered by constant awareness of customs (*'urf*) and of the *al-maslahah* in support of its own legitimacy. The social environment can either open up or restrict the prospects of a verse or *hadîth*: one can see that in the case of women—because the issues are sensitive and necessarily linked to traditions and relations to power and authority a relations-restrictive projection almost always prevailed since existing cultural practices had to be preserved or legitimated. Access to the power of knowledge, to intellectual and financial autonomy, to the job market, and to political choice and commitment was often restricted and denied, not in the light of the texts alone, but through the decisive refraction of cultural contexts.

It is imperative here to work out a process exactly the opposite to what I mentioned in the second section. Early scholars' knowledge of their environment, that is, their confidence in taking it into account when interpreting texts, enabled them to approach the latter primarily to extract their objectives. Taking cultures and societies into account here contributed to integration, openness, and dynamism. In the case of power and authority issues and of women, the cultural posture was the exact opposite: the aim was to confirm, restrict, and legitimate established relationships and customary practices. Thus, the same dialectical relationship between text and context made for flexibility in one case and rigidity in the other. *Fuqahâ'* (both women and men) as well as anthropologists, historians, sociologists, and ethnologists (again, both women and men), must work together in an extensive process of critical studies, reinterpretations, and analyses of the societies for which and in which the texts are to be understood and implemented. In the light of the higher goals of *personal integrity*, *dignity*, *education*, *autonomy*, *development*, *freedom*, and *welfare*, we must study all that, in the past, resulted in literalist reduction and cultural projection, to regain hold of the texts' possible meaning and undertake to implement them in contemporary societies while, here again, taking into account the customs and habits, what is tacit, or the power and subjection logics that could visibly or subtly hamper the quest for the ideal of higher goals. We should not only draw up a reading grid regarding traditional cultures but also analyze all the processes that can, in modern societies, produce implicit power relations or alienating forms of logic about women's fulfillment and rights.

Goals, Discourse, and Commitment

We must imperatively protect ourselves from possible distortions and reductions of Islam's message in all fields, and as far as women are concerned. The work of inference just mentioned and for which I presented a methodology in the third section is crucially important here. The corpus of higher objectives (and the corresponding applied ethics) must be established before any circumstantial analysis of texts and environments to avoid running the risk of being misled by the letter of some texts or the cultural shackles of past or contemporary societies. Only in this way can the deductive work of implementing injunctions become meaningful: being faithful to the message without fearing to disturb social frameworks, power relationships, and the traditional roles placed on women as a result of partial under-standing of the message (or more prosaically, of the will to preserve clearly understood male interests). Reconciliation with the liberating substance of Islamic teachings requires this.

One should begin by clearly defining the fundamentals and order of discourse about women. Most commentaries, analyses, and accounts, as we have seen, focus almost exclusively on the different roles and functions of women in family and social units. No in-depth, structured, dialectical reflection puts forth about women as beings, about womanhood, about women's relationship to meaning, about their religious practice, or about how they relate to the social body as a whole. The approach through objectives that requires thinking about *being, dignity, development, freedom, equality, justice, bal-ance, love,* and *welfare* does not allow us to overlook speaking about women's being, their spirituality, autonomy, and responsibility, and the essential and social meaning of womanhood. Men, *fuqahâ',* can sometimes touch on those dimensions, but it is women who must, from within, refuse to accept that religious discourse about them should be merely legal and, in effect, curtailed, since it deals with interpersonal relations without elaborating anything about *wom-anhood.* Such curtailed, reductive discourse, once again, is danger-ous on several levels: not only is its ambition to codify, and thereby delimit women's various social functions; it also grants norms such predominant importance that it can lead to strictly ritualistic recom-mendations regarding religious practice (e.g., behavior rules, dress) and purely formal ones regarding social affairs (e.g., wives' rights and duties, mothers' family responsibilities). Therefore, the first liberation that should be worked out—and that can lead the whole community of believers the world over to evolve—consists of pro-ducing a discourse on womanhood that restores the link with mean-ing rather than single-mindedly focusing on norms. This can indeed be observed everywhere today: the spiritual awakening and revival that run through Muslim societies, and in which women are particu-larly active agents, require new discourse about the meaning of faith, worship, freedom, and social commitment. It is also true that some confuse this quest for meaning—at the heart of the global culture and with the loss of former points of reference—with a return to the most rigid traditional sources that seem to protect both meaning and norms. Resolving the complex equation of the present by referring to an idealized past model is typical of crisis situations, loss of confidence, and the need for protection against social evolutions that escape the control of those involved. This is why the discourse must rely on in-depth studies of all the dimensions of women's being in the light of the higher objectives. This means, beyond norms, raising such issues as the acquisition of *knowledge* (about texts and all the other sciences) for women; the meaning of their *dignity* and *welfare* in all that has to do with their minds, hearts, and bodies; their inalienable *autonomy* and the essence of their *freedom* in the mindscape of social representations as well as in group structures, without overlooking the question of the essence of womanhood and related factors. The initial liberation process is demanding, but it is imperative if we aim to establish a social dynamic respecting objectives and resisting the most subtle and/or paradoxical alienations.

Even before turning to the issues of social discrimination and power structures in human groups, earlier reflection about faith, spirituality, and the quest for meaning is required. This approach is often lacking in classical studies and debates, which involve almost immediately possible forms of discrimination affecting women at the heart of the collective mindscape or of social dynamics. Nothing, or very little, is said and worked about the issue of the meaning of the quest and of the encounter with a spirituality that should be a promise of liberation and autonomy. The higher objectives of ethics about the inner being require educating the *conscience*, respecting the being's *dignity,* and seeking inner *balance, love, sincerity, humility,* and *contemplation*; this is an invitation to elaborate a fundamental, feminine philosophy of *being*, of *autonomy,* and of *freedom* likely to deal with both the most rigid traditional representations and the most modern subjective projections. Suggestions must be offered for a social presence and for the involvement of women enabling them to become reconciled with their inner beings and the essence of their freedom, refusing reductions and alienations, whether in the woman as function of the past or in today's woman as sex object. A social and political feminism projecting this reflection about being, spirituality, meaning, and the goals of womanhood, in itself and in society, would be in danger of being mistaken about its essence and its possible alliances; reflection about women as subjects must be combined with fundamental reflection about women's being itself. The latter determines the essence of womanhood in its dignity, while the former grants women the means to be free. The point is not only to fight discrimination—although this struggle is imperative—but also to make society change in the light of the questions today's women ask about themselves and ask societies about the quest for meaning, their welfare, and the freedom of their being.

We need in-depth debates without formalist restrictions, for what is at stake is the meaning of practices beyond mere respect for norms. Much has been said in the West about Muslim women's dress, intended by these women as an expression of modesty and by some in modern societies as a sign of discriminatory submission. Often in reaction, Muslim institutions or scholars have been seen to offer dress as the ultimate expression of faith or as an act of resistance against Western cultural imperialism. In all cases, the debates have reduced the meaning of modesty itself in the order of means and ends. In the spiritual order, in reflection about being and freedom, understanding the meaning of modesty (whether for men or for women) cannot be limited to the issue of visible modesty in dress. This latter must be part of a much more fundamental approach integrating the meaning of spiritual, psychological, and intellectual modesty along with modesty in dress. At a time when women are too often confined to either strictly normative or mainly aesthetic representations, this reflection about the essence and meaning of modesty smacks of protest and liberation. Resistance begins in such depths.[14]

This does not prevent fundamental reflection about social questions—quite the opposite. For reasons that have to do with being, conscience, but also simply physiology, women relate quite specifically to life, commitment, children, and education. Never have our societies been in such urgent need of this feminine input in approaching some issues that are indeed broader than the "mere" question of women. Yet one of women's major contributions to their cause may well lie not merely in resisting the discriminations and alienations that directly affect them but in their specific way of approaching the social crises that involve all of us. Here again, the issue should be approached from the source, which may result in a new way of defining the priorities of social and political commitments. This means starting by refusing to enter men's political Universe by approaching politics in the same way as men do.[15] This would be nothing less than another form of alienation. This issue is highly specific and requires deep, global questioning about the cause and contribution of women in modern times.

From the point of view of *fuqahâ'*, of men and of women themselves, the priority is to get rid of social and media representations about the "West," which restrict debates to the issues of models or forms. Thus, the Western cultural model is seen to require resistance through emphasis on an "Islamic answer" essentially relying on the formalism of social roles or of dress. The answer is insufficient; it can be observed every day. Far from any formalism, then, or rather in opposition to all formalisms, commitment for the recognition of women's being and involvement must start by questioning goals and not only representations. Prior to any collective, social, or political commitment process, women must—along with men—determine the outline of a religious and humanist understanding and discourse reconciling women with their function as free, autonomous, and responsible spiritual agents. By relying on this approach, which rereads the texts in the light of higher goals, it becomes possible to think about women's presence and major contributions to the development of contemporary societies while undertaking reforms of the discriminations they continue to suffer. We must clearly refuse to accept that a woman with the same training and skills as a man should experience job discrimination or be paid only 70 percent of a man's salary, that she should be barred from responsible posts because of being a woman, that pregnancy should be considered a handicap, or that she should be compelled to submit to the male imagery that still dominates the job market. *Fuqahâ'* legal councils including women scholars, specializing in texts as well as in the study of social logistics, must speak out on those questions of rights, justice, and equality. This is part of the long-run reform of mind-sets and social dynamics; it requires determined commitment in education, social work, and the collective psychological dimension of representations. That is why the temptation to transform the cause of women into a contemporary media struggle can turn out to be dangerous and counterproductive, quite profoundly and on several levels: first, because we are at the heart of a Universe of imposed representations that must be cast aside, but also because the risk is great—and so often verified—of producing a perverse media presence of women *subjects* who have been transformed into *objects* of representation.

Religious formalism will not be able to resist the onset of global culture that disrupts morals and imposes a specific idea of women and their functions. In-depth reflection about meaning and objectives is an urgent priority in terms of women. Restrictions, deadlocks, and perversions of the message insensibly affect all Universes of reference, and the Muslim world, torn between rejection and imitation, does not at present make any major contribution to this fundamental reflection. Women should not wait passively for something to happen: they must look after themselves and develop new approaches in the light of higher objectives to protect their *being*, their *integrity*, their *femininity*, and their *rights*. They must struggle against all formalist dictatorships, both that which imposes the headscarf without belief in the practice coming from the heart and that which imagines all objectified female bodies fit into a size six dress,[16] that which compels women to stay at home for religious reasons and that which sends them back home after the age of forty-five for aesthetic reasons.

Society and Mosques

One should sometimes begin with simple, tangible, very concrete matters. However, they are not always the easiest. Muslim-majority societies and Muslim communities in the West, in Africa, or in Asia are often constituted around mosques, which in one way or another play a very important part in the group's thought and non-thought. Their role has often been minimized when addressing the issue of women: dress, family status, and social presence have been focused on—and rightly so—but this space has often been overlooked while, in effect, it concentrates and symbolizes the bulk of the problems that undermine Muslim societies today.

The mosque is a religious space expressing a certain idea of authority, the substance of a discourse, and distribution of roles. Those three aspects are essential: they have an impact on Muslims' collective psychology and they radiate attitudes and behaviors in daily life. This is nothing new, and the mosque's centrality can be observed from the beginnings of Islam. Indeed, in the Prophet's time, mosque building marked the meaning of the Muslims' presence or, even more, of their adoption of their new place of residence. Social life was quick to become organized around the mosque, as in Medina, with daily prayers, education and training circles, receiving men and women as well as visitors, supporting the poor, and related activities. From the beginning, the place's accessibility, spatial distribution, and the involvement of women and men took on specific significance: the Prophet's mosque welcomed women, their educational commitment was similar to men's, and their social role was naturally recognized, like that of Um Salamah and Fâtimah (respectively, the Prophet's wife and daughter). Today, the relationship to mosques should be placed at the heart of a global approach to assess the reforms needed and the priorities that must be respected.

Mosques today are essentially men's places, and this does not correspond to the higher objectives of Islam's message. Indeed, some Prophetic traditions (*ahâdîth*) express the idea that it is preferable for women to pray at home, but the bulk of Islam's message as well as the Prophet's practice suffice to show that the mosque's space must absolutely be open to women. In the Medina mosque, men would line up in front and women at the back, because the postures of prayer require modesty. They were together in the same place, and women could express their views.[17] In the course of history, the spaces have been separated, with sometimes different entrances to make access easier: those evolutions can be understood (they are due to culture, and to the considerable number of faithful flocking around bigger mosques) and it would be difficult to reverse the trend as far as space management is concerned (even though I think it would be a necessary step). However, what remains imperative is to allow women equal access to a place of worship that is clean, well-kept, and equipped with the sound system equal to that of the men's facility. This is not so today: not only do some mosques simply have no facilities for women, but when these are available, their state of upkeep is often shocking. The facilities are too small, not always kept up or equipped, the sound system is often poor, so that women are almost being discouraged from attending the mosque. During festival times, when the number of faithful increases, women's facilities may actually be taken over by men while women are invited to pray elsewhere or at home. In some Muslim countries or communities, women wait in the car while their husbands, brothers, or sons pray: nothing is available for them, and sometimes the time for prayer goes by and they cannot pray. This attitude speaks volumes about the underlying state of mind: this is simply not acceptable!

Not only is it difficult for women to get to mosques, their involvement in the management of mosques is rare, exceptional, and sometimes altogether unthinkable. The management councils, presidents, and members of the organizations that run places of worship are almost exclusively men, who choose its activities according to a specific vision of the roles of men, women, and children and of the mosque itself. Women must be integrated into mosque management committees in the same way as their presence is necessary in reflection and *fatâwâ* (legal rulings) councils. Those councils, much more than the imams' actual speeches, orient the activities of places of worship, impart its meaning to religious discourse, and influences (or failure to influence) the social commitments of women and men. In those mosques where women *are* involved, one can feel, more than elsewhere, greater care for teaching essentials as well as practically relating to reality: this double contribution is most needed. Women, more than men (and this is verified everywhere), encourage spiritual, meaning-oriented teaching, rather than formalistic approaches confined to rites, obligations, and prohibitions. Their presence in mosque management committees should first of all lead to reforming problems related to mosque access and poor upkeep, but then they should also be involved in organizing activities for the faithful in general, for women in particular, and for the young imperatively.

The role of imams is often stressed, and indeed it is crucial because of imams' proximity to the faithful, their knowledge of the social environment, and their fluency in the languages of non-Arabic speaking countries. It remains, however, that the most influential event in mosques and within Muslim spiritual communities occurs prior to weekly speeches; what actually gives shape to the group is the way mosque managers conceive the mosque and its role, influence, and relationships to authority. This is where women and men must work together, in equal numbers, to answer the community's spiritual and practical needs: making the mosque accessible to women, giving lessons oriented to the quest for meaning and spirituality, promoting a positive influence of the mosque over the social environment where it is situated, training the young, welcoming the poor, and establishing an open, active social presence. Numerous mosques the world over have achieved and are achieving impressive things, and those initiatives must be duly praised. It is clear, however, that women are still too often absent from those dynamics, and this

results in a state of mind that in one way or another seems to disqualify women from religion and, *a fortiori*, from positions of authority
and management. Distortions begin at just this point, and their consequences can be observed daily in mosques themselves as well as in
Muslim-majority societies. A goals-oriented approach—as described
in the previous section—would require a truly radical reform of the
practical management of mosques. This also requires women to get
involved and claim a right to play their legitimate part; whether in
the Muslim world or in the West, such involvement is very rare, and I
have met mosque officials who also complained of women's passivity
in this respect. Women, like all victims of discrimination or alienation, often come to accept, or even create, the processes that exploit
them, in mosques as in life, at work as in parenthood.

The Family

Most of the comments about women in classical works and traditional discourse focus on the crucial importance of the family in
Islam. It is therefore to protect the latter that many *fuqahâ'* repeat the
norms instituted by the texts and insist on the central role of women
in maintaining the family unit. As for the family's being fundamental
to religious teachings, there is no doubt about that: it is important
to stress the goals and framework within which its essence must be
thought out and promoted as at the heart of traditional or modern
societies. Here again, nevertheless, the issue should be considered
globally in the light of the different social environments the reflection involves. When studying the different legal productions and the
various *fatâwâ* issued by the different councils throughout Muslim-
majority countries—as well as in Western societies[18]—one can
observe an impressive discrepancy between, on the one hand, the
stress on norms and on women's roles and duties within their families, and, on the other, the present state of families with crises, tensions, divorces, violence, and so much untold suffering. If repeating
norms can provide formal reassurance, the study of actual, experienced, concrete, daily situations produces exactly the opposite effect
and cannot but be unsettling and cast doubt on the smooth, oversimplified, conventional discourse about family ideals. The crisis is deep

and the malaise is widespread among Muslim families East and West. Repeating norms, duties, and rights in a literalist manner—without considering reality—can help blind oneself but does not solve any of the problems confronting Muslim couples and families today. If, in addition, only the responsibility of women and mothers is focused on solving family problems (which some *'ulamâ'* claim have no other cause than women's carelessness and "modernization"), this is evidence that current crises have not been fully measured, and in particular natural social transformations, which require returning to scriptural sources. What is needed, ultimately, is to devise an implementation that will respect higher goals and have the concrete means to reform things for the better. Whether one lives in Africa or in Asia, in the United States or in Europe, constituting a balanced, harmonious family and being able to resist the stresses of personality and time require permanent effort; it is a struggle, a *jihâd* that cannot be won through normative injunctions but rather by relying on deep understanding of the objectives of married life, parenthood, and love.

A Prophetic tradition states that someone who marries has achieved "half the religion"[19]: this points out the importance of religion in confirming the individual's personality and faith. The *hadîth* clearly focuses on the goals of marriage, which must both fulfill a being's needs and answer the ethical requirements of religious and spiritual teachings. This cannot be reduced to the defensive, formalist discourse that is heard today about the meaning of marriage in Islam: confronted with the excesses of current permissiveness, marriage is presented as a duty, with its rules and rights which, by uniting believers, should be sufficient to guarantee a union's success. These are, here again, purely normative teachings and advice, which fail to answer the needs of the women and men who wish to start a family or avoid a break-up. Speaking of marriage certainly implies speaking of a common aspiration beyond oneself, but it also means, for oneself and self-accomplishment, tackling the issues of love, dialogue, listening, physical attraction, and sexuality as related to cultures, habits, and wider family circles. A lasting, loving marriage cannot be achieved through prescriptive religious reminders, *fatâwâ*, or lists of duties and rights. Yet, unfortunately, Islamic discourse on marriage does mainly amount to just that and men very often make use of this fact: quite often indeed, men who never pay attention to any of Islam's spiritual teachings (regarding daily or married life) insist, when crisis comes, on their Islamic rights as husbands, relying on a tradition that they know is favorable to them and that they can bend to their wishes. Such formalism, which relies on a religious and cultural tradition to justify its commands, results in a vicious circle that maintains suffering and nurtures hypocrisy. Whether in traditional societies or in the West, men remind women of their duties and do not hesitate to draw a list of their own rights to choose, decide (for the couple), or even engage in polygamy without considering women's rights and the social and religious conditions that absolutely must be respected. *Fuqahâ'* very often remain silent and sometimes even share in such hypocritical male deviations.

What must be reformed and revised is the whole approach and such teachings about marriage. Women and men—scholars, psychologists, social workers—must engage in this together, on the basis of everyday life and in the light of scriptural sources. Couples must be advised and supported by insisting on the freedom to choose one's spouse based on love which, once felt, should be nurtured, maintained, and deepened through *thoughtfulness*, *dialogue*, and the personal *fulfillment* of each of the partners. We must tackle the sensitive yet essential issues of how difficult it is to be a husband or a wife today, of the efforts that must be made: to establishing dialogue, to weathering crises, to recalling the doubts and pains that must be lived through at the heart of an experience that brings as much happiness as it requires self-questioning and sacrifice. Islam does not make marriage compulsory, and anyone can choose celibacy if this is where he or she finds proper balance and welfare, but what comes out as the most natural choice for most people remains a life of shared *love* and *fulfillment*. Nevertheless, one should remain oneself, a woman or a man, beyond being another person's partner: giving the other everything while fulfilling oneself. This is, ultimately, what the *hadîth* and its higher objective express: it is through shared life and love that individuals, both women and men, attain their personal faith, their intimacy with God, with themselves, and with their spouse. Within a couple, human beings find complete spiritual, physical, and human fulfillment and this cannot be reduced to a mere code of conduct repeating the rights and duties of the spouses and in particular of women.

Regaining awareness and understanding of higher objectives (*maqâsid*) is imperative, insofar as it restores meaning to the norms and injunctions that are repeated by scholars and in mosques without considering the state of society and societal difficulties. Times have changed, and continuing to claim that families break up because of women and "their new freedoms" is clearly failing to be aware of the deep crisis running through fatherhood in modern times. Being a father today is difficult and complicated. Such issues as presence, transmission, relating to the mother and to authority, to exemplarity, and to the process of children's acquiring autonomy raise profound questions; it is thus quite wrong and reductive to make women and their liberation responsible for this "crisis of fatherhood" and those upheavals.[20] *Fuqahâ'* and *fatâwâ* councils never deal with those issues: all is as if, to solve family problems, one had to remind the spouses of their duties and in particular stress the role of the wife, threatened by the colonization of global Western culture. The approach is oversimplified; it is above all dangerous since it cannot help us face problems and analyze them in their depth and day-to-day reality, by assessing the reforms needed today about understanding the message in the light of contemporary challenges. Muslim families suffer, as others do, from the "absent father" syndrome,[21] from lack of communication, from emotional distress, divorces, runaway children, abuse, and suicide attempts. This is what we must discuss boldly, ceasing to blame those crises on the shortcomings of women who no longer play their role and irresponsibly seek emancipation.[22]

It is surprising (but not so much really) to find *fuqahâ'* and thinkers who are so ready to promote *ijtihâd* and social and political reform literally come to a deadlock when the issue of women in Muslim-majority countries and in other Muslim communities is brought up. This seems to be forbidden territory, where not only are the texts sacred, but also are the cultural traditions and habits, which cannot be questioned. Yet the problems are deep, complex, and reveal many failings both within families and in the way *fiqh* is thought and transmitted in our time. Beyond those clear stands that must be taken—and are slowly beginning to be discussed—about the prohibition of forced marriages, domestic violence, or genital mutilation,[23] for instance, it is important to look into daily realities and decree the law coherently in the light of the message's higher objectives. Making marriage, divorce, and polygamy so easy for men (unlike women) and moreover repeating bluntly that inheritance rules are based on final, incontrovertible (*qat'iyyah*) verses maintains a state of blindness that makes it impossible to solve problems. Men increasingly take advantage of religion to justify their shortcomings and supposed privileges, while women are victims of the misuse of a religion whose essence was to liberate them. Choosing a husband, seeking divorce, refusing polygamy, studying, or working are rights granted to women in the texts themselves. It may be necessary, in different social contexts, to insist on those rights, because abuse and hypocrisy are becoming so frequent amid unacceptable, consenting silence. Goals and rules must then be repeated, and in the name of the former, one should dare suggest new solutions to the latter's implementation.

The most emblematic case is that of inheritance. In many cases, a woman may receive as much as a man, or more. In direct filiation (parents–children), however, a daughter receives half the son's share. All *fuqahâ'* have repeated that this can be explained through the goals and the Islamic philosophy of the respective responsibilities of men and women: women keep their money for themselves while men spend theirs to provide for the whole family's needs as well as their own. This sharing of wealth should therefore be understood in the light of a broader framework determining the different responsibilities and roles within the family and society; the case is logical and well supported. But what should be done when, in contemporary families and societies, this logic of solidarity no longer works, when men have (willingly or not) abdicated their financial responsibilities and women find themselves alone, sometimes without an extended family, with several dependent children? Is it enough to repeat the "final, incontrovertible norm," without paying attention to context, and thus support obvious injustice? Or should we, on the contrary, revise the implementation of the texts or suspend their application, or ask for clear compensation from the community—whether the State or local authorities—as I have been suggesting for years? Those are practical, day-to-day, precise issues that require more specific treatment—one more in touch with reality, its complexities, and the difficulties encountered by women and men in contemporary societies.

My conclusions are again the same here: a more global approach is required regarding the issue of women in the Islamic Universe of reference. Awareness of the Message's higher goals, a deeper (as well as more feminine) reading of the texts, and knowledge of the daily life and difficulties facing women, men, and families must produce a renewal in Islamic thought, avoiding both defensive, timorous formalism and a hypocritical, often unfair maintenance of the *status quo*. The field of law and jurisprudence (*fiqh*) cannot remain an exclusively male domain; neither can it be thought about independently, outside societies and their crises. This requires, at the same time, speaking about being a man in our time, about the roles of men, of fathers, and, of course, the education that must be equally given to girls and boys. Those wide platforms of critical debates, of deep, holistic approaches, of specific reflections in touch with reality, are lacking everywhere among Muslims today, whether in the East or West.

The New Female Leadership

Whether in Muslim-majority countries or in Muslim communities in the West, in Africa or in Asia, one can observe everywhere the emergence of a new feminine conscience or, more broadly speaking, of an understanding of the issues linked to the question of women. The fact itself is not new, indeed, but the process has gained in scope and speed. Women and men have taken full measure of the problems facing contemporary Muslim societies and have decided to address the issue directly, by stating first of all that there was clearly a problem in the way texts about women were approached and, consequently, in the general Islamic discourse and the concrete implementation of its teachings.[24] A reform was necessary from within, and had to begin by questioning the most traditional legal positions as well as the statements and standpoints of early scholars about women. To that end, it was necessary to begin by identifying what actually pertained to the texts and/or to the culture in which one scholar or another was immersed, and could explain this or that interpretation. This process of deconstructing *fatâwâ* at the same time required the verses and *ahâdîth* and the aforesaid legal rulings to be read in the light of the higher objectives of the global message. Women and men have engaged in this imperative undertaking: some have described it as "Islamic feminism" while others have preferred to place it within a process of "reform" or "reappropriation" of Islamic teachings against historically dated or biased masculine readings. Those latter reject the concept of "feminism," which refers to a given historical experience in the West with no equivalent in Islam. This debate is open, and it is highly interesting since it represents a struggle for women's rights, in quest both of an Islamic identity and of historical legitimacy. The issue of the movement's nomenclature and the limits of demands and reforms is a major one, for in the name of the same process of stating women's rights, deeply different approaches emerge. Some women and men have accepted and integrated the approaches, discourse, and terminologies advocated by feminists in the West and have imported them into the Islamic Universe of reference; others think of Muslim women's struggle in exceptional terms, from within, strictly through the categories of Islam's message, its goals and its legal apparatus; others still—and this is my own position—seek a balance between faithfulness to the sources and Islamic ethics on the one hand, and, on the other, integrating all the social, economic, and political analyses that may account for the dynamics of power, alienation, marginalization, or liberation.[25] All those trends are committed to the cause of women but their visions, limits, and outcomes of their demands are not identical; the debates, though still too rare, are already strained and may even sharpen and intensify. The movement, shot through by deep tensions and multiple suspicions, is nevertheless underway and the major demands that can be found throughout are restoring women their legitimate rights in the light of Islam's fundamental teachings and enabling them to reach the empowerment necessary to their personal *development, autonomy,* and *welfare.*

In this respect, the issue of access to education is essential. The levels of illiteracy among women in Muslim-majority societies are appalling, and totally unacceptable in the light of Islam's message.[26] It is all the more so when one knows that women's education more than anything else plays a regulating role in the management of families, family planning, social development, and the evolution of mind-sets in general.[27] If we add to this that when girls and women have access to schooling they usually achieve better results than boys and men (and this is true both in poor societies and in economically more advanced ones), one cannot but be shocked—and outraged—at their lagging so far behind in this field. Very encouraging evolution can nevertheless be observed the world over: women study and receive training—from Saudi Arabia to Indonesia as well as in Africa, Europe, the United States, or Turkey—and are increasingly found in universities or in the job market with higher and higher skills. Many also undertake Islamic studies, read the texts, ask questions, and seek adequate answers. Women's keenness and dynamism may indeed lead (and is already beginning to lead) to serious imbalance in Muslim societies and communities (in which men are less and less well trained or less so than women), but one must admit that a rich and interesting dynamic has set in. At a very deep level, in the slow motion of the evolution of mind-sets and societies, far away from the media (in particular the Western media that are more interested in *visibly* "Westernized" Muslim women), women are establishing a new relationship to religion: the issue matters to them, they feel they have the right to study it and ask questions, and they offer new proposals while striving to remain faithful to Islamic teachings, to the higher objectives of the Message, without agreeing to remain confined to traditional, literalist, or cultural masculine readings. Men are not absent from this process, as I have pointed out; some of them, scholars or thinkers, support it in the very name of Islamic teachings and their higher objectives.

Along with women's involvement, the priorities of the intellectual and social reform process are being revised. Leadership itself is changing; it is becoming more feminine, and one can observe new ways of approaching the problems of education, youth, marriage, or family relations. The point is less to insist on formalist norms than on the meaning and earnestness of commitments: there is clearly in the world over—both East and West—a new feminine leadership that is part of dynamics at the grassroots level but has not yet sufficiently emerged in academic and/or popular intellectual production.[28] All over the African continent, in Asia, in Europe, and in North America, one can observe the emergence of forces in society questioning the texts, their interpretations, and the nature of proposed reforms; women are increasingly present in civil society, on university campuses, and in social and political organizations. These changes are bound to become even more visible in coming years, even though it clearly appears that this movement is in need of thinking of itself in a more global, coordinated, and organized manner, of coming to terms with its plurality, and of performing its own critical self-assessment. In the long run, its efficacy will lie in its ability to set up permanent channels of communication between the different experiences and actually turn into a field of study and analysis in which women, men, *fuqahâ'*, thinkers, and the different social agents should be fully involved. This requires reconsidering the terms of the debates but also, and above all, the places and agents of their promotion: carrying out reforms within and through Islam for Muslim women implies that the latter should take responsibility for themselves and become—with men, I repeat—autonomous subjects of their history, striving to remain faithful to objectives, which entails criticizing deep-set and questionable traditions, formalism, sham, and all forms of hypocrisy. These may come from inside the Muslim world or from some Western governments who, along with their patented ideologues, are only too happy to be able to make use of a "reform of Islam" to transform it (relying on a few carefully selected Muslim women and men) into outright abdication faced with their economic domination and cultural imperialism. This means, in practice, that women should now be (more) present in *fatâwâ* councils throughout the world, both as text scholars and as experts specializing in social dynamics and daily realities. Their presence and the results of their reflection should be formalized, without compromise, in all constituted Councils throughout the world, East and West. This is a major challenge, just as the cause is a major one.

14

Ecology and Economy

The entire reflection developed in the third section of this book about the importance of the Book of the Universe, as well as the reform of law methodology I have suggested, should be enough to convince us of the importance of the Creation and of nature in the Islamic Universe of reference.[1] However, reality seems to suggest that this is not the case and that reflection about respecting the environment or about how animals should be treated is virtually nonexistent in contemporary Islamic intellectual discourse. Organizations or publications focusing on the subject can indeed be found here and there,[2] but such publications remain marginal, and seemingly more "serious" issues are being addressed "elsewhere." As a matter of fact, this phenomenon reveals the shift toward more and more generalized formalism, more and more out of touch with reality; I keep repeating that Islam teaches us to respect nature and living things, but ultimately, obsession with norms focuses our attention on technicalities (in particular, as we shall see, in regard to the treatment of animals) and not on higher goals. Muslims' silence over the great contemporary ecological issues is indeed highly significant: in effect, it deeply betrays the revealed message.[3]

Awareness that the Universe is in fact a Revelation that must be respected, read, understood, and protected should reform our minds and our attitudes toward nature, animals, and therefore also to an economy focused on economic production and the mad logic of economic growth at all costs to society. We are still very far from that and reflection about the outcomes of human activity, of levels of consumption, and of development is either absent or else remains very superficial or oversimplified: little communication has been established with the non-Muslim agents and organizations who specialized in such issues and gave us more concrete and less structural or formalistic answers. Muslim women and men, wishing to be faithful to the deepest essential teachings of Islam, should be primarily interested in the studies—and real-life experiences—which raise questions about our development and consumption models, our utilitarian relationship to nature, and our ecological carelessness. Instead of that, consciences are stifled by heaps of legal rulings, of *fatâwâ* which address formal or secondary issues (such as, for instance, the strictly lawful character of ritual slaughter techniques in the production of meat), without considering far deeper issues such as reflection over ways of life and modes of behavior and consumption.

And yet, what should we remember of those Quranic verses that speak so beautifully of the signs in the Creation? What should we understand, when reading those verses that drew tears from the Prophet, such as that over which he pondered until dawn: *"In the creation of the heavens and the earth, and the alternation of night and day, there are indeed signs for all those endowed with insight."*[4]

The Messenger's spiritual initiation began by transforming his outlook on the world, causing him to perceive signs that spoke to him and called on him to ponder, understand, and get closer to the One. He never forgot it, and when looking into his Prophetic experience we cannot but become convinced that there can be no spiritual path without the heart and mind relating more deeply to time, space, nature, and animals. The One appealed to hearts, starting by transforming believers' outlooks on the elements, then on themselves, to turn again to the Universe. This is the meaning of the verse: *"We will show them Our signs on the horizons and in themselves, until it becomes clear to them that this [Revelation] is the truth."*[5]

The Prophet of Islam continuously reminded his Companions of the importance of the signs in Nature and of respecting it totally.[6] One day, as he was passing by Sa'd ibn Abî Waqqâs, who was performing ritual ablution, the Prophet scolded him: "What is this waste, o Sa'd?" "Is there waste, even in ablution?" Sa'd asked. And the Prophet answered: "Yes, even when using the running water of a stream."[7] Water is a central element in all teachings and ritual practices since it represents the purification of body and heart, in both the physical ("real") and spiritual worlds. But the Prophet taught Sa'd and his Companions that neither water nor any element in nature should ever be considered merely as a "means" toward their spiritual edification; on the contrary, respecting them and using them moderately was already in itself a form of spiritual exercise and elevation, a "goal" in their quest for the Creator.

The Prophet's insisting on refusing to waste even "the running water of a stream" shows that he places respect for nature on the level of a primary principle, of a higher objective that must regulate behavior whatever the situation and the consequences of human action may be. This is not an ecology stemming from the foreboding of catastrophes (set off by human actions) but a source of an "ecology at the source" in which humankind's relation to nature rests on an ethical bedrock linked to understanding the deepest spiritual teachings.[8] A believer's relationship to nature can only be based on contemplation and respect. This is what led the Prophet to say: "If one of you holds a [palm] shoot in his hand when Judgment Day arrives, let him quickly plant it."[9] The believing conscience should therefore feed on this intimate relationship with nature to the very end, so that even one's last gesture should be associated with the renewal of life and its cycles.

The same teaching runs through the Prophet's life: he kept drawing his Companions' attention to the necessity of respecting all animal species. He once told them the following story: "A man was walking along a road, in very hot weather. He saw a well and went down to quench his thirst. When he climbed up again, he saw a dog panting with thirst and said to himself: 'This dog is as thirsty as I was.' He then went down the well again, filled his shoe with water and climbed up, holding it between his teeth. He gave the dog to drink and God rewarded him and forgave his sins." The Prophet was then asked: "O Prophet, are we rewarded for treating animals

well?" And the Prophet answered: "Any good towards a living crea-
ture gets its reward."[10] Through such traditions and his own example,
the Messenger pointed out that respecting animals was part of the
most essential Islamic teaching. He used all opportunities to stress
this dimension.

Numerous verses and Prophetic traditions express this: they
clearly set forth the terms of an Islamic ethics that should be spelled
out according to the higher goals of the message as a whole. We are
far from the often superficial, chaotic, if not contradictory, reflections proposed today by Muslim societies and communities, their
scholars, their thinkers and their institutions, to the notable exception of a few individuals or organizations that spend a large amount
of their energy swimming against the tide.

Ritual Slaughter

I am starting this chapter with this issue because it most significantly
reveals the current reduction, if not the betrayal, of Islam's message
and the serious confusion between means and ends. *Fuqahâ'* councils
the world over have sought to determine the lawful (*halâl*) nature of
slaughter, focusing almost exclusively on the technical modalities of
slaughtering and cutting the animals' throats. The point was (and still
is) to determine when, and in which conditions, an animal slaughtered by Muslims (or non-Muslims), with what technique or what
equipment, could (can) be considered as "*halâl.*" The debates and disagreements—beyond establishing whether the "People of the Book's"
(Jews' or Christians') meat is permissible—focus on very technical,
often highly specific details: Can the animal be stunned? How can
its being alive be determined? Must the sacrifice formula be actually
spoken, or is an audio recording sufficient? Does the slaughterer have
to be a Muslim? Those issues are indeed important and meaningful,
but in all it is as if the necessities of slaughtering and consumption
themselves were wholly overlooked.

However, the Prophet did not simply command us to respect
the ritual and say the formula "*BismiLLah, Allahu Akbar!*" ([*I begin
with*] *In the name of God, God is the greatest!*) with which animals
could be killed for food. He required animals to be treated in the best

possible way and spared needless suffering. As a man had immobilized his beast and was sharpening his knife in front of it, the Prophet intervened to say: "Do you want to make it die twice? Why didn't you sharpen your knife [away from the animal's view] before immobilizing it?"[11] Muhammad had asked everyone to do their best to master their range of skills:[12] for a man whose task was to slaughter animals, this clearly consisted of respecting the lives of the animals, their food, their dignity as living beings, and sacrificing them only for his needs, while sparing them unnecessary suffering. The formula accompanying the sacrifice was only to be understood as the ultimate formula that, in effect, attested that the animal had been treated in the light of Islamic teachings during its lifetime. This formula was certainly not sufficient to prove that those teachings were respected: an animal slaughtered correctly according to Islamic ritual but ill-treated during its lifetime therefore remained, in the light of the Islamic principles transmitted by the Messenger, an anomaly and a betrayal of the message. The Prophet had threatened: "He who kills a sparrow or any bigger animal without right will have to account for it to God on Judgment Day."[13] The Prophet thus taught that the animal's right to be respected, to be spared suffering and given the food it needed, to be well treated, was not negotiable. It was part of human beings' duties and was to be understood as one of the conditions of spiritual elevation.

When returning to the texts and Prophetic tradition and taking into account the consequences of contemporary productivist reasoning, one can perceive that a formalist, technical approach empties the spiritual message of all its substance. Being obsessed by the techniques of *halâl* and *a fortiori* saying nothing and proposing nothing about the issue of the outrageous treatment of animals in our societies marked by overconsumption and excessive productivity (in some factory-breeding farms, in slaughterhouses), as well as the ill-treatment of animals in poorer societies, all this is most illogical, astounding, and simply deranged. We remember the great Prophetic teachings, which are revered and glorified, but they have hardly any effect on the way we manage the matter of the treatment of animals on a day-to-day basis. The consumption of *halâl* food is reduced to a technicality, without any fundamental consideration for the necessities about sacrifice, according to which one should only be allowed to take life after respecting it and sparing it ill-treatment and suffering. Here, "adaptation reform" regarding the means to the end is transformed, through a major perversion, into actual betrayal: strict respect for the form of the message; obvious infidelity to its substance.

The paroxysmal contradiction in terms of this is reached during the festival of sacrifice ('*îd al-Adhâ*) which commemorates Abraham's sacrifice at the end of pilgrimage. Not only can one witness appalling scenes in terms of lack of respect for animals and their ill-treatment, but one is also shocked at the amount of waste, at both national and international levels. Indeed, progress has been made regarding the distribution of meat, in particular to people in poorer countries, but chaos still rules. Mistreating animals, wasting food—is this being faithful to the higher goals of Islam's message? Where are the *fuqahâ'* councils—integrating specialists in slaughtering techniques but also those with up-to-date knowledge of development, who can stress the goals and priorities firmly and vigorously while suggesting new approaches to those issues? Because respecting the lives of living animals is more important than the "techniques" used to slaughter them, because wasting food is unacceptable, because higher goals cannot be ignored in the name of means and productivity! For all those reasons, it is important to produce more coherent reflection and practices, and to issue circumstantial legal rulings, taking applied ethics into account in the light of the challenges of our times.

Proposing breeding techniques on a small, medium, or large scale;[14] developing new types of slaughterhouses allying respect and efficiency; issuing legal rulings (*fatâwâ*) that, in some areas, more clearly encourage monetary compensation rather than ritual sacrifice (which remains a recommended act—*sunnah*) are all initiatives that may help the Muslim world to reconcile itself with the higher objectives and meaning of its ethics rather than hiding behind insistence on norms and means that guarantee only false respect of the requirements of Islam's message. Ritual slaughter is a simple, day-to-day example, which perfectly reveals the contradictions within contemporary spiritual teachings. It emblematizes the whole problem: obsession with form regardless of substance, confusing means and ends, adoption of reform that is not suitable for transformation, and overdetermining norms while neglecting meaning: it is the heart of all contradictions.

Growth and Sustainable Development

The month of Ramadan ought to be a school enabling the Muslim conscience to return to what is essential in the message, its objectives, and the questionings necessary to grasp higher goals. For if we are to respect an *Islamic conception of life and death* and humankind's *common welfare and interest,* as well as the individual's *development, freedom, welfare,* and *solidarity* and human *brotherhood,* it is important to engage in fundamental reflection about the growth and development models offered to contemporary societies. This is indeed the very essence of fasting: for a month, believers take a break from their usual lives to return to meaning and essentials, breaking with their habits of consumption, the rhythms of everyday life, and the deep-seated ideas about competing to acquire and possess material things. Beyond the act of worship and its spiritual dimension, the fundamental teaching of this exercise consists of understanding that the way we relate to wealth and consumption (and therefore to growth) should be questioned in the light of the goals human beings set for themselves. The month of Ramadan is an awakening of conscience that must result in a quest for the *welfare* of being, of *qualitative development,* contrasting, spiritually and critically, with the quest for the welfare of having and of strictly *quantitative development.* The ethical goals of fasting, clearly stated in the texts or put together by inference, require us to question our choices in life, development, and individual and collective growth. Yet, an appalling perversion can be observed: this month, which ought to "produce meaning," has been taken over—like so many ecological and humanitarian projects—by the logic of an imperialistic economy based on growth and productivity. Rather than being a month for awareness of goals by questioning development models and consumerist ways of life, that month, and its nights in particular, turn into an increasingly neglectful fair encouraging consumption, even in poorer societies. This is deep, almost complete alienation. The point was to consume *less,* to consume *better* in terms of conscience and quality, and we end up consuming less during the day to consume without moderation and with total abandon at night. This is yet another example of formalist perversion: norm and form are maintained while the religious practice's ethical goals are lost.

What is highly surprising is the silence of *'ulamâ'* and *fuqahâ'* on such issues. So many books critical of the West denounce "Western" models of excessive consumption and self-abandon, but one can find no Islamic reflection, from within, about those fundamental issues. It is repeated again and again that Islam advocates *respect* for nature and animals, calls for respecting people's *dignity*, and promotes human *solidarity* and *brotherhood*, but one can find but very few critical studies which, in the name of higher ethical goals, question the growth and development models forced on both industrialized or poorer developing societies. Some United Nations programs, within the United Nations Development Program (UNDP), have been working in this direction since 1990, striving to develop new tools meant to measure societies' human development on the basis of welfare and quality of life (human development index) rather than calculating quantitative growth, gross national product (GNP), or gross domestic produce (GDP).[15] Economist Amartya Sen, long committed to a humane, humanistic approach of matters related to the economy, says exactly this: "Development cannot be divorced from ecological and environmental concerns. Indeed, important components of human freedoms—and crucial ingredients of our quality of life—are thoroughly dependent on the integrity of the environment."[16] If spirituality has a meaning and if ethics has a function in contemporary times, it indeed lies in questioning structures related to development projects, and to models according to human approaches. But we cannot be content with idealist discourse, completely out of touch with the world's realities, and suppose that the issue of ecology, that is, the urgent need to save the planet, is but a structural question that only requires a few ethical adjustments within the dominant economic model based on the obsession with technical and economic growth, productivity, and quantitative development. The very idea of "sustainable development" must be analyzed, criticized, or at very least questioned.

The participation of Muslim scholars and thinkers is marginal or virtually absent, while debates, standpoints, and arguments have developed considerably since the 1970s and in particular since the 1992 Rio de Janeiro summit.[17] Indeed, very noble statements are made about Islamic principles—and I have mentioned them—but in effect, Muslims' contribution to an ethical approach to development is very poor. Yet, everything in Islam's teachings and practice ought to lead to fundamental reflection about those issues, while all is as if they were wholly secondary. *'Ulamâ'* and governments in Muslim-majority societies thus seem to have accepted that dominant economic models were self-evident and that they were to be reproduced and imitated, adding a little sprinkling of Islamic points of reference and ethics without any other fundamental reflection. This is the same formalist deviation that produces normative discourse without any concrete action stemming from meaning and goals. Those are purely adaptative reforms.

In-depth reflection is required. Respect for *life, nature,* and the culture of *peace* that must be promoted and taught along with the aforementioned higher goals (*dignity, personal development, freedom, welfare, solidarity, brotherhood*) requires looking at the world as it is and proposing substantial, and not merely structural, alternatives. Stating that a balance must be found involving "economic development," "respecting the environment," and "adjusting social balances" (the triangular philosophy of sustainable development) does not take the reflection far enough. Numerous firms and multinational corporations have, sometimes with the help of international institutions, appropriated buzzwords related to the idea of "sustainable development," "human development," "sustainable growth," or "ethical growth" (integrating a few ecological and humanitarian considerations into their take-over of new markets), but their philosophy and interest prevent them from questioning the philosophy of quantitative, technical development itself, which almost naturally imposes itself everywhere and to everyone. Oil-producing countries, the governments of Muslim-majority societies, and the greatest economic agents are driven by the same craving for profit, productivity, and consumerism. Subject to this philosophy and proposing only cosmetic, marginal adjustments, sustainable development is quite simply improbable. Currently, it is mostly empty words, mere fiction. The contemporary Muslim conscience suffers from the same crisis: a lack of reflection about goals, no alternative proposal, and in effect, acceptance of development models imposed from without.

The facts are alarming. In addition to the poverty of women, children, and men and the existence of astounding illiteracy rates, societies are faced with daily ecological tragedies. Deforestation, desertification, pollution, and immoderate use of natural resources are part of the daily lives of women, men, communities, and societies who yet refer to a very demanding spiritual and ethical message. The poverty of the Islamic contribution to this debate rivals the schizophrenia and hypocrisy of behaviors and practices. Those issues should be examined in priority, and in depth, in the councils I have called for, bringing together *fuqahâ'*, thinkers, scientists, and economists. Text scholars and experts in the human, social, economic, and ecological areas should join efforts to devise local and global alternatives, by questioning not the form and structures of development models and/or the techniques of economic practices, but their essence, their substance, and their goals. The global coherence of Islamic teachings calls for this; our schizophrenic recklessness holds us back.

An Islamic Economy?

There is no "Islamic economy," just as, as I said, there is no "Islamic medicine." What *can* be found in the Islamic Universe of reference is a series of principles outlining an ethics, a general philosophy of the economy's goals, but there is no such thing as an economy that is "Islamic" by essence or through some specific disposition.[18] There is no "Islamic economy," therefore, but an "Islamic ethics" of the economy. The observation may seem trivial, obvious, simple, but its consequences are particularly important in terms of the discourse and practices of Muslim economists and economic functionaries. What has been represented, and is still being represented today, as an "Islamic economy" is in fact a set of principles and techniques (rejecting interest—*ribâ*, imposing a purifying social tax—*zakât*, risk sharing—*mushârakah*) that are applied within the classical economic system and are supposed to represent an alternative. In effect, the aim is to achieve the same results—in terms of economic stimulation, efficiency, return, and profit—while avoiding practices seen as unlawful to Islam: essentially charging any interest, but especially usury and speculation in currencies and foodstuffs. The fact that the same objectives can be reached with financial and economic techniques labeled "Islamic" is moreover considered as proof that this represents a true alternative.

This is the same formalist confusion as that I had criticized in so many other fields of endeavor. By giving the label "Islamic economy" to a set of techniques based on two or three general principles totally out of touch with the framework of ethics and the general philosophy of Islamic teachings on the subject, one manages to propose formal, technical adjustments without questioning the higher goals of economic activity. The perversion goes even deeper and is particularly dangerous: this "Islamic economy," along with its sister "Islamic finance," suggest a series of reforms of the techniques and modalities of transactions at the heart of the classical system, which they do not question in its essence, but which on the contrary they confirm both in its philosophy of productivist profitability and in its global domination. Presented in this way, the great catchphrase "an Islamic economy" is far from being an alternative. At best it is simply a "marginal option" whose function is insensibly to confirm the preeminence of the "mainstream"—that is to say, the liberal market economy. We are here at the heart of the in-depth debate I mentioned at the beginning of this book: are we speaking about an adaptation reform, which—in its undeniable movement—confirms that to which it adapts, or are we trying to undertake a transformational reform that questions existing practices and suggests other ways in the name of the higher goals of ethics? In other words, we should be less pompous and bombastic in our rhetoric and more ambitious and bolder in our fundamental reflection and our practical, concrete proposals.

The principles of ethics put forward in the third section of this book, which require us to respect the *dignity* of humankind, nature, and all living species, to protect their *welfare*, their *development*, their *diversity* as well as *fraternity*, *justice*, and *solidarity*, are among the many objectives that characterize a philosophy of economy. The prohibition of some means or techniques should be understood in the light of this general philosophy: the texts have confirmed and allowed some practices (ownership, trade) and have prohibited others (interest, speculation) in the light of the higher goals of ethics. Communities, firms, or economic functionaries should be aware of that and try to achieve those outcomes rather than simply being content with making techniques "lawful" (*halâl*) while aspiring to the same profit levels and soulless consumerism. The point is, of course, not, in the name of a spiritual disposition or idealistic ethics, to advocate an economic activity that would turn its back on efficiency and profitability (which are the natural and essential driving forces of trade) but rather to associate ethical conscience with economic action, its source and origin, to question its goals, intentions, and priorities. Legitimately seeking profit or trying to make money is one thing; accepting a global economic system blindly and madly driven by the accumulation of wealth, growth, quantitative development, privatization, and the commercial exploitation of beings, goods, and services is quite another. When a society's *welfare* and *health* are measured exclusively through its GNP or its GDP, ethics and higher goals are dangerously absent from our thinking. In economic matters, contemporary Islamic thought seems to have accepted this major contradiction since its objectives seem to be to achieve the same GNPs or GDPs, albeit reached by different means.

However, the problem lies far deeper than that: the relationship between higher goals and the means to achieve them, which together must be "lawful" (*halâl*), requires fundamental reflection about the meaning and objectives of economic activity. The dominant neoliberal economy cares little about cosmetic adjustments and so has no difficulty in integrating them into its business plan. Thus, the experiences, techniques, and terminology of Islamic finance are being studied and integrated by great international banks (HSBC, Crédit Suisse, City Bank, etc.) not because this constitutes an efficient alternative, but because the "Islamic" label opens new markets. The dominant logic of all-out profitability integrates in its dynamic all the initiatives which, by presenting themselves as alternatives or resistances to its own logic, open new and particularly profitable markets. This is a perversely vicious circle, but it is efficient: one just has to suggest labels, change the terminology, and adapt the techniques. The garb is ethical but the content (i.e., obsession with return and profit) is exactly the same: the operation is nothing more than an exercise in pure marketing techniques.

I should modestly begin by saying that there is today no "Islamic" alternative to the dominant neoliberal economic model. The Muslim world does deliver harsh criticism of the common charging of interest, of stock trading, manipulation and speculation of currency, and of injustices in international trade, its order and imposed terms; but in effect—apart from a few initiatives that remain highly marginal— the economic order forces itself on everyone. What can be found in the Islamic Universe of reference is, as I said, a set of higher goals and means that calls for fundamental reflection about the meaning and essence of economic activity today. Islam's teachings question our consciences rather than requesting us to "retool ourselves" while thinking only about the lawfulness of techniques and practices. If one is coherent and determined about the issue of economic and social justice and the global ecological challenge, this is indeed where we must begin. What is proposed here is a radical reform both of mind-sets and of the philosophical and ethical fundamentals of the economy that imposes itself on everyone today. The mad spiral that widens the increasingly indecent gap between a very small, very rich minority and an ever-growing number of poor people, which leads us to destroy the planet in the name of immoral profit for the privileged few, which presents horrific financially motivated wars as "moral"— stopping this mad spiral requires more than just formal, marginal adjustments. Indeed nobody, no government and no economist, has offered a viable alternative model, but fundamental reflections concerning the need for a radical approach in terms of the philosophy and outcomes of the dominant neo-liberal economy have grown in number and substance. The latter's unwavering advocates have come to look down most condescendingly on those "wide-eyed dreamers" who criticize the world economic order by resorting either to the older categories of "outdated, vanquished Marxism," or to "idealistic principles" that they cannot implement efficiently in the real world.[19] This last criticism is not quite unjustified; the ability to put forward a worked-out, efficient, and coherent alternative model is questionable, but it by no means reduces the legitimacy of the fundamental criticism leveled at the neoliberal economy. People may smile today at those who raise the issue of goals, but ultimately time and crises will catch up with us and we will have to face the issues of meaning: can we go on encouraging consumerist ways of life in industrialized countries, which will have serious consequences in terms of social imbalances and on the planet's health? Can we relentlessly promote economic growth without caring about the consequences of that logic on commercial and social policies, matters related to mass migration phenomena, the pauperization of whole areas of both rich and poor societies, as well as the serious ecological consequences? The dogmas of the new religion of the laissez-faire economy—or "market fundamentalism," as it is termed by one of its former advocates George Soros[20]—are undermining democratic societies, breaking up the social fabric of poor or traditional societies, and destroying nature. If we do not raise those issues out of principle, we will be compelled to do so by the imminence or the reality of the deepest crises and break-ups: global warming, rampant poverty, massive migration, wars, terrorism, and other still unknowable disasters.

Numerous philosophers and economists, in alterglobalization circles, and well beyond, have denounced the global economic order in fundamental, radical terms. They have also criticized those initiatives which, in the name of "sustainable" or "human" development, claimed to reform or humanize classical economic practices by seeking to establish a balance among economic, social, and ecological issues, while they retained the same productivist, technique-centered approach. Without actually proposing a model, they have developed thorough criticism of the capitalist economy in the name of ethics and humanist goals. This criticism remains legitimate, relevant, and necessary to any real reform in the future. What is most surprising and shocking today is the absence of any Muslim contribution to those reflections. Ethical principles and higher objectives are known and identified—even though they have never been clearly ranked and classified—but this has only led to mere rejection of the capitalist economy (with theoretical and highly generalizing overtones). Moreover, as I said, the proposed reforms about alternative "*halâl*" techniques have only confirmed the dominant model's highly materialistic objectives.

Even so, the Muslim Universe is well-equipped, in ethical and philosophical terms, to question the dominant economic order and undertake fundamental reflection about this issue. However, this requires refusing formalism and formulaic cant and tackling multidimensional and complex fundamental issues. Faithfulness to the ethical goals, as I have mentioned, requires undertaking an in-depth *transformation reform* of the dominant model and this involves a thorough, specialized study of the economy, its instruments, and the interaction among the various spheres of human activity. Committing oneself to ethics, to humankind, to ecology, to respect for nature, repeating the great principles of respect for Life and all living organisms without criticizing the fundamentals of a market economy— which is supposed to regulate itself through the balance of "freely" competing forces striving to earn more, and faster, and before others do[21]—is meaningless and amounts to wishful thinking. It is as extravagant a delusion as it would be to call for the respect of democratic rights in a country where a military curfew was enforced. Terms and objectives should therefore be redefined in the light of higher goals: redefining the essence of *welfare, freedom,* and *solidarity* in other than quantifiable, productivist terms. Taking matters even further than the mere revision of development indexes carried out by UNDP, it is important, from within, to criticize the economic concept of "development" and integrate this into broader reflection of humankind's *dignity, balance,* and *autonomy* as a being and subject. Reflection about the economy and ecology must be taken to such lengths, since higher goals call on us to give shape to a certain idea of humankind, the constraints upon it, its freedom, and its responsibilities.

This is clearly very far from simple technical adjustments that are so often presented as the "Islamic economy." If its only specificity is to guarantee the same results as the neoliberal economy with "*halâl*" means, this raises serious questions. The effects of this economy, which produces injustice, death, and the destruction of the planet, are anything but "*halâl.*" The saying goes that "the ends do not justify the means"; in the order of the "so-called Islamic economy," we should say that the lawful character of the means can never justify the foreseeable immorality of ends, objectives, or results. The formula, as well as the awareness it implies, should put an end to deceitful formalist dumb shows. What we need today are long-term, thorough, detailed studies, a global vision to be spelled out in detail, enabling local step-by-step resistance approaches to link the various sectors of social and economic activity. It is also important that *fuqahâ'* councils and Muslim economists stop working in isolation and involve non-Muslim specialists who are in the vanguard of this critical approach to the dominant economic model. This decompartmentalization is imperative and should be carried out on two levels: First, issues of fundamental applied ethics (higher goals) require concerted work about mind-sets, education, revisited traditions, assessment of the quality of life. Second, local or international real-world experiences must be shared in managing alternative projects, small self-managed businesses, ethical investments, banking cooperatives, small banks that offer microcredit, and other endeavors. Such exchanges and collaboration must of course be carried out as the same time as the fundamental reflection already mentioned above, which lies at the heart of ethical principles and shared (or debated) higher goals.

It is important to share the experiences of people in the Southern Hemisphere: development cooperatives, promotion of small businesses, trade at the local and international levels, management of microcredit institutions, and, in Muslim-majority countries, distributing *zakât* or establishing *awqâf* (sing. *waqf*, public charities) for the benefit of the society.[22] Those projects are often handled in isolation and those involved rarely share details about their successes and failures. One should however take matters further and establish actual North-South relations across cultures and religions. Universes of resistance to the dominant economic order remain divided or remain in ignorance of one another. Muslim thinkers hardly seem to have studied or integrated Western criticisms of the system produced by the West itself: it is as if, to acknowledge criticisms as relevant, one needed to ask about the faith of the woman or man who had written them. Thus, the "atheistic" critique of the capitalist economy has almost been dismissed because of its intellectual origin, without its fundamental interest and historical achievements receiving proper attention. Yet, nothing serious can be thought and achieved in terms of resisting the dominant model without resorting to a critique "from within" that works out the stages of an alternative "from within." We should integrate the system to try to free ourselves from it and not, in an arrogant or utopian manner, consider ourselves as standing apart on a margin that is or should be protected.[23]

"Halâl" Consumption?

Much has been said about the work scholars should produce about root causes, that is, about the fundamental critique of the dominant economic system. They should understand the system's complexity and define the role of the different areas that combine to strengthen it. It is probably in the area of consumption (seen as a crucial element of economic logic) that the scope and multidimensional character of this task can best be measured. Once again, we are faced with serious, far-reaching distortions of Islamic teachings in the name of formalism and obsession with norms, causing any reflection to go astray and perverting the substance of the reform. Consumption lies at the nexus formed by awareness of goals, and ethics, respect for human dignity, nature, and animals, and—even at some superficial level—understanding of how the global economy works. Consumption (food, beverages, clothing, but also housing, transportation, and entertainment) is any human activity that reveals the individual's degree of awareness, priorities, and general philosophy as to the person's relationship to being and having. Buying commodities (clothes, cosmetics, games, music), food, or beverages (rice, fruit, vegetables, coffee) that are produced by multinationals that take over traditional markets and exploit local workers, especially children, is fundamentally different from choosing to consume more ethically and pay attention to ends as well as means.

The "*halâl*" market and an economy of "Islamic" products have undergone extraordinary development in the past few years. One can observe the same deviations, which consist in trying to obtain the same results with means and commodities considered as "*halâl*" without questioning the productivist, mercantilist, materialistic points of reference and state of mind produced by such processes. Little thought has been given to the squandering of natural resources, to the exploitation of men, women, and children, to the outrageous treatment of animals. All that matters, at the end of the day, is the lawfulness of the product that is to be consumed or worn and the "Islamity" of the commercial transactions through which it is marketed. Islamizing the means in this way while legitimating an unethical capitalism interested only in end results is the most perverse expression of the counterproductive formalism that acts against the values it claims to defend. This global "Islamized" capitalism, as it can be seen on the African continent, in Arab countries, or particularly so-called emerging Asian countries as in Malaysia, or today in Dubai, results in an Islamized Americanization under a coat of very *halâl* terminology and financial techniques.

Reform, alternative ideas, and resistance are reduced to market-oriented variations on the theme of Islamized labels. Fast food is profitable, therefore Islamic, *halâl* fast-food restaurants are put into operation, from McDonald's to other famous brands. Coke dominates the soft drink market, so a line of products labeled as "Cola" emerges (Mecca Cola, Zem Zem Cola, Medina Cola) to recall the "taste" of the parent company's product while they are alleged to resist the actions of the foreign company or constitute an alternative! There is no resistance in this, no alternative thought, and indeed no originality:

marketing methods have merely been "Islamized" (although not always), as well as brands...and that is supposed to do the trick. Not only is this logic too basic, it is above all dangerous, for behind a veneer of "Islamity" it hides objectives that care little for ethics, sometimes paying little attention about the collateral damage produced by such economic processes. Just as people are satisfied with the mere technical and "Islamic" aspect of slaughtering without paying attention to the way the animals were treated in their daily lives, little thought is given to the way in which workers are exploited, in all the sectors of economic activity, to provide the new "Islamic" products (as is also shown by Fulla, the *hijâb*-clad doll, an Islamized duplicate of the Barbie doll complete with a line of accessories that, like it, is made in China). Not only are those serious aspects minimized, but in addition, the same attitude and the same logic of all-out profitability and blind productivity are maintained. Where ethical awareness and understanding goals should bring more soulfulness and reflection about the meaning and quality of life, the "Islamic" label is exploited then sullied to enable market logic to work on minds but invested with additional religious legitimacy. Ultimately, the "Islam" label, marketed freely, brings money, loads of money. We have come full circle: the capitalist system has managed to efficiently take over an ideational frame of reference that was supposed to resist it, with the collaboration of its operators and of Muslim consumers themselves.

Thus, from one end of the chain of economic operations to the other, problems are far reaching, multiple, and complex. Coherence requires the issue should first of all be approached holistically, in the light of the higher objectives pointed out earlier. This is the only way not to be deceived by technical, formalist adjustments that ultimately change nothing, or even confirm the dominant global economic system. Raising awareness among economic operatives is necessary, but it is no less imperative to educate consumers so that both the former and the latter become more fully aware of the issues involved and ask themselves about the outcomes at the heart of their commercial ventures and of their day-to-day consumption. National and international legal councils, here again including *fuqahâ'*, women, and men, and (Muslim or non-Muslim) specialists in those different disciplines, must produce thorough, comprehensive reflection about the goals of economics, of consumption, and about the use of the "*halâl*" label as applied to techniques, productions, and products (regardless of ends). Fundamental issues emerge from simple, day-to-day life choices. For instance (and in the light of the different legal opinions about the issue of meat), let us ask an interesting question: which is ethically more "Islamic," more "*halâl*"? A chicken that has been mistreated when alive, that may never have seen the light of day and that has been force-fed before being slaughtered according to Islamic norms with the ritual formula, or an animal that has been kept in a healthy environment respecting its development accord-ing to "organic food" label norms, but for which no ritual formula has been declaimed? Many *fuqahâ'*, single-mindedly focusing on technical norm implementation, would not even understand such a question's being asked, and yet, all things considered, in the light of outcomes, before God and human conscience, this question is meaningful and may rightfully be asked in the name of the refusal of too often hypocritical formalities. Ideally, of course, both aspects should be combined, but such projects remain marginal, as experi-ments in different parts of the world demonstrate. Without having to push people into such radical choices, would it not be appropriate, nevertheless, to declare—after detailed study of course—that truly "organic" products are "*halâl*" in their essence and principle, and that Muslim consumers must be invited to add, before eating, the usual and simple formula "*Bismi-LLahi ar-Rahmân ar-Rahîm*" (I begin with [In the name of] God, the Merciful, the Most Merciful) with-out further ado? We are still quite far from taking such fundamental stands, and yet the contemporary Muslim conscience needs to be awakened and redirected on such issues.

When considering all the issues mentioned in this chapter, one can ascertain that the needs are many. True commitment by '*ulamâ*', scientists, economists, and other specialists is necessary to develop an in-depth reflection. Besides, a sweeping awareness and reeduca-tion campaign should target consumers to lead them to transcend formalities and develop an ethics of consumption consistent with the aforementioned higher goals.[24] The Muslim world must under-take this radical reform and free itself from the misleading exclu-sively normative approach, which often adds injustice to hypocrisy. Everywhere symbols, techniques, and products are put forward and presented as "Islamic" while the whole economic system they stem from fails to respect any of the aforementioned ethical goals. This hypocrisy of "formal faithfulness" is as true in product development as it is in punishments under the law: the economies of oil-rich kingdoms, which are fully integrated into neoliberalism, based on speculation and the accompanying corruption and injustice, receive no specific "Islamic" or "ethical" condemnation while poor Pakistanis or Filipinos who steal are "Islamically" punished for example's sake...or for form's sake. Reforms must begin and education must absolutely be put to rights.

The Planet, Poverty, and Genetically Modified Organisms (GMOs)

The aim of this book is reform and coherence: reform in the name of coherence. One should know what one wants. If we aim to return to scriptural sources and extract higher objectives and ethical goals, we should then equip ourselves with the means to respect them across history and the diversity of societies. In a time of complex globalization where all the fields of human activity interact and have multidimensional consequences, there can be no question of having an isolated, partial, or formalist approach. Twofold action is necessary in the light of the ethical goals to which we strive to remain faithful: on the one hand, we must redefine—for our time—the outline of the Way, the vision, in terms of the *Islamic conception of life and death* (*ad-dîn*) and of the *common good and interest* of humankind (*al-maslahah*), generally but also for the different areas of human activity (the sciences, education, economy). On the other hand, more detailed specialized studies should be undertaken to get up-to-the-minute knowledge about new developments, and of their relations and actual interactions, and thus determine the most realistic and efficient way of acting on the world in the name of ethics and reform for the better. This is the profound, essential meaning of the *sharî'ah*: following the Way toward the ideal while giving ourselves the means, through study, efforts, and reforms (that are forms of *jihad*) to fulfill as best we can the sacralities of the message. The point is not to implement a few laws (often the most repressive) symbolically, but to think through actions and laws in the name of the ethical goals of the Way.

It is impossible, in present-day circumstances, to undertake reforming human realities, mind-sets, understandings, and societies without having a broad view of what the problems are and becoming intercurrently involved on several levels, with the issues being so interrelated. But when construing contemporary Islamic thought, one cannot but observe that it is strangely—albeit most significantly—absent from some contemporary essential debates, or, at least, lagging far behind developments. The reasons are always the same, I think: a very timid, defensive attitude about issues that *fuqahâ'* have poor knowledge of; the lack of a general, well-structured, fully developed vision among scholars, thinkers, and workers in various fields of expertise; and finally, the tension within the whole community, which is obsessed with maintaining the most visible and restrictive norms. This is most glaring in the matters related to the economy and ecology: an earnest, realistic ethical thought cannot approach either of them in isolation, and one must not fail to note all the necessary conclusions and all the concrete consequences that such a combined approach leads to in either field of activity.

Nature suffers because of some forms of human behavior. This is mainly due to the way of life of some societies, the richest and most industrialized, which squander natural resources, pollute the planet, deplete the ozone layer, and produce astounding amounts of greenhouse gases. This results in the effects that can be observed today, foremost among which is global warming with the accompanying outrages, for those populations who suffer at first hand from the effects of climate change or the slow progress of the desert (due to frenetic deforestation) are the poorer societies: in effect, they are twice made the victims of a global economic system that keeps them in poverty and exposes them most directly to the consequences of richer societies' way of life. The latter are still protected and in effect, the 2.6 billion people living on less than two U.S. dollars a day are the most directly affected by drought (with the loss of wooded areas) and the progress of the desert on the one hand, and by cyclones, floods, and natural disasters on the other. Moreover, forecasts announce a more than 25 percent drop in agricultural productivity for African countries (Sudan, Niger, Kenya), which are already destitute.[25] With sea levels rising and increasing threats of cyclones, the twenty-first century is shaping up to be a time of forced mass migrations, with populations compelled to flee or be displaced (the mind-numbing figure of four hundred million people in one century has been adduced). Dealing with such issues (global warming, pollution, desertification) requires developing a general ethical approach focusing as much on economy, solidarity, and overconsumption as on respecting nature and species, because all these dimensions are linked. This is what is required of the contemporary Muslim conscience: a comprehensive, earnest, far-reaching, realistic, and efficient contribution about the educational, economic, and ecological policies that would make it possible to reform the situation and better respect the dignity of Men and nature.

Faced with poverty, global warming, the destruction of natural resources, and an accelerating scale of natural disasters, we are redirected back to higher goals, and thus to our fundamental ethical references. The point here is to reform our general approach of problems, our ways of life, our modes of consumption, and our relationship to human solidarity; in other words, our fundamental education. In this sense, such catchphrases as "sustainable development" or "human development" are sometimes to the Western Universe of reference what the "halâl" or "Islamic" labels have become for Muslims: an ethical smokescreen that—badly—hides the greedy, productivist deviations or distortions of those systems into which those strategies integrate and are supposed to reform.

It would take too long to mention here, one by one, all those problems on which we should focus as a priority, but it seems most urgent to deal with the issue of global warming whose consequences can already be observed in climatic change and the nature of recent natural disasters. Mind-sets must be made to change by developing a popular awareness and a spiritual and secular education integrating those issues. Day-to-day behavior, the use of water, electricity, cars—and all that has to do with consumption in general—are daily habits to which we must restore meaning and gravity in our relationship with applied ethics and respect for the planet. Islamic reflections, productions, and guidelines about those issues are very scanty and the handful of experts specialized in those fields are often out of touch with the populations of Muslim societies or communities. It is as if this were not actually part of Islam's fundamental teaching. Internationally, the same lack of commitment can be observed, and *fuqahâ'*, scientists, and governments in Muslim-majority societies are by no means a constructive, innovative force in debates about ecology and climate.

Their absence is most telling. Debates over issues related to climate change started more than twenty years ago and led to international agreements such as the United Nations Framework Convention on Climate Change (which became effective in March 1994) or the Kyoto Protocol (which became effective in February 2005 and is notorious because the government of the country that causes the most elevated levels of pollution, the United States, failed to ratify it). Yet, there are very few serious, thorough studies providing suggestions or establishing principles and a framework to approach such issues in the light of the higher goals of Islamic ethics.

The same can be said about the struggle against poverty and national and international programs involving solidarity. I keep repeating that Islam has integrated the dimension of respect for the poor and solidarity into religious practice through *zakât* (purifying social tax) or the institution of *awqâf* (sing. *waqf*, endowment, a donation turned into a public commodity or charity). This can only be true if paying, collecting, and distributing *zakât* and establishing *awqâf* are organized taking into account a global strategy that integrates ethical requirements into economic practice and thinks through those stages through which the poor can become autonomous (instead of remaining dependent on handouts). Such reflection that must incorporate local, national, and international dimensions remains very sketchy among *fuqahâ'* and legal councils. Principles, norms, and antiquated practices are endlessly repeated without being integrated into a global strategy of popular reeducation, struggle against poverty, or even the decree of new economic policies for the people in countries in the Southern Hemisphere. As I said, the higher objectives of Islamic ethics require fundamental reflection about the characteristics of economic activity, as well as the principle of welfare and human solidarity. It is definitely not just a matter of compensating through charity what the system maintains through injustice. Islamic teachings tell us that the poor have rights which they must be given without going through the humiliation of begging for them.[26] This is expressed in the Quranic verse that mentions the "right of the poor" to the wealth of the rich, educated, and cossetted by the believing conscience: *"In their wealth there is a right [a stipulated share] for the beggar and the deprived."*[27] In the light of general ethical principles and on the basis of the spiritual and humanist teachings linked to available means (refusal of interest and speculation, *waqf, zakât*), it is imperative to propose a critical approach to the neoliberal economy, the management and redistribution of wealth, and the way the issue of world poverty is addressed. Adjustments and reforms can only be structural; the very fundamentals of the system must be thought through and reconsidered.

The same greedy motivations, mainly prompted by profits and increased productivity, have enabled scientific research to produce new hybridized plant and vegetable species. Genetic engineering (GMOs, or genetically modified organisms) has made it possible to increase productivity with plants whose genetic material has been altered to make them more robust, more resistant to pests or herbicides. If traditional agriculture were sufficiently protected and if crops were more fairly distributed, there would be enough food for all humankind. However, this would entail reconsidering both our economic practices and our ways of life in richer countries and this has not been on the agenda. The most efficient way to avoid recognizing our selfishness and injustice, to keep producing more and increasing greatly the profit margins of production of foodstuffs by major international agribusinesses, is to require scientists to transform nature and its species, and to tamper with their genes and alter them at will, because we refuse to alter our blind, greedy policies. The logic of revered profit and growth is always the same, unfortunately. GMOs therefore flood markets while most people stand idle, as is the case in North and South America, in Asia (China, India), and slowly but increasingly, in Europe and in a few African countries (mainly Egypt and South Africa).[28] Europe has shown the greatest resistance to the use of GMOs, with movements and organizations that oppose manipulations whose consequences have not yet been construed and that would like the "precautionary principle" to be applied. The phenomenon of GMOs is a recent one and has gone into rapid, exponentially growing exploitation without anyone's taking the time to ascertain its possible consequences on nature and biodiversity and of course, in the long run, on human health. The fact that emerging countries like China or India naturally integrated those products in the wake of their economic expansion speaks volumes about the imperatives and requirements of competitiveness imposed by the exigencies of the "free" market and laissez-faire capitalism. The economy has its reasons that reasonable precaution does not know. Poorer countries have and will have no choice: ultimately, they will have to grow and consume what is forced on them to live and survive. Without sci-entific means to check the reliability of research, without financial resources to resist imposed economic policies and products, they will soon fall into line and will do so even more in the future.

Have the contemporary Muslim conscience in general and *fuqahâ'*, scientists and experts councils in particular, so much as looked into these issues? Have they raised awareness among women and men about ethical consumption choices? Have they taken a clear legal stand about those genetic manipulations whose motivations are not always as noble as they may seem and whose risks remain a legiti-mate preoccupation? Many *'ulamâ'* and thinkers answer that they have far more urgent concerns than those, and that Muslim-majority societies are faced with such curses as illiteracy, poverty, corruption, and so many other difficulties that, after all, the economy, GMOs, and the quality and quantity of consumption remain secondary issues. One can hear and understand such arguments, yet their logistics and their conclusions remain highly debatable. First of all, as I said, these problems are now interrelated and the ethical approach requires comprehensive reflection. Second, it is not true that all Muslim-majority societies are poor, yet even in oil-rich kingdoms or Mus-lim communities in the West, such reflection is absent or unfocused, and the same reflexes of ritualistic and ethical formalism have set in everywhere. Finally, one cannot but notice the isolation of Muslim thought in which publishing continues to focus on higher goals and Islamic ethics with no effect on believers' practical, day-to-day lives. Whenever they can, Muslims consume with the same frenzy as others, obey the same requirements of the dominant economy, take an equal share in polluting the planet, in deforestation, in mistreating animals, and in creating nonrecyclable waste. Where is the "ethical distinc-tion" that constitutes the essence of Islam's message, the fundamen-tal notion that everyone must be "a witness" in her or his being and actions? Who fashions and teaches the knowledge of higher goals that requires each conscience, in its life and daily consumption, to resist economic, productivist, and consumerist deviations?

If Islam and Muslims can provide a meaningful contribution today, it lies in questioning the goals of life and in the requirement of improving its quality. In all cases one should get rid of blind imita-tion: the imitation of past scholars (*taqlîd*) that makes us believe that we can avoid facing today's challenges by taking refuge in the past;

and the imitation of the dominant economic model and ways of life that delude us into believing that we may be saved by melting into the dominant positions and fashions of the present. Those are the essential teachings that we must become reconciled with, and that we must call on *fuqahâ'* and scientists to put into practical use in our individual and collective daily lives. This is what the reform, renewal, and contribution of the Muslim world requires, unless one is deluded by words, catchphrases, and formulas about the "*halâl*" or "Islamic" character of this or that practice or technique while, willingly or not, remaining blind to the betrayal of sacralities. To criticize knowledge cut off from its sources, Rabelais used the apt expression: "Science without conscience is but the ruin of the soul." In our present Islamic Universe of reference, which is muddled with often misleading normative formalities, one should recall that the morality of means is never sufficient guarantee of the ethicality of ends. That is indeed why the human conscience must never stop questioning means and ends and adding *soul* to knowledge, science, and economy. Only through this effort can we eradicate poverty and preserve the planet's future: that is what being stewards on earth (*khulafâ' fî-l ard*) requires.

15

Society, Education, and Power

It is certainly in consideration of the issues about the vision of society and of the directions of education and political management that my reflections ought to start the broadest and most intense debates and thereby lead to the most important consequences. Calling for the reconsideration of the sources of Islamic law and jurisprudence (*fiqh*), for an imperative rebalancing in which the Universe, history, and human societies would become sources of *fiqh* in their own right, and for a shift in the center of gravity of authority in Islam, can only have serious, far-reaching consequences on thought and on social, educational, and political commitments. This reassessment, this radical reform of Islamic thought and of Muslims' commitment in the contemporary world, are absolutely necessary conditions for renewal and for reconciling Muslims with the ethical goals and higher objectives of the Way (*ash-sharî'ah*).

When reading those works produced by contemporary *'ulamâ'* and Muslim thinkers, when visiting Muslim-majority societies and communities the world over, one cannot but observe a state of deep, general crisis. Reflection struggles to renew itself, visions for society are partial and fragmented, and the challenges presented by the

West's economic and cultural domination seem insurmountable. The breakdown of political institutions appears irreversible and civil society seems paralyzed: the former categories of Islamic thought are no longer sufficient and everywhere one can feel that we are reaching the end of a cycle that may, one hopes, foretell a renewal, a new way to reform. I am far from having the answers to all those questions, but it seems that to formulate the latter, the contemporary Muslim conscience must (while reconsidering the sources and fundamentals of its inspiration) think of new approaches, new methodologies, and perhaps critically reassess some postulates and rhetoric, as to both the elaboration of its thought and the management of its affairs.

My effort here is therefore, humbly, a step toward transition: the aim is, at the end of a cycle composed of intense crises, questionings, and failures, to equip ourselves with the intellectual and methodological means to think and achieve necessary reform. This does not at all mean cutting ourselves off from scriptural sources and the long and rich spiritual, legal, and philosophical tradition in Islam's history—quite the contrary. What is attempted here is, on the one hand, to work toward *reconciliation* with the general message and its higher intentions and on the other, to think about its *coherence* in a globalized world that has increasingly complex and interdependent societies. It is to put the Islamic tradition in motion and build bridges between the revealed Book and the Book of the Universe, between text and context scholars, between the Islamic Universe of reference and other religions or civilizations, between women and men, between the agents of change in both East and West. It is to prepare favorable ground, with determination, faithfulness, and openness, but without oversimplification or naivete.

To this end, one must begin with the critical study of deep-set truths and commonly accepted formulas, particularly regarding the relationship between religion and politics and, more generally, between the private and public spheres. Issues such as education, civil societies, and the management of the different religious and political powers must also be addressed. Such issues as democracy, citizenship, implementation of the law, and elections lie at the heart of the in-depth debates that must be started, or rather restarted, in Muslim-majority societies but also among all Muslims who are faced with the challenges of modernity and globalization.

I have said over and again that to be serious and efficient and have a real impact on visions, practices, and strategies in the field, such reflections and debates must be carried out in a more open manner. *Fuqahâ'*, theoreticians, politicians, thinkers, and experts in the social sciences must meet, exchange their experiences and ideas, then further the discussion and come up with new suggestions. This is what we have the right to expect, not only from Muslim elites but also from the various agents in civil society. If shifting the center of gravity of authority has any meaning in the Islamic Universe of reference, it is precisely because it is necessary to enable ordinary women and men, members of the spiritual community, to feel more concerned about it and to become involved as forces for questioning and proposing a quest for solutions. The Islamic world suffers from those failings: Muslim-majority societies and communities that are essentially driven by emotional reactivity may follow certain recognized and/or charismatic scholars or leaders, but they become totally incapable of producing critical, constructive, and/or dissenting collective thought, as autonomously elaborated from the grassroots. Leaders may be individuals, women, men, by hundreds or thousands; there is no lack of them among Muslims. What is deeply lacking, however, is *leadership*,[1] a vision nurtured by a collective aspiration and very concretely expressed through a common movement in which all those involved take part intellectually and practically, transversally, and from the grassroots to the top.

Religion and Politics

The ready-made formulas stemming from the two Universes of reference are well known: in the West, it is suggested that religion has nothing to do with politics, while some Muslim *'ulamâ'* and thinkers claim that Islam makes no distinction between religion and politics. Those two propositions are clear and simple, but they are both reductive and misleading through their very oversimplification and apparent clarity. There is no religion or spirituality whatsoever that is not in one way or another related to politics, to a conception of politics, or to more or less elaborate discourse about the issue. Similarly, there is no political system or practice, even in the most secularized and ideologically atheistic, agnostic, or nonbelieving societies, that is completely cut off from religious points of reference, even if the latter are only represented in the society's cultural background—France is culturally Roman Catholic just as China is nurtured by Confucianism—and political systems and politicians cannot neglect or ignore those dimensions. The relationships between politics and religion are even more palpable in most of the world's other societies, East and West, and they bear the influences of respective national histories.

What matters here is not to know whether religion has anything to do with politics—since they are always related—but rather to know what type of relation should be considered and encouraged. The central issue is that of authority and what is meant by the separation of church and state. Some Muslims avoid the question by stating that in Islam, there is no church, so that it is impossible to separate the state from another entity that does not itself exist. This amounts, intentionally or not, to diverting the meaning of the proposition: the point is not to know whether there is in Islam an institutional body managing religious affairs (as the Roman Catholic church does), but to question the source, management, and legitimacy of authority and power. In other words, is there a locus where authority is legitimated from above (through a Revelation or a religious institution) and imposes its dogmas and decisions, as opposed to another place where power is subject to pluralistic management and open to negotiation among the group members, and where legitimacy comes from institutions involving procedures consultation? What matters here is to ascertain whether religious dogma is indeed separated from political thought or whether, on the contrary, the former bluntly and authoritatively imposes itself on the exercise of the latter. Hence, the relationship that was gradually established between dogma and reason, between religious authority and political power, must be studied in its complexity and historical background. The issue is not simple and the answers are many, often singular, and always fashioned by the different national or continental historical experiences.

Those are the terms in which the debate must be stated, for the point is truly to distinguish between two powers, two orders of authority, and hence, two intellectual attitudes: that which, in its relationship to the divine, submits to revealed truths in the name of the heart, and that which, in the name of its autonomy and freedom, claims its rights and its share in the community's decisions. The confusion of orders occurs when the mind longing for divine truths turns into a dogmatic mind and wishes to impose its truths on the political and social community. What endangers political pluralism is indeed, on the one hand, the imposition of a religious power whose legitimacy is seen as transcendent, and on the other, emergence of a dogmatic mind deaf to other people's beliefs. The nature of this "dogmatic mind" is not only religious, however: recent history abounds in such distortions of atheistic, agnostic, or secular ideologies that virtually turn into religious references, with their undisputed order, their dogmas, and even their "priests," "rabbis," or "imams." Closed, dogmatic thinking is not absent from the minds of some self-proclaimed "rationalist" thinkers both right and left, or some advocates of French or Turkish forms of secularism (to mention only the most striking examples) changed into outright religions with their undisputable truths, their sacred spaces, and their polarized discourse distinguishing the elect from the reprobate. Reflection about the relationship between politics and religion requires us to take the study of the subtlety of those relations very far, up to their possible perversion.[2]

Contemporary legal councils, including *fuqahâ'*, thinkers, politicians, and political scientists, must definitely look into this issue and put forward approaches that are faithful to scriptural sources but above all are in touch with contemporary challenges. It is important first of all to return to the sources and undertake a true clearing of the terminological ground, moving beyond rhetoric ("In Islam, there is no distinction between religion and politics") and simplistic oppositions ("Unlike the West, Islam opposes the separation of religion and politics") that are so quickly formulated both by some Muslim thinkers and by Orientalists fond of distinctions and oppositions. Such concepts as "*ash-sharî'ah*" (the Way or the Law, according to interpretations), "*al-'aqîdah*" (creed), "*al-'ibâdât*" (worship), "*al-mu'âmalât*" (social affairs), and "*al-maqâsid*" (objectives) must not only be defined but revisited in the light of the legal tradition and integrated into a general methodology that enables us to take up the challenges of our time. Unfortunately, this task has not been performed and one keeps hearing rhetoric whose relevance ought to be examined. Thus, it is quite wrong to claim that Islam makes no distinction between the field of religion and that of politics: from the outset of legal reflection (which was the first science applied by scholars), *'ulamâ'* have established a clear difference in methodology between separate spheres.

The orders of creed and worship (al-'aqîdah and al-'îbadât) are subjected to the sole and ultimate authority of the revealed texts. Here,
one bends to what the Revelation and Prophetic traditions transmit:
all believers are called on to say, with faith in their hearts and consenting minds, *"We have heard and we have obeyed."*[3] In Christian
terminology—although the perspective is not similar and the comparison remains relative—we are in the order of "dogma" in the sense
of truth imposing itself on reason. The methodology is the exact
opposite of that found in the sphere of social affairs (al-mu'âmalât),
where the whole range of possibilities is open, up to the limits of what
is definitely prohibited by the texts or scholarly consensus. In this latter field, only broad guidelines and general principles direct people's
intelligence (some precise rules are stated, but they are always linked
to conditions that in turn should be taken in the light of fundamental
principles and higher goals). Hence, the door is wide open for human
intelligence, its creativity, and quest for solutions in the light of the
principles stated: it is this freedom offered to human intelligence that
has enabled Islamic civilization to produce so much scientific and
philosophical knowledge in the course of history.[4] One can therefore
understand that if scriptural sources determine the ethical coherence
of the whole range of human action by fixing objectives and higher
goals, they do not standardize the spheres of this action under the
authority of a single institution or of closed dogmas.

Such reflections are not new; they are indeed as old as the
Islamic legal tradition itself. All early works of *fiqh* clearly distinguish the chapters dealing with *'ibadât* and those dealing with
mu'âmalât, because their essence and the methodologies applied
in them are differ. Muslim theoreticians, contemporary *fuqahâ'*,
as well as legal councils, have not fully developed their reflections
about the concrete consequences of such distinctions on present-
day management of political issues. Since colonization ended, the
need to oppose political, economic, and cultural imperialism has
been such an obsession that it seemed imperative—as can be ret-
roactively understood—to insist on Islam's fundamental otherness
that could not bend to the secularization that was being forced on
it. Through the colonial experience, imposed secularization meant
rejection of the Islamic reference, "de-Islamization" of the masses,
and mostly, after independence occurred, the takeover of power by
dictators and tyrants, never by democrats.[5] The Western equation

secularization = freedom = religious pluralism = democracy has no equivalent in Muslim-majority societies where, through the historical experiences of the past century, the equation has tended to associate other representations that would rather sound like: *secularization = colonialism = de-Islamization = dictatorship*. The need to oppose Western imperialism and its efforts to impose on society development models has been such that Muslim thought has settled into a role of rejection and denial based on otherness, having lost the ability to reconcile this with its own points of reference and develop a vision from within, relying on its own richness and assets. Compelled to oppose others, it has ended up ceasing to be true to itself.

As to the central issue of the relationship between religion and politics, reform therefore requires from the contemporary Muslim conscience a far-reaching process of self-reconciliation. We should return to the sources and carry the reflection about the higher goals of ethics to its logical extent. Although Islamic teachings do indeed show general consistency about higher objectives and ethical goals in all fields of human action, they nevertheless require orders to be clearly characterized and methodologies to be kept separate. There is definitely an area of faith and rituals where the principles and models of practice are imposed on human reason, and there is also a vast field of human action open to intelligence, to creativity, and to the diversity of social, political and economic organization models in different societies, cultures, and histories. At the same time, Islamic teachings never separate the ethical reference from the whole range of human action—whatever the field—but within it, they distinguish, from the outset, the strict modalities of religious practice from the rational and open modalities of social, political, cultural, and economic activity. Respect for higher goals and ethics must therefore be instituted in all fields: ethics in politics, ethics in economy, ethics in communication, ethics in citizenship, among other areas. But this is never to be confused with a dogmatic approach that tells its divine truth and imposes it without consultation.

Thus, Islam establishes a clear distinction between the field of dogma that imposes itself and that of rationality that intervenes, between religion and politics as those two entities are defined in the Western Universe. Legal councils should begin by elaborating more thorough reflections of those realities in the light of contemporary challenges. What Islamic teachings resist lies on a wholly different level: it is not the distinction between religion and politics, between dogma and rationality, between imposed and negotiated authority, but rather—in the name of the final separation of orders—the disappearance of ethical references from the fields of politics, rationality, and negotiated authority. It is at this depth in the debate that real issues lie, beyond the ideals and rhetoric that the caricatured and artificial "civilizations" of the West and Islam throw at each other. These are, ultimately, the old beliefs of Machiavelli (died 1527) as to politics and Rabelais (died 1553) about science: does not everything become possible when one separates morals from politics and conscience from science? How indeed can one effectively separate religion (and its morals) from political and scientific action while avoiding any mad rupture of politics and moral certainties? Do not contemporary times insistently beg this question? What is the deep, critical contribution—aside from any formalist staging of Muslims— to this debate today?

Public Sphere, Private Sphere, and Rights

The reflection I have started here should have consequences on two different but complementary levels. Reconsidering and rebalancing the sources of law will result in shifting the center of gravity of authority in Islam, and this of course is directly related to the issue of power and its management within that community. Bringing to light all the higher objectives of Islam's general message, with the categories of its ethical principles, should also lead to in-depth reflection about the relationship between ethics and social organization, religious references, and social visions and, more generally, the role of civil society. We must begin with this latter dimension to take the step-by-step reflection from the social to the legislative fields and eventually turn to political power itself. Once again, the present reflections are inferred based on fundamental reforms that I think are imperative, and which I have mentioned in the first three sections of this book: those reflections must be taken further and deeper in those new places for consultation and research we have called for, where the expertise and experience of *fuqahâ'*, thinkers, and agents of a civil society will be brought together, consulted, and put to sound use to produce new, dynamic thought able to meet today's challenges.

Some intellectuals and thinkers, influenced by debates over "civilizations" (their possible confrontation or their hopeful alliance) find themselves compelled to overemphasize the distinctive features of what is supposed to represent the specificities of their own civilization or culture. One of the most recurrent themes in debates within Western, liberal, and democratic societies is the distinction made between the private and public spheres. Indeed, this is quite appropriately presented as the continuation of the reflection about the relationships between religion and politics and processes of secularization in general. At the heart of Western societies, which are going through true identity crises (because they must face the presence of new religions and cultures and massive, continued immigration that is nonetheless necessary for them to survive), sociologists are compelled to assess achievements and reaffirm founding principles, if not completely rethink religious and cultural pluralism. Those reflections feed contemporary debates[6] within but also between the Anglo-Saxon and French schools of thought, in particular with the contributions of John Rawls, Charles Taylor, Will Kymlicka, Tariq Modood, Jean Baubérot, Régis Debray, Olivier Roy, among so many others.[7] For some, like Rawls, pluralism can only exist by stressing the need for public space to be neutral—seeing this as the achievement of secularization and liberal democracies—while others insist that no public space can be totally neutral (as Modood thinks). The gist of those debates about pluralism, multiculturalism, and the common principles founding our modern societies is interesting and relevant to all human communities in the globalized world, including Muslim-majority societies. Nevertheless, global factors (relations between civilizations, mass migrations) influence these debates, as do national considerations (cultural identity, majority vs. minority relationships, power relations) that lead some thinkers and sociologists to take surprising positions, some of which verge on caricature.

As noted earlier, no public sphere can be wholly neutral culturally or religiously. Each nation has a history, a tradition, a collective psychology that naturally imposes a specific cultural shading to the given nation's public sphere. Eastern Christians living in Muslim-majority societies are influenced by what the Islamic reference has infused into the common culture. The same is true for French Muslims and Roman Catholicism, for American Muslims and Protestantism, and for British Muslims and the Anglican tradition. The cultural features of India and Hinduism, or of Indonesia or Malaysia and Islam, fashion the language and symbolism common to members of those societies. This phenomenon is natural and certainly inevitable, and it has never been seen as standing in the way of religious and cultural pluralism. The heated debates that are arising about the neutrality of public space in terms of religion and culture are oversimplified and misleading, because such mythical neutrality simply does not exist, and in fact obfuscates another real issue that is thus avoided, which is *equal* rights (and in a way, shared power). The same applies to Muslims' repeated statements about the pluralism said to have been accepted by Islamic civilization throughout its history: from medieval Andalusia in what is now Spain to the Ottoman experience under Süleyman the Magnificent (died 1566), cultural diversity and the peaceful coexistence of religions are presented as evidence in itself of the power of Islam's teachings. It is true that one can only admire and respect the social organization and open use of religious references that allowed such tolerance toward religious and cultural minorities. But when speaking in this way of this pluralism as inscribed in history (sometimes to answer questions produced by another contemporary debate about multiculturalism), the heart of the matter is also avoided—acceptance of cultural and religious diversity does not at all guarantee equality in rights—although this higher objective ought to be foremost in motivating our reflections. Thus, in the West or in the East, social and political issues are either *dis*placed to the religious and/or cultural fields, or *re*placed within a history that fails to provide clarity about the modalities of social organization and of rights protection.

Such questions should first of all be stated in terms of rights and laws, then only afterward in terms of power. Thus, it is imperative, in the West, to make a radical turnabout and produce "postintegration"[8] thought and discourse that do not equate socioeconomic issues with problems of uneasy or failed religious or cultural integration. The involved citizens and their children have long been culturally and religiously "integrated" and are faced with structural, institutional, or occasionally socioeconomic and racist discrimination that must be analyzed for what they are. We should refuse to accept cultural projections based on issues that are not cultural. Moreover, contemporary Muslim thought must approach those issues in the light of the higher objectives inferred from the texts, contexts, and history. We must be faithful and remain consistent. What in effect, in contemporary societies and apart from confused digressive discourse about religious and cultural pluralism, does the respect of *dignity, welfare, freedom, equality,* and *justice* mean for individuals within a given society (and between interacting societies on the international level)? Those are the higher objectives of the Way (*maqâsid ash-sharî'ah*) and it is in their light and in their respect that visions of society and the institution of common laws must be considered. This must begin with thorough reflection from within about the meaning and outline of a contemporary implementation of *sharî'ah* understood in terms of norms aiming to fulfill the higher goals of the global message. The issue is complex and the challenge is a major one.

Concretely, this means thinking through the common legislation of societies with permanent concern for protecting the *dignity* of people, their *beliefs* (with all this entails as to private and public needs and the specific needs of faith communities), but also the exercise of their practices and the expression of their ethics within the public sphere. Indeed, the essence of the objectives of *welfare* and *freedom* is to allow women and men to reach fulfillment and this means allowing them, in their public involvement, to remain faithful to their personal beliefs and values. Whether one is an atheist, agnostic, or a believer, this is what everyone wishes and calls for. A public space aiming to be so neutral as to forbid its members' free quest for coherence would soon become oppressive and inevitably discriminatory since it would necessarily allow its majority to enjoy such expression. But this is only one of the dimensions of the reflection: it is also important to undertake a critical analysis of all that, in social logistics, collective symbolisms, and institutional management, can hinder access to *justice* and *equality.* Fundamental reflection—far more sophisticated than the formulas of the Islamic ideal and of good human intentions—should be developed about racism and its structural dimension (which sometimes systematically targets religious affiliations): institutionalized or tacit discrimination against the poor, women, immigrants, or foreigners. In the Muslim world as in the West, discussions about cultural and religious pluralism that fail to address the real issues of rights, discrimination, and the relationship between power and domination are but delusions, mere smokescreens.

Because the higher objectives of the Way are very demanding about such issues, contemporary Islamic thought should be the first to put forward its views of such matters. But here again, absence and silence lurk behind discourse, recalling the ideal objectives expressed by scriptural sources or the greatness of Islam's universalistic past. One should be critical, self-critical, and innovative, in the very name of faithfulness to higher objectives. In our time, there can be no question of using terminology without questioning its substance in the light of past or present context. Whether in the structures of nation-states or in their possible disintegration into bigger systems (or, on the contrary, faced with increasingly restrictive identity claims motivated by the fear the effects of globalization), it is important to define clearly the status of the members of structured communities, and to recognize and guarantee all their aforementioned rights (*dignity, welfare, freedom, equality, justice*). What in the past was sometimes a need, sometimes a possible choice about the contractual integration of "protected people" (*ahl adh-dhimmah*), no longer corresponds to contemporary realities and sociopolitical structures. Hence, it is important to define a clear status for members of the community, not only to protect their legitimate rights but also to secure them the legal power to defend those rights adequately. The concept of "citizenship" (*al-muwâtanah*) is now the commonly accepted reference, although some literalist or traditionalist *fuqahâ'* hesitate to use it or reject it altogether (because it is not part of classical Islamic terminology). The promotion of *citizenship*, conceived here as a legal status, is fundamental but it remains incomplete if it does not integrate a broader, more thorough approach to all the social dynamics and symbolic, structural, and institutional processes that cause discrimination.[9] It is also important to look critically into other forms of civic status, those of "non-citizen," "foreigner," "resident," and "immigrant," which justify far more serious issues of determination, exploitation, and domination—in both Eastern and Western countries.[10] Thus citizenship, a status that ideally should encompass all the higher ends of ethics, itself needs an ethics to become fully validated so as to deal with the risks of its own disruption and/or of the similarly transgressive shift of discriminations to another sort of victim, the "non-citizen" in all his or her variants. This *ethics of citizenship*[11] must of course, along with equality, guarantee the possible sharing of power according to laws and rules while remaining respectful about outcomes.

Those difficult questions involve far-reaching debates, but they are only marginally approached in Islamic circles. Knowledge and experience exist, as do theoretical and practical expertise, but what is lacking today is awareness of the issues and the concrete will to deal with their complexity.

Laws, Power, and Civil Society

In the Islamic Universe of reference, as the present study indeed makes clear, reflection about the law occupies a central position. *Fuqahâ'* jurists have even, as a result of their specialization, reduced *sharîah* to a mere body of laws to be implemented: indeed one can often read and hear, from Muslims and non-Muslims alike, a translation of *sharîah* as meaning only and strictly "Islamic law." This understanding and translation are significant: they reveal one of the reductions that took place within Muslim thought over the course of centuries. This reflects the process already mentioned among the different stages in the evolution of the science of the fundamentals of *usûl al-fiqh*: a fixation on texts stemming from a doubly defensive posture, towards the evolution of society and the domination of other people. The phenomenon began very early on, as we have seen in ash-Shâfiî's reaction when writing his *Risâlah*. Originally, even scholars who naturally tended to remain close to the letter of the texts integrated the environment (*al-wâqi'*) and the people's common interest (*al-maslahah*) into their understanding of the law and their subsequent formulation of legal rulings (*fatâwâ*). The meaning of the higher objectives of the Way was naturally taken into account through the no less natural integration of the social and human environment into their legal thought. As time went by, and as the risk was perceived about principles' being neglected, confident faithfulness to the higher goals of the Message gave way to wary faithfulness to the letter of the texts. *Ash-sharîah*, which had been the Way to the light from which the implementation of laws over time and in different environments was thought out, came to be reduced to a set of laws to be implemented formally, as they then were. Those laws were becoming and have often become, in their formalism, the exclusive identifying mark of the "Islamic" character of the collective vision. As can be seen, this understanding and translation reveal reductions that have critical consequences.

The return to goals and higher objectives requires us to approach the issue of the Way and of the laws from a necessarily more comprehensive standpoint, since what matters in effect is to relate respect for outcomes to the real situation of societies and the human environment to think through the relationship to laws, and to legislation in general, both realistically and consistently. I have shed light on a number of higher goals that could be inferred from the texts: principles such as people's *maslahah*, respect for *life*, *peace* (particularly social peace in this context), *dignity*, *welfare*, *knowledge*, *equality*, *freedom*, *justice*, and *solidarity*, which constitute the fundamentals of Islamic ethics. One should then add more specific objectives such as guaranteeing *education*, protecting *health*, *subsistence*, *work*, *belongings*, *contracts*, *neighborhood*, and, on the social and collective level, promoting the *rule of law*, *deliberation*, *pluralism in religions*, *cultures*, *and memories*, the natural *evolution* of society and the *independence* of nations. This long list of higher goals must be consistently associated with reflection about the social and political vision that it must inspire, but regarding which it determines no specific preestablished model. This is an important remark: the goals-oriented approach here again requires us to distinguish between goals and universal principles on the one hand, and historical models on the other. The latter, such as the Prophet's experience in Medina, were models through which goals were implemented at a precise moment in history; since this latter is changing, models must necessarily change as well.[12] Relating to ethical goals and seeking consistency in action forbid us to idealize the past, to sanctify the thought of *ulamâ*, and to remain at a standstill in social and political matters; this is clearly an invitation for critical reason to remain always watchful about possible betrayals or perversions of ideals, and at the same time creative about solutions to be found or historical models to be fulfilled.

For decades, sharp contradictory debates have been ongoing among scholars, thinkers, and politicians about whether it was right to refer to the term "democracy" as a model of political organization for Muslim-majority societies. Some refused the term they considered as "Western," others saw in it an essential distortion of the relationship to "divine power" (*al-hâkimiyyah lil-Lah*), and still others wanted to qualify it and speak of "Islamic democracy"; finally, others accepted the notion without considering that it was contradicting Islamic principles.[13] In recent years, advocates of the last position have become far more numerous, but some leaders or movements today still oppose using this concept in the name of a certain idea of the implementation of the *sharî'ah*. We are indeed at the heart of the matter, and the dispute over the concept and its use brings to light the twofold reduction that occurred during the debates: the understanding of laws is disconnected from higher outcomes, and they are associated with specific historical models. Contemporary Muslim thought finds it difficult to escape formalism or immobilism. The study of the higher goals of ethics and their possible categorization on the level of social and political vision bring to light five founding principles which are also those underlying democratic models in their diversity: rule of law, equal citizenship, universal suffrage, accountability, and separation of powers. Muslim-majority societies should thus normally, in the light of those principles and higher goals, begin a process of democratization by considering the implementation of laws according to objectives and, most important, crafting a model according to those same goals and to the condition of the social environment. A general process must therefore be set off, taking into account the whole range of ethical viewpoints that must be respected. In other words, the process of democratization must generate its own critical and self-critical constructive analysis of contemporary democratic models' shortcomings in achieving their ideals. We cannot engage in immoderate use of a concept and in blind imitation of models without, in the very name of the ethics that calls on us to begin the process of social and political reform, undertaking a critical analysis of the contradictions, inconsistencies, and shortcomings of contemporary democratic models.

I shall return to those essential issues later in this chapter, but this concept sheds light on the nature of the reflection that is expected and required of *fuqahâ'*, thinkers, and politicians. It is, in effect, not an adaptational reform but a transformational reform, and it must be radical. Civil society, that of ordinary women and men, needs to wake up and call for legal councils and intellectuals to provide comprehensive, but precise and consistent answers to their social, cultural, economic, and political questions. The population, through its commitment and its legitimate demands, must take it on itself to seize control of the authority to which it is entitled. The shift in the center of gravity of authority that I am calling for also involves—indeed mainly involves—the return of ordinary women and men to full civic commitment, uncompromising critical questioning, and a collective, practical search for solutions. This is one of the aspects of the crisis and of the shortcomings that can be observed today in the Islamic Universe of reference, always with the same reflexes of defensive formalism as obsessed with otherness, whereas what should be initiated is a confident, universalistic reform movement, which is both wholly inclusive and positively assertive.

The Islamic Penal Code (Hudûd) *and the Moratorium*

In March 2005, I launched a call for a moratorium on the death penalty, corporal punishment, and stoning in the Muslim world[14] and the subsequent reactions were incredibly revealing. During the seven years that preceded the *Call*, I had discussed it privately or in small groups with various scholars from Egypt, Morocco, Jordan, Pakistan, and Indonesia who largely found the arguments interesting, apt, and constructive. When the appeal was launched and the media in East and West reported it, silence was almost total among *'ulamâ'*, except for the al-Azhar *'ulamâ'* council, who denounced the meaning of the *Call* in terms that unfortunately did not correspond to its substance. The Webmasters of the *islamonline.net* site—who hastily, and most strangely, assimilated this move to a "Western" viewpoint—instantly appealed to some scholars, thinkers, or Islamic organization leaders, who often reacted virulently and most of the time (this is obvious when reading their arguments) without reading the nine pages of the *Call*. The controversy displeased the polarizing forces of both Universes of reference: some Western thinkers thought that my approach was insufficient and that *hudûd* had to be denounced outright, while conversely some *fuqahâ'* and intellectuals saw it as an excessive compromise in that it was in contradiction to Islam's principles. Some critics even claimed, in the name of a very dangerous reductive approach, that the *Call* was an attack against *sharî'ah* produced by an "over-Westernized" mind "trying to please the West." Some voices cast me out of Islam, doors were closed, and organizations stopped inviting me and questioned both the terms of the *Call* and my own credibility, using bizarre arguments and ascribing to me thoughts and positions I had never taken nor defended. I was faced with an emotional reactivity stemming from reductive understanding and a lack of critical reading: a summary of the very evils I have been describing since the beginning of this discussion. The Mufti of Egypt, Shaykh 'Alî Jum'ah, answered the *Call*'s arguments in detail, recognizing its substance as legitimate while objecting to its form;[15] one can understand this, considering his function, but debating the substance does remain a priority.

Opponents to the *Call* claimed that it questioned definitive (*qat'î*) texts of the Quran and Prophetic tradition, that I opposed the implementation of *sharî'ah*, and that this was a Western approach that did not stem from arguments defended on the basis of the "Islamic sciences" of *fiqh* and *usûl al-fiqh*. Not only does the *Call* begin by asserting the undisputed character of the texts referring to the death penalty and corporal punishments (in the Quran and Sunnah) and to stoning (in the Sunnah), but it explains the source of my approach to the Islamic penal code (*hudûd*), which is but a very restricted part of the Way (the meaning of *ash-sharî'ah* as I explained already). Moreover, I relied on the methodology of *usûl al-fiqh* to ask *'ulamâ* in general, and *fuqahâ'* in particular, three fundamental questions: What do the texts really say? What are the conditions required for implementation? In what social context? It is indeed strange to observe that the *Call*'s critics, some of whom argued that it substituted itself for the opinions of specialists and *fuqahâ'*, did not even notice that the *Call* ends with three questions, specifically so as to open the debate with *'ulamâ'*.

While this debate must be started and carried out, it is necessary to take measures guaranteeing justice and respect for the dignity of humankind, particularly of the poor and of women in Muslim-majority societies, for they are the first victims of the literal and often hasty implementation of the texts. My position defended the idea that whatever the number of poor people or women who were executed, physically punished, or stoned in the world (the argument of opponents to the *Call* insisted on observing that such implementations were marginal, which in any case is statistically highly questionable), a moratorium (*ta'lîq*) needed to be decided on to end to the implementation of penalties that today represent complete pure injustice. The proposal was not directed against Islam's teachings or against the texts—quite the contrary. In the name of the higher objectives of the message that call for respect for the *life* and *dignity* of women and men, *equality,* and *justice*, it was urgent to put an end to an instrumentalization of religion through literalist, formalist implementations that continued to affect poor people, women, and political opponents who have never had the means to defend themselves and who are punished for example's sake and without justice. It was therefore a *Call*, a stand taken from within, in the light of the texts and of social and political contexts, taking into account higher goals, determined to achieve the suspension of unfair implementation while calling upon *fuqahâ'* to debate the issue. Was this falling short of Islamic principles or betraying the texts? Only a superficial or partial reading (or no reading at all, as could be observed from some *'ulamâ'* who took position without reading the text of the *Call*) could lead to different conclusions.

Numerous *'ulamâ'* who had understood, or even agreed with, the meaning of this move later chose to oppose it or to remain silent, after the launching of the *Call* brought passionate debate and polarization both within the Muslim world and in the West. Some showed concern about the *Call*'s Islamic justifications (which is precisely the debate it was intended to start), but most were afraid either of losing their credibility with their base and communities or of giving the impression of yielding to impositions that seemed to come from the West. During encounters with *'ulamâ'* or scholars in the West, in Morocco, in Pakistan, in Indonesia, or in Africa, many approved the presentation of my position in private, but then refused or simply avoided speaking out about it. In this sense, debates about the moratorium have significantly revealed the state of reflection and its profound shortcomings in the Islamic Universe of reference. Fear of emotional popular reactions or the power relationship with the West negatively interfere with our reading of our own scriptural sources and with the imperative concern for consistency beyond formalism and the necessary critical debates between *fuqahâ'* and other experts. What matters is to avoid losing face, to save appearances even by sacrificing criticism and self-criticism, as well as the lives of women and poor people whose supposedly limited number is thought to justify silence. A thousand times have I heard "this is not a priority!"

Not only is this argument unacceptable in the light of the ethical requirement that does not bend to the logic of numbers, but the critical approach must be taken further. The debate, or the consenting silences over *hudûd*, reveals deep-set tensions, and facing such issues squarely may well help promote other debates, question a number of certainties, and open up some situations. How is faithfulness to the Way to be understood, what role must higher goals and objectives play, how must the implementation of laws be thought about in the light of the Way? Those questions are broadly dealt with in the present chapter, and the debate (and sometimes the nondebate some tried to impose) that followed the *Call* is highly revealing evidence about the need for a radical reform of our approaches. Only open, critical legal councils, less timid about forms and more radical about consistency, can take the reflection further. This must nevertheless be attempted, with determination and patience: the *Call* was launched in March 2005, several million people have heard about it in the past few years, but its first effects cannot be expected to appear until at least the next generation, if and only if Muslims take up the challenge of deep questioning and fundamental critical and self-critical reflection in the name of faithfulness to the Way, of ethics, justice, consistency, and peace. Beyond the issue of *hudûd*, the very essence of faithfulness to Islam's message is at stake here. We must become reconciled with ourselves, whatever the positions expressed in the West where some, unable to uncouple themselves from their own Universe of reference, have claimed that this move was insufficient and where others have intentionally simplified the terms of the debate to maintain polarization and suspicion about Islam. Thus, their arguments runs, the moratorium was presented as a trick imagined by a perverse mind that played on words and wanted to gain time, hoping that in the end those "barbarian customs" would be implemented. Those critical voices were not heard—and suddenly became very laudatory—when French President Jacques Chirac called for an international moratorium on the death penalty,[16] and most of them naturally supported the Italian initiative of an international moratorium that was eventually voted on by the United Nations General Assembly in December 2007,[17] despite a resistance and refusal front coming from . . . "Muslim" governments!

Education

I have brought to light the higher goals to which we must try to remain faithful while working out the details of a social and political project. This commitment to faith therefore requires us to engage in a far-reaching movement to reform societies in the light of ethical principles, of course, but also on the basis of a critical assessment of contemporary achievements and models. Muslim-majority societies as well as communities living in Asia, in Africa, or in the West must absolutely accept and deal with diversity; they must be open to pluralistic, contradictory debates, both internally and with the outside world; they must give voice to the base in general and to women in particular. A vast movement of intellectual, social, and political openness must be initiated, a *democratization* movement in the sense of sharing speech, legitimacy, and powers. This opening up can only be meaningful if equipped with some means of respecting the conditions for its success, by opening places for debate, consultation, and critical assessment. Such consistency can only be possible if it promotes an education whose substance, form, and scope answer the ends of openness itself. This also requires thinking about the coherence of democratic institutions and, for our own time, studying the links between media, freedom, and power.[18] When we turn to the contemporary Muslim world, it seems as though those issues "had nothing to do with us" or were quite secondary. The West's educational systems are criticized while their philosophy is often being copied, and the great Western media are vilified while the al-Jazeera channel, their alter ego, is praised. There are always the same contradictions, the same lack of a vision.

Official, state educational systems in Muslim-majority societies are virtually all deficient and in crisis. From Africa to Asia and throughout the Middle East, one can observe either unacceptable illiteracy rates or systems and methods that kill critical thinking and reinforce rote learning and social injustices. Reforms are urgently needed, for any opening or democratization project is bound to fail if populations are kept illiterate or functionally illiterate, or if their education is based on the lack of critical thinking, on reinforcing social divides, and on protecting the interests of an elite. East and West, private school projects, often for Islamic schools, have appeared; their promoters wished to propose an alternative to state systems (that did not answer their expectations regarding curricula or whose organization was unsatisfactory). The principle of private schools making up for the shortcomings of the public state system is not bad in itself, although one should primarily strive to reform the system and its structures which, in effect, educate the vast majority of children. East and West, this is where the community's efforts should focus. Reflections and initiatives in this direction unfortunately remain marginal. As for private school projects, I am baffled: indeed they add subjects and teaching hours related to religious education (they teach the Quran and *ahâdîth*, the lives of Prophets, morals, and good behavior) but the general philosophy of teaching philosophy continues to imitate the goals of Western social and economic systems based on selection and performance. Willingly or not, an elite is targeted and taught—along with the integration of formal religious knowledge—the culture of success, efficiency, profitability, the quest for "first place," for material social success, and other goals. What is supposed to prove the success of those schools is assessed through such criteria (percentage of successful examinations, ranking in the lists of schools that "produce" top students). One can understand that those schools cope with crisis and emergency situations and that they perpetuate the vicious cycle by first of all responding to shortcomings, then taking into account "what matters to parents" and end up following the same performance logic, adding Islamic formalism.[19] Fundamental reflection is required here: in the light of the aforementioned higher goals, and observing the nature of the crises occurring in Muslim societies and communities, is it really this kind of alternative education that we need? Should we not be doing "something different"? Returning to the sources of ethics, so as to foster a will to succeed, indeed, but one that is not reduced to formula and to the cult of academic performance and has more to do with *personal development, welfare*, developing *critical thinking, creativity, solidarity*, and the *knowledge* and *respect* of others. We are very far, today, from considering the alternative in those terms. Contemporary Islamic thought is very critical of "Western models" in the name of a particular philosophy of life and a strong conception of ethics, but in effect it ends up imitating the technically highest performing models in terms of quantitative success and, without true critical assessment, reproducing systems based on productivist conceptions that are very little concerned with the quality of ethical requirements.

What is called "an Islamic school" is very often a school for an elite in the East or a school exclusively for Muslims in the West. "Islamic" subjects are added, but those schools rarely excel for their philosophy of education, their original teaching methods, and their concern for practical consistency with the higher principles of ethics. Yet the aim should be to develop pedagogic concepts—and there should be a similar general movement inside state and public school systems—that both impart knowledge and awaken pupils' *consciences*, shape their *critical minds*, lead them toward *autonomy*, and awaken them to personal and collective *responsibility*. A society that is intellectually, culturally, and politically open, that experiences true qualitative and human *development*, needs a school system and schools that promote such values and ethical principles and above all that do not end up yielding to the dictates of economy by being privatized or becoming obsessed with the specific, standardized production of "gray matter" just as some firms focus on producing raw materials. Respect for *diversity*, human *solidarity*, and cultural and artistic *creativity* should also be taught; such are the schools we need today, and they should combine traditional methods with more innovative approaches in order to take up the challenges of contemporary times. Several school planners and teachers have examined those issues, but again, the reflection too often remains formalistic, technical, and/or superficial. What motivates those projects is often fear and the desire to protect children from globalized culture or behaviors little involved with ethics. This defensive approach is everywhere showing its limits and often its counterproductive character.

Democracy and Media

One can argue on and on over the use of the concept of "democracy" and lose sight of the essence of the discussion over and above semantic differences. What matters is, once again—beyond models—to remain faithful to fundamental principles (rule of law, equality before the law, universal suffrage, limited mandate, separation of powers) and to the numerous higher outcomes presented and studied (*dignity, welfare, freedom, equality*). On the basis of those principles, each society, each nation can—and has the inalienable

right to—determine its own model and mode of institutionaliza-
tion on the basis of its history, culture, and collective psychology. To
reach those objectives, however, some conditions absolutely must
be met, particularly at the heart of all contemporary societies South
and North, East and West. Democratization has prerequisites (e.g.,
education, instruction, as we have seen) and requirements whose
absence makes it wholly impossible for the reform process to succeed. The Muslim world needs *fuqahâ'* and specialists in the study of
societies to examine those issues, developing a holistic approach that
takes into account interactions between the different fields (education, civil participation, political commitment, development of civil
society, elections). We have text scholars who speak and legislate
about the need for a legal reference framework or ethical norms but
who are completely out of touch with reality and its requirements:
their thought relies on structural normative schemes, whereas at
present reforms can only be devised as a gradual process and on
a temporal basis. Societies and the fields of human action are too
complex and interdependent to be considered as isolated normative
frameworks, from which and for which jurists could legislate. Only
a formalist thought can be content with those idealistic, inefficient
reductions.

Democratization processes are everywhere in need of popular
education, teaching and mastery of the language, as well as a minimal knowledge of history, laws, and institutions. This generalized
elementary civic education is the *sine qua non* condition for the
process of political openness, democratization, and eventually the
formation of a civil society that is intellectually well equipped and
politically active. This also means for citizens in general to be aware
of their responsibilities and of their rights, to pledge to respect their
obligations toward the community, and to never hesitate to demand
their legitimate rights. It also requires critical speech, participating in
elections (or calling for them to be held and to be transparent in most
Arab-Muslim, Asian, and African countries) and establishing areas
and meeting places where power can be challenged. Democratic ideals must offer such consistency of means and ends to the population
in general and individuals in particular. On a more general level, it
is also important to engage in critical assessment of the shortcomings and potential deviations of contemporary models in the West
or elsewhere.

At the heart of the "conflict," "debate," or "dialogue" between civilizations, democracy is often presented in the West as "a value" supposed to be either "Western" or "universal," or, with no fear of contradiction, both at the same time. Thus presented, "the critique of democracy" becomes suspicious and its instigators tend to be lumped with old-time idealistic Communists defending the "dictatorship of the proletariat" or new Muslim radicals advocating a theocratic implementation of the *sharî'ah*. A neologism has even been coined in the field of political movements to account for the emergence of this new and dangerous "antiliberal" alliance: Islamo-leftism. By lumping the critique of democracy together with the rejection of liberal values, hence of democracy itself, assimilations and reductions occurred, preventing critical debate by oversimplifying it in a dualistic manner: for or against democracy—this is the sole operative equation and one must choose one's camp. The perversion is clear here: liberal thought becomes dogmatic and cleverly stifles critical and *democratic* debate.

However, democracy is not a value but a generic system encompassing a set of organizational and institutional models for universal, fundamental values and principles. Democracy could only be a "value" if it guaranteed the respect of a series of other higher "values": it would then be a "value" that could only be relative, being subject to *a priori* conditions that must be assessed on a case-by-case basis. It is therefore not a *value in itself* but the product and consequence of the human attempt to propose a consistent collective project, respectful of the aforementioned fundamental values. It should be remembered that in political philosophy, any attempt to absolutize models—by turning humankind's historical experience into an absolute value—tends to a kind of "theocratization" (and this is true even of wholly atheistic models) and reveals the dogmatism of some minds that nevertheless claim for themselves the ideals of modern, "liberal thought." Dogmatic liberal thought is unfortunately a very real creation of our time, an intellectual hybrid that promotes its political ideology to the rank of a universal philosophical (and almost religious) theorem.

The critique of democracy, in the sense of criticizing its dysfunction and the perversion of its models and institutions, is a necessity today. If one approaches the issue on an international level, one very quickly realizes that the high-sounding dialogue between civilizations that would reduce the terms of the debate to accepting democracy or not is most misleading: one knows, or should know historically that being a democracy has never been enough to guarantee the promotion of *peace*, the respect of human *rights*, *dignity*, *freedom*, *autonomy*, etc.[20] From the outset, Athenian democracy was forever at war with its neighbors (besides, its discriminatory treatment of women, the poor, and "Barbarians" is well known) and today as well, U.S.-style democracy keeps getting involved in conflicts and wars that, as in Iraq, completely fail to respect fundamental values and human dignity (moreover, that the discriminatory treatment of Native-American and African-American citizens still endures within the system is well known). The constructive critique of contemporary democratic models must be undertaken on that *wider* level, first of all, by identifying what they do not guarantee in terms of respecting values, which must absolutely be reformed if we are to be consistent. Repeating that it is the least bad system cannot justify passivity about denouncing its perversions and excesses.

On the level of the internal functioning of democracies and their institutions, the critique must be just as thorough and constructive. Populations no longer trust the politics of ideas and are eventually swept away and seduced by politics as a form of show business. Such phenomena as superficial training in civics, increasingly sketchy knowledge of history and civic institutions, and insignificant rates of participation in social debates and elections (when these are not merely media events) undermine democracies, eventually betray their ideals, and backfire against the powers of the people who were supposed to be sovereign. When to this we add that the less salutary areas of economy, finance, and the practices of multinationals and giant firms (where the democratic and consultative character of decisions is not a prerequisite) often decide and impose general political orientations, alliances with some nations (even dictatorships), and involvement in conflicts and wars without consulting the people, the picture darkens. Idealistic discourse about "democracy" as a value struggles to hide the need for debate about democracy as a system apt to be both perfected and alienated. In these times of "global war against terrorism," one must also add most dangerous declines and perversions: by relying on and instrumentalizing fear—and producing a real "ideology of fear"—governments have been able to take increasingly freedom-suppressing security measures against citizens. Surveillance, search, and the loss of long-fought-for rights are becoming standard—and accepted—practice in the name of the fight against terrorism and to guarantee people's security. Terrorism indeed exists and its evils must be fought with determination, but it is no less clear that this bugbear is sometimes used to justify the most anti-democratic policies. Fear and doubt are spread, and then populations are told that they are being watched and that a number of their rights are being suppressed for their own good. Minds forcefed threatening discourse and pictures eventually atrophy and accept them, yet such generalized intellectual atrophy and passive acceptance are contrary to the democratic ideal.

A reflection must urgently be carried through about the role and power of the media in contemporary democracies.[21] People speak of freedom of the press, simply counting the number of newspapers on the market or the number of television channels available. Yet one hardly hears about the far more restricted number of those who actually own those media outlets and their real involvement in the world of economy and politics. The same people who produce and sell weapons own the media—with a few ideas to defend. It is often argued that there is no direct link and that no real censorship is practiced. It is indeed true that there is no censorship of the kind used in past and present dictatorships, but editorial policies, influences, and interests are nonetheless promoted and protected. To this must be added the dictatorship of speed: one must be quick, be the first to supply instant news, before anyone else does. Critical elaboration and detailed reports are seen as out of step with the common vision and becoming more and more difficult to produce: speed imposes a subtle standardization of thought because it is no longer possible to take the time, and risk, of explaining diverse points of view. Speed now has a political function, both in political thought and strategies. Contemporary politicians have understood this, and the most efficient among them are now those who express the ideas of their program (that may or may not include many ideas) in "media events," in communication strategy (where strategy is often more important than the substance conveyed). Reflection about contemporary democracy cannot function without such analyses.

Muslim thinkers and intellectuals should engage in comprehensive thought about those achievements and those distortions of human experience, through history to contemporary events. One cannot be content with repeating the ideality of "Islamic values" outside and beyond the world's complexity. The West is facing deep crises and some are expecting its more or less imminent implosion, but such an attitude is unfair and dangerous. It is unfair for the populations who are affected by those crises and by the system's perversions that sometimes break them up or manipulate them; it is dangerous because, in this global age, no one can or will be spared those risks and their consequences. Moreover, such a critical stance fails to observe and analyze the nature of the crises and potential breakdowns that also undermine Muslim-majority societies. Frequently corrupt political authorities, curtailed freedoms and rights, unbridled consumption (bordering on overdose) of global culture and media—such is the reality we must humbly face, and then radically reform while involving all fields of expertise and all people of goodwill respectful of fundamental values and shared higher goals.

This also means engaging in reflection about the media and an ethics of communication for our time. We cannot be satisfied with television channels (like al-Jazeera in Arabic or in English) that seem to present another point of view while using the same information methods and the same market and propaganda logistics. Considering that today almost 70 percent of the information broadcast in the world is relayed by Western news agencies and that increasing speed has become the measurement of efficiency and competence (about publishing news and their "media truth"), it has become important to engage in thorough reflection about the media, and particularly the alternative media. Businesspeople, journalists, and communications specialists should be able to bring their skills together to think through and produce new strategies and new modes of communication on the local level (i.e., local media), through the Internet or in association with larger newspaper, radio, or television projects. We must also commit ourselves to an ethical stance in the media and mass communication that is one of resistance, and that must, to be efficient, become specialized, professionalized, and institutionalized the world over.[22]

Powers and Counterpowers

Globalization has transformed the nature and weight of the different powers and their interactions within human communities.

From more industrialized to poorer societies, consequences are real, multidimensional, and very far reaching. Yet people in the Islamic world, whether *'ulamâ'*, thinkers, social organizations, or Islamist movements, continue speaking about the dynamics of power distribution, political power, scholarly authority, and relations to people, as if nothing had truly changed. They would like to reform societies by relying on classical, visible powers, without noticing the extent to which this approach is not only outdated but also dangerous. Single-mindedly focusing on the relationship to "political power," some Islamist movements (after the dictatorial turn taken by Arab regimes in the wake of independence) have gone so far as to reduce the reference corpus of the texts to a series of injunctions establishing the framework of what an Islamic structure and state should be. Such organizations as, formerly, al-Jama'ât al-Islamiyyah or al-Jihâd in Egypt, or today Hizb at-Tahrîr or al-Muhâjirûn, have developed a binary thought process that distinguishes societies in terms of their structure and political power. According to them, Islam first and foremost imposes an "Islamic system" purified of Western failings and that it is by setting up such a system that society as a whole can be reformed. Transnationalism, through the creation of a supranational entity, the caliphate, copied on the historical model, should make it possible to start a general transformational movement. Other movements and organizations with more sophisticated and less dualistic thought—Islamist organizations like the Muslim Brotherhood in Egypt, an-Nahda in Tunisia, Justice and Development (JDP) in Morocco, an-Nahda or Hamas in Algeria, parties like Refah and, very differently, Justice and Development (ATK) in Turkey, PAS or ABIM in Malaysia as well as the various Indonesian Islamist parties and large movements and organizations such Nahda al-'ulamâ' or even al-Muhammadiyah in Indonesia or the ideologues of the Iranian regime—have all, despite the great diversity of their intellectual approaches and sociopolitical strategies, determined a relationship to the texts and to political power based on analyses that date back to the early or mid-twentieth century; they find it difficult to evolve and make a comprehensive reassessment. Indeed some thoughts and practices are being transformed through the exercise of power and the requirements of *realpolitik*, as in the evolution of Iranian reformists or in the Justice and Development party in Turkey, but such reassessments directly result from political pressure of politics, the practice of power, or the relations that must be maintained with it. The history of *political Islam* in the twentieth century began with necessary reflection about the relationship between political power and the people, and between the people and political power. The finally divergent positions of Jamâl ad-Dîn al-Afghânî (1839–1897) and Muhammad 'Abduh (1849–1905)[23] were radically reformist, because they examined systems and power distributions (colonization, subjected local powers, and alienated peoples) that were effective and actually oppressive and from which the oppressed needed to break free. The issues of independence, dictatorship, and the perversion of the regimes set up after independence, the failures of development, rampant corruption, and social injustices throughout the Muslim world have caused political Islamic thought to evolve toward the primary dimension of politics as the groundwork and stake of real power. Grassroots education and social commitment have been and are still conceived of in terms of getting political power, either to hold on to it or at least to influence it. Contemporary Islamic political thought has been altered by those approaches and the adaptation of social and political strategies has not led to the necessary reforms and to the critical reassessments of vision and thought that our globalized world requires today. It seems to be deeply out of touch with our time.

What was already true in the past from the political viewpoint has now become a far more tangible reality: strictly political power is highly relative, subject to impositions, pressures, and influences that reduce, undermine, or altogether prevent its actual exercise. In this age of globalization, the means of communication and culture and the autonomy of politics have shrunk away. The facts are the same everywhere, nationally and internationally: economic (and banking) forces, the stupendous power of multinationals (which influence legislative and executive powers in different ways), and the media's determining role have transformed politics and the role of politicians in richer and more industrialized societies. The situation is even worse in the poorer societies of the Third World, since not only are they faced with the same phenomena, but their political power is subjected to economic forces over which they have no real control. Political ideologies, the former categories of right and left, are breaking down and losing their meaning, for ultimately, political ideals and the concrete practices of a political power devoid of any determining influence compel governments and politicians in office to bend to the realities of the real power of the market, of profit logistics, of requests from powerful multinational firms, and of the media that fashion perceptions, making extensive use of opinion polls and thus influencing political choices. Populations no longer believe in political discourse: they are increasingly aware of the unhealthy, opaque activities of women and men who love power, who are ready to lie to get it and keep it, but who ultimately change little about the reality of things. The political radicalisms of the past are perceived as outdated utopias; today's political pragmatism is akin to administrative management. Nevertheless, politics still stirs up the crowds, particularly through the media's capacity to create political figures and represent conflicts through pictures rather than ideas. National political meetings and demonstrations stir up the crowds and summon emotions, and participation in presidential or national elections sometimes reaches record rates (when they are really free). Such phenomena are presented as evidence of the "good health" of democracies. Is this really so? Really "political" debates of ideas, confronting ideologies, programs, visions for the future are rare and increasingly amount to rhetoric built around a few symbols. The highly efficient power of contemporary media, and foremost among them television, of course, consists in creating politics, in continuing to give the impression that this is where everything is decided, according to the regular rhythm of political agendas and elections. This is akin to an optical illusion, which leads people to believe that political authority, which has lost so much of its power, remains the essential seat of decisions and power issues. If we add to this the emotional hypertrophy that sometimes turns political affiliations into scenes of passion that call to mind the level of agitation seen at sporting events or popular music concerts, one can fully measure the deviations and perversions of political activity as such.

Modern times virtually give us a live show of the breakdown of political ideologies, the increasing relativity of politicians' power, the standardization of thought and strategies, while, behind the scenes, the undemocratic seats of real, stupendous powers stir. If to this we add that the social and political reforms that are necessary today in all societies, and should be politicians' responsibility, require long-term commitment and are not necessarily popular, one can measure even more closely how restricted the power of politicians is, both nationally and internationally. The time of social reforms does not correspond to the time and rhythm of elections (or of the media): in effect, politicians can choose either to start bold social reforms (which are sometimes unpopular in the short run), which require time and may lead them to lose in the next election cycle, or to bend to the general trend, to accept majority discourse and the classic interplay of influences that will change nothing in the condition of society (but may ensure their potential reelection).

The point here is not to downplay the importance of political power but to develop a comprehensive approach enabling us to identify those areas where issues of power are truly expressed. The concern for consistency between the higher outcomes of ethics and human action in the social and political arenas requires just such a general, multidimensional approach. Globalization is a reality and has truly changed things: we must reassess our analyses, readjust our visions, and revise our social and political strategies to avoid being misled, focusing solely on political power that has become less efficient and less credible. This may indeed be the greatest danger: social, economic, cultural, and political commitment in the name of ethics can lose all legitimacy in people's eyes and all real efficiency if it is obsessed with political power. The latter has become so relative and limited, as we have seen, that exerting it may be the most direct way of losing or being made to lose credibility before the people to whom one had committed oneself. Political power devoid of real authority, which necessarily involves compromise, if not surrender, ultimately disqualifies its advocates, however honest, sincere, and devoted they may have been or even remain. Political power may indeed corrupt people, but political power without authority certainly leads even the least corrupt to lose their credibility. The recent experiences of social and political movements in Muslim-majority countries, including those of Islamists, abound and should be enough to convince us.

What could be the alternative, then? How can we reform humankind and societies by elaborating a vision that does not choose the wrong target or strategy? Here again, text and context scholars, thinkers, and scientists must work together to create the outline of efficient thinking and commitment at the local, national, transnational, and international levels. Committing oneself in the light of higher objectives, taking into account the global environment, adapting strategy to the realities of individual countries, of their history and culture, of the prognoses for them, require an increasingly important mastery of increasingly numerous and decisive influence factors. The political stands of the past, former right-left, secular-Islamist divides are no longer operative and require new fundamental reflection. The front lines of resistance to an unjust economic order, to jungle politics, to dishonest or illegal wars, to terrorism in all its forms (group or state), to the alienation of standardized global culture—those front lines have shifted and diversified so that alliances must diversify as well, just as objectives must look beyond the issue of political power. The Muslim world is far from having created this intellectual mutation, and thus often discourses in the victim's role, according to which Islam and Muslims are the eternal targets of everything and everyone.

Our world may well need a wholly new approach, developing a systematic, organized management of counterpowers wherever they exist. Equipped with ethics, with critical resistance in the name of ethics, a sweeping movement should mobilize civil societies nationally and internationally. It is important—beyond age-old divides—to initiate movements embodying the awakening of multidimensional ethical counterpowers touching on all sectors and all levels of intellectual, social, political, economic, cultural, and ecological activity. At the heart is a globalization that blurs national boundaries and elicits a tendency to withdrawal, faced also with gloomy prognoses about the future of the planet that require us to consider our actions more globally, so that the issue of meaning is everywhere coming back to the forefront. What matters today is to impart *meaning* and to resist in the name of meaning: the objectives-driven approach is now the only mechanism that imparts value to resistance. For some it awakens the conscience, for some it enlightens faith, and for others it stirs their minds and hearts.

Status-seeking or the obsession with taking power that is exclusively political (and devoid of real authority) or economic (and without any alternative model) can only undermine the credibility of thinkers, leaders, and organizations. Moreover, the temptation to organize counterpowers or, in other words, to give oneself the power to manage counterpowers, always eventually jeopardizes political ethics itself. Recent examples showed alterglobalist movements moved by the idea that "another world is possible," being headed by some leaders who use the same old opaque management methods of controlling power. Ideological preserves, populist deviations, and the urge to control causes this possible new world to be as redolent of alienation as the existing one. In South America, in Africa, in the United States, as well as in Europe and Asia, the same can be observed, and the finest ideas of alterglobalism seem to be stalling because of the very nature of their politics-oriented management. Contemporary Islamic thought must assess those experiences, both within Muslim-majority societies and in the West, in Africa, or in Asia. Beyond controlling one organization or movement, what matters is setting off a general, broadly sweeping movement of ethical awareness, of multidimensional mobilization whose agents should now, humbly and modestly, do their best in their own fields of competence. No more, but no less.

Ethical counterpowers must emerge at the heart of civil societies as minds struggle against propaganda, lies, and disinformation. We must reconcile these factors with complex, in-depth debates and serious reading. This turn of mind must be allied to national and international actions that fight for the dignity of women and men, of citizens, foreigners, and immigrants; for the right to *welfare, health, education, freedom, justice*, and *solidarity*; and more broadly for the *rule of law, independence*, and *pluralism*. Those intellectual, social, and political commitments must be completed with the study of financial and economic alternatives starting from the small business level, and possibly moving into bigger multinational groups. But that is not all: cultural resistance (food, films, songs, music), the use of alternative media, of the Internet, of radio and television channels with new, original programs, must be considered both locally and internationally. All available expertise and skills must be called on in a sweeping awareness movement that raises the issue of meaning and summons everyone everywhere to act in the name of higher outcomes. In this multidimensional movement, the various dimensions will be theorized but, ultimately, its strength will lie in the lack of a single source of control and center of management. We must be ambitious without illusion and humble without naivete; the road will be very long, and the nature of today's multiform globalization must result in a globalization of multidimensional ethical counterpowers. This is because the ambition to resist must be combined with humility about projects undertaken and results achieved. This is in keeping with fundamental spiritual teachings: the imperative requirement of resisting with one's heart, conscience, and skills; determined patience and active perseverance to go on; confidence in the name of meaning, regardless of results. This is how Muslim spirituality, echoing all the spiritualities in the world, teaches the meaning of dignity. We should never turn into dreamers or idealists finding legitimacy in aspirations to a hereafter. We must look squarely at humans, hypocrisies, and lies; we must simplify nothing. Nothing will be changed, for instance, by denouncing wars and promoting wide-eyed, improbable pacifism. Lucidity requires us to denounce all aspects of the business of war and promote a profound, uncompromising ethics of peace. Victims have this right over our intelligence and commitments. What spirituality and meaning first and foremost require are competence, realism, consistency, and earnestness.

16

Ethics and Universals

The reform presented in the course of this book must begin with reconciliation with the texts, their meaning, and their higher goals considered in history and in various human societies. In the five broad areas I have chosen to focus on (from among so many possible others), from medicine to politics, it has become clear that it is imperative to struggle against the two phenomena of restrictive imitation (*taqlîd*) of past scholars and contemporary literalist reduction (*qirâ'a harfiyyah*). It has also become clear that those two intellectual attitudes were often motivated by fear of deviations, of the texts not being respected, or of excessive influence from the West, or from homogenized global culture. That is not all, however; along with this protective fear, major confusions can be observed between what pertains to religion and what pertains to culture; between respecting higher outcomes and a normative and technical ethics of the means; between a reading presented as the only "objective" one and a purely "masculine" reading; between the meaning of the general message and approaches that are so categorized and segmented that they lose all practical efficiency. Those shortcomings have often been encountered and pointed out in the course of the previous discussion of each of the practical cases. The major general consequence of those phenomena as an entity (although they are also serious problems in themselves in each of the fields studied) has been to consider and present faithfulness to Islam in terms of the mode of exclusiveness and otherness, far more than in terms of shared universals.

The first step toward fundamental reconciliation may well be reconsidering this intellectual attitude that has been present in the minds of Muslims for centuries. Fearing the dissolution of principles and rules and of domination by others, Muslim thought regrouped around some symbols, principles, rules, or cultural features that essentially stood out as singular, specific, and different. Being one-self meant—and still does—expressing, repeating, and reinforcing one's otherness. East and West, whether Muslims are a majority or a minority, this intellectual disposition remains the same. Islamic values are indeed claimed to be "universal" and operative for all ages and all societies, but they are often conceived only in their typically "Islamic" character, in relation to their exclusive source and practice. In the course of history, as crises, fears, and foreign dominations came and went, the Muslim conscience was led to consider its universalist teachings from the standpoint of its otherness: in other words, Muslims consider and speak of universals and of their values like provincials, or more precisely, like provincialists.

It clearly appears, however, when considering the higher goals related to human communities, religious traditions, and cultural systems, which require respecting the *rule of law, independence, pluralism, cultures, religions,* and *memories,* that this attitude too must be reconsidered. If the One has willed the diversity of *"nations and tribes,"*[1] the plurality of religions, of skin colors and languages, of cultures and memories, it means that the universality, which according to Muslims emanates from the last revealed religion, is necessarily open, shared, inclusive, and dynamic, rather than fearful, exclusive, rigid, and closed. Such should indeed be the essence of this religion: stating and repeating again and again the values that the historical cycles of prophethood had confirmed one after the other, and which humankind's analytical reason, in its critical autonomy, has discovered, formulated, and claimed as its own.

We need to reconcile with an Islamic universality whose essence is pluralistic. The function of its truth, naturally acknowledged by believers, is not to standardize truths and values beyond Islam itself, but to establish correspondences, intersections, bridges. Confirming its universality as the last Revelation does not mean denying what came before it or what appeared elsewhere outside of its Universe of reference, but rather being able to say and repeat what was formulated in the past and/or establish positive interactions with what is produced by other traditions or civilizations today. Concretely, this entails engaging a twofold movement that consists in determined self-assertion allied to confident opening up to all civilizations and religions but also to the different subjects of thought that were long considered dangerous precisely because of fears about dilution or transgressions against the text. This has been discussed in terms of the experimental and social sciences, but with respect to the present discussion, such areas as philosophy, mysticism, and, of course, interfaith dialogue must also be added. Those debates open the way to deep, constructive understanding of such issues as universals, values, and shared or singular ethical concepts.

Texts, Faith, and Reason

Islam is a religion of the Book, a religion of texts. The written Revelation, which Muslims accept as the literal revealed word of God, tells of Meaning and of the Way, of morals and good behavior. This relationship to scriptural sources is quite specific: it shapes the hearts and minds of the faithful in the light of the faith it inspires, and orients not only their reception of the texts but also their whole behavior in the world and in humankind. The written Revelation addresses the intelligence, which receives it in a very particular way through the prism of faith that imparts to it a specific status, substance, and essence. Faith receives and projects on this Revelation a landscape of meaning, intuitions, emotions, and hopes that nurture the heart and also fashion the inner self and its relationship to God's signs and to life. The love of God and His Prophet, the relationship to one's parents and family, to others, to life and death, are, of course, fostered by this particular relation of faith to texts which in their turn sustain, reinforce, and illuminate faith. It is truly a matter of heart and love that imparts meaning.

In this process, reason receives, reads, understands, and inter-prets in a way that is not wholly autonomous. The first reason that receives the Revelation is not analytical reason but the reason of the heart. This is what the Quran refers to when it says about those who deny the truth: *"They have hearts with which they do not understand; they have eyes with which they do not see; they have ears with which they do not hear."*[2]

What is involved here is the inner dimension, a faith that enlight-ens and causes one to see things "differently" in oneself and beyond the self. This is, of course, true of the manner in which the written Rev-elation is read and understood, but also the manner in which the book of the world is approached. Here again, analytical reason is not suffi-cient to receive the signs, meaning, and hopes anchored *a priori* in the essence of the created world. The contemporary Muslim conscience, from those of ordinary people to those of the intellectual elite, has not separated itself from this most specific relationship to the two Books that enlighten life and give it meaning. Analytical reason searches on and on, but the conscience and heart give it information pertaining to another order—that which explains why and of goals, ethics, and limits. Reason receives the reasons of the heart, the lights of faith.

The two Books, which echo one another, prevent the world from becoming "disenchanted," in the words of Marcel Gauchet,[3] and preclude strictly technical uses of reason and science without con-science. This approach and those assets nevertheless involve risks of deviations, which unfortunately course through the history of Islamic civilization. Fear of the texts' being neglected or of Muslim popula-tions being alienated by the domination of others has encouraged defensive, almost exclusively normative, readings of the revealed texts. Such readings, relying on faith and on the reasons of the heart just mentioned, often came to reduce the use of analytical reason to the mere function of quoting or repeating the text's literal or apparent reasons. This is, however, a clear confusion of orders. The revealed text indeed expresses norms, but in so doing it does not enclose ana-lytical reasoning within a role as the "guardian of limits" (in the name of a faith that would no longer be a guiding light but a prison). The two Books summon the intelligence and justification to experience the quest for meaning through signs and to reconcile it with essen-tial questions and critical thinking. Just as faith cannot be imposed, meaning cannot be dictated and the human conscience must search, progress, question, and criticize, in a to-and-fro movement. Neither can reason be compelled to humility: it encounters humility—or it does not—in the course of its peregrinations and through its quest for meaning, knowledge, and the sciences. The strictly normative approach developed by text scholars specialized in fundamentals (*usûl al-fiqh*) or in law and jurisprudence (*al-fiqh*) has—even though their fears can and must be understood in times of crisis—reduced the scope and restricted the skills of the exercise of autonomous analytical intelligence. The question of meaning then became pointless and critical thinking dangerous. In the course of history, *fuqahâ'*, by focusing on one book only and reducing its substance and circumscribing faith to acceptance of norms, eventually developed a formalistic approach to the texts. And yet normative, technical formalism in dealing with the texts is as dangerous as analytical, technical reason in dealing with the world: in both cases, the issue of outcomes is sacrificed. Paradoxically, the two approaches converge: *fuqahâ'* and scientists eventually overlook the issue of "why" and of outcomes because they come to adopt a reductive, utilitarian approach. Some *fuqahâ'* and some scientists understandably dislike philosophy. Yet the two Books, taken together, call on us to develop a philosophy of faith and of knowledge, in the name of faith and meaning.

The absence of critical thinking and of meaning is indeed a great danger. There is another, which consists in resorting to mere inclusion. The Revelation informs us that nothing has been left out:

> *"And We have explained for men in this Quran every kind of similitude…"*
> *"We have sent down to you a Book explaining all things."*
> *"We have omitted nothing from the Book."*[4]

This is understood to mean that it says everything, particularly in scientific study. The Revelation is then transformed, not into a book of norms as above, but into a scientific handbook. What analytical reason works out is supposed to be already present in the Book, and such concordance is seen as apt to confirm faith. That the Book contains nothing that contradicts science is one thing, but turning it into a scientific work is quite another matter. The "concordist" approach that seeks to confirm the Revelation through its concordance with scientific knowledge is very successful among Muslims, and scrupulous caution must be encouraged in this respect. The greatest circum-spection is required here, because the revealed Book's function is to tell and recall the goals of the sciences and not their contents. The Book orients the conscience without determining reason and scien-tific practice. The experience of faith regarding the Books must not find expression in such an instrumentalization of reason, whether to state the norms or to confirm (or confirm itself through) acquired knowledge. This confusion of orders is a dangerous reduction.

Religion and Philosophy

The relationship between text scholars and philosophy (*'ilm al-kalâm*) has long been difficult. Let us recall that Abû Hâmid al-Ghazâlî (died 1111) spoke out very harshly in *The Incoherence of the Philosophers* against Greek philosophy of Aristotelian inspiration, which he had formerly studied and practiced, and that Ibn Rushd (Averroes, died 1198) responded with *The Incoherence of the Incoherence* to defend the practice of philosophy.[5] The issue was an important one, for the aim was, at that time, to restrain or counter the influence of Greek thought, metaphysics, and logic in the Islamic Universe of reference, which had begun as early as the ninth and tenth centuries with Abû Yûsuf al-Kindî (died 873), Muhammad al-Farabî (died 950), and then, of course, Abû 'Alî al-Husayn Ibn Sînâ (better known in Western thought as Avicenna, died 1037). Many Muslim scholars felt that the Revelation and Prophetic tradition had provided Muslims with instruments sufficient to deal with the issue of meaning, of morals, and of humankind's behavior in the Universe. Philosophical thought, whether self-contained or influenced by Greek rationalism or Chris-tian theology (itself bearing the influence of Hellenistic philosophy), was seen to be useless and dangerous. Protecting against such study was necessary.

Muslims have, for centuries, retained this paradoxical, suspi-cious relation to philosophy. Indeed, the Quran raised and then answered the question of meaning, but analytical reason was not meant to deal with it independently. It is indeed because the Revela-tion tackled the issue and gave a clear answer through the expression of *tawhîd*, the principle of divine oneness, that human attempts to deal with the issue were pointless and could only be counterproductive. In this sense, philosophy could only create a dangerously arrogant desire for autonomy, a shaky faith, or entry into the Universe of useless, futile debates. Yet, very early on, the works of the greatest critics of philosophy such as Abû Hâmid al-Ghazâlî or Taqî ad-Dîn ibn Taymiyyah (died 1328) included highly important fundamental philosophical analyses. Al-Ghazâlî's reflection on doubt in his work *Al-Munqidh min ad-Dalâl* or in *Mishkât al-Anwâr* was to have decisive influence on the methodic doubt established by Descartes in his search for truth (both in the *Discourse on Method* and in the *Meditations on First Philosophy*).[6] Ibn Taymiyyah was less interested in theoretical philosophy, but he developed a social and legal philosophy that, by inference, reveals at its source a philosophy of knowledge and meaning that indeed develops in the light of the revealed Book but with an independent, rationalistic, and systematic approach.

This apparent renunciation of philosophy, of metaphysics, and hence of theoretical philosophy was far from being the only response of text scholars and *fuqahâ'*. They may have taken very severe stands against Greek-influenced metaphysics—that presented itself as rationally autonomous as to the quest for truth—but, in effect, they often, directly or indirectly, produced metaphysical reflection and they almost systematically tackled the issue of meaning in an almost systematic way. This opposition between religion and philosophy results from a misunderstanding and is but a false debate. Closer to our own time, Jamâl ad-Dîn al-Afghânî (died 1897) revisited this issue, which he considered to be crucial to the awakening of the contemporary Muslim conscience. In a lecture in Calcutta in 1872, he presented philosophy as the mother of sciences; he did not set it against its relationship to the Revelation, but on the contrary integrated it into an interesting hierarchy of references. He said:

> It is therefore indispensable that there should be a mother science which could be considered as the collective soul of all the other sciences, in order to be able to safeguard them and to use them as needed while granting each of them the possibility to progress. Now, the only science that can claim to constitute the collective soul, the preserving force and the cause of the others' survival is philosophy, that is *hekmat*, for it deals with everything and in general terms.

He added, referring to Abû Hâmid al-Ghazâlî,

> In his book *Deliverance from Error*, Imam al-Ghazâlî, called
> Hojjat-el-islam, argued: anyone who claimed that Islam
> was against geometrical evidence, against philosophical ar-
> guments and the laws of nature, would be an obscurantist
> friend of Islam. Now, the damage caused to the Islamic reli-
> gion by such a friend would be more serious than that caused
> by heretics. For the laws of nature, the evidence of geome-
> try and philosophical arguments can only be considered as
> self-evident truths. He who claimed that his religion denied
> self-evident truths would necessarily have admitted his reli-
> gion to be invalid.[7]

This relationship to philosophy makes it possible to raise the issue
of reason's relation to Revelation. In the early twentieth century,
Muhammad Iqbâl (died 1938) in his seminal work *The Reconstruction of Religious Thought in Islam* places the issue of faithfulness to
the texts and of the dynamism of Muslim intelligence in the world
and its evolution at the center of a general relationship to philosophy,
meaning, and outcomes.[8] Philosophy should not be considered as the
antithesis of the religious viewpoint (it is the antithesis of the strictly
normative approach); it should, to the contrary, restore the latter's
comprehensive dimension of relating to the One, to meaning, and to
goals. The Revelation has not ended the quest for meaning; it accompanies and nurtures it, because progress in grasping that knowledge
is never completed. The Revelation is an answer, but it must remain
a question in one's relationship to learning, to knowledge, to action,
and to ends. The formalist and normative reduction prevents such an
approach and impoverishes the relationship to the human quest for
meaning. The latter is universal and Revelation never extinguishes
it; it indeed orients it, but without ever governing its intensity and
depth.

This reconciliation with philosophy is essential. The point is to
return from a *sharî'ah* reduced to a set of laws to a *sharî'ah* understood as a Way stemming from the two Books and questioning
consciences in the process. Focusing and projecting on the conclusions, it questions the means and constitutes a true metaphysics of
the sciences, of all those sciences mentioned in this book. Muslim

thinkers must reconcile the contemporary Islamic conscience with those questionings and those fundamental reflections. A philosophy of quest, of legislation, an epistemology of the sciences in the light of the Way, may open prospects for contemporary Muslim thought and avoid its timidly and fearfully withdrawing into itself. Reading the two Books in the light of the ends makes it possible to reconcile with the universality of the quest rather than be obsessed with the specificity of the means. The latter should not be minimized, but restored to their proper place: they outline the limits and norms on the Way, but they are not the Way.

Sharî'ah, *Sufism, and Ethics*

In the course of centuries, the geography of the "Islamic" sciences was determined by their fields of specialization. As the legal function became preeminent, other distinct areas emerged for some scholars, regarding the relationship to the divine, to texts, and to knowledge. In the now classical tradition, three main branches were distinguished: Creed (*al-'aqîdah*), Law (*ash-sharî'ah*), and Truth (*al-haqîqah*). Some *fuqahâ'* in the course of time, especially the contemporary advocates of literalist *salafî* thought or of traditional legal schools, have opposed the idea that there could be a distinct path reaching to the Truth through an initiation leading to gnosis (*al-ma'rifah*), an intimate knowledge of God, in proximity and sometimes in annihilation of the "I" and of the self. According to them, such approaches, Sufism or "Islamic mysticism," are inventions created outside the belief system of Islam, mainly deriving from Christian influences, which have added innumerable innovations (*bida'*) to fundamental Islamic rules. They see this as nothing but a way of undermining Islam from within, with a vocabulary, practices, and rules that do not respect the Islamic framework, nor its norms and requirements. They consider the mere mention of the word "Sufism" as a fundamentally suspicious act.

It is true that over the course of centuries, and to an extraordinary extent today, numbers of self-proclaimed Sufi circles have appeared and one may wonder what remains "Islamic" in their fundamental beliefs, practices, and norms. Some circles establish a relationship to the *shaykh*, the guide, or "master," which is akin to sanctification, to *shirk* (association) or to superstition, and which ascribes to him the role of an infallible saint or of a necessary intermediary between the pupil or aspirant (*al-murîd*) and God (whereas Islam makes it clear that the relationship must be individual and direct). Others offer their followers highly surprising lightening of religious practice: no compulsory ritual prayers, paying *zakât* to other beneficiaries (including sometimes the *shaykh* himself or his circle), relatively easier practices of fasting, and entirely revisionist codes related to behavior and dress. Exclusionary discourse can also be denoted in some Sufi trends, claiming that their way is the only faithful one, excluding all others. Today, some schools combine all those features and promote a Sufism that it is difficult to relate to Islam. One can understand the fears of some *'ulamâ'* and *fuqahâ'* and their attempts keep such deviations from being considered as Islamic and sometimes encouraged in the West because they are supposed to represent the open, modern face of an Islam of the heart (and no longer an Islam of norms).

Because of such fears, some *fuqahâ'* nevertheless reacted too strongly, criticizing and rejecting Sufism as a whole for being a fundamental distortion of Islam's teachings. Yet, many mystical traditions, from the very beginning, insisted on scrupulous faithfulness to Islam's teachings. They may have developed specific language, their own terminology, a particular method of spiritual education, or determined for their followers the steps, stations, and states of mystical initiation, but this was meant to be followed in addition to ritual practice, while the rules prescribed by the texts were never to be substituted or curtailed. Such traditions as *al-Qâdiriyyah, ash-Shâdhiliyyah, an-Naqshbandiyyah,* the *Tijâniyyah,* or the *Murids* were initially, with their respective founders, very strict and respectful of Islamic practices and norms; later, some of their secondary followers and some of *their* offshoots did sometimes fall into excess and distortions, but it would be unfair to condemn Sufi traditions as a whole. In the course of the history of Islamic civilization, mystics—for instance, the Prophet's Companion Abû Dhar al-Ghifârî—played the central role of recalling the heart of Islam, its essence, and the goals of spiritual education.

Most of the great jurists of Islam were affiliated with Sufi circles, and the master work of Abû Hâmid al-Ghazâlî in the twelfth century, *Revival of the Religious Sciences (Ihyâ' 'ulûm ad-dîn),* reconciles the orders of spirituality and of law. So does the work of

'Abd al-Qâdir al-Jilânî (died 1166), *Sufficient Provision for Seekers of the Path of Truth* (*Al-Ghunia li Tâlibi Tarîq al-Haq*), or that of Shâfi'i scholar Ahmad ibn Naqid al-Misrî (died 1368), *Reliance of the Traveller* (*'Umdat as-Sâlik wa 'Uddat an-Nâsik*), that couples presentation of the law and rules with fundamental Sufi spiritual teachings.[9] Very early on, Indian scholar Ahmad as-Sirhindî (died 1624)[10] had challenged the idea that consisted in distinguishing between the fields of knowledge and action, between *al-'aqîdah* seen as including the principles of faith (*arkân al-îmân*), *ash-sharî'ah* dealing specifically with laws, and *al-haqîqah* seen as the path to intimate knowledge of God. For as-Sirhindî, in keeping with the discussion developed throughout this study, *ash-sharî'ah* encompasses the dimensions of gnosis, the education of the heart and the elevation toward the One. *Al-ma'rifah*, intimate knowledge of God—that is, The Truth—lies at the heart of the *sharî'ah*: it is its essence and light, and *al-haqîqah* and *ash-sharî'ah* stem from one *'aqîdah*, which is a single clear creed. This approach has the advantage of again citing several truths to which Muslims must return—spiritual education, the demanding task of reforming and transcending oneself that is the essence of Islamic mysticism, and also of Sufism—and that represents the heart of Islamic teachings. In light of those teachings, with growing knowledge, following the Way (*ash-sharî'ah*) absolutely mandates that exertion (*jihâd*) of the self on itself—that is, on the ego. This practice and its requirements constitute the circumstance and light of commitment to the Way. Moreover, they represent the best ways of struggling against the formalistic reduction repeatedly mentioned in the book. Restoring education and continuing a spiritual quest at the center of the understanding and implementation of the *sharî'ah* mean resolving to reconsider the priorities and goals of human action and of ethics. This perspective may seem paradoxical, but remains fundamentally true: it is by emphasizing intimate individual experience that Islam can reconcile with the common universal quest.

It is important to reconcile the *sharî'ah* with all forms of mysticism and with Sufism by restoring the latter to its proper position, provided normative principles are respected (no sacralization or worship of the *shaykh*, no accepted breaches of practice, no encouraged superstitions). Moreover, Sufism should be reconciled with ethics, so that the goals of self-transcending are concretely allied with the higher goals as regards presence and action in the world and in human societies. To this end, *'ulamâ'*, *fuqahâ'*, *shuyûkh* (plur. of *shaykh*) and/or the initiated in Sufi circles (*turuq*, plur. of *tarîqah*) as well as thinkers in general should agree to start a dialogue, to speak together, and to circumscribe the common good and groundwork that impart meaning to their commitment. Such dialogue does not yet exist, which paves the way, in disorder and division, for the emergence of exotic Sufi movements that exploit people's credulity, sincerity, and naivete; support the most unethical (and supposedly most "modern") behavior; and respond to the legitimate quest for meaning with an offer that allows for minimum effort with the approval of *shuyûkh* who take the pupil's hardships and difficulties on themselves in return for the aspirant's blind submission and, sometimes, tidy sums of money.

Dialogues

Contemporary Muslim intelligence suffers a crucial lack of dialogues and debates on several levels. We have just seen how important it is to begin open, constructive intra-religious dialogue, between the various schools and trends, to transform the ignorance of others, oppositions, rejections, and general divisions into better-accepted and better-managed diversity. Like the Companions, we should learn again that God's uniqueness, the Prophet's unique exemplarity, the similarity of scriptural sources, the community of faith, of principles and of practice never suggested the standardization of thought. The universality of Islam requires, within its own Universe of reference, that a diversity of understandings, approaches, and schools should be experienced, composed, and fostered. Questions of legitimacy (between legal schools and trends of thought), religious authority (in terms of determining festival dates, modes of representation), and political position (on the national and international levels) foster divisions and stand in the way of fundamental critical debates about the relationship to the texts, about concrete contemporary issues, or simply about diversity in Islam itself. Muslims are unable to tolerate divisions and thus need to open a critical dialogue that can accept a diversity of views and above all identify those areas or issues for which fundamental agreement exists. They have long since lost the ability to agree intellectually *for* (i.e., about) something (an idea, a project, a commitment); they only come together emotionally and then sometimes show apparent unity when mobilizing *against* a potential enemy, a provocation, or an attack. Without critical dialogue, their union is indeed emotional, often excessive, punctilious, and short-lived. Some *'ulamâ'* see this as evidence of the strength of the Islamic "*ummah,*" but going beyond appearances, it actually reveals unparalleled fragility and weakness. Popular demonstrations, so excessive in the Muslim world, against the Danish cartoons or Pope Benedict XVI's speech in Germany,[11] reveal far more about societies where critical debate is lacking, where civil society is muzzled (and sometimes cunningly instrumentalized to vent its anger on the outside world, on the West), where hypocritical formalism is institutionalized, than they do about the specific object of the anger. The same is true of mobilizations against the war in Iraq or of opposition to the Israeli government's repressive policy toward the Palestinians. From the top leaders to the grassroots of Muslim societies and communities, one can observe emotional mobilizations determined by the timing and intensity of media coverage. There is no in-depth debate between trends of thought, no critical dialogue, no long-term strategy ... and always the same lack of vision and coordination.

Clearly, it is impossible—and it may indeed be counterproductive—to engage in a "dialogue of civilizations" if one does not simultaneously carry out this imperative *intra* dialogue among Muslims. Indeed both must and can be mutually enriching; one should enter dialogue as one looks at oneself in a mirror, and manage to draw on the amount of information that dialogue with the other reveals about oneself. The whole reflection about higher outcomes already developed is essential in this respect, for one should indeed, when starting a critical, constructive dialogue with other civilizations, ask oneself about one's own meaning and objectives. After answering this question one can, inductively, determine the conditions and means of dialogue. It is strange, and all-in-all unacceptable, to observe the lack or poverty of the Muslim contribution to this attempt at dialogue between civilizations and cultures. Referring to ethical outcomes should give rise to a collective, critical, and constructive approach of the very notion of "dialogue" and its meaning. Instead of such fundamental reflection, idealistic reflections appear here and there about common values and respecting diversity.

Our times require far deeper and more earnest commitment than that, although Muslim scholars and intellectuals engage in the debate in a chaotic and most naive manner. Before accepting such terms and themes as "dialogue," "alliance," "civilizations," "cultures," with all the related themes such as "identity," "integration," "affiliation," the framework and rules of the game must be established. The debate over "civilizations" and "cultures" must not act as a screen and be a pretext behind which the other real problems of contemporary times are hidden—and displaced by. Depicting the "dialogue of civilizations" as the positive ideology of our time to avoid discussing the strategies of political, economic, cultural, and military domination is a smokescreen and, when all is said and done, nothing but hypocrisy. No strong political ideology being available, a twofold displacement is being performed in the North: a kind of ideology of fear[12] is created, fixing attention on differences and on potential disruptions and clashes between religions and cultures, then debates focus on issues concerning civilizations and values, far from any general political or economic considerations. This clever strategy encloses the agents of dialogue in an isolated Universe where issues that suddenly seem the most important are discussed without dealing with previously existing real problems that nevertheless remain essential. The strategy is the same both internationally and nationally: as we have seen, in many European countries, problems are being "culturalized," "religionalized," or "Islamized" while they are in actuality primarily social and political in nature. Rather than proposing real social policies that promote equal treatment and ending job and housing discrimination, the problem is displaced and transferred into terms related to "integration."

The second flaw that can be observed in this "dialogue between civilizations" pertains to the construction of one's "own" civilization and of that of "the other." Western and Islamic civilizations are shown, according to the needs of this dialogue, as closed, monolithic entities, thus initiating another dialogue with a different Universe presumed to represent fundamental otherness in its thought and values. Yet nothing could be less true historically, scientifically, and philosophically than such a self-representation whether now or in the past. History books too often present the Middle Ages as an intellectually dark period, almost a black hole, before the luminous period of the Renaissance preceding the age of Enlightenment and of free rationality that is seen as the archetypal distinguishing feature of the West. This vision is purely a historical and ideological reconstruction that ignores the presence and contribution of Muslims at the heart of Europe for centuries, in the fields of the sciences, law, art, philosophy, architecture, and other disciplines. Such reduction of the past and roots of the West and of Europe, in the manner of Pope Benedict XVI who only relates to its Greek and Christian heritage, is not innocent intellectually and ideologically; it represents a selective memory, an identity construction based on a major "historical disregard," and the choice, in the past and today, of reducing Islam to otherness. The West should therefore, simultaneously, start a dialogue with itself to rediscover and reclaim the whole of its heritage including the Islamic sources it has hidden from itself; only at such cost can deep, relevant dialogue develop. The same must be done in the Muslim world, which has long been nurtured and influenced by Greek, Roman, Jewish, and Christian thought from all areas in the West. As I have said again and again, it is impossible to start earnest dialogue about present diversity if one persists in denying the plural reality and the diversity of one's own past, and this applies to each of the world's civilizations.

Another requirement for dialogue between civilizations must be added: ideas and values should not only be discussed, but measured through their concrete implementation in reality. It is unfair, as I said, to compare one's "own" ideal values with the failings and shortcomings observed in "the other's" societies; similarly, it is of little interest, in the long run, to isolate a debate of ideas and values from the realities of the world. We must undertake a true critical and self-critical analysis to measure the gap between our values and our practices. Dialogue between civilizations is meaningful only if it compels its agents and involved parties to ponder the inconsistency between ideals and respective concrete policies. Intellectual probity calls for such self-awareness in the mirror of the other's questioning. One can then realize that the problems encountered have less to do with values, which have often been historically or philosophically shared, than with disagreements about their ideological use or with the inconsistency observed everyday in political, social, or economic practices. Both Universes refer to *dignity, justice, equality,* and *freedom* and in both Universes—to various degrees—one can observe undignified or wrongful treatment of human beings (from immigration policies to torture), conspicuous injustice (between the rich and the poor, various forms of discrimination), persistent inequalities (between women and men, of various origins, and skin colors), breaches of freedom (dictatorships, enhanced security policies, increased surveillance). When the "dialogue between values and ideals" is approached and translated into a "dialogue between policies and practices," it takes on quite another character: it becomes meaningful because it requires outcomes to be assessed in terms of concrete realities. This is what I have been calling on the Muslim conscience to do throughout this book; it is an exercise that the members of each society, each religion, each culture, or civilization should constantly compel themselves to do. That is how, through an open, critical, and constructive dialogue with the other, one can measure the extent of the reforms to be undertaken about oneself.

Good intentions in dialogue are not sufficient. One must insist on *a priori* conditions that alone can enable the dialogue's objectives to be achieved. Those conditions do not lie in means or ends but in the attitude and frame of mind, that is, in the mind-set that the women and men taking part in such debates must maintain. First of all, they should approach those debates with *humility*, realizing that no civilization was ever established without influence from others and that no society perfectly respects its ideals. *Concern for coherence and self-criticism* that must be uncompromising and constructive must naturally be included in those conditions if one wants to reach beyond formalistic, idealistic dialogue buried in the great achievements of the past or in utopian aspirations to a future more dreamed of than actually prepared for. Finally, dialogue requires *respect*, without patronizing tolerance—one based on knowledge, trust, and here again, a free critical relationship. Dialogue approached with *humility, concern for coherence and self-criticism*, and *respect* for the other, can enable the parties to go beyond flimsy flights of lyricism and keep them focused on the real issues related to this dialogue, to social, political, and economic questions; to ideological construction of the past; and to shared universal values. This self-critical, dialectical relationship to oneself and others precludes leaving out sensitive issues, those that, after all, made the dialogue necessary in the first place and that are—intentionally or not—forgotten along the way.[13]

Interfaith dialogue is also crucial and must be conducted with the same intellectual and critical rigor. I have dealt with this issue at length in a previous book[14] and presented the fundamental conditions for necessary, fruitful dialogue. What matters therefore is to avoid being deluded into engaging in dialogues whose outcome, in an age of globalization and multiple tensions, would be dialogue itself. Just as "an ideology of fear" devoid of real ideas or ideals has developed, it could be answered by a kind of new "ideology of dialogue" whose only idea would be to promote a dialogue of civilizations far removed from the hot issues of economy, politics, domination, and power. The "politics" of dialogue thus produced from the outset multiply the chances for encounters and exchanges between agents who either share common views (in which case this is not dialogue but what I have long called "interactive monologue"), or confront one another to measure their degree of flexibility toward their own Universe of reference. Nothing about this is without difficulties, and although dialogue as such must not be refused or rejected, because it is imperative and inescapable, it is important to reconsider the "terms of dialogue" in the same way as the "terms of exchange" are criticized in economic discourse.

Muslim *'ulamâ'* and thinkers have not contributed as they should to the reflection that should have accompanied this dialogue. Problems are interdependent and connected: the intellectual attitude that consists of considering Islamic universality in exclusivity and otherness; the cartoon construction of an imaginary West; propensity to formalism to elude self-criticism; a focus on the rules coming from the revealed Book without properly understanding the Book of the Universe; neglecting higher objectives, so that *sharî'ah* becomes a closed, static system of laws to be implemented almost literally. All those distortions prevent the Muslim world from comprehending issues in their full depth and complexity. Above all, they prevent it from deriving actual benefit from a constructive critical encounter with "the other," through their differences and the viewpoint the latter offers, for the point is ultimately to construct oneself by oneself and through this "other" (and help her or him construct himself or herself as well). This requires breadth of vision about values and an open prospect as to outcomes, confidence, and a permanent effort to subject ideals to the instrument of the critique of reality. This is the meaning of the Prophet's appeal: "O God, we ask you [to grant us] useful knowledge!"[15] Such useful knowledge is, intellectually and in daily life, knowledge allied to applied ethics. This intellectual breadth recognizes universal and shared values, and identifies higher goals, but requires scientific rigor, thorough self-criticism, and concern about coherence in identifying problems and assessing concrete practices. A radical reform of minds is therefore required.

Spirituality and Intelligence

The great question about the relationship between religion and philosophy has brought to the heart of the debate the relationship between faith and reason already discussed. This important theme is worthy of in-depth, ever-renewing reflection. However, in the order of reflection about the higher goals of ethics, another equation must be examined, discussed, and solved. I am not referring to the strict relationship to the question of truth, but more fundamentally to the issues of meaning and coherence that must, as we have seen, fuel our dialogue with ourselves and with others. When related to religion, spirituality is faith that, projected on life and on the world, imparts meaning to being just as it makes meaningful and orients the actions of human beings. Intelligence is the act of reason that observes, comprehends, and attempts to understand being, the self, the Universe, and life. In the order of action, driven by meaning, demanding coherence, one must go further than the discussion between faith and reason and find those ways that make it possible to combine spirituality and intelligence. In terms of the classical categories of philosophy, this is the order of the philosophy of action that completes the order of knowledge and leads to the quest for harmony.

Such a quest for meaning and understanding makes it possible to avoid the two primary failings elucidated in the preceding pages and more generally throughout the present book. Placing spirituality, the intimate quest for meaning, light, and peace, at the center of the religious experience makes it possible to overcome the formalistic reductions that turn religion into a closed, restrictive Universe of norms, limits, and prohibitions. There are, to be sure, rituals, obligations, and morals, but they pertain to a *conception of life and death* that imparts to them a meaning and substance that one must perpetually recall to avoid becoming deluded by the presence of a formal set of rules emptied of the heart of their meaning. This is what the

Prophet of Islam indicated in a tradition that should be understood both literally and figuratively: "God does not look at your bodies or at your image but God looks into your hearts."[16] Intelligence enables analytical reason to rise to the understanding of complexity, the order of relativities, and the requirement of coherence. More than "knowing," what is involved is "understanding,"[17] putting things into perspective, and multiplying angles and standpoints to attain intellectual empathy. Intelligence is contrasted with dogmatism in all its forms, from exclusivist, sectarian positions to binary, simplistic readings. It is often hastily stated that faith is by nature dogmatic (or is the most liable to become so), yet this is not true: with or without faith, what makes the mind dogmatic is a particular disposition of the intelligence. Produced by an atheistic or a believing conscience, the dogmatic mind tells nothing of its own intellectual capacities (which may be numerous and sophisticated), but it reveals its whole reductive mode of functioning about the order of truth. The oneness of truth, both by essence and by definition, is in such action confused with exclusively possessing it with privilege and authority. Understanding complexity, about the relationship of reason to knowledge and truth, opens prospects of diversity by linking a single truth to the order of multiple outcomes, of individual quests, and of singular evolutions driven by a common and universal aspiration to knowledge.

Allying spirituality and intelligence, and meaning and understanding, is a major challenge of our time. Postmodernism is defined through the rejection of universals and the apprehension of relativity through innumerable approaches including structuralism (or "poststructuralism") and constructivism (or "deconstructivism" or "postconstructivism"). By questioning the claim to truth, the fundamentals of ethics seem to have been undermined. Yet our societies, our ways of life, and the state of the planet compel us, because of impending natural catastrophes, of troubled identities, of mistreated Nature, to reconcile ourselves with the shared universality of goals and values. Whether our truth is theoretically one or theoretically relative, it can only have substance if it calls on the practical conscience for meaning and coherence. Far from any theoretical, formalistic religion or philosophy cut off from the world, and from any dogmatic, exclusivist faith or rationality imposing itself on everyone, we must rediscover the ways to depth and complexity: a luminous, profound, and humble faith allied with an insightful, critical, determined mind.

This involves a paradoxical and yet highly necessary alliance: that of humility with regard to power, and ambition with regard to projects. Ambitious humility wards off passivity and fatalism while humble ambition protects from arrogance and dogmatism.

Understanding the texts on the basis of higher objectives is a highly demanding spiritual and intellectual exercise. Knowledge of texts and contexts, a comprehensive vision allied to specialized skills, mastery of the order of ends and priorities are necessary conditions to be able to produce and practically implement an ethics that can claim some efficiency—an ethics of transformation and not of adaptation. Allying spirituality and intelligence therefore requires a perpetual effort at coherence; this implies profound knowledge of goals, permanent self-criticism about one's own practices, and a particular disposition for intellectual empathy that consists of comprehending the other's points of references from her own point of view (without ever hesitating to offer constructive criticism of that other's practical inconsistencies). What is meant here is not to relativize one's own relation to God, to truth, and to the meaning of life, but to iterate this relation within an aspiration that orients intelligence and human behavior towards consistency with outcomes, which is never fully achieved and must constantly be reassessed. The ethical requirement necessitates permanent questioning.

We are then heading for the Way, for universals that integrate and feed on diversity and differences and combine the various viewpoints and competences—both from within the same religious family and from outside. Important work remains to be achieved from within, however, as the present book has attempted to show. Radical internal reform, the liberation of hearts and minds, would make it possible to reconcile the substance of the texts and to meet the challenges of our time. This involves grasping higher goals and questioning monopolized or entrenched authorities and powers to impose consistency about values, norms, and practices in all fields of human activity. What applied ethics imposes by inference, beyond all the "post" philosophies (postmodernism, poststructuralism, postconstructivism) is to reconsider the meaning and substance of universals from within and with regard to the other. Similarly, it requires reflection about meaning and coherence and calls for dialogues with one's own and with other civilizations, and to be apt to tackle the respective inconsistencies of practices rather than the ethereal ideals of theories. Goals and ethics train the heart to the intensity of questioning and the mind to the construction of bridges—between self and self, oneself and others, values and behaviors, and means and ends. This however requires speech to be free, minds to be called on or to call themselves to debate, to criticize and to question openly and honestly! All minds, those of every faith, should at last accept their responsibilities and stop adopting a victims' stance and blaming governments, *'ulamâ'*, the West, and all "the others." The spiritual community of Muslims, the *ummah*, holds such a wealth of human and material resources, so many intelligent minds, so many skills and potentialities, that it has the objective means to face its numerous crises. For this, each heart and mind, women as well as men, with their respective assets, need to contribute to this deep, radical reform. They must, in the name of responsibility, claim their share of authority.

Conclusion

The reflection that has been developed over the course of this book operates on several levels and is not easy to comprehend. As has been shown, one must, on the one hand, immerse oneself in the Islamic Universe of reference and assess its sources, instruments, and (interpretative, legal, or ethical) methodologies, and on the other, take into account the history of their concrete implementation, going so far as to measure their relevance and efficacy in terms of the challenges of our time. This is a thorough, critical study from within, which states that we are in need of radical reform.

My questionings and proposals about the nature and categorization of the sources and fundamentals of *usûl al-fiqh* entail nontrivial concrete consequences. First, our relationship to the texts and to the Universe must be revisited: we are faced with two Revelations that need to be read and understood in parallel. Each has its rules, principles, and requirements, and the scholars and scientists that deal with each of them open for us, together, the ways to faithfulness and coherence toward the divine teachings inviting humankind to its humanity. Building on this approach, our outlook changes spiritually and intellectually: what is involved is no longer simply respecting the teachings of a book standing outside history, but expressing a deep reverence of the heart and mind toward nature, societies, and cultures through all time and in all their diversity. This mirror reading of the two Books, of the two Revelations, requires us to think through the higher objectives of Islam's message in a new, more rigorous, specialized and necessarily dynamic manner: applied Islamic ethics must take into account not only the texts' explicit norms and prohibitions but more systematically the requirements of contexts and of human, social, and scientific environments. This is a major shift that involves reconsidering the modalities of text reading and interpretation, the methodologies of the rules' extraction (from the texts), and above all the nature of the areas and competencies used to carry out that task.

Text *'ulamâ'*, specialists in the fundamentals of law and jurisprudence (*usûliyyûn*), or in applied law and jurisprudence (*fuqahâ'*) are not the only people who must engage in this reform (just as they are not the only ones to blame for present difficulties). Indeed, the shift in the center of gravity of authority just mentioned must lead to mobilizing all manner of participants: those of ordinary Muslims and those of women (and not just so-called women's issues); those of scientists as well as of specialists and experts (Muslims or non-Muslims). In the light of those teachings and of the higher goals revealed by the Book, all areas of knowledge, all intellectual energies must be mobilized, along with the creativity of women and men, to impart concrete, practical meaning to spiritual and ethical coherence in history as well as in societies, both rich and poor, Muslim-majority or not, whatever their cultures. In this sense, a new presentation of ethical goals is particularly demanding: it requires allying the comprehensive vision of the message with rigorous specialization in each area of human knowledge and action to grasp issues in their complexity and enable applied ethics to respond adequately to the inconsistencies and challenges of our time.

That is the price for "transformation reform." The meaning and function of the Quran's message—in keeping with all divine, spiritual, and philosophical messages—lies in its capacity to educate our hearts and minds to resist the aberrations of humankind and societies and seek to transform and fashion the world into what is best for human beings: *dignity, justice, love, forgiveness, welfare,* and *peace.* From this standpoint, being modern cannot be synonymous with "adapting" to evolution and progress, however mad and inhumane they might be. What is needed is to awaken consciences, to question, to assess, and ultimately to free ourselves from the mirages of time and the pressure of fashion, however liberated they may seem. We are quite aware of the elevated, multidimensional nature of the challenges we are collectively setting for the contemporary Muslim conscience, but this seems to be the only method to ensure deep faithfulness to the Way and its ethical goals. Resistance must indeed be on two fronts: against evolution and progress devoid of conscience or soul on the one hand, and against literalist immobilism (rigid imitation, *taqlîd*) and misleading formalism on the other. In this sense, aspirations for reform can be most misleading and lead to renunciations and alienation that are just as dangerous as the evils they were meant to cure: in their obsession to follow "the West," some thinkers simply change their referent, their model, "god" or master, but the process of closing oneself off in imitation is the same thing, or maybe even worse, because it disguises itself in the cloak of freedom. Reconciliation with oneself, with higher objectives and with universals, is far more demanding. It involves spiritual but also deeply intellectual introspection: extracting universals from one's innermost experience and thus bringing the individual inner self into harmony with the collective and plural human conscience. Such reconciliation requires humility, critical and self-critical coherence, and a deep sense of listening and of respect, for oneself and for others. Our ethics is one of liberation.

As the various chapters in this book tried to show, the transformation reform proposed involves multiple requirements: a new outlook on texts and human and social contexts, mobilizing knowledge and skills, and rebalancing legitimacy and authority in the production of norms and ethics. It clearly amounts to refusing immobilism, formalism, blind imitation (of all kinds), or fatalism. No human reality is irreversible, no human power is absolute and eternal, no challenge is final, for the believing conscience, as ought also be the case for the humanist conscience, *everything remains possible*. Faith is confidence. Here, intelligence is resistance. The alliance of faith and intelligence, of confidence and resistance, must liberate intellectual energies and give life to true freedom, which refuses alienation and mobilizes knowledge, human creativity, and ethical sense to transform the world and make it a better place. I have attempted to outline a framework and present a reading grid that could make such a renewal possible. I am thus setting out on a path and these initial proposals are far from final; I shall go on examining the various possibilities lying ahead, but the law of life and of history, the divine tradition (*sunnat Allah*), teaches us every day that it is up to subsequent generations to develop, deepen, and improve the insights and reflections of those who came before them. Along the way, I have conveyed an insight and a thought: may God, the Most Near, protect them if they are of any use, or cause them to be quickly forgotten if there is no good in them.

In practice, I have mentioned the long work that lies ahead in such fields as medicine, culture, and the arts; the issues of women and gender relations; educational, social, and political prospects; economy, and ecology. Those various topics have not been examined thoroughly and many others could still be added. A choice was imposed by limited time and space. I have sometimes suggested answers, but most of the time I merely raised specific, often complex, questions, which require answers if I want to remain coherent about the higher goals of Islam's message and its applied ethics. I mentioned creating spaces for study, institutions, and training centers, where text scholars (*usûliyyûn, fuqahâ'*) could meet, debate, and consult with other scholars in the experimental and social sciences, and specialists and experts in the different areas of expertise. This, I think, is an urgent priority, on the local level as well as nationally and internationally. Initiating exchanges, creating opportunities, developing projects, institutionalizing the vision are imperative. In some countries, or even locally in some cities, interesting projects and new and sometimes strikingly original collaborations have been set up: I have seen such instances in Africa, in Asia, in the Middle and Near East, as well as in the United States, Canada, Europe, and Australia. Visions are not always clear, projects are not always carried out in synergy, but intuitions are present, visible, and palpable. Those real-world initiatives fill me with hope. For one who travels around, who meets women and men, ordinary people as well as scholars, it is clear that this is as much a time of crisis as of intellectual and spiritual effervescence. All feel the need for renewal and each on his or her own level does the best possible to seek insight into a vision for life. I wish to pay tribute to all those women and men, ordinary people, organization leaders, intellectuals, *'ulamâ'*, scientists, or scholars, who give so much of their hearts, of their sincerity, of their energy, and of their time to make things change, move, and progress. The intellectual groundwork underlying this book owes them a great debt: the road is a long one, but there is no lack of spiritual and intellectual energy. Radical reform, in any case, with its exacting ethical requirements and its demand for liberation, essentially consists of recalling that, through faith in the One, confidence, and determination, *everything is always possible.*

Acknowledgments

This book owes so much…to so many people. To so many minds, so many scholars and intellectuals as well as the numerous Muslim societies and communities I have visited throughout the world. This book was born of spiritual communions and of much intellectual sharing. It is also the singular outcome of a plural progress: reading, teaching, encountering, debating, and fulfilling commitments in the field have provided the substance of the present study and I wish to thank all those who have, in one way or another, contributed to nurturing me, to challenging me, and to stimulating my thought. To them, to "you," I inscribe this book, intimately, individually, and collectively.

Special thanks go to my colleagues at Oxford University, Saint Antony's College, Walter Armbrust and Eugene Rogan (Middle East Center), Kalypso Nicolaidis and Timothy Garton Ash (European Studies Center), and the staff at the Faculty of Theology where I teach and where I was able to test part of the substance of this study. Nor will I forget Han Etzinger and Dick Douwes with whom I team up at Erasmus University, Rotterdam, within the scope of the "Citizenship and Identity" chair I have been holding for the past two years, of the Ph.D. projects we supervise together and of the municipality's

Citizenship and Sense of Belonging project. Those collaborations have been most fruitful for me and have directly or indirectly made it possible to complete this book.

I wish to thank Yasmina, who was my personal assistant for five years and who dedicated her efforts, heart, and time to making my office efficient and well-organized. New roads are now opening for her: my heartfelt thanks! Marjolein, my assistant in Rotterdam, has also been remarkably devoted and I can never thank her enough for her presence and commitment. Cynthia Read of Oxford University Press is a friend and a sister along the road: the best present a publisher can give an author. This book would not be what it is without the permanent, unconditional commitment of Muna Ali who assists me from the United States and who read, discussed, corrected, and put forward suggestions at each stage in its production. Her humility and reliability are unequaled: thank you, I do not forget, I forget nothing. In the same breath, I would like to express my deep gratitude to my appointed translator and demanding reader, Claude Dabbak: a noble presence, impressive and discreet learning, and always apt remarks that have helped me improve formulations and/or the substance of my thought. I know how lucky I am.

And then, there are my relatives. My family. Iman, Maryam, Sami, Moussa, and Najma…they are the first to bear the weight of my commitment. They have been by my side, encouraging me, for so many years: if this book is in any way useful, a large share of the merit will be yours! For my mother, my sister, my four brothers, and the large family who follow me, encourage me, read and support me, these pages will I hope be evidence that the tree produces some fruit. Its qualities are yet to be proved…not my love.

London, July 2008

Notes

Introduction

1. *To Be a European Muslim* (Leicester, UK: Islamic Foundation, 1997).
2. *Western Muslims and the Future of Islam* (New York: Oxford University Press, 2004).
3. *Islam, the West and the Challenges of Modernity: Which Project for Which Modernity?* (Leicester, UK: Islamic Foundation, 2000).
4. Muhammad Iqbâl, *The Reconstruction of Religious Thought in Islam* (London: Oxford University Press, 1934). See especially chapter 6, "The Principle of Movement in the Structure of Islam."
5. See the text of that *Call* (and the ensuing reactions) on the homepage of my Web site: www.tariqramadan.com.
6. These are the higher principles related to the protection of religion (*dîn*), life (*nafs*), the intellect (*'aql*), progeny (*nasl*), wealth (*amwâl*), and, according to some, dignity (*'ird*). I shall return to this in parts II and III.

Part I

1. Abû Hâmid al-Ghazâlî, *Ihyâ 'ulûm ad-dîn*, 5 vols., 3rd ed. (Beirut: Dar al-Qalam, [in Arabic], n.d.).
2. See my book *Aux Sources du Renouveau Musulman*, 2nd ed. (Paris: Bayard, 1998).

Chapter 1

1. A verb of the same form, whose root is "*ja-da-da*," is sometimes used to convey the idea of "innovating," or "modernizing."
2. The Arabic word "*man*" used in the original can mean either an individual or a group; this text uses the more inclusive "*humankind*," unless gender is specific.
3. *Hadîth* reported by Abû Dawûd.
4. Quran 11:88; 16:103; 26:195.
5. The author then would be the Prophet Muhammad or, from a more global methodological viewpoint, the text should be dealt with as a human work taking into account its chronology, or even its evolutions or possible contradictions.
6. It must be added here that the heated debate that opposed Mu'tazilî rationalists and Ibn Hanbal, during the reign of al-Ma'mûn (died 833), about the created or uncreated nature of the Quran, was totally separate, for the advocates of both camps, from the question of whether the Quran should be given contextualized interpretation. Discussions today carry in a most biased and superficial manner the terms of the debate that began in the ninth century and went on through the tenth and eleventh centuries, among Hanbalî, Ash'arî, and Maturidî about the status of the Quran. The point was to determine the status of the Quran in relation to the principle of God's oneness (*at-tawhîd*), and not the legitimacy of interpreting revealed verses in the light of the Prophetic experience and history that endow them with meaning. Thus, Ahmad ibn Hanbal, a fierce advocate of the uncreated nature of the Quran, never questioned the need for a contextualized legal reading: essentially, what he opposed was the elaboration of dogmatism and of a theologico-philosophical theory (*kalâm*) that tended to acknowledge only human reason as its ultimate reference. The classical Islamic tradition (whether Sunni or Shi'i) was quick to establish—beyond the disputes about the status of the essence of God's Word, qualities, and names—that if the Word (the Quran) comes from God, the Word is not God, and the text's Revelation within human history requires the mediation of human intelligence to grasp and understand it and to remain faithful to it through time. Once more, the central issue was to determine the nature and limits of interpretation confronting the revealed text.

7. *Salafî* literalists refuse the involvement of the legal schools and their scholars of reference when approaching and reading texts. They call themselves *salafî* because they are keen to follow the *salaf,* which is the title given to the Prophet's Companions and the pious Muslims of the first three generations of Islam. The Quran and Sunnah should therefore, according to them, be interpreted directly, bypassing the divisions of legal schools.

8. Those prescriptions have five distinct categories: at the two ends of the scale of prescriptions one can find *al-wâjib* (or *al-fard,* although some scholars, particularly of the Hanafî school, make a distinction in status and value between *al-wâjib* and *al-fard*) and *al-harâm*: the first term refers to an action that is considered as mandatory, whereas the last means that which is absolutely forbidden. If, for instance, a Quranic injunction is stated in the imperative (e.g., *"Perform prayer and give the social purifying alms"* Quran 2:43) or in the negative imperative (such as *"And do not come near to adultery"* Quran 17:32), those injunctions would be identified as, respectively, an obligation (*wâjib*) or a prohibition (*harâm*). Between those two extremes, 'ulamâ have identified three other classes of human actions: what is "recommended" or "preferable" (*al-mustahab, al-mandûb*), what is "reprehensible" (*al-makrûh*), and what is permitted (*al-mubâh*).

9. Those are serious accusations that make a scholar or thinker thus qualified to be considered as an enemy from within, that is, as an apostate (*murtad*) or a traitor.

10. See my discussion and analysis in *Western Muslims and the Future of Islam* (New York: Oxford University Press, 2003), 43.

11. See my presentation in *Western Muslims,* 31.

12. The aim of this book is to show that, nevertheless, *ijtihâd* is not limited to that dimension. In other words, although the necessary textual expertise must be recognized and respected, it is also urgent to reassess the importance of expertise about knowledge of the environment, and of the clinical, humane, and social sciences.

13. The verb *ajtahidu* comes from the same root (*ja-ha-da, ij-ta-ha-da*) as *"ijtihâd."*

14. *Hadîth* reported by Abû Dâwud, Ahmad, at-Tirmidhî et ad-Daramî.

15. The Prophet once said: "The man in my community with the best knowledge of the licit and the illicit is Mu'âdh ibn Jabal." (*Hadîth* reported by at-Tirmidhî, Ibn Mâjah and Ahmad.)

16. Quran 16:89; 6:38.

Chapter 2

1. The syllabus of this initial work was published in my *To Be a European Muslim* (Leicester, UK: Islamic Foundation, 1999).

2. Muhammad Iqbâl, *The Reconstruction of Religious Thought in Islam* (London: Oxford University Press, 1934).

3. Prominent among whom are Shaykh Yûsuf al-Qardâwî and his seminal book *Fî Fiqh al-Aqalliyât al-Muslimah* (Cairo: Dâr ash-Shurûq, 2001, in Arabic) and Shaykh Taha Jâbir al-'Alwânî's work, including his book *Ijtihâd* (Herndon, VA: International Institute of Islamic Thought, 1993). The Fiqh Council in the United States and the European Council for Fatwa and Research have been working for several years to provide such answers according to that methodology.

4. See my preface to the French edition of the first volume of *fatâwâ* issued by the European Council for Fatwa and Research, *Recueil de Fatwas: Avis Juridiques Concernant les Musulmans d'Europe* (Lyons: Editions Tawhîd, 2001). While noting the positive contribution of such an approach, as a first step in providing context-specific answers, I raised the issue of its evolution and limits.

Part II

1. To this corresponds the bulk of the *fatawâ* produced to answer the needs of Muslims in modern times, whether in a majority or minority situation. This is a first step, as I said, but carrying the reform process further is a necessity, as I shall try to demonstrate in the next section of this book.

2. For further reflection into the concept of *sharî'ah*, see my *Western Muslims and the Future of Islam* (New York: Oxford University Press, 2003), 31–61.

Chapter 3

1. The first date refers to the Islamic lunar calendar that starts with *Hijrah* (622): this date is of interest in that it enables us to situate scholars in the time lapses since the time of the Prophet Muhammad.

2. Two books stand out as references as to ash-Shâfi'î's life: Ibn Abî Hâtim ar-Râzî, *Kitâb Adab ash-Shâfi'î wa Manâqibuh*, ed. Muhammad Zâhid ibn al-Hassan al-Kawtharî (Cairo: n.p., 1953), and Abû Nu'aym al-Isfahanî, *Kitâb Hilyat al-Awliyâ' wa Tabaqât al-Asfiyâ'* (Cairo: Al-maktaba al-arabiyya, 1938). One should also mention the first general synthetic presentation of his life drawn up by al-Fakhr ar-Râzî, *Kitâb Manâqib ash-Shâfi'î* (Cairo: n.p., 1933), based on the earlier works of al-Bayhaqî (died 458/1065) who had written a biography with the same title. Those various works sometimes contain important differences about the dates, places, and stages in Imam ash-Shâfi'î's life, but the general framework and the main circumstances about the elaboration of his thought are nearly alike.

3. Mentioned above, see the chapter subsection "What Reform Do We Mean?"

4. This criticism (which should be understood in the context of that time) is in itself questionable and should be subjected to a thorough analysis that is beyond the scope of the present discussion.

5. This does not mean, as we shall see, that Mâlik ibn Anas was not considering the human and social environments. He was at the same time strict with the reference texts when they exist and very open to taking into account the context when said texts were silent.

6. Ash-Shâfi'î himself does not seem to have given it that title and does not refer to it as such.

7. Although respect for, and constant reference to, the Quran and Sunnah (tradition and *ahâdîth*) stand out as objective features of the Hanafî school that it would be wrong to deny or underrate.

8. See Ibn Abî Hâtim ar-Râzî, *Kitâb*, pp 165–166.

9. The Arabic quotation is concise and dense: *"al-'ilm bil-ahkâmi ash-shar'iyyah al-muktassab min adillatiha at-tafsiliyyah."* See the detailed analysis of this definition in Dr. Wahbah az-Zuhaylî, *Al-Fiqh al-Islâmî wa-Adillatuhu* (Dâr al-Fikr, Lebanon, 1989), 3rd ed., in Arabic, 16–18. The introduction as a whole gives a thorough and necessary explanation of the outline of *fiqh* studies.

10. Ash-Shâfi'î, *ar-Risâla*, ed. Ahmad Muhammad Shâkir, al-Maktabah al-'ilmiyyah (Beirut: al-Maktabah al-'ilmiyyah, n.d.), in Arabic, 21–25; ash-Shâfi'î, *al-Risâla* (Cambridge, UK: Islamic Texts Society, 1987), trans. Majid Khadduri, 67–80.

11. Ash-Shâfi'î, *al-Risâla*, in Arabic, 21; in English, 67.

12. It is from that perspective, as well as in relation to the debates of his time, that in the following chapter he studies the question of the abrogation of verses, establishing the primacy of the Quran and the secondary status of the *ahâdîth* that can never abrogate a verse (this position contradicts that of the Hanafî school).

13. Quran 7:163; also see the analysis of this verse in ash-Shâfi'î, *ar-Risâla*, in Arabic, 62; in English, 102.

14. That is by, referring to something else than the text itself: either another text or the surrounding reality.

15. *Istihsân*, legal preference, is for ash-Shâfi'î a (highly controlled) extension of analogical reasoning (*qiyâs*) that remains the norm about the implementation of rulings in situations about which the text says nothing.

Chapter 4

1. Interesting biographical facts and comments can be found in Muhammad Abû Zahrah, *Abû Hanîfah, Hayâtuhu wa 'asruhu, arâ'uhu wa fiqhuh* (Cairo: Dâr al-Fikr al-'Arabî, 1991); in English, *The Four*

Imams. Their Lives, Works and Their Schools of Thought (London: Dâr at-Taqwâ, 2001), trans. Aisha Bewley, 113–254.

2. See Muhammad Abû Zahrah, *Abû Hanîfah*, in Arabic, 202; *The Four Imams*, 240.

3. See Muhammad Abû Zahrah, *Abû Hanîfah*, quoting ash-Sha'rânî in *al-Mîzân*, in Arabic, 236–237; *The Four Imams*, 246.

4. That is, "our opinion is worth as much as theirs." See Muhammad Abû Zahrah, *Abû Hanîfah*, 237 (passage not translated into English). It should be noted that the criticism stating that Abû Hanîfah neglected Prophetic traditions is most unfair; he was indeed one of the first legal Scholars who relied on single-chain traditions (*ahâdîth âhâd*) when formulating his legal opinions.

5. One should also mention, beside his books commenting the works of his predecessors (and in particular ash-Shaybânî), his exegesis of the Quran (*tafsîr*), *Kashf al-Asrâr*, which is highly enlightening about the interpretation of a number of rulings and the contextualizing of interpretation and understanding.

6. The reference work concerning the life, works, and sayings reported from *Abû Hanîfah* is that of Abû al-Mu'ayyid al-Muwaffaq al-Makkî (died 568), *Manâqib al-Îmâm Abî Hanîfah*, in Arabic, 2 vols. (Beirut: n.p., 1981).

7. The use of *istihsân* remains very restricted, and must be seen as an extension of analogical reasoning. Ash-Shâfi'î used to speak of his work *al-Um* as a book challenging the validity of *istihsân* (*kitâb ibtâl al-istihsân*): cf. Muhammad Abû Zahrah, *Manâqib al-Îmâm Abî Hanîfah*, in Arabic, 302; *The Four Imams*, 252.

8. Even though the categorization and terminology used draw clear distinctions about the classification of the sources and the Quran's particular status. Thus, a command stated in the Quran is called "*fard,*" while it is called "*wâjib*" if it is based on a Prophetic tradition (similarly, prohibitions are termed "*harâm*" when stated in the Quran and "*makrûh*" when stated in the Sunnah). Those distinctions are quite specific to the Hanafî school.

9. Mâlik is reported to have said that *istihsân* represents "nine-tenths of [legal] knowledge." See Muhammad Abû Zahrah, *Manâqib al-Îmâm Abî Hanîfah*, in Arabic, 302; *The Four Imams*, 252.

Chapter 5

1. The same is true of Imam Mâlik's principle of "closing—by interdiction—the paths potentially leading to what is prohibited or harmful (*sadd adh-dharâ'i*). Here again, it would be impossible to achieve a kind of "legal projection" if one had not identified the meaning, that is,

the intention of the initial prohibition on which the whole reasoning is based.

2. Abû al-Ma'âlî al-Juwaynî, *al-Burhân fî Usûl al-Fiqh*, 2nd ed. (Cairo: Dâr al-Ansâr, 1979), in Arabic.
3. Ibid., 2: 923.
4. Ibid., 2: 1151.
5. Abû Hâmid al-Ghazâlî, *al-Mustasfâ min 'Ilm al-Usûl* (Baghdad: Muthanna, 1970, in Arabic).
6. Ibid., 1: 286–287.
7. Cf. Shihâb ad-Dîn al-Qarâfî *Sharh Tanqîh al-Fusûl* (Cairo: Manshûrât Maktabat al-Kulliyât al-Azhariyyah wa Dâr al-Fikr, 1973), 391, in Arabic.
8. Cf. Tâj ad-Dîn Ibn as-Subkî, *Jam' al-Jawâmi'*, Dâr Ihyâ' al-Kutub al-'Arabiyyah, Cairo, no date (in Arabic), where Ibn as-Subkî himself refers to Hanafî scholar Tâj ad-Dîn at-Tûfî about that issue on page 280 of the second volume.
9. On the other hand, the *'ibadât* (the practical acts of worship) are to be implemented as such, in their essence, and in the light of their inherent objectives, without taking time and differences of time and place into account.
10. No source gives reliable evidence about his place of birth but he is known to have lived in Andalucia most of his life.
11. See in particular Ahmad al-Raysuni's outstanding contribution, *Imam al-Shatibi's Theory of the Higher Objectives and Intents of Islamic Law* (Herndon, VA: The International Institute of Islamic Thought, 2005), trans. N. Roberts, 73–105.
12. Abû Ishâq ash-Shâtibî, *al-I'tisâm* (Beirut: Dâr al-kutub al-'ilmiyyah, 1995), in Arabic.
13. The methodology of objectives also applies, of course, to the rulings of the four practical pillars of Islam (*al-'ibadât*), as ash-Shâtibî himself stresses: see Abû Ishâq ash-Shâtibî, *al-Muwâfaqât fî Usûl ash-Sharî'ah* (Beirut: Dâr al-Ma'rifat, 1996), vol. 2, *Kitâb al-Maqâsid*, in Arabic, 324–326.
14. Ibid., 2: 324.
15. The intellect can understand that being enchained to the prison of one's ego, desires, and passions is harmful, and that, consequently, the divine Lawgiver's intention to set us free from thus is a good one. Still, one's being, heart and will must be made to accept the meaning of that objective and this requires spiritual education and constant awareness of what motivates our actions.
16. Ash-Shâtibî, *al-Muwâfaqât*, 2: 324.
17. Ibid., 2: 326. The order that ash-Shâtibî suggests in this respect is noticeably different from that found in al-Ghazâlî: according to him, what is to be protected is "religion (*ad-dîn*), human life

(*an-nafs*), progeny (*an-nasl*), property and belongings (*al-mâl*), and intellect (*al-'aql*)".

18. Ibid., 2: 476–673.
19. Ibid., 2: 681.
20. *Hadîth* hassan (good) reported by as-Darâqutnî, al-Bayhaqî (10/13), al-Hakîm (2/122), at-Tabrîzî in *al-Mishkât* (197), al-Hâfiz in *al-Matâlib al-'âliyyah* (2909); considered "hassan" by at-Tirmidhî.
21. See the important work of principle extraction carried out by al-Raysûnî, *Imam al-Shatibi's Theory of the Higher Objectives*, 317–323 (more specifically, point 7 on page 318).
22. These are the five categories that qualify all the actions of responsible human beings; they are known as *al-ahkâm at-taklîfiyyah*.
23. Ash-Shâtibî, *al-Muwâfaqât*, 4: 268–270.
24. Ibid., 1: 33–42 and 4: 392–434.
25. Ibid., 1: 95–115.
26. Ibid., 4: 477 (also see pages 640–679). See also my analysis in *To Be a European Muslim* (Leicester, UK: Islamic Foundation, 1999), 86–89.
27. Al-Raysûnî, *Imam al-Shatibi's Theory of the Higher Objectives*, 264.

Chapter 7

1. Quran 96:1–5.
2. The second surah revealed, according to the most recently accepted chronology, again refers to that same knowledge: "*Nûn. By the Pen and by that which they write. You [Muhammad] are not, by the grace of your Lord [Rabb-Educator], possessed. Verily, for you is an unfailing reward. And surely you have sublime morals. You will soon see, and they will see, which of you is afflicted with madness*" (Quran 68: 1–6).
3. Quran 64:1; 81:15–20; 87:1–5.
4. Quran 22:46.
5. Quran 55:1–6.
6. Quran 3:190.
7. Quran 5:4–5.
8. Quran 2:168.
9. See my book *Western Muslims and the Future of Islam* (New York: Oxford University Press, 2003), chapter 2.
10. Quran 16:114.
11. For a more detailed reflection about *al-fitra*, see my book *Western Muslims*, chapter 1.
12. Ibid., Ramadan, *Western Muslims*, 17.
13. Quran 55:5; 21:33; 36:40; 21:30.

14. Quran 21:35.
15. Quran 13:4.
16. Quran 32:27.
17. Quran 41:39.
18. Quran 40:67.
19. Quran 30:22.
20. Quran 49:13.
21. That is, as to their own, *per se* existence, for those signs (whether clear verses or fundamental natural principles) can always give rise to a broader interpretation relative to their environment: social and human for the former, physical for the latter, as the theory of relativity or quantum physics teach us today.
22. Quran 5:48.
23. Quran 10:99. The root of the verb used here, "*tukrihu*," is "*ka-ri-ha*" and it is the same in "*ikraha*" in the verse quoted below, that lays down the principle of religious freedom.
24. Quran 2:256.
25. Quran 10:78.
26. Quran 33:62; see among the most explicit verses in this respect: Quran 35:43; 48:34; 30:30.
27. Quran 3:140.
28. Quran 3:137.
29. See chapter 8 in my book *In the Footsteps of the Prophet: Lessons from the Life of Muhammad* (New York: Oxford University Press, 2007).
30. *Hadîth* reported by al-Bukhârî; *hadîth* reported by Ibn Mâjah; *hadîth* reported by Muslim.
31. One could mention other situations such as the frequent instances when the Prophet stressed his status as a human being who was not endowed with final authority over the whole range of human action, especially when specific worldly knowledge was involved. Thus, one can recall the incident that occurred soon after he arrived in Medina: when the Prophet arrived in the city, he saw local people grafting their palm trees. He told them: "It might be better not to do so." The *Ansâr* (Muslim inhabitants of Medina) dropped the practice, but the date crop decreased. They went to inform the Prophet who said: "I am but a human being. So, when I tell you to do something that pertains to your religion, accept it; but when I tell you something from my own personal opinion, remember that I am a human being. You are better informed of your worldly affairs." (*Hadîth* reported by al-Bukhârî and Muslim; two versions reported by Râfi' and Anas.) Many other similar situations have been reported, and they shed light on the Prophet's particular status: despite being the depositary of the divine norm and, as such, the reference in religious affairs, he remained a fallible human being in all other fields.

32. Quran 4:82.
33. Quran 47:24.
34. Quran 33:72.
35. Quran 59:21.
36. *Hadîth* reported by at-Tabarânî; *hadîth* reported by al-Bukhârî.

Chapter 8

1. Quran 14:32–33.
2. One can see clearly here the passage from "God" to "We" that aims to prevent the personalization of God through the use of one single personal pronoun. In the Quran, God can randomly be referred to as "God," "He," or "We."
3. Quran 35:27–28.
4. This has nothing to do with the temptation of "concordism" that would attempt to turn the written Revelation into some sort of "science" book imposing or confirming the knowledge acquired in one field or another of scientific research. This approach seems to me inappropriate both from scientific and strictly religious viewpoints: the Revelation simply is not a scientific text.
5. See my analysis in *Western Muslims and the Future of Islam* (New York: Oxford University Press, 2003), 55–61.
6. As to the concept of science, one can add they are considered as "sciences" only by believing Muslims.
7. I shall examine the serious (and negative) consequences of such an approach later in this book.
8. Or, to the contrary, it is wholly and absolutely "Islamic" insofar as it involves the intelligence submitting to the structured, imposed order of the two Books and "submitting" to each of them. Any natural act could thus be "Islamic": such an approach, attractive though it is, does not allow for any operating categorization *a posteriori* and therefore voids our reflection through its overly general character.

Chapter 9

1. This debate is essential and reveals a real, profound crisis as to the question of authority in Islam: who is entitled to speak in the name of Muslims? According to which criteria? With what legitimacy?

Chapter 10

1. This approach is based on the Quranic verses instructing to "enjoin what is right and forbid what is wrong and harmful" (Quran 3:104)

and on the Prophet's injunction: "Make things easier [for Men] and do not make them more difficult." (*Hadîth* reported by Muslim.)

2. Mohammed Hashim Kamali, *An Introduction to Sharî'ah* (Kuala Lumpur: Ilmiah Publishers, 2006), 118.

3. Ibid.; the contribution of Shaykh Muhammad At-Tâhir Ibn 'Âshûr (1879–1973) in the field of *usûl al-fiqh* is crucial. In his book *Maqâsid Ash-Sharî'ah Al-Islâmiyyah* he proposed a new approach and categorization of the higher objectives that is very useful for us today. See *Maqâsid Ash-Sharî'ah Al-Islâmiyyah* (Tunis: dâr al-Islam, 2006), in Arabic, in English, *Treatise on Maqâsid Sharî'ah* (London: International Institute of Islamic Thought IIIT, 2006).

4. Mohammed Hashim Kamali, *Freedom of Expression in Islam*, rev. ed. (Cambridge: Islamic Texts Society, 1997), 16–24.

5. Ibid., 1–6.

6. Mohammed Hashim Kamali, *Introduction to Sharî'ah*, 118.

7. Ahmad al-Raysûnî, *Imam al-Shatibi's Theory of the Higher Objectives and Intents of Islamic Law* (Herndon, VA: The International Institute of Islamic Thought, 2005), trans. N. Roberts, 363–366; Ahmad ar-Raysûnî, *Al-Kuliyyât al-asâsiyah li-sh-Sharî'ah al-Islâmiyyah* (Rabat: At-Tawhîd wal-Islâh, 2007), 72–81.

8. As clearly appears from the arguments and textual evidence (*al-adillah*) put forth by scholars since al-Juwaynî. In the case of the priority of religion, they essentially referred to the sanctions the majority of scholars considered as established for those who left their religion (*hukm ar-riddah*). However, not all scholars agreed: for a discussion about this issue, see my book of dialogues with Professor Jacques Neirynck, *Peut-on Vivre avec l'Islam?* (Lausanne: Favre, 1999, 2004). Cf. also on my Web site the article for the *Washington Post* and *Newsweek*, "Muslim Scholars Speak Out: On Jihad, Apostasy and Women," www.tariqramadan.com/article.php3?id_article=1163&lang=en.

9. Quran 30:30; 5:32; 4:119.

10. See, in this respect, my *In the Footsteps of the Prophet: Lessons from the Life of Muhammad* (New York: Oxford University Press, 2007), 200–204.

11. Quran 2:208.

12. See my book *Jihâd, Violence, Guerre et Paix en Islam* (Lyons: Tawhid, 2000) and my collection *Non-Violence?* (Paris: National Federation of Yoga Educators, Dervy, 2000).

13. Respecting living species and Nature is fundamental in the different scriptural sources and this point will be mentioned again later when we come to discuss ecology.

14. Quran 17:70; 22:78.

15. *Hadîth* reported by al-Bukhârî and Muslim.
16. Quran 55:4; *Hadîth* reported by Muslim, Abû Dawûd and at-Tir-midhî.
17. Quran 17:15; 16:90.
18. Quran 2:251.
19. For a critical study of the very use of the concept of modernity see the introduction to my book *Islam, the West and the Challenges of Modernity: Which Project for Which Modernity?* (Leicester, UK: Islamic Foundation, 2000).

Part IV

1. One can add the work done in management and business by Rafik Beekun, such as his book *Islamic Business Ethics* (Herndon, VA: International Institute of Islamic Thought [IIIT], 1996). Such titles are interesting and at the forefront of an effective applied Islamic ethics.

Chapter 11

1. The concepts in italics refer to the higher objectives in the categorization proposed in the third section; this format is maintained throughout this section.
2. See figure 10.3 of this book. The goals mentioned here are drawn from the different levels, naturally distinguishing what pertains to the relationship to the body, to health, and to medicine in general.
3. Quran 41:44.
4. Quranic references to the "ailments of the heart" are numerous (e.g., Quran 2:10).
5. Quran 26:88–89.
6. Quran 10:14.
7. *Hadîth* reported by al-Bukhârî and Muslim.
8. Quran 5:32.
9. *Hadîth* reported by al-Bukhârî.
10. *Hadîth* reported by al-Bukhârî and Muslim.
11. Quran 2:156: *"To God we belong and to Him we shall return."*
12. *Hadîth* reported by al-Bukhârî and Muslim.
13. See his article "What Is Islamic Medicine?" (www.islamset.com/hip/i_medcin/index.html): the five criteria he set forth to differentiate the two medicines can in fact be summarized in the second (the references to faith and "divine ethics"), of which all the others are direct or indirect consequences. In this sense it is not the medicine that is Islamic but rather the ethics.

14. *Medical Ethics of Medieval Islam with Special Reference to Al Ruhawi's "Practical Ethics of the Physician,"* ed. and trans. Martin Levey, *Transactions of the American Philosophical Society* (Philadelphia: APS, 1967), 1–100.

15. See for instance this version of the oath written in 1964 by Louis Lasagna, Academic Dean of the School of Medicine at Tufts University, and used in many North American medical schools today:

> I swear to fulfill, to the best of my ability and judgment, this covenant: I will respect the hard-won scientific gains of those physicians in whose steps I walk, and gladly share such knowledge as is mine with those who are to follow. I will apply, for the benefit of the sick, all measures [that] are required, avoiding those twin traps of overtreatment and therapeutic nihilism. I will remember that there is art to medicine as well as science, and that warmth, sympathy, and understanding may outweigh the surgeon's knife or the chemist's drug. I will not be ashamed to say "I know not," nor will I fail to call in my colleagues when the skills of another are needed for a patient's recovery. I will respect the privacy of my patients, for their problems are not disclosed to me that the world may know. Most especially must I tread with care in matters of life and death. If it is given me to save a life, all thanks. But it may also be within my power to take a life; this awesome responsibility must be faced with great humbleness and awareness of my own frailty. Above all, I must not play at God. I will remember that I do not treat a fever chart, a cancerous growth, but a sick human being, whose illness may affect the person's family and economic stability. My responsibility includes these related problems, if I am to care adequately for the sick. I will prevent disease whenever I can, for prevention is preferable to cure. I will remember that I remain a member of society, with special obligations to all my fellow human beings, those sound of mind and body as well as the infirm. If I do not violate this oath, may I enjoy life and art, respected while I live and remembered with affection thereafter. May I always act so as to preserve the finest traditions of my calling and may I long experience the joy of healing those who seek my help.

16. All those documents can now be found on the Internet, on the various sites dealing with those issues, in particular that of the Islamic Organisation for Medical Sciences (in English and in Arabic). See www .islamset.com/ethics/code/index.html.

17. See the whole code and the oath (in English and Arabic): www .islamset.com/ethics/code/index.html.

18. Muwaffaq ad-Dîn Abû Ibn Ahmad Ibn Qudâmah, *Al Mughnî fi-l-Fiqh* (Beirut: Dâr al-'arabî, 1983).

19. *Hadîth* reported by Abû Dâwûd.
20. See the series *The Islamic Vision of Some Medical Practices* (Kuwait City: IOMS, 1981–1999); see also their Web site, www .islamset.com/ioms/pricelis.html.
21. *The Islamic Vision* (1989), 238.
22. *Hadîth* reported by al-Bukhârî and Muslim.
23. *Hadîth* reported by Muslim.
24. Ibn Hajar al-'Asqalânî, *Fath al-Bârî fî Sharh Sahîh al-Bukhârî*, 18 vols. (Cairo: Dâr al-Rayân, 1988), in Arabic.
25. See the commentary of Abû Dâwud's *Sunan* by Shaykh Abd al-Muhsin Al-'Abbâd (Cairo: al-Matba'a as-Salafiyyah, 1970), in Arabic.
26. *Hadîth* reported by al-Bukhârî and Muslim.
27. Quran 17:31.
28. *Hadîth* reported by al-Bukhârî and Muslim.
29. This is the case with the *hadîth* reported by Muslim (in the chapter about the creation of human beings) that refers to "forty-two nights." The opinions of *fuqahâ'* often take into account those two references and decide on the opinion that seems the most plausible, considering individual situations.
30. See in particular Yûsuf al-Qardâwî, *Al-Fatâwâ al-Mu'âsirah*, vol. 2 (Cairo: Dâr al-Wafâ', al-Mansûra, 1993), in Arabic, 546; and Heba G. Kotb's PhD dissertation, *Sexuality in Islam*, 2004 (posted on the Internet: www2.hu-berlin.de/sexology/GESUND/ARCHIV/kotb2.htm).
31. Quran 17:33.
32. Quran 4:29.
33. *Hadîth* reported by Muslim.
34. *Hadîth* reported by al-Bukhârî and Muslim.
35. See the opinions mentioned by Ibn Taymiyyah in *Al-Fatâwâ al-Kubrâ*, vol. 4 of al-Matba'ah (Cairo: al-'ilmiyyah, n.d.), in Arabic, 260–265.
36. See the interesting article by Ari R Joffe, MD, Philosophy, *Ethics, and Humanities in Medicine* (2007), www.peh-med.com/articles/browse .asp?date=&sort=&page=2.
37. With several countries now passing laws of "presumed consent" where everyone is a donor unless the individual specifically opts out (while most people don't know how or what to do), where organ procurement and advocates for organ transplantation pressure families and the obtaining of consent is not transparent, it would seem that these points violate the very conditions *fuqahâ* initially put on organ donation.
38. This itself has disastrous public health consequences because in hiding their infection, the infected tend to spread the disease even more to spouses and other family members, so the question is not just about compassion for the sick, it should also be about proactive/preventive public health.

39. The international organization Islamic Relief organized an International Conference on AIDS in Johannesburg in November 2007, bringing together text scholars, specialists, physicians, thinkers, and social workers, to consider how to tackle the disease on the basis of Islamic references. The positions expressed made it clear that there is still a long way to go. A Web site has been set up and is open for consultation and debate (www.islamandhivaids.org). A working document, *Case Studies* (also posted on that site) was distributed on this occasion and served as working material for various commissions. The only thing that this ever so welcome initiative can be reproached for is, once again, constituting a work group exclusively composed of text specialists (*'ulamâ'* or *fuqahâ'*) who could not rely on physicians or specialists to share in their discussions. *'Ulamâ'* had to deal with some astounding questions: is it legitimate, according to Islamic principles, to seek a divorce if the spouse has AIDS? Can a child with AIDS be disinherited, or can a mother be separated from her child if she has the disease (or the reverse)? Physicians or practitioners could probably have helped *'ulamâ'* avoid engaging in legal discussions about issues indirectly linked to the disease (while this involves knowing what the disease is but also mere common sense and humanity). It is sometimes important to state clearly that some questions are by essence pointless and absurd and are to be rejected out of hand. We must refuse the inflation of *fatâwâ* that formulate legal rulings on just about any subject and, most important, without careful consideration. Addressing such matters implies giving legitimacy to reflections and attitudes whose very essence is humanly, islamically, and ethically unacceptable: discrimination, stigmatization, banishment from the family, from society, and ultimately, from life. This is antithetical to Islamic ethics. In some areas of life and of medicine in particular, it would, paradoxically, be a good thing to think of issuing a *fatwâ* about a series of naturally groundless and dangerous questions that precisely do not need *fatâwâ*.

Chapter 12

1. See my categorization of trends (about text interpretation) in *Western Muslims and the Future of Islam* (New York: Oxford University Press, 2003), 24–30. See also, in consideration of methodology and interpretation, Khaled Abou El Fadl, *Speaking in God's Name: Islamic Law, Authority and Women* (Oxford, UK: Oneworld Publications, 2001).
2. See Olivier Roy's interesting book, *Globalised Islam* (New York: C. Hurst, 2004). (Its approach and some of its conclusions are, however, questionable and/or debatable.)

3. Quran 5:48.
4. For reflection about those cultural adaptation situations, see my *In the Footsteps of the Prophet: Lessons from the Life of Muhammad* (New York: Oxford University Press, 2007), 84–87.
5. *Hadîth* reported by al-Bukhârî and Muslim.
6. My commitment to Africa over the last twenty-five years has given me practical knowledge of the extent of the problem and the religious and cultural issues involved. In Burkina Faso for instance, most Islamic organizations and *'ulamâ'* have taken a firm stand against female genital mutilation, while in nearby Mali, which has a huge Muslim majority, the *Council of 'ulamâ'* has been opposing all prohibitive action, because it is regarded as a plot coming from some Western-influenced circles of Mali's elite or from the government itself. In such a situation, it is impossible to achieve serious work through normative reminders: the problems are complex, and they are not only normative but also political, legal, and psychological.
7. Such attitudes are sometimes found among scholars but are particularly frequent among their pupils: literalist, traditionalist, reformist, Sufi, or strictly political movements here and there claim to be the sole holders of the truth and do not hesitate to pronounce others "outside" Islam or to cast heavy doubt on their intentions and projects.
8. For contemporary times, see my *Aux sources du renouveau musulman* (Paris: Bayard, 1998; Lyons: Tawhid, 2000).
9. See the short and highly interesting study by Saba Mahmood, *Secularism, Hermeneutics, and Empire: The Politics of Islamic Reformation*, in the journal *Public Culture* (2006); in this respect, see my preface to the *Translation of the Quran* (Lyons: Tawhid, 2005); published also by the *New York Times* as "Reading the Koran" as part of its report on Islam (January 6, 2008; published on www.tariqramadan.com/article.php3?id_article=1320&lang=en).
10. See in this respect, Alan J. Scott's highly interesting book *On Hollywood: The Place, the Industry* (Princeton, NJ: Princeton University Press, 2004), which shows what a major stake culture has in globalization and how it operates globally.
11. This is the fine experiment (and success) of Aminata Traore's neighborhood project in Bamako, Mali. Primarily relying on political will and popular energy, streets have been paved, cleanliness restored, and a central market that sells only local produce, fruit, vegetables, and drinks has been set up. This initiative, as Aminata Traore once explained to us, is a local commitment that sprang from general reflection about global deculturation, particularly in Africa.
12. In this respect, read Kenneth White's interesting *Une Stratégie Paradoxale: Essais de Résistance Culturelle* (Bordeaux: Presses universitaires de Bordeaux, 1998).

13. Quran 49:13.

14. It is by relying on the sense of belonging to both the collective culture and mind-set that Switzerland's foremost political party, the Union Démocratique du Centre (UDC), launched a popular initiative against building minarets in Switzerland. The symbol of the minaret is presented as "non-Swiss" and most importantly as the expression of "Islam's arrogance" and Muslims' attempt at domination. The reference to "symbols," to their visibility and their belonging, or failing to belong, to the shared culture is not a minor point, and is echoed in collective emotions in times of identity crises. The party gained ground despite all the women and men of good will, who stood helpless before the sweeping power of such extreme discourse.

15. Umberto Eco, "From Play to Carnival," in *Turning Back the Clock: Hot Wars and Media Populism*, trans. Alastair McEwen (New York: Harcourt, 2007), 71–76. See also the interesting book by Xavier Couture, *La Dictature de l'Émotion: Où va la Télévision* (Paris: Xavier Audibert, 2005).

16. *Hadîth* reported by al-Bukhârî and Muslim.

17. See my *To Be a European Muslim* (Leicester, UK: Islamic Foundation, 1998), 198–212; see also the whole of my biography of the Prophet, *In the Footsteps of the Prophet*.

18. Friedrich Nietzsche, *The Birth of Tragedy*, trans. R. Speirs (Cambridge and New York: Cambridge University Press, 1999); includes major reflections about Greek art and the figures of Ariadne and Dionysus; Dostoevsky's various works are filled with reflections about art, poetry, and meaning. His longest work *The Brothers Karamazov* is very rich about the relationship to meaning, ethics, and arts. It includes the tortured Dimitri's famous answer to his brother Alyosha the saint: "Beauty is a terrible thing. God and the Devil are fighting there, and the battlefield is my heart"; see my *Islam, the West, and the Challenges of Modernity* (Leicester, UK: Islamic Foundation, 1999), the whole of part 3 dealing with values and cultures.

19. Between absolute rejection of art and music and mimetic production, a critical choice must be made, or at least an in-depth debate must be started. The two most prominent productions today are those of Sami Yusuf (who is very successful with Muslim audiences) and Yusuf Islam (formerly known as Cat Stevens), who has returned to popular music and song and uses his name to reach an audience beyond Muslim communities. The first associates Eastern music with words exclusively focused on Islamic themes, while the latter uses Western rhythms with texts that in one way or another are keyed to religious themes. Those two examples are interesting for their very visibility but they call for in-depth

reflection over musical typologies and above all, the themes and words of the songs that are considered to agree with Islamic ethics: is it not "Islamic" to tell of life, pain, suffering, love, separation, and doubts simply, humanly, and universally? And how is that? Besides, where is creative originality when one imitates the modes of production, publicity, and concerts that condition survival in that Universe? The two aforementioned artists have opened very interesting doors and, ultimately, their art itself raises a number of questions that must be given serious and thorough consideration to avoid falling into an age of *artistic taqlîd* (imitation) just as *fiqh* has been (and still is) paralyzed by that other form of dangerous imitation, *legal taqlîd*. I have been recently introduced to two promising artistic productions: these of Kareem Salama (a young American Muslim musician who plays in the country music genre) as well as of the American Sufis living in Indonesia (whose music/instruments are fusion of East/West and lyrics from Sufi poetry in three languages). With Yûsuf Islam, Sami Yûsuf, and many others less well known are the first steps in that long artistic journey.

20. Quran 55:1–4.

Chapter 13

1. Even though, on the level of fundamentals, the reflections and critical input of the West's feminist movements cannot be ignored. From Clara Zetkin in Germany to Virginia Woolf in England and Simone de Beauvoir or Christine Delphi in France, reflection about women's condition (autonomy, social status, voting rights, identity, power relations) is crucial whether one is in total agreement with those approaches that may be atheistic, communist, or ideologically extreme. What matters, as in Simone de Beauvoir's long study, *The Second Sex*, is the analysis of the logic and representations that must be criticized. Not everything in the Islamic Universe of reference can be reduced to the same categories, but studying the complex nature of the relations among the cultural, social, and political levels is bound to have some relevance to Muslim societies and communities.

2. This is what Fatima Mernissi has attempted to do in several of her books, in particular *Beyond the Veil: Male-Female Dynamics in Modern Muslim Society* (London: Saki Book Publishers, 1985) and *The Veil and Male Elite: A Feminist Interpretation of Women's Rights in Islam* (New York: Perseus Books, 1991). The author raises a number of essential questions with analyses that may be debatable or challenged (especially as to the relationship to scriptural sources)

but remain relevant on the issue of women's status and the Muslim psyche.

3. Benoîte Groult's various critical comments (and assessment) about feminist struggles are most interesting in this respect. See also Helen Hirata, Françoise Laborie, Hélène Le Doaré and Danièle Senotier, *Dictionnaire critique du féminisme* (Paris: PUF, 2000). Besides, the rifts that have appeared within the feminist camp (in France, Spain, Britain, or the United States) over how the issue of Muslim women should be tackled, regarding the headscarf, marriages, and other issues, reveal hitherto unsuspected (religious, cultural, psychological etc.) divides within the Western cultural realm. The most significant case is that of Christine Delphi, a historical figure of French feminism: her commitment to the cause of Muslim women in France (in particular regarding the issue of access to schooling for veiled girls) has for example caused her former feminist partners to decide to marginalize her thinking and her struggle.

4. Quran 33:35.

5. See my chapter "The Question of Women in the Mirror of the Revelation" in *Islam, The West and the Challenges of Modernity* (Leicester, UK: Islamic Foundation, 2000), Appendix 4.

6. Quran 2:187.

7. Quran 30:21.

8. *Hadîth* reported by Muslim.

9. Very early on, for instance, comments about women's rights can be found in all four (now majority) Sunni law schools stating that women were not at all obliged to look after their husbands, serve them, and do the housework or the cooking. The most explicit on this point was the Andalusian scholar Ibn Hazm (died 1064) from Cordoba. The Shiite tradition's various schools also held innovative positions about marriage, women's rights, and other topics at a very early stage.

10. *Hadîth* reported by Ibn Mâjah.

11. See my *In the Footsteps of the Prophet: Lessons from the Life of Muhammad* (New York: Oxford University Press, 2007), 211–216.

12. 'Abd al-Halîm Abû Shuqqah, *Tahrîr al-mar'ah fî 'asr ar-Risâlah* (Kuwait City: Dâr al-qalam, Kuwait, 1990), in Arabic, and translated into French as *Encyclopédie de la Femme en Islam*, trans. C. Dabbak (Paris: Al Qalam, 1998–2002).

13. All studies in the social sciences, in sociology or in the field of education and instruction are useful in this respect whatever the context. This inclusive approach to the social sciences, among other things, must help further the reflection.

14. In several mosques in the United States or in Europe (and particularly on one occasion during the month of Ramadan in Lille in Northern

France), I have surprised many Muslims by calling for deeper and broader reflection about the meaning of modesty in the light of the challenges in our societies. There can be no culture of dialogue or of peace without the emergence of a spirituality or a general philosophy of intellectual, psychological, and dress modesty. In the age of communication and mass media, it is important to weigh the impact of images as conveyor of political and cultural messages. One should add to this the mastery of technical means that may subject thought either to pressure or to the temptation of arrogance. When Universes of reference are led to interact in such a permanent and intricate manner, modesty must in all cases become a faithful companion of intellectual, psychological, and of course dress commitments. Modesty has to do with meaning, goals, and symbols: it tells of one's relation to oneself and to the world, and this should be studied and understood. Inner and outer modesty are at the heart of this fundamental reflection.

15. In a male Universe, women always have to "do more" than men to prove their abilities. This is also often the case for blacks in the Universe of whites or for new citizens, that is, former immigrants, in constituted societies (East or West): they have to "integrate." The never-achieved integration of women, of citizens of "immigrant background," of blacks, or of converts to a religious community, reveals power issues underlying sustained representations. Studies by feminists, by thinkers, or by activists analyzing (or affected by) the processes of racism (from Frederick Douglass to Martin Luther King or Malcolm X) have observed the same constant everywhere: discrimination and racism have to do with perceptions associated with the logistics of power. As far as women are concerned, it is important for them to refuse resembling a particular image of men, having to resort to the same relationship to power, or trying to be tougher or more inflexible in the way Margaret Thatcher, the "Iron Lady," did or Condoleezza Rice does today. Women's approach to politics should be new and different, both in their methods and in their priorities. One should indeed remember that the main Quranic reference to a woman of power, the queen of Sheba (in surah 27), presents her—unlike so many kings and leaders—as open to consultation, reasonable, wise, and trying to avoid conflict and war at all costs. This teaching should be pondered over.

16. I heard this from some feminists during a meeting in the Brussels European Parliament organized by socialist members of the European Parliament. An Italian feminist had expressed the hope that feminisms could converge, especially that of Muslim women and the old Western tradition. She saw clear complementarity between women criticizing male imagery from a religious moral standpoint

and the necessary resistance against what she called "the dictatorship of size 10."

17. See my *In the Footsteps*, 146–148.

18. Whether for the *fuqahâ'* councils of al-Azhar in Egypt, of Saudi Arabia, of Kuwait, or of Indonesia, or of Europe or America, the same discrepancy can be observed.

19. *Hadîth* reported by al-Bayhaqî.

20. I was invited to a Convention in London in 2004, on the issue of fatherhood and its critical prospects, in particular the question of authority today. See the interesting work developed by numerous organizations that specialized in the subject, in particular the Fatherhood Institute (www.fatherhoodinstitute.org). Muslim thought hardly ever deals with those issues: yet parenthood is in crisis in Muslim-majority societies, particularly in Europe. Jobless fathers, immigrants or not, find it difficult to come to terms with their responsibilities as parents, and such situations are common. Legal thought remains silent and here again it seems content with repeating the norms that protect the family ideal.

21. See these interesting works: Claudio Risé, *Le père absent: Enquête sur la place du père dans les familles occidentales* (Paris: Perrin, 2005); Patrick Guillot, *La cause des hommes* (Paris: Viamedias, 2005); and *Quand les hommes parlent* (with Guy Corneau) (Gap, France: Souffle d'Or Eds, 2002), and, in English, Guy Corneau, *Absent Fathers, Lost Sons: The Search for Masculine Identity* (Boston: Shambhala, 1991).

22. As part of the social project of the city of Rotterdam (linked to the creation of the "Citizenship and Identity" chair I hold at present) in which I am involved, I have taken part in many encounters with women and in particular women from Muslim families, of Moroccan, Turkish, or Berber background. In January 2007, on the premises of the regional education and training organzation ROC Zadkine, I heard women (of different social backgrounds) comment on the absence, abdication, or neglect of fathers, which they thought required a campaign to reaise awareness and responsibility. They confirmed, with vigor and energy, what we have similarly observed in Morocco, Senegal, Mali, Burkina Faso, Egypt, Indonesia, and Malaysia: men, fathers, are essential to solving the family crisis and to the success of educational projects. The point is not here to look for culprits (or simply shift to new culprits) but to make sure we do not choose the wrong target, methodology, or discourse.

23. For example, a local campaign against forced marriages has been launched by the umbrella Islamic organization SPIOR (Stichting Platform Islamistische Organisaties Rijnmond) in Rotterdam. It

has published a booklet to combat such practices and started a popular education action. This initiative led to a "European campaign against forced marriages" in May 2008, press conferences and debates were organized in the major cities (Rotterdam, Brussels, Paris, Rome, London, and Berlin) with publications in eight languages (including Turkish and Arabic). The initiative started from within Islamic organizations and relied on Islam-based arguments to be heard and be efficient. See *Hand in Hand against Forced Marriages*, translation from the Dutch, May 2008; a sort of extraordinary Council of about fifteen *'ulamâ'* gathered around the Mufti of Egypt, Shaykh 'Alî Jum'ah, in a conference held in Cairo on November 23 and 24, 2006, and issued a legal ruling (*fatwâ*) stating that the practice of genital mutilation was not Islamic and that it was reprehensible. It was the first time such a collective ruling was issued.

24. This was what motivated the long critical work of text study and compilation produced by 'Abd al-Halîm Abû Shuqqah throughout the six volumes of *Tahrîr al-mar'ah fî 'asr ar-Risâlah*. Scholars and thinkers such as Muhammad 'Abduh at the beginning, in the late nineteenth century, or all through the past century 'Abd al-Hamîd ibn Bâdîs, 'Allâl al-Fâsî, Muhammad al-Ghazâlî, Yûsuf al-Qardâwî, Râshid Ghannûshî, Hassan at-Turâbî, 'Alî Jum'ah, and, in the Shiite tradition, Murtadah Mutahharî, 'Alî Sharî'atî, Muhammad Fadl Allah, and Mohsin Khodivar (among so many others who cannot be fully listed here), have clearly contributed to furthering the debate and reflection about the issue of women. One can, of course, be critical of the different approaches and the limitations of some viewpoints, but no one can deny the importance of those contributions in the last century.

25. It is impossible to classify this or that position or contribution in an isolated category. Some trends, however, appear in the debate between women themselves. The interesting contributions (although on some points they require thorough critical discussion) of committed women thinkers such as (to list but a few names and books) the writings of Nawâl Sa'dawî; Fatima Mernissi (in all her writings, besides the two books I have already mentioned); Leila Ahmed, *Women and Gender in Islam* (New Haven, CT: Yale University Press, 1992); Asma Afsaruddin, *Hermeneutics and Honor: Negotiating Female "Public" Space in Islamic/ate Societies* (Cambridge, MA: Harvard Center for Middle Eastern Studies, 1999); Asma Barlas, *Believing Women in Islam: Unreading Patriarchal Interpretations of the Qur'an* (Austin: University of Texas Press, 2002); Amina Wadud, *Qur'an and Woman: Rereading the Sacred Text from a Woman's Perspective* (New York: Oxford University Press, 1999); *Inside the Gender Jihad:*

Women's Reform in Islam (Oxford, UK: Oneworld Publications, 2006); Kecia Ali, *Sexual Ethics and Islam: Feminist Reflections on Qur'an, Hadith and Jurisprudence* (Oxford, UK: Oneworld Publications, 2006); Saba Mahmood, *Politics of Piety, The Islamic Revival and the Feminist Subject* (Princeton, NJ: Princeton University Press, 2004); Ziba Mir Hosseini, *Iran: Emerging Feminist Voices*, in *Women's Rights*, ed. Lynn Walter (Westport CT: Greenwood, 2001); or Zainah Anwar (an activist and feminist, who heads the Malaysian organization *Sisters in Islam*, which organizes conferences and seminars on a regular basis). All those contributions are not equal in value and do not reflect standardized thought: approaches are varied, and sometimes quite different if not contradictory, but they stand out by the strong influence of Western social sciences and the (sometimes critical) acceptance of the theses, of some demands and/or of the methods of feminism in the United States or in Europe (occasionally also with analyses stemming from African-American struggles, such as the case of Amina Wadud). Other trends exist, which may or may not share in some of the criticisms and demands voiced by the aforementioned authors, while more clearly wishing to remain within the classical Islamic frame of reference. The writings and/or commitments of Zaynab al-Ghazâlî as early as the 1930s: see her autobiography *Ayâm min hayâtî*, translated into English as *Return of the Pharaoh, Memoirs in Nasir's Prison* (Leicester, UK: Islamic Foundation, 1994); Fatima Nacif in Saudi Arabia (*Droits et Devoirs de la Femme Musulmane* (Paris: IIFSO, 2001); Heba Rauf Ezzat (see *Women and the Interpretation of Islamic Sources*, in *Islam 21*, available at www.islam21.net/pages/keyissues/key2–6.htm); Khadija Mufid (the president of *Hidn* organisation in Morocco, she resigned with a bang from the Party for Justice and Development [PJD] and has appeared several times in Arab media on women-related issues and organizes training courses in the field); Nadia Yassine (a member of the movement *Al-Adl wa-l Ihsân* in Morocco, she is involved in reform from within; see her book *Full Sails Ahead* [Iowa City, IA: Justice and Spirituality Publishing, 2006]; Asma Lamrabet's *'Aïsha, l'islam au féminin* (Lyons: Tawhid, 2003), and *Le Coran et les Femmes, Une lecture de libération* (Lyons: Tawhid, 2007) are part of that trend. New generations are involved in those dynamics the world over, and in particular in the United States and Europe (with for instance Ingrid Mattson in the United States, Sheema Khan in Canada, city councillor and psychologist Salma Yacoub in the United Kingdom, Malika Hamidi in Belgium [she coordinated the European Parliament symposium about *Feminist Muslims: from paradox to reality* on March 3, 2004] and in France Saida Kada or Zahra Ali [who was a very young and active member of the organization *Feminists for equality*]). Less visibly in terms of people, deep and broad trends can be perceived in the civil societies and Islamic organizations of Muslim-majority countries; their irreversible evolution can only be measured in the long run: in West and North Africa, in the Middle East, or in Asia. The diversity of approaches, reflections, and even objectives is as real as the lack of critical (and constructive) internal and wider debates among the various trends.

26. See in this respect two reports issued in 2000: one by UNICEF (*State of the World's Children*) informs us that almost two-thirds of the 130 million unschooled children in the world are girls (and this is often the case in Muslim-majority countries); the second by UNESCO (*2000 Statistical Yearbook*) confirms the trend for adults: two-thirds of the 875 million adult illiterates are women. In Southeast Asia, three women out of five are illiterate, and one of two in Africa and the Arab world. The figures are profound and speak for themselves: this most clearly betrays the higher objectives of Islamic ethics.

27. See Isabelle Guerin, *Les femmes et l'économie solidaire* (Paris: Éditions La Découverte, 2003), which presents surveys from France and Senegal, as well as Saskia Everts, *Gender and Technology: Empowering Women, Engendering Development* (London: Zed Books, 1998) and Devaki Jain, *Women, Development and the UN, A Sixty Year Quest for Equality and Justice*, preface by Amartya Sen (Bloomington: Indiana University Press, 2005). See also the exhaustive synthesis by Margaret C. Snyder and Mary Tadesse, *African Women and Development: A History: The Story of the African Training and Research Centre for Women of the United Nations Economic Commission* (London: Zed Books, 1998). Highly interesting information can also be found in the CD-ROM entitled *Femmes du Sud, Genre de Développement: Quelques Repères Historiques, 1975–2001* produced by the *Association Femmes et Développement* (AFED, France). See also the Web site listing all the entries about this subject on the web: *Women and Development Resources on the Internet* (www.gdrc.org/gender/link-resources.html). Another Web site presents similar synthesis of the books available on the issue of women and development since: www.womenink.org. Everywhere, the conclusions are the same: women, their education, and involvement, are essential factors to both qualitative (*welfare*) and quantitative development (growth) in all societies the worldwide, and overlooking (or even denying) this runs against the very essence of Islam's teachings.

28. I have observed this phenomenon all over the world. In sub-Saharan Africa, from Senegal to Cameroon as well as in Mali, Niger, or Togo, in Belgium (where the conference about Islamic

feminism mentioned was held in March 2004), in Britain, in Sweden, in Australia, as well as in Malaysia and Indonesia, the issue of women is central and their involvement is an undeniable constant.

Chapter 14

1. I have considered some economic challenges in my book *Western Muslims and the Future of Islam* (New York: Oxford University Press, 2003), 177–199. My critical approach got some strong reactions while I was proposing a "radical reform" of the too-often formalistic and technical reforms presented as the new and alternative "Islamic economy" and "Islamic finance." I shall not repeat these analyses here: what I have been saying remains, of course, accurate today and in line with my current study.

2. The London-based Islamic Foundation for Ecology and Environmental Sciences is carrying out very interesting work in this field: see its Web site and its newsletters (*Ecoislam*): www.ifees.org.uk. See also the local work produced by the London Islamic Network for the Environment, which has undertaken some interesting activities and has a Web site providing a lot of practical information (www.lineonweb .org.uk).

3. A few interesting contributions can however be noted in this field. See, for instance, Mawil Y. Izzi Dien, *The Environmental Dimensions of Islam* (Cambridge, UK: Lutterworth Press, 2000) and, by the same authors, *Islamic Environmental Ethics, Law, and Society* in *Ethics of Environment and Development: Global Challenge, International Response*, ed. J. Ronald Engel and Joan Gibb Engel (Tucson: University of Arizona Press, 1990), 189–198; and Seyyed Hossein Nasr, "Islam and the Environmental Crisis," in *Spirit and Nature: Why the Environment is a Religious Issue*, ed. Stephen C. Rockefeller and John C. Elder (Boston: Beacon Press, 1992). See also, as a general introduction, the article by Frederick M. Denny of the University of Colorado, "Islam and Ecology: A Bestowed Trust, Inviting Balanced Stewardship," on the Harvard University Web site (http://environment.harvard.edu/ religion/religion/islam/index.html). The detailed, discerning critical reflection of Soumaya Pernilla Ouis, of Lund University in Sweden, is particularly welcome in this field: see, in particular, "Global Environmental Relations: An Islamic Perspective" (*The Muslim Lawyer*, vol.4, issue 1 [May 2003]: 12–16; *Association of Muslim Lawyers*, www.aml .org.uk/journal/4.1/SPO%20-%20Global%20Environment%20Relatio ns.pdf) as well as "Islamic Ecotheology Based on the Qur'an," *Islamic Studies* 37 (Summer 1998): 153. See also her interesting critical account of Mawil Izzi Dien's book mentioned above: "Review of The

Environmental Dimensions of Islam by Mawil Izzi Dien," *American Journal of Islamic Social Sciences*, vol. 19, no. 2: 113–116; and finally "McDonald's or Mecca? An Existential Choice of Qibla for Muslims in a Globalised World?" *Encounters*, vol. 7, no. 2 (Islamic Foundation, Leicester, UK, 2001): 161–188.

4. Quran 3:190.
5. Quran 41:53.
6. See my *In the Footsteps of the Prophet: Lessons from the Life of Muhammad* (New York: Oxford University Press, 2007), chapter 15.
7. *Hadîth* reported by Ahmad and Ibn Mâjah.
8. The two ecologies' concerns are bound to converge, ultimately, even though their sources are different.
9. *Hadîth* reported by Ahmad.
10. *Hadîth* reported by al-Bukhârî and Muslim.
11. *Hadîth* reported by al-Bukhârî.
12. "When you want to do anything, do it by mastering it [in the best possible way]" (*hadîth* reported by al-Bukhârî and Muslim).
13. *Hadîth* reported by an-Nasâ'î.
14. Important alternative experiments are appearing in various parts of the world. In Muslim societies, the phenomenon remains marginal, but ecological breeding and bioethical production initiatives, especially in the United States and in Britain, are worth mentioning and supporting. Some Muslim organizations have become involved in the Farm Animal Welfare Council (FAWC) in Britain and try to find better options regarding animal treatment in general. See for instance, in Britain, the initiative of Muhammad Ridha Payne who, shocked at the treatment of animals in "*halâl*" meat processing, has launched the first network of firms producing organic *halâl* food (organic *halâl* businesses): Abraham Natural Produce. There are many other such initiatives the world over, but they remain marginal, and far removed from the priority preoccupations of Muslim societies and communities.
15. See UNDP's successive annual reports, *Human Development Reports*, available on the Web site: http://hdr.undp.org/en.
16. This quotation appears on the aforementioned Web site in support of the whole approach of human development.
17. See the interesting article by Thomas Davis, "What Is Sustainable Development?" and the whole of his "partial bibliography" (www .menominee.edu/sdi/whatis.htm) as well as the whole series of articles by Edgar Morin and Serge Latouche about the issue of sustainable development: www.decroissance.info/LES-CRITIQUES-DU-DEVELOPPEMENT. See also the works of Latouche from *The Westernisation of the World: The Significance, Scope and Limits of the Drive Towards Global Uniformity* (Cambridge, UK: Polity Press, 1996) to the latest *Le pari de la décroissance* (Paris: Fayard, 2006). The

article with the same title "What Is Sustainable Development?" by Jeffrey Brown, executive director of *Global Learning* organization, advocates a different and interesting approach (www.globallearningnj .org/iste.htm). See in this respect: World Commission on Environment and Development, *Our Common Future* (New York: Oxford University Press, 1987).

18. This appears very quickly when one reads the numerous contributions and studies produced by Muslim economists. See, in particular, Umer Chapra, *Islam and the Economic Challenge* (Leicester, UK: Islamic Foundation and Herndon, VA: the International Institute of Islamic Thought, 1992); "The Role of the Stock Exchange in an Islamic Economy," in Sheikh Ghazali Abod et al., *An Introduction to Islamic Finance* (Kuala Lumpur: Quill Publishers, 1992) and "Money and Banking in an Islamic Economy," in M. Ariff (ed.), *Monetary and Fiscal Economics of Islam* (Jeddah, Saudi Arabia: King Abdul Aziz University, 1982); Muhammad Nejatullah Siddiqi, *Muslim Economic Thinking: A Survey of Contemporary Literature* (Leicester, UK: The Islamic Foundation, 1981); Taqi M. Usmani, *An Introduction to Islamic Finance* (Karachi, Pakistan: Idaratul Ma'arif, 1998); Rodney Wilson (ed.), *Islamic Financial Markets* (London, UK: Routledge, 1990). Some works offer detailed approaches to some development issues: see Muhammad Akram Khan, *Rural Development Through Islamic Banks* (Leicester, UK: Islamic Foundation, 1992); Munawar Iqbal (ed.), *Distributive Justice and Need Fulfillment in an Islamic Economy* (Leicester, UK: Islamic Foundation, 1984). The list ought to be much longer, but one should also mention the interesting and constructive study by the academic Charles Tripp (of the School of Oriental and African Studies [SOAS], *Islam and the Moral Economy: The Challenge of Capitalism* (Cambridge, UK: Cambridge University Press, 2006). Numerous texts produced by classical contemporary scholars such as Muhammad al-Ghazâlî or Yûsuf al-Qardâwî deal with economic issues in the light of scriptural sources and are often quoted by economists (particularly those mentioned here). Other studies go in the same direction but deal with firm management, for instance, Rafik Beekun's impressive *Islamic Business Ethics* (Herndon, VA: International Institute of Islamic Thought [IIIT], 1996).

19. Such criticisms are frequently leveled at the international alterglobalization movement. The yearly organization of the World Social Forum or of continental forums has made it possible to voice radical criticism, but the reproaches leveled at the movement are partly legitimate: ceaseless internal struggles over power and influence, recycled old ideas, lack of clear proposals as to political and economic issues, and other issues.

20. His book is highly influential and attacks the dogmas of market economy, proposing a systematic criticism of its fundamentals: see *The Crisis of Global Capitalism: Open Society Endangered* (New York: Public Affairs, 1998). See also Robert Reich's *The Work of Nations: Preparing Ourselves for 21st Century Capitalism* (New York: Knopf, 1991), which has already raised the most relevant questions for our time.

21. This is the myth denounced by Soros and with him, by the whole alterglobalization movement.

22. Many field experiments exist in all countries of Africa, South America and Asia. Integrated development projects, cooperative networks, small self-managed businesses, as well as microcredit lending, which has become famous through Muhammad Yunus's successes in Bangladesh with the Grameen Bank (see his book with Alan Jolis, *Banker to the Poor: Micro-lending and the Battle Against World Poverty* (New York: Public Affairs, 1999); and with Jacques Attali, *Portraits de Microentrepreneurs* (Paris: Le Cherche Midi, 2006). It should be noted that the Islamic Development Bank has developed interesting projects the world over, integrating new instruments and establishing new partnerships: such sectors as Islamic economy, insurance, microcredit, etc. See its Web site where those projects are presented and the different reports (www.isdb .org). A critique of the commitment's approaches and fundamentals remains relevant but the quality and success of some projects cannot be denied.

23. In this respect, see the proposals I have already made about the economic issue, which drew abundant criticism from Muslim scholars but without any actual argument about a possible alternative: my *Western Muslims*, part II, chapter 8, and *Economic Resistance*, 177–199.

24. Many organizations the world over try to raise consumer awareness through campaigns about "fair trade," "organic products," or buying recyclable products. My assistant at Erasmus University Rotterdam, Marjolein Kooistra, is very much involved in the movement and the international organization network Slow Food (see their Web sites www.slowfood.com, www.slowfoodfoundation.com, and www.terramadre2006.org), which insists on biodiversity and the ethical character of the entire food production chain: from the treatment of nature and animals to seeking balanced, healthy consumption (as opposed to the fast food concept). The first European fair-trade conference, *Fair Trade in Europe*, which was held in Lyons, France on February 1–3, 2008, is part of this general consumer awareness campaign: exhibitors from all over the world, involved in various areas of economic activity, presented their philosophy and ethics and their innovative achievements (see www

.salon-europeen-commerce-equitable.org/-SALON-EUROPEEN-
DE-COMMERCE-.html). All these initiatives are interesting
because of the increased awareness they lead to, even though they
have sometimes been criticized either for some of their methods
(as in the case of Max Havelaar) or for the idealistic, utopian character of their initiatives. Consumer responsibility and awareness
remain essential, however, if one wants to reform mindsets and
strictly economic logistics. Beyond the prohibition of consumption of specified products (pork and alcohol), the Muslim contribution is very poor in this respect.

25. In this respect, see the interesting article by former high commis-
sioner for Human Rights Mary Robinson and UNDP official Kevin
Watkins, who draw the link between the measures that must be
taken about global warming and the meaning of the human rights
struggle. They state forcefully that rich countries are responsible
and need to reform their ways of life: "Clear objectives are required. We must bring down world CO_2 emissions, at present about 7
tons per person, to 2 tons in 2050. To this end, rich countries will
have to reduce their emissions by at least 80%." See their article
published in *Le Temps* (Switzerland), on December 28, 2007, at
the time of the difficult Bali agreements. See also two interesting
studies: the collective work by Machiko Nissante and Erik Thor-
becke (eds.), *The Impact of Globalization on the World's Poor;
Transmission Mechanisms* (London: Palgrave Macmillan and United Nation University, 2007), and Paul Spicker's simple and enlightening introduction, *The Idea of Poverty* (Bristol, UK: Policy Press,
2007).

26. See in this respect my October 2005 article in the British magazine
EMEL: "One Day, Our Poor People Will Ask": www.tariqramadan
.com/article.php3?id_article=482&var.

27. Quran 51:19.

28. See Jeffrey Smith, *Seeds of Deception* (Yes! Books, 2002), and *Genetic Roulette: The Documented Health Risks of Genetically Engi-
neered Foods* (White River Junction, VT: Chelsea Green, 2003);
Hervé Kempf, *La Guerre Secrète des OGM* (Paris: Seuil, 2003);
Gilles-Eric Séralini, *Ces OGM qui changent le monde* (Paris: Seuil,
2004).

Chapter 15

1. This phrase belongs to Belgian sociologist Felice Dassetto who pointed out, during one of our debates in Barcelona (May 30, 2007), when
speaking about the Muslim community in Belgium, that it had "many
leaders" but suffered a "lack of leadership." The phrase is apt.

2. Elements relevant to this issue can be found throughout the debates that have developed over the past two years, in particular between on the one hand Ian Buruma (author of the most interesting *Murder in Amsterdam* [Harmondsworth, UK: Penguin, 2006]; see also his article "The Dogmatism of Enlightenment" and Timothy Garton Ash, and on the other hand, Pascal Bruckner and Ayaan Hirsi Ali. All the contributions can be found on this Web site, www.signandsight.com/features/categories/31_Multiculturaslim.html. See also Jean Baubérot's reflection in the French context, *L'intégrisme républicain contre la laïcité* (Paris: de l'Aube, 2006).

3. Quran 2:285.

4. The medieval period is most revealing in this sense, on both the philosophical and legal levels. See in this respect the most interesting and particularly enlightening contribution by French philosopher Alain de Libera, *Penser au Moyen Age* (Paris: Seuil, 1996), as well as the more introductory work *La Philosophie au Moyen Age* (Paris: Presses Universitaires de France, 2004).

5. See my article about "The Relationship Between Religious Authority and the State" ordered by the Spanish foundation ATMAN and translated into English and French on my Web site: www.tariqramadan.com/article.php3?id_article=989.

6. See the large number of interesting debates in recent publications (which it would be impossible to mention here) and in a dazzling array of Web sites. The opendemocracy.net Web site, to cite only one example, has reported some comments over the reflections of Tariq Modood and some of his critics: see www.opendemocracy.net/faith-europe_islam/response_madood_4630.jsp.

7. See Charles Taylor, "Multiculturalism and The Politics of Recognition," in *Multiculturalism and The Politics of Recognition*, ed. A. Gutmann (Princeton, NJ: Princeton University Press, 1992); Tariq Modood, *Multiculturalism: A Civic Idea* (Cambridge, UK: Polity Press, 2007); Bhikhu Parekh, "Redistribution or Recognition: a Misguided Debate," in *Ethnicity, Nationalism and Minority Rights*, ed. S. May, T. Modood, and J. Squires (Cambridge, UK: Cambridge University Press, 2005); W. Kymlicka, *Multicultural Citizenship* (Oxford, UK: Oxford University Press, 1995); A. Amin, "Ethnicity and the Multicultural City: Living with Diversity" in *Environment and Planning A* (2002), www.envplan.com/abstract.cgi?id=a3537; S. Benhabib, "Nous" et 'les Autres': The Politics of Complex Cultural Dialogue in a Global Civilisation" in *Multicultural Questions*, ed. C. Joppke and S. Lukes (Oxford, UK: Oxford University Press, 1999); A. Barry, *Culture Equality* (Cambridge, UK: Polity Press, 2001); Jean Baubérot, *De la Séparation des Églises et de l'État à l'Avenir de la Laïcité*, with Michel Wieviorka (Paris: de l'Aube, 2005); Régis Debray, *L'Enseignement du Fait Religieux dans l'École Laïque, Rapport au*

Ministre de l'Éducation Nationale (Paris: Odile Jacob, 2002); *Le Feu sacré, Fonctions du Religieux* (Paris: Fayard, 2003); Olivier Roy, *Secularism Confronts Islam*, trans. G. Holoch (New York: Columbia University Press, 2007).

8. See my article on my Web site (www.tariqramadan.com): "For a 'Post-integration Discourse,'" written as part of the city of Rotterdam's "Citizenship, Identity and the Sense of Belonging" project.

9. See in this respect the different works that subject such logistics to thorough, enlightening analysis: Jean Lau Chin (ed.), *The Psychology of Prejudice and Discrimination: Race and Ethnicity in Psychology* (Westport, CT: Greenwood, 2004) and *Race, Identity and Citizenship: A Reader* (Oxford, UK: Blackwell, 1999); Joseph Castel, *La Discrimination Négative* (Paris: Seuil, 2007); Eric Maurin, *Le Ghetto Français* (Paris: Seuil, 2004); Stéphane Beaud and Michel Pialoux, *Emeutes urbaines, Violentes sociales* (Paris: Fayard, 2003); Alain Renaut, *Egalité et Discriminations* (Paris: Seuil, 2007); Daniel Sabbagh, *L'Égalité par le Droit: les Paradoxes de la Discrimination Positive aux États-Unis* (Paris: Economica, 2003).

10. Very few studies can be found concerning the status and treatment of immigrants in Muslim-majority countries, in particular the oil-rich kingdoms. Hardly anything exists about their acquiring citizen status: this absence is most revealing. In the Gulf countries, citizenship is based on ancestral belonging, so that no immigrant South Asian or Arab—regardless of time there or if even born there—can petition for citizenship.

11. See my reflection about the "ethics of citizenship" in *Western Muslims and the Future of Islam* (New York: Oxford University Press, 2003), 165–171.

12. Just as there is no developed alternative "Islamic economic model" that could replace the existing dominant economic model, there is (contrary to what some Islamic organizations with a simplified, simplistic political vision assert) no developed alternative "Islamic political model." The idea that there is, for our own time, an "Islamic state" concept whose structure and organization are found to enable the fulfillment of the higher goals mentioned is outdated, wrong, and quite dangerous: it allows the advocates of binary political thought to oppose two systems and two models, "the Islamic system and model" vs. "the Western system and model" and perilously simplify the terms of the debate. They then go on to compare the ideals of the "Islamic model" with the shortcomings observed and experienced in the "Western model," to prove the former's greatness as the only future alternative. The comparison is intellectually unfair and scientifically wrong, and its conclusions are superficial and risky. The Muslim world, its *fuqahâ'*, thinkers

and politicians, have no alternative model to suggest, but they do have a set of higher objectives to which they must remain faithful through history and societies: hence, they must, starting from their own points of reference, study all social and political human experiences, past and present, Muslim or non-Muslim, critically assess, them and then suggest ways that might lead to greater faithfulness to the Way and greater coherence in the management of human affairs. Once again, we must refuse to idealize the past or sanctify the words of early 'ulamâ', and compel ourselves to face the challenges of modern times: with a critical mind, we must highlight all forms of formalism and hypocrisy. This requires humility, because we should integrate all interesting experiences and all original ideas wherever they come from. It requires ambition and determination because we have to assume those responsibilities at the heart of our own time.

13. On this point, see the interesting contribution and synthesis by John Esposito and John O. Voll, *Islam and Democracy* (New York: Oxford University Press, 1996) as well as François Burgat, *Face to Face with Political Islam* (London: I. B. Tauris, 2003), and Azzam Tamimi, *Rachid Ghannouchi: A Democrat within Islamism (Religion and Global Politics)* (New York: Oxford University Press, 2001).

14. See the whole text of *The Call* (in five languages) and the reactions it elicited on my Web site: www.tariqramadan.com/call.php3?id_article=264?lang=en The islamonline Web site (islamonline.net) has also allotted a page to the debate and published some reactions, but it failed to publish my answers to scholars or organization leaders. See also my synthesis "The Call for a Moratorium" in Kari Vogt, Lena Larsen, and Christian Moe (eds.), *New Directions in Islamic Thought: Exploring Reform and Muslim Tradition* (London: I. B. Tauris, 2008).

15. See his answer and my own on my Web site: www.tariqramadan.com/article.php3?id_article=323.

16. See my press release: "Le noble 'moratoire' de Jacques Chirac, l'ignoble moratoire de Tariq Ramadan?" (October 7, 2004): www.tariqramadan.com/article.php3?id_article=86.

17. See Italy's resolution proposal for a universal moratorium on capital executions, voted on by the United Nations Assembly in December 2007.

18. See my study of education and Islamic schools in my *Western Muslims*, 126–144. In the social project carried out with the city of Rotterdam, the first axis linked to the reflection over citizenship and diversity was that of education. It seemed essential to work on three areas: representation, communication, and targeted actions. The essence of citizenship and of young people's integration into

civil society requires major efforts in education; this is true in both East and West.

19. Numerous discussions with school officials and teachers about the philosophy and nature of private Islamic school projects in Morocco, Egypt, and Jordan as well as in the United States, Canada, France, Sweden, Britain, Belgium, and other European nations reveal that many questions as well as doubts can be raised about the true nature of those alternative schools and their initiators' outlook on the surrounding society as a whole. Numerous contradictions exist.

20. See the link between the cult of performance and democracy in Greece: *Performance Culture and Athenian Democracy*, ed. Simon Goldhill and Robin Osborne (Cambridge, UK: Cambridge University Press, 1999); John Thorley, *Athenian Democracy* (London: Routledge, 2004); Josiah Ober, *The Athenian Revolution: Essays on Ancient Greek Democracy and Political Theory* (Princeton, NJ: Princeton University Press, 1998).

21. See Noam Chomsky, *Media Control* (New York: Seven Stories Press, 2002); Robert McChesney, *Rich Media, Poor Democracy: Communication Politics in Dubious Times* (New York: New Press, 2000); and in the French context: Groupe médias d'Attac, *Médias et Mondialisation Libérale*, 2002), www.homme-moderne.org/societe/media/divers/GMattac.html; Antoine Schwarz and Henri Maler, *Médias en Campagne* (Paris: Editions Syllepses, 2005); Serge Halimi, *Les Nouveaux Chiens de Garde* (Paris: Raisons d'Agir, 2005); Pierre Bourdieu, *Sur la Télévision* (Paris: Raisons d'Agir, 1996).

22. See my various contributions about the media and Islam (whose image is largely negative in Western media today). I have undertaken a reflection on this subject since the early 1990s: a number of articles and lectures are posted on my Web site (www.tariqramadan.com) in different sections, in particular in the "Lectures" (audio & video) section.

23. See in this respect my book *Aux Sources du Renouveau Musulman* (Paris: Bayard, 1998), reedited by Editions Tawhid (Lyons, 2000), 50–132.

Chapter 16

1. Quran 49:13.
2. Quran 7:179.
3. Marcel Gauchet, *The Disenchantment of the World: A Political History of Religion*, trans. Oscar Burge (Princeton, NJ: Princeton University Press, 1997).

4. Quran 17:89; 16:89; 6:38.
5. Abû Hâmid al-Ghazâlî, *Tahafut al-Falasifah* (Cairo: Dâr al-Ma'ârif, 1958, in Arabic), translated into English as *The Incoherence of the Philosophers*, trans. Michael E. Marmura, rev. ed. (Salt Lake City, UT: Brigham Young University Press, 2000); Ibn Rushd, *Tahafut at-Tahafut (The Incoherence of the Incoherence)* (Cairo: Al-Matba'ah al-Islamiyyah, 1884); see www.muslimphilosophy.com/ir/tt/index .html.
6. Abû Hâmid al-Ghazâlî, *Al-Munqidh min ad-Dalâl* (Cairo, Al-Maktabah al-Anglo-Misriyyah, 1962), translated into English as *Deliverance from Error and Mystical Union with the Almighty* (Washington, DC: Council for Research in Values and Philosophy, 1995); Abû Hâmid al-Ghazâlî, *Mishkât al-Anwâr* (Cairo: Ad-Dâr al-Qawmiyyah, 1964), translated into English as *The Niche of Lights*, trans. David Buchman (Salt Lake City, UT: Brigham Young University Press, 1998). In the first four parts of the *Discourse on Method*, Descartes sets forth the stages of methodical doubt then outlines what his commentators were to term "hyperbolic doubt," which he was also to develop in the *Meditations on First Philosophy*, in particular in the *Second Meditation* that returns to the issue of doubt and builds a system of truths on the "clear and distinct ideas" self-evident to reason and the subsequent categorization process. See also, concerning the relationship between al-Ghazâlî and Descartes: Hani Ramadan, *Une critique de l'argument ontologique dans la tradition cartésienne* (Paris: Publications Universitaires Européennes, and in London: Peter Lang, 1990).
7. Quoted in my book *Aux Sources du Renouveau Musulman*, respectively pages 64 and 67. See the whole of al-Afghânî's reflection about the sciences, philosophy, and Islam, 63–72.
8. Muhammad Iqbâl, *The Reconstruction*, chapter 6. See also his creative, insightful representation in *The Book of Eternity—Javid Nama*, www.allamaiqbal.com/works/poetry/persian/javidnama/transla tion/index.htm.
9. The complete work is available in English: *Sufficient Provision for Seekers of the Path of Truth*, 5 vols., trans. Muhtar Holland (Ft. Lauderdale, FL: Al-Baz Publishing, 1997); Ahmad ibn Naqid al-Misrî, *Reliance of the Traveller, a Classical Manual of Islamic Sacred Law*, in Arabic with English translation and commentary by Nuh Ha Mim Keller (Beltsville, MD: Amana Publications, 1991, 1999).
10. For a study of his thought on the issue at hand, see Muhammad Abdul Haq Ansari, *Sufism and Sharî'ah: A Study of Shaykh Ahmad Sirhindi's Effort to Reform Sufism* (Leicester, UK: Islamic Foundation, 1995).
11. See my various articles about those two matters published in newspapers in the United States or in Europe: most of those contributions are still accessible on my Web site (www.tariqramadan.com).

12. See "The Global Ideology of Fear or the Globalization of the Israel Syndrome" on my Web site: www.tariqramadan.com/article.php3?id_article=523&var.

13. I have taken part in an important number of conferences about the issue of dialogues among cultures, religions and civilizations the world over. I have often repeated those remarks, calling on those involved to go further in their critical relationship but also in their choice of themes. We have had a few detailed discussions with Federico Mayor or Jorge Sampaio, the former president of Portugal who is in charge of the "Alliance of Civilizations" project first launched by Spain, then in association with Turkey, and finally with the United Nations. This dynamic is interesting; all dialogue projects are of course useful in themselves. It is during one such encounter, for instance, that I debated with Cornelio Sommaruga, former president of the International Committee of the Red Cross, who on that occasion very aptly added to the first four conditions of intimate and collective peace I had stipulated (the *question of meaning, education, coherence, justice*), a fifth one: *forgiveness*. This addition is most welcome and the remark is profound and relevant. I will not, therefore, ever forget the rich and positive nature of such encounters, but we wish to point out the potential danger of transforming them into pretexts to avoid dealing with fundamental political and economic issues.

14. See my *Western Muslims*, 200–213.

15. *Hadîth* reported by Ahmad and Ibn Mâjah.

16. *Hadîth* reported by al-Bukhârî and Muslim.

17. In keeping with the distinction that exists in Arabic between *al-'ilm* (knowledge) and *al-fahm* (understanding). One should also add, in the order of the intellect's relation to its object, the general and initial meaning of *al-fiqh* (deep understanding) and the alliance of heart and reason with *al-furqân* (discernment).

Glossary

1. Concepts Used in Islamic Sciences

Al-'aqîda. Faith and all the matters related to the six pillars of *al-imân* (God, His names, His attributes, the angels, the prophets, the day of Judgment, and predestination). In general, it studies that which is beyond sensory perception. It does not exactly include the sphere of theology or that of Christian dogmatics, although some orientalists attempt to suggest it does. It also does not correspond to the sphere of philosophy, as understood in the sense of Western philosophy.

Al-fiqh. Islamic law and jurisprudence. It comprises two general sections that are based on different and opposed methodological approaches: *al-'ibâdât*, worship, where only what is prescribed is permitted; and *al-mu'âmalât*, social affairs, where everything is permitted except what is explicitly forbidden.

Ash-shahâda. The profession of faith and its testimony through a formulation with the heart and intelligence of "I bear witness that there is no god but God and that Muhammad is His prophet." It is the foundation of "being a Muslim."

Ash-sharî'a. There is not a single definition of *sharî'a*. Scholars have generally circumscribed its meaning from the standpoint of their own sphere of specialization. Starting from the broadest to the most restricted exceptions, there are the following definitions:

1. *Ash-sharî'a*, on the basis of the root of the word, means "the way" ("the path leading to the source") and outlines a global conception of creation, existence, death, and the way of life it entails, stemming from a normative reading and an understanding of scriptural sources. It determines "how to be a Muslim."

2. *Ash-sharî'a*, for *usûliyyûn* and jurists, is the corpus of general principles of Islamic law extracted from its two fundamental sources (the Qur'an and the Sunnah). *Ash-sharî'a* also uses other main (*al-ijma'* and *al-qiyas*) and secondary (*al-istihsân, al-istislâh, al-istishâb, al-'urf*) sources.

At-tasawwuf. Sufism. It is, in fact, the science of mysticism, which has a specific framework, norms, and a technical and specialized vocabulary. Membership requires an initiation rite. Synthetically, it comprises the studies of different scholars or schools about the stages and states that allow intimate progress toward God. It is the dimension of *al–haqîqa*, of truth, of ultimate spiritual Reality, which only those nearest to it may know.

Usûl al-fiqh. The fundamental principles of Islamic law. Usûl al-fiqh expounds principles and methodology by means of which the rules of law and jurisprudence are inferred and extracted from their sources. It involves the study and formulation of rules of interpretation, obligation, prohibition, and global principles, *ijtihâd* (*ijmâ', qiyas*).

2. Technical Terms

Ahâdîth (plur. of hadîth). Reported and authenticated traditions about what the Prophet said, did, or approved.

Ahkâm (plur. of hukm). Rulings, values, prescriptions, commandments, judgments, or laws stemming from Islamic law.

Asl (plur. usûl). Root, origin, source, or foundation.

Ayah (plur. âyât). Sign or indication; also, verse.

Dalâla. Meaning or implication.

Dalîl. Proof, indication, evidence, scriptural support, or source.

Dhannî. Not explicit, leaving room for conjecture about its origin and/or allowing scope to interpretation as to its meaning.

Dhâhir. Manifest or apparent: the literal meaning of the text.

Far' (plur. furû'). Branch, subdivision, or secondary element as opposed to roots or foundations (*usûl*). It also means a new case in the practice of *qiyâs*.

Fard 'ayn. Personal duty or obligation.

Fard kafâ'î (kifâya). Collective obligation. If part of the community takes care of it and fulfills it, the rest of the community is relieved of it.

Fatwâ (plur. fatâwâ). Specific legal ruling. It can be a mere reminder of a prescription explicitly stated by the sources or else a scholar's determination on the basis of a text that is not explicit or in the case of a specific situation for which there is no scriptural source.

Hukm taklîfî. Restrictive law defining rights and obligations. It is based on human responsibility.

Ijmâ'. Consensus of opinion, in the sense of unanimous or majority opinion.

Ijtihâd. Literally, "effort." It has become a technical term meaning the effort made by a jurist, either by extracting a law or a ruling from scriptural sources that are not explicit or by formulating a specific legal opinion in the absence of texts of reference.

'Illa. The actual cause of a specific ruling. It makes it possible to understand a ruling through its cause and thus opens the way to elaborating other rulings through analogy or extension.

Istihsân. Judging something as being good; it is, in fact, the application of "legal preference."

Istinbât. Both inductive (inferential) and deductive extractions of the implicit or hidden meaning of a given text. More broadly, it means extracting or pointing out the laws and rulings specified by a scriptural source.

Istishâb. Presumption of continuity of what was previously prescribed.

Istislâh. Consideration linked to general interest.

Jumhûr. Majority trend, when referring to the majority opinion among the conflicting views of scholars; this does not affect the validity of a minority opinion if it is justified.

Kalâm. Literally, "speech." In *'ilm al-kalâm,* it is linked to Islamic philosophy but also concerns fields that, according to the Western partition of intellectual domains, are based in theology or dogmatics. This science is, in several aspects, situated at the intersection of the three above-mentioned spheres.

Madhhab (plur. madhâhib). School for the teaching of Islamic law.

Makrûh. Abhorred.

Mandûb (or mustahab). Recommended.

Maqâsid (sing. maqsûd). Objectives or goals.

Maslaha. Consideration of public interest.

Mubâh. Permitted.

Mukallaf. Someone who has reached the age of puberty and is in full possession of his or her mental faculties.

Muqayyad. Limited, restricted, defined, determined, or circumscribed. This also qualifies a *mujtahid* who formulates legal rulings within a specific school for the teaching of Islamic law.

Mutlaq. Absolute or unrestricted. Also qualifies a *mujtahid* who is competent to formulate legal rulings beyond schools for the teaching of Islamic law, directly from the sources.

Qat'i. Clear-cut, explicit, or definite, leaving no scope for speculation as to its interpretation.

Rukhsa, rukhas Mitigation in the practice or implementation of prescriptions due, for instance, to age, illness, income, social conditions, or other factors.

Rukn (plur. arkân). Pillar or fundamental principle.

Sahîh. Authentic, meeting specific authentication criteria.

Shart (plur. shurût). Condition, sometimes criterion.

Shûrâ. Consultation.

Takhsîs. Restriction from a general to a specific meaning.

Taklîf. Responsibility or obligation.

Taqlîd. Imitation. In legal matters, it means the blind imitation of one's predecessors without questioning, assessing, checking, or criticizing their legal opinions.

Ta'wîl. Interpretation, more specifically in the sciences of faith: allegorical or metaphorical interpretation.

Tazkiyyah (an-nafs). Effort at spiritual purification or initiation to spiritual elevation.

Ummah. Spiritual community, uniting all Muslim men and women throughout the world in their attachment to Islam.

Wâjib. Obligation; often used as a synonym of *fard* except by Hanafi jurists.

3. Terms Used to Qualify the Status of Scholars

'Alim (plur. 'ulamâ'). Literally, "the one who knows." A scholar in a broad sense, who may be a specialist in one particular branch of Islamic sciences. It can qualify those who graduated from a university with a degree in a field related to Islamic sciences (the term *mawlâna* is also used to express the idea of "scholar," or *sheikh*).

Faqîh, fuqahâ. Literally, "one who understands deeply." Generally defines the jurist who masters the sciences of law and jurisprudence, but this title is sometimes used for scholars of very diverse abilities. By referring to etymology, one may apply this term to an individual possessing great religious knowledge, without thinking of a particular field of specialization. In the language of specialists, the term refers to someone who knows legal matters without necessarily being competent to develop and formulate specific and/or new legal rulings. His knowledge may relate to one particular school or to several; he may know the views expressed about a given legal issue; he may know the points on which scholars disagree; he may also express one or several already formulated legal rulings, but this is generally where his competence stops. The *mujtahid* or *muftî* are generally acknowledged *fuqahâ'* but a respected *faqîh* is not necessarily a *mujtahid* or a *muftî*.

Imâm (plur. a'imma). Literally, "the one who is placed at the front." Applies to any person, specifically trained or not, who directs prayer or officiates during Friday sermons. More particularly, this term is used to qualify a scholar who has historically left a mark on the development of Islamic sciences and knowledge, especially in the field of law and jurisprudence. One thus speaks of the "great imâms (a'imma)" when thinking of Abû Hanîfa, Mâlik, ash-Shâfi'î Ibn Hanbal, or Ja'far as-Sâdiq, for instance. This may express the recognition of the community as a whole or sometimes, more specifically, of the circle or the school of thought or organization in which the said scholar may have been involved.

Muftî. Some scholars have often made undifferentiated use of the terms *mujtahid* and *muftî*. The link indeed seems natural since the practice of *ijtihâd* is necessary to the formulation of a *fatwâ* (same root as *muftî*). A *muftî* is therefore someone who formulates specific legal opinions on the basis of texts that are not explicit or in the absence of specific texts. Three slight specificities were pointed out by scholars to justify the differences in denominations and functions. The *muftî* is clearly at the disposal of the community or of individuals; his function is to *answer* questions and have these answers direct his reflection. This is not the case for the *mujtahid* who is not necessarily asked questions and can work independently. More than the *mujtahid*, since he interacts more directly with his environment, the *muftî* must know the people and society he lives among; this is also required of the *mujtahid* but less expressly. Finally, some have noted a mere institutional difference: the *muftî* is a *mujtahid* who has been employed by the state or who serves a specific institution to formulate legal rulings and direct the administration of affairs. The *muftî* would thus simply be a *mujtahid* who has become a civil servant. The same distinctions exist among scholars regarding the *muftî mutlaq* and the *muftî muqayyad*.

Mujtahid. A scholar working on scriptural sources to infer or extract judgments and legal rulings. He is recognized as competent to practice *ijtihâd* (same Arabic root, *ja-ha-da*) on texts that are not explicit or in the absence of specific texts. Numerous qualities are required to reach this level of competence: (1) knowledge of the Arabic language; (2) knowledge of the Qur'an and *hadîth* sciences; (3) deep knowledge of the objectives (*maqâsid*) of the *sharî'a*; (4) knowledge of the questions for which a consensus exists, which makes it necessary to know the substance of the works on secondary questions (*furû'*); (5) knowledge of the principle of analogical reasoning (*qiyâs*) and its methodology; (6) knowledge of the historical, social, and political contexts; that is, the situation of his society (*ahwâl an-nâs*); and (7) recognition of his competence, honesty, reliability, and uprightness. Scholars have distinguished two types of *mujtahid* for whom the required competence criteria differ:

1. *al-mujtahid al-mutlaq* (absolute): Extracts legal rulings and opinions directly from the sources and beyond all specific school criteria. His recognized knowledge of texts and methodological principles enables him to formulate views that do not necessarily refer to schools that teach Islamic law and their rules.
2. *al-mujtahid al-muqayyad* (limited): Extracts prescriptions within the framework of a specific juridical school. The conditions required for the latter are, of course, less demanding; they also include the knowledge of the rules of deduction linked to the school that teaches Islamic law to which he belongs or refers.

Sheikh (plur. shuyûkh). Literally, "old." Denotes people who have a degree in one branch or another of Islamic sciences. It is also very broadly used to express students' respect or recognition of teachers' abilities even if the latter do not have an official degree. One can note some obvious instances of excess in this respect. In mystical paths and circles, the *sheikh* is the initiating master who guides and accompanies the *murîd* (the initiate in quest of knowledge) on the path to knowledge and elevation.

Usûlî (plur. usûliyyûn). A scholar knowledgeable about the fundamental principles of Islamic law. He works on the Qur'an and Sunnah and he must master the instruments of Islamic law and know the principles and methodology by means of which the rules of law and jurisprudence are inferred and extracted from their sources. He studies rules of interpretation, the fields related to obligation and prohibition, as well as rules about general orientation. The principles of implementation of *ijtihâd*, *'ijmâ'*, or *qiyâs* also fall within his province although this does not mean he is competent to implement them. His knowledge is essentially theoretical. A *mujtahid* or a *muftî* necessarily masters the field of knowledge and competence of an *usûl* scholar but the latter is not immediately or necessarily a *mujtahid* or a *muftî*, since his knowledge may be only theoretical, merely enabling him to identify the instruments of extraction and deduction without being competent to make use of them.

Index

Page numbers in italics refer to illustrations.